362.1
Im 7

D1206935

Imperialism, Health
and
Medicine

Edited by Vicente Navarro

POLICY,
POLITICS,
HEALTH AND
MEDICINE
Series

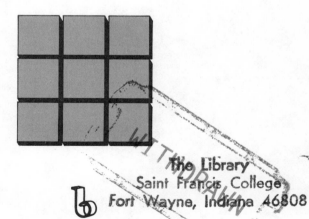

WITHDRAWN

The Library
Saint Francis College
Fort Wayne, Indiana 46808

Baywood Publishing Company, Inc.
Farmingdale, New York 11735

83-737

Copyright © 1974, 1975, 1976, 1977, 1978, 1979 in The International Journal of Health Services by Baywood Publishing Company, Inc., Farmingdale, New York. All rights reserved. No part of this book may be reproduced in any form, by mimeograph or any other means, without permission in writing from the publisher. Printed in the United States of America.

Library of Congress Catalog Card Number: 80-67832
ISBN Number: 0-89503-019-5

© 1981 Baywood Publishing Comapny, Inc.

Imperialism, Health
and
Medicine

Edited by Vicente Navarro

Baywood Publishing Company, Inc.
Farmingdale, New York 11735

Weineiz 0221 0775 82 1805 16880 0180376

INTRODUCTION

The Nature of Imperialism and Its Implications in Health and Medicine

Vicente Navarro

In trying to understand poverty, death and disease in the world of underdevelopment, a reader may go through the extensive bibliography existent in developed capitalist countries on health and medicine in what is usually called the Third World and rarely, if ever, find categories such as capitalism and imperialism presented as possible causes of that poverty, death, and disease. In most references on underdevelopment of health, published by western academic centers or international agencies, there is a deafening silence about those concepts and realities. And on the rare occasions when they appear, they are usually placed in an introductory notice of dismissal in which those terms are placed in quotation marks as if to alert the reader that they are irrelevant or subject to suspicion, i.e., of concern only to incorrigible ideologues who are supposedly oblivious to the passage of time. Serious scholars and/or international officials are supposed to ignore or dismiss such "ideological" terms and concepts. In its stead, they are supposed to explain the overwhelming poverty in which the majority of humanity lives today by referring to the assumingly ever present scarcity of resources in the underdeveloped countries, a scarcity that is made all the more devastating by the continuous growth of their population. According to a prevailing interpretation of poverty, popular in the centers of orthodoxy of the developed capitalist world, the cause of the overwhelming poverty of the majority of the world's population is their reproductive behavior, i.e., they have too many children, keeping those populations stuck in the mud of poverty. Consequently, population controllers continue sowing pills, condoms, intrauterine devices, diaphragms and marked calendars to the ever-growing poor populations. The western system of power, unable to multi-

5

ply the dinners, does what it can to suppress the diners. Meanwhile, Latin America, Africa, Asia, and Oceania's children obstinately continue to be born, claiming, as the Uruguayan writer Eduardo Galeano has said, their natural right to a place in the sun in those magnificent lands which could, under a different system, give to all what is now denied to most. Erland Hofsten's and Bonnie Mass' essays in Part 3 of this volume show why the Malthusian and neoMalthusian theories continue to be sold in the international marketplace of ideas. They serve to reproduce the power relations that are the primary cause of underdevelopment.

The theory that poverty is due to lack of resources has increasingly become untenable, considering the enormous importance that the resources—raw materials, products, and capital—coming from those supposedly poor countries have had for the enrichment of capitalist developed ones. Therefore, a new series of explanations have appeared in the centers of orthodoxy that attribute the underdevelopment of health in underdeveloped countries to an absence of not physical but intellectual resources, i.e., of "know-how." This know-how is assumed to be, for the most part, value free and neutral. Thus, technological transfer has become the "name of the game," the "in" thing in circles of development. That technological transfer has taken many different forms in medicine and public health, from Flexnerian transfer to nutritional aid. Key agencies in that transfer have been U.S. foundations, U.S. and international agencies of aid, and academic institutions of capitalist developed countries. Peter J. Donaldson's, Michael Taussig's, and Jaime Breilh's essays in Part 2 of the volume analyze the modus operandi of those agencies, foundations, and institutions that transmit technologies from developed countries to underdeveloped ones. These authors also show that those technologies, far from being neutral, carry with them ideologies and relations of power that are not only foreign but harmful to the interests and needs of the majorities living in the underdeveloped world. A point worth stressing is that the transmission belt function of intellectual and technical institutions does not respond to an "international conspiracy" to keep down the poor populations. There is no need for such a conspiracy. The western system of power has a logic of its own in which the ideology of the dominant classes in the dominant capitalist countries is transmitted as the only universally valid ideology—an ideology that is, of course, presented or perceived not as an ideology but as a factual and accurate vision of reality, i.e., the vision that is needed to solve poverty's problems. The reality, however, is different. As the essays in Part 2 show, the values transmitted in those technologies and ideologies are not solving the problems of underdevelopment but, rather, are contributing to reproduce and strengthen the pattern of power relations that determines underdevelopment. As one of the authors, Donaldson, indicates,, "the shortcomings of these programs is not that they create the inequality associated with professional services throughout the developing world but that they so neatly serve those who maintain it." (p. 122)

The failure of technological transfer to break with underdevelopment has created in response an entire series of ideological positions that explain underdevelopment as an outcome of too much technology or of the wrong type of technology. A whole array of theories has appeared—from the "small is beautiful" or "intermediate technologies" to the "back to nature" type—in which all share the same lack of awareness of the political determinants of that technology. In these and other related theories—and even in their radical versions such as in Susan George's, Frances Moore Lappe's, and Joseph Collins'—we also find a studious avoidance of explanatory categories such as capitalism and imperialism (1). Those categories are either ignored or considered as being irrelevant to the issue in question. A recent example of that avoidance is Ivan Illich, who has recently explained the well-known mass starvation in the Sahel in West Africa as an outcome of the usage of wrong technology (2). But, as Nicole Ball shows in her article in Part 1, the actual cause of that drought and of that starvation was in the power relations of capitalism and imperialism existent in that part of the world.

It is the intention of the essays in this volume to challenge the prevailing explanations of the underdevelopment of health, presenting them as ideological explanations that serve to reproduce and sustain the western system of power and its concomitant distribution of economic and political control, a system of power that we call *capitalism and imperialism.* By capitalism, is meant a social formation in which a class—the capitalist class or bourgeoisie—has a hegemonic dominance over the means of production, consumption, and legitimation; and by imperialism, is meant a world-wide system of power, characterized by the political, economic, ideological, and cultural domination of one or more nations by another nation(s), a system of power which follows the interests of the dominant classes and groups in the dominating nation and, also, sectors of the ruling classes of the dominated nations. The essays in this volume, and especially those by Michel Chossudovsky, Nicole Ball and myself in Part 1, further elaborate on the nature of capitalism and imperialism and on the political and economic determinants of the underdevelopment of health and of health services.

In summary, the position presented in this volume is that the major cause of death and disease in the poor parts of the world today in which the majority of the human race lives *is not a scarcity of resources, nor the process of industrialization, nor even the much heralded population explosion but, rather, a pattern of control over the resources of those countries in which the majority of the population has no control over their resources.* As a beautiful Colombian folk song puts it, "Oh love, oh my love, tell me, are we poor because we do not have riches or is it that we don't have riches because we are poor?" The peasants who sing that know quite well that if they and their families are poor, it is not (as foreign consultants keep telling them) because they have too many children but, rather, because of the pattern of control over the land, credit, and capital in their village, country, and continent, a continent in which the wealth shared by 6 million Latin Americans at the top of the social pyramid is the same as the amount shared by 140 million at the bottom. This volume shows that that reality applies to most of the underdeveloped world. Contrary to prevailing orthodoxy, the contributors in this volume believe that capitalism and imperialism, far from being passé categories of analysis, are very much needed concepts for our understanding of underdevelopment and its health and medical problems. They are, as Neruda would put it, "at the center of things."

Imperialism as a world-wide system is a continuously changing pattern of world-wide relations. The increasing economic integration among nations has meant not only an expansion of foreign trade but also the rapid growth of foreign investment, via the multinational corporations which have become the hallmark of modern capitalism, and the primary vehicle of imperialist relations between developed and underdeveloped countries. Several essays in this volume, particularly those by Elling, Bader, Lall, and Bibile in Part 4, analyze the impact of the multinational corporations on the health of the populations.

Needless to say, all the contributors of this volume are aware that the analyses presented here will be quickly dismissed in the corridors of power as "rhetorical," or "ideological." Meanwhile, the orthodox voices will continue with their own rhetorical solutions for poverty, not less ideological by being couched in sociologuese or technologuese. Their ideological apparatuses will continue their discourse in an almost surrealist language. In wealthy lands that are empty, they will keep proposing the limitation of births, in wealthy countries with plenty of capital that is wasted, they will continue saying that capital is lacking, and they will keep describing as "aid" those deforming orthopedics of loans and the draining of wealth that results from foreign investments. It is the aim of this volume to provide alternative analyses and suggestions to the ones prevailing in the current asphyxiating climate of orthodoxy.

A further point needs clarification. The essays published in this volume do not provide a homogeneity in terms of style nor in terms of ideological positions. Nor are they presented as definitive pieces but, rather as exploratory positions that, indeed, may need further elaboration. They have been chosen as representative of the different positions and concerns that have appeared in the *International Journal of Health Services* during the last few years. For reasons of space, many other articles also relevant to the topic "Imperialism, Health and Medicine" appearing in the *International Journal of Health Services* have not been included. The reader who is interested in further exploring the topics covered in this anthology is referred to the many other articles published on these subjects in the pages of that quarterly.

Last but not least, it is worth stressing that it is not the intention of this volume to present "models" for breaking with underdevelopment. Paraphrasing Karl Marx, we perceive the intention of this volume "not to create a plan for the future that will hold for all times [but, rather] to do an uncompromising critical evaluation of all that exists, uncompromising in the sense that our criticism fears neither its own results nor the conflict with the powers that be." (3) The oppressed masses suffering from imperialism and capitalism will be the ones to create their own future. Many of them are already doing it. It is worth noting that those oppressed masses who have broken with those oppressive realities have been able to do so only by using revolutionary force, enabling them to break with the institutionalized violence represented by capitalism and imperialism. The reason for making explicit this historical reality is that so much has been written by the established press and academe equating revolutionary movements with violence, while remaining silent about the enormous institutionalized violence that capitalism and imperialism represent. Imperialist and capitalist forces will always oppose by all means available to them the transformation of the realities of oppression. Let us not forget that the peaceful road to socialism in Allende's Chile became the bloodiest counter-revolution known in Latin America. The violence represented by imperialism is clear for all to see. In numbers of preventable deaths, the equivalent of six Hiroshima bombs explode every year, without making a sound, in the world of underdevelopment. About that violence, the organs of communication remain silent. There are many other examples of such silence. When an earthquake killed 20,000 people in Nicaragua, the international press carried the news and mobilized public opinion to assist the victims of disaster. But that same press was silent about the 18,000 deaths a year due to hunger in Somoza's Nicaragua. Those deaths were so normal that they did not make "news." But when the oppressed Nicaraguan masses used force in their rebellion against Somoza and his imperialist allies, an outcry of condemnation appeared in that same press against "violence" and "extremism." Examples are many of the mobilization of public opinion against revolutionary forces that are opening the doors of justice. It is hoped that this volume will help to clarify that ideological mystification by showing the enormously violent nature of capitalism and imperialism, the primary cause of poverty, death, and disease in today's world. Thus, this volume is dedicated to those of our fellow health workers who, in the world of underdevelopment, are being killed, tortured, or persecuted because of their belief that the only way of breaking with the underdevelopment of health is to break with the sickness of imperialism.

REFERENCES

1. World Agricultural Research Project. "Review Article: The Political Economy of Food and Agriculture," *International Journal of Health Services,* Vol. 10, No. 1, 1980, p. 161.
2. Illich, I. *Medical Nemesis.* Calders and Boyers. London, 1975.
3. Marx, K. letter to Arnold Ruge, 1844, Marx Corresponde. Krause Pbs. 1964.

TABLE OF CONTENTS

Introduction: The Nature of Imperialism and Its
            Implications in Health and Medicine
        Vicente Navarro   5

Part 1: The Political and Economic Determinants of the
         Underdevelopment of Health and Health Services

1. The Underdevelopment of Health or the Health of
    Underdevelopment: An Analysis of the Distribution of Human
    Health Resources in Latin America
        Vicente Navarro   15

2. Human Rights, Health, and Capital Accumulation in the Third
    World
        Michel Chossudovsky   37

3. The Economic and Political Determinants of Human (Including
    Health) Rights
        Vicente Navarro   53

4. Drought and Dependence in the Sahel
        Nicole Ball   77

Part 2: U.S. Foundations, U.S. Foreign Policy and
         International Health

5. Foreign Intervention in Medical Education: A Case Study of the
    Rockefeller Foundation's Involvement in a Thai Medical School
        Peter J. Donaldson 107

6. Nutrition, Development, and Foreign Aid: A Case Study of U.S.
    Directed Health Care in a Colombian Plantation Zone
        Michael Taussig 127

7. Community Medicine Under Imperialism: A New Medical Police?
        Jaime Breilh 149

Part 3: Critiques of Malthusian and Neo-Malthusian
Population Theories and Their Political Function

8. Population Growth—A Menace to What?
   Erland Hofsten 171

9. An Historical Sketch of the American Population Control
   Movement
   Bonnie Mass 179

Part 4: Corporate Power and
Underdevelopment

10. Industrialization and Occupational Health in Underdeveloped
    Countries
    Ray H. Elling 207

11. Breast-Feeding: The Role of Multinational Corporations in
    Latin America
    Michael B. Bader 235

12. The Political Economy of Controlling Transnationals: The
    Pharmaceutical Industry in Sri Lanka, 1972-1976
    Sanjaya Lall and Senaka Bibile 253

Contributors 283

PART 1

The Political and Economic Determinants of the Underdevelopment of Health and Health Services

CHAPTER 1

The Underdevelopment of Health or the Health of Underdevelopment: An Analysis of the Distribution of Human Health Resources in Latin America

Vicente Navarro

Oh love, oh my love,
tell me
are we poor because we do not have riches
or
is it that we don't have riches because we are poor?
(translated from an old Colombian folk song)

Assuming that a first step in analyzing the present maldistribution of human resources in the health sector of a country and a continent is to understand the nature of that condition and the reasons for it, I will focus in this paper on the causes of that maldistribution in our Americas, placing special emphasis on that part south of the Rio Grande—the Latin American continent—usually referred to as the underdeveloped America.[1] I am aware, of course, of the great diversity among the Latin American

This paper is based on a presentation at the Pan American Conference on Health Manpower Planning in Ottawa, Canada, September 10-14, 1973. A modified version of this paper appears in the Spring 1974 issue of *Politics and Society*.

[1] The term "underdeveloped countries" will be used interchangeably in this paper with such terms as poor countries or nations and developing countries. At the same time, I am aware of the lack of a precise term that would define not only the state of poverty of the majority of our human race, but also the process that determines it. For an interesting discussion on this very point, see reference 1.

economies. However, I believe that all the Latin American countries (with the exception of Cuba) exhibit certain patterns of economic, social, and political structures and behaviors that, in the context of the distribution of resources, are more similar than dissimilar. I feel that these similarities justify the consideration of these different countries as a group in this paper.

Also, because the underdevelopment of poor nations is closely related to the development of the rich ones, I will also touch, although very briefly, upon the present maldistribution of human resources in the health sector of North America.

In addition, because, and as I will show, the distribution of human health resources follows and parallels the distribution of most of the resources in underdeveloped countries, I will analyze the distribution of resources in the health sector within the context of the parameters that determine underdevelopment and explain that distribution. In other words, I will examine the tree, the distribution of human health resources, in the context of the forest, underdevelopment. Indeed, the thesis I will develop in this paper is that the present maldistribution of human health resources is brought about by the same determinants that cause the underdevelopment of Latin America.[2]

In so doing, I will try to close a gap in the ever increasing bibliography on health and health services in developing countries which is rich in description, but scarce in analysis. Indeed, in looking back on this large body of literature, we can see quite a number of scholarly and very elegant descriptive studies and reference works on the health and health services of developing countries. Yet, what most of these publications lack, as Ruderman (2) pointed out when he reviewed one of them, is an analytic explanation of why underdevelopment of health and health services came about in the first place. I would postulate that this omission is not an accidental one. Indeed, had they analyzed and begun to explain the underdevelopment of health and health services, those scholars and researchers might have come to the conclusion, uncomfortable as it may be, that the main cause of the underdevelopment of health was the state of health or lack of it, of the political, social, and economic structures that determine the underdevelopment in the societies studied. Avoidance of this analysis led these scholars to consider the maldistribution of health resources in a vacuum, as if its analysis could be explained separately and independently from the analysis—admittedly sometimes embarrassing, and always sensitive—of those structures which determine that distribution to begin with.

Let me give an example. In the 1960s, a very thorough, elegant, and complete study—one of the most complete surveys that has ever been carried out, either in developed or developing countries—was carried out on the production and distribution of human health resources in Colombia (3). One finding of this study was that by social classes and by regions, the distribution of human health resources in that country was highly askew. Another fact brought out by this and other surveys was the highly skewed distribution of wealth and income in Colombia, with 5 per cent of the population owning 52 per cent of the wealth (4). It would have seemed logical to explore the possible correlation, and even causality, that might exist between the highly skewed distribution of wealth, income, and political power in that society and the highly skewed distribution of human health resources in the country. Yet, in a seminar arranged to discuss the

---

[2] In my analysis of economic underdevelopment, I owe a great intellectual debt to André Gunder Frank, Paul Baran, and Charles Bettelheim. Actually, an intention of this paper is to show that their interpretative model of economic underdevelopment is also useful in explaining social underdevelopment in general and health resources underdevelopment in particular.

meaning and conclusions of that health manpower study, and attended by prestigious scholars and researchers, not only was there no attempt to relate the distribution of wealth and human health resources, but the highly skewed distribution of wealth was not even mentioned, let alone discussed by these scholars (3). Oblivious and inattentive to the parameters within which this maldistribution of human health resources took place, their conclusions were empirically invalid and ineffective policy-wise.

The attitude detectable in this seminar reflects what Birnbaum (5) has called recently the tranquilizing effect of social research (and I would include a large percentage of health services research) in the 1960s. Indeed, social research in this period was characterized by the dominance of the empiricist, i.e. the expert on the trees who fails to see the forest.[3] It was the time, you may remember, when Daniel Bell wrote his *End of Ideology* (7), an end which, as Blackburn (8) indicates, was not so much the end but the victory of the ideology of empiricism and pragmatism.

This empiricism led the major part of studies on health services development and planning to emphasize the method, the method as the "unideologic," "value-free" instrument for distributing resources. Thus, the emphasis within the analysis, study, and application of the planning of the distribution of human health resources was on the methodologic aspects, without analyzing and/or questioning (but rather taking as "given") the social, economic, and political structures that determined and conditioned that underdevelopment. Cost-benefit, cost-effectiveness, PPBS, and the all-encompassing health planning CENDES method, were actually products of the "apologist" ideology that sustained those structures responsible for the maldistribution of resources.[4] A significant exception to this situation in Latin America was Cuba, which was exploring an alternative road to the one prevalent in Latin America for breaking with underdevelopment.

As for the rationale and explanation for underdevelopment, it was considered that the condition of Latin America was determined by the scarcity of resources. In this respect, the main assumption underlying the analysis of development has been that development is the transformation of one mode or type—the underdevelopment—to the other—the developed. In the analysis of development, the general features of the developed countries are abstracted as an ideal type and compared or contrasted with the equally typical features of the poor societies. Development comes about, in this view, by the replacement of the features of the latter with those of the former. As a consequence of this interpretation, the model the underdeveloped countries are expected to follow contains all the features of the developed ones. Parsons (10), Hoselitz (11), and others have elaborated this model,[5] and recently Kahn and Weiner (13) have popularized it. Due to the great influence—and even control of ideas—that these sociologists and popularizers have enjoyed, their analyses have affected most writings on health services in underdeveloped countries. For instance, in a large number of references, most of the indicators of health services in underdeveloped countries, such as bed-population ratios, are compared with indicators from the developed ones, often accepting the premise that indicators of developed countries can be used as models or targets for the underdeveloped ones.[6]

[3] For a critique of empiricism and pragmatism, see reference 6.

[4] For a critique of the CENDES method and its limited application in Latin America, see reference 9.

[5] For a thorough and critical review of the U.S. sociology of development, see reference 12.

[6] For a representative study using this analysis, see reference 14. For an excellent critique of this approach, see reference 15.

A further elaboration of this approach can be seen in the stages of growth theory, popularized by Rostow's *Stages of Economic Growth* (16). According to Rostow, development is the process whereby a country changes its characteristics in five stages. The writer assumes the stages to be universal and to apply to all countries.

Because of the great influence that the Rostowian interpretation of development has enjoyed, it merits examination in some detail.

> It is possible to identify all societies, in their economic dimensions, as lying within five categories: the traditional society, the preconditions for take-off, the take-off, the drive to maturity, and the age of high mass-consumption. First, the traditional society. A traditional society is one whose structure is developed within limited production functions, based on pre-Newtonian science and technology, and on pre-Newtonian attitudes towards the physical world. . . . The second stage of growth embraces societies in the process of transition; that is, the period when the preconditions for take-off are developed; for it takes time to transform a traditional society in the ways necessary for it to exploit the fruits of modern science to fend off diminishing returns, and thus to enjoy the blessings and choices opened up by the march of compound interest. . . . the stage of preconditions arise(s) not endogenously but from some external intrusion by more advanced societies. . . . We come now to the great watershed in the life of modern societies: the third stage in this sequence, the take-off. The take-off is the interval when the old blocks and resistances to steady growth are finally overcome. The forces making for economic progress, which yielded limited bursts and enclaves of modern activity, expand and come to dominate the society. Growth becomes its normal condition. Compound interest becomes built, as it were, into its habits and institutional structure. . . . [The] take-off is defined as requiring all three of the following related conditions: (1) a rise in the rate of productive investment from, say, 5 percent or less to over 10 percent of national income (or net national product (NNP)); (2) the development of one or more substantial manufacturing sectors, with a high rate of growth; (3) the existence or quick emergence of a political, social and institutional framework which exploits the impulses to expansion . . . (17).

In the Rostow interpretative model, the major factor in development is contained in his third or take-off stage, and this is characterized by a rapid rate of investment and growth.

Rostow visualizes two major agents of change, determinants of the process of development. The first agent of change identified is the *diffusion of values* (entrepreneurial values) from the developed societies or metropolises to the under-developed societies, initially to the national capitals of the underdeveloped societies, then to their provincial capitals, and finally to the peripheral hinterlands. Development is thus perceived as a phenomenon of acculturation and diffusion of institutional and organizational values, together with the transmissions of skills, knowledge, and technology, from the developed to the developing countries.

The second agent of change is the *diffusion of capital*. According to Rostow and the previously mentioned authors, the underdeveloped countries are poor because they lack investment capital and therefore cannot develop and escape from their poverty. As a consequence of this assumption, they believe it essential for the development of the poor countries that the richer, developed countries diffuse capital to the underdeveloped ones, thereby stimulating their economic development. Thus, foreign capital, according to the Rostowian interpretation, creates a "market, entrepreneurial economy" in the form of an "enclave," similar to the one in the developed or metropolis society, which evolves first in the poor nation's capital, and from there expands its positive and economically stimulating influence to the rest of the country.

This interpretation leads the authors to the conclusion that development takes place in, is stimulated by, and is channeled through an "enclave" of the developed, metropolitan economy within each of the underdeveloped countries. Indeed, they consider that there are dual economies in the underdeveloped countries; one, the "enclave," urban-based, well developed market economy, with technical, entrepreneurial, and cultural values diffused from the developed metropolis; and the other, "the marginal economy" that includes those rural-based sectors of the population, sometimes its majority, that have not been incorporated into the "entrepreneurial market economy."

Because of the great influence of the Rostowian school of thought in the sociology of underdevelopment, inside as well as outside the health sector, the three characteristics of the Rostowian theory, (a) the need for cultural and technologic diffusion, (b) the scarcity of national capital, and (c) the dual economies, all appear in most of the literature dealing with distribution of general resources, and also human health resources, in developing countries.[7]

Indeed, the *cultural diffusion* argument is reflected, in health services literature, in the heavy emphasis placed on the necessity of training different types of personnel in underdeveloped countries following the curriculum and educational resources prevalent in the developed countries. The second Rostowian argument, on the *scarcity of capital*, is presented with different interpretations but usually appears under the rubric "that poor countries *cannot afford* to provide whole health care to the whole population" or also under the argument that poor countries can "only afford social security for a few sectors, and mainly the industrial urban based sector, because investment capital determines the overall important growth of the take-off stage." The concept of *dual economies and societies* is reflected in the existence of an unequal distribution of health resources between the cities and the rural hinterlands, with Western "hospital based" medicine in the cities and the indigenous and "less developed" form of medicine in the rural areas. This dualism is considered to have come about, first, because of the lack of diffusion of Western, developed medicine to the rural areas (argument 1 of the Rostowian interpretation) and, second, because of the lack of resources and investment capital in those areas (argument 2).

Rostow's "stages of growth" theory is the most accepted theory for explaining development and analyzing the distribution of resources, both within and outside the health sector. Its popularity in the corridors of power and academic circles in developed countries (as well as in the leading circles in developing countries and in the international agencies) is attributable partially to its rationalization and justification of the present relationship between the developed and the developing nations, presenting the developed countries as "models" to be emulated by poor countries and showing underdevelopment to be due to an assumed scarcity of resources in underdeveloped areas and not to economic structures and the pattern of economic relationships between poor and rich countries. The "fault" of underdevelopment is therefore left squarely on the shoulders of the poorer nations.

THE FALLACY OF SOME OF THE THEORIES OF UNDERDEVELOPMENT CURRENTLY POPULAR INSIDE AND OUTSIDE THE HEALTH SECTOR

Frank (18), Baran (19), and Griffin (20), however, have all shown the Rostowian model and its derivatives to be empirically invalid when confronted with reality, and to

---

[7] For the most comprehensive, empirical study of the "stages theory" of social (including health services) and economic development, see reference 14.

be theoretically inadequate when called upon to explain the process of development and its concurrent distribution of resources. This inadequacy explains why such theories are ineffective policy-wise for promoting development.

Let us analyze each of the three basic postulates of the Rostowian theory and check them against the empirical evidence available to us from sources outside the health sector, as well as from data gathered within the health services.

First, regarding the supposed lack of diffusion of cultural values, available evidence shows that, quite contrary to the Rostowian assumption, there is a very large diffusion—so much so that some may even refer to it as dominance—of cultural values abstracted from or generated from developed to developing societies. As several authors have pointed out, the media (television and the press) in Latin America are on the whole very heavily influenced by the values of North America. As Frank (21) notes, in Mexico the Spanish version of the *Reader's Digest*, for instance, has a higher circulation than the entire circulations of Mexico's eight largest magazines put together. And, according to a recent UNESCO report (22), 70 per cent of the TV programs shown in Latin America originate in the United States.

Another important element of cultural diffusion is institutional education. The system of primary, secondary, and university education, patterned after the systems in developed countries, is usually alien to the needs of poor countries. A recent UNESCO report (23) states, for instance, that while most inhabitants of underdeveloped nations live in agricultural, rural sectors where there is a need for a collective sense of solidarity, most of the values expounded in primary and secondary schools are urban, and are, as in most Western, developed societies, individually, entrepreneurially, and urban oriented. Cultural diffusion also takes place at the university level. As Garcia (24) has shown, in a comprehensive review of medical education in Latin America, most medical curricula in Latin America have been patterned on German, French-Spanish, and, more recently, American models, and these are models that, as McKeown (25) has indicated, reflect an engineering approach to the understanding of the body and its diseases and tend to ignore the understanding of the socioeconomic environment that brought about the diseases. The emphasis on hospital-based, technologically-oriented medicine and especially individual, acute-episodic care, typical of the medical education of Western, developed societies, is replicated in the developing societies. Rural, ambulatory, social, and continuous care is underrepresented, if not nonexistent, in the curricula of medical institutions in developing societies. When the rural type of medical care is taught, student exposure is apt to be more symbolic than real (26).

Thus, quite contrary to the Rostowian claim, there is a very heavy diffusion of cultural values from developed to developing countries. Moreover, it can be postulated, again contrary to Rostow's assumption, that this cultural diffusion—defined by Candau, the late Director-General of the World Health Organization, as "cultural imperialism"—is, as I will try to show later on, more harmful than beneficial to the process of development.

Complementing this observable cultural diffusion is technologic diffusion. Let me underline, incidentally, that I believe false the dichotomy commonly drawn between cultural diffusion and technologic diffusion. Indeed, technology is a value-laden (and not value free) process in which cultural values are assumed and subsumed. According to the United Nations Economic Committee for Latin America (UN-ECLA), most of the technology of Latin America has been imported from the developed areas, and primarily from North America. Actually, Fucaraccio (27) has stated that 80 per cent of Latin

American equipment is imported. And, as Illich (28) has indicated, this technology, which is foreign to the parameters of underdevelopment, can harm more than benefit the process of development. The labor-saving technology of developed society actually contributes to the creation of unemployment in the underdeveloped countries.[8] Moreover, the investment needed for this technology diverts vital investment from less glamorous, but more efficient and much more needed projects. Not long ago I estimated, for example, that with the annual operating expenditures of the three open heart surgery units in use today in Bogotá, a city with a population of over 2 million, a quarter of the children living there could receive a half liter of milk each day for one year. I should underline here that the main public health problems in the city of Bogotá are not heart conditions but gastroenteritis, infectious diseases, and malnutrition (30). Furthermore, if indeed the experience of developed countries applied to developing ones, it is highly probable that, considering the high density of units for such a small catchment area, the care provided by these units is not really needed.

Once again, to refute Rostow's theory, it can be postulated that there is too much, rather than too little, cultural and technologic diffusion from the developed to the developing countries.

THE MYTH OF THE SCARCITY OF RESOURCES

As for the second Rostowian assumption, on the lack of capital and the need for more capital investment by developed nations in the developing countries, several authors have shown that the Rostowian model is inaccurate as an explicative model of underdevelopment. Indeed, Fucaraccio (27), and others (31), have shown that there is no scarcity of capital in Latin America, but rather an underuse and misuse of capital. Fucaraccio points out that Colombia and Argentina, for instance, invest 20 per cent and 23 per cent of their domestic gross national products, respectively, which compares quite favorably to the lower percentages of 16 per cent and 18 per cent invested by the U.S. and France in their respective domestic economies. But, for an analysis of the ramifications of a country's investment process, the nature and control of investment is more important than the size of investment.

As for the nature of these investments, a large proportion is financed from domestic savings. This leads to the question of which people are saving. To answer this question, it is necessary to examine the levels of income distribution in Latin America, where

> . . . (a) a large part of income is concentrated in a minority of the population . . . which generates the savings subsequently converted into capital goods; and (b) at least 50 percent of the population not only do not have the ability to save but lack sufficient income even to satisfy their most basic needs which are estimated at about $190 per annum per capita (27).

This distribution of income and corresponding use of savings determines the structure of investments, production, and consumption, where

> . . . the construction sector accounts for between 40 and 50 per cent of gross domestic investment, depending on the year and the country concerned. A considerable part of such construction represents residential units which do little to solve the low-income housing shortage in Latin America and in no way help to increase productive capacity.

[8] For an analysis of the harmful effects of Western technology on the economies of Latin America, see reference 29.

The remainder comprises construction related to productive capacity and to public works. Equipment accounts for between 50 and 60 per cent of investment, of which half is for transportation and the remainder machinery and spare parts.

This distribution of investment suggests that Latin America could increase its rate of growth and assume a less vulnerable position if it were to change its pattern of investment accordingly. However, since the pattern of investment is conditioned by the pattern of savings, which in turn is conditioned by income distribution, a substantial modification in the pattern of investment could mean breaking the rules under which the system operates, insofar as it may conflict with the criteria of profitability.

Also, there is a quite marked underutilization of capital, the factor allegedly in scarce supply. According to an ILPES-CELADE (UN-Latin American Institute for Socio-Economic Planning-Latin American Commission for Development) study, between 1960 and 1963, only 58.2 percent of industrial productive capacity was utilized. This situation, which tends to perpetuate itself, is attributed to distribution and levels of income and to causes of a technologic nature (27).

Furthermore, the emergence of the highly controlled economy in the international economic sphere has resulted in strong links between domestic and foreign capital, and this has constituted a relationship that has meant an external decapitalization, where private investment, as the Foreign Ministers of Latin America (except Cuba) indicated in the Viña del Mar meeting in 1969 (32), has meant,

... and now means, that the sums taken out of our [Latin American] countries are several times higher than the amounts invested. Our potential capital is being reduced. The profits on investment grow and multiply, not in our countries but abroad. So-called aid, with all the well-known restrictions attached to it, means markets and further development for the developed countries, but it does not compensate for the sums which leave Latin America as payment for external indebtedness or as profits produced by direct private investment. In a word, we know that Latin America gives more than it receives.

Contrary to Rostow's thesis, the diffusion of capital does not go from developed to developing countries, but rather, from developing to developed. In 1969, the same year the Foreign Ministries meeting took place, U.S. companies took out of Latin America roughly $1 billion more in profits than they invested there (33). And as Frank (21, p. 50) has noted, the largest part of the capital

... which the developed countries own in the underdeveloped ones was never sent from the former to the latter at all but was, on the contrary acquired by the developed countries in the now underdeveloped ones.

THE FLOW OF HUMAN CAPITAL IN THE HEALTH SECTOR FROM DEVELOPING TO DEVELOPED COUNTRIES

Here, again, reflecting what occurs in other sectors of the economy, there is a pattern of diffusion and flow of human health resources from Latin America to North America that represents a savings for the North American economy. Indeed, it has been estimated that the overall saving for the U.S. as a result of the inflow of 5756 physicians from developing countries in 1971 was equivalent to the yearly output from fully half of the 120 U.S. medical schools (34).

Foreign-trained doctors presently represent 20 per cent of all practicing physicians in the United States, and some states have a higher proportion, e.g. New York, with 38 per cent (35). In some specialties and types of practice these percentages are higher still. For instance, preliminary data from a recent survey of mental hospitals conducted by the American Psychiatric Association, indicated that two-thirds of filled psychiatric positions were held by foreign-trained physicians (35). All before mentioned figures, incidentally, include only permanent U.S. residents and exclude interns, residents, fellows, and exchange visitors. When we include all these categories, then, the annual inflow of foreign physicians who entered the United States in 1970, 1971, and 1972 was far greater than the number the country produced in each one of those years (36). Of those who stayed and became permanent residents during the decade 1960-1970, 35 per cent came from Latin America (37), representing an annual direct and indirect savings during that period of approximately $400 million—a superior amount to the annual "aid" in medical care and hospitals that went from the U.S. to Latin America in the same time period, estimated to be $20 million (38). It is worth underlining that this medical "aid" is mainly focused on teaching hospitals, perpetuating the pattern of production that benefits the consumption of the donor country and of those groups in the recipient country that Frank calls the lumpen-bourgeoisie. (By lumpen-bourgeoisie is meant those domestic social groups in underdeveloped societies that control most of the wealth of their society and who, at the same time, have identical interests to those of foreign industry and commerce. The expression "lumpen" is added to the term bourgeoisie because their economic, social, and political power is dependent on the power of the bourgeoisie of the metropolis (18, p. 5)).

The pattern of production prevalent in the health sector of developing countries, as we will see later, is hospital-based, technologic and specialized medicine relevant to the needs of the lumpen-bourgeoisie but not to the majority of the population.

The exodus of human health resources implies a very serious decapitalization for each donor country. Ozlak and Caputo (36) have estimated that the annual loss for the whole of Latin America due to the flow of physicians to the United States is $200 million, a figure which is equal to Chile's education budget for 1970, or to the total medical aid given by the United States to Latin America throughout the decade of the 1960s. This decapitalization is particularly accentuated in some countries, such as the Dominican Republic, where one half of that nation's newborn children die before reaching the age of five, and from which country 30 per cent of medical school graduates each year emigrate to the United States (39).

THE CAUSES OF UNDERDEVELOPMENT OF HUMAN RESOURCES INSIDE AND OUTSIDE THE HEALTH SECTOR

The main reason for underdevelopment in Latin America, as a recent UN-ECLA report (40) states, is the nature, subject, and control of economic and social investment leading to a pattern of production and consumption aimed at optimizing the benefits of the foreign and national controllers of that capital, and not at stimulating the equitable distribution of resources in the particular Latin American nations. The report emphasizes that these patterns of investment

> . . . determine a structure of production in the modern sector which is mainly characterized by the production of consumer goods, particularly consumer durables of a luxury type. Even the relatively small scale production of capital goods is designed to reinforce production machinery that is geared to consumption, to the detriment of a possible expansion of the capital goods sector which might boost the development of the rest of the economy and ensure its ultimate capacity for self-sustained development.

Also, in another UN-ECLA report (41) it is said that

> ... the establishment or expansion of a sector of consumer durables or luxury goods, such as automobiles, television sets, or refrigerators—the base of mass consumption in developed countries—tends to depend upon the expansion and broadening of credit and loan facilities. In substance, savings and cash assets of various types, including foreign loans, are absorbed by these activities and diverted from a hypothetical, direct role in the formation of productive capital.

These patterns of production and consumption repeat themselves throughout the primary, secondary, and tertiary sectors of the economy, with the tertiary sector, including health services and education, supporting the secondary and primary sectors. Furthermore, within the tertiary sector (as with the other two sectors), the public sector is, on the whole, aimed at strengthening the private sector.

Indeed, parallel to what occurs in the overall economy, the same social groups that determine the patterns of production and consumption in the primary and secondary sectors also shape patterns of production and consumption in the health sector. And it can be posited that these are patterns that do not benefit the majority of the population. In addition, as in other economic sectors, the public sector exists to take care of and strengthen (some may say so as to avoid its collapse) the private sector. Finally, the overall cause of the lack of health services coverage of the whole population is not the scarcity of capital and resources in the health sector, but the maldistribution and maluse of those resources.

THE FALLACY OF UNDERDEVELOPMENT

In summary, the cause of underdevelopment and its consequent maldistribution of resources is not (a) the scarcity of the proper "values" and technology in poor countries, (b) scarcity of capital, and (c) the insufficient diffusion of capital, values and technology from developed society to the underdeveloped country's enclave and from the enclave to the rural areas, but quite the opposite. The cause of underdevelopment in poor nations is precisely the existence of Rostow's "conditions for development" in these countries. That is, (a) too much cultural and technologic dependency, and (b) the underuse and poor use of existing capital by certain national and international groups who have control of those resources. Moreover, factors (a) and (b) determine factor (c), the "dual economies" with the advanced, urban-based entrepreneurial market sector and the underdeveloped, rural-based, "non-market" marginal sector. The so-called "marginal" and "market" sectors of the economy, in fact, are intrinsically linked, so one cannot explain one sector without explicating the other. The development of the "market" model is determined by the underdevelopment of the "marginal" form. Indeed, the wealth of the enclave is based on the surplus generated by the "marginal" rural sector. And contrary to Rostow's assumption, it is the intrusion of the values of the developed countries along with their technology and "entrepreneurial, market, international" capital into the poor societies, that creates the source of underdevelopment. As Frank (21, p. 8) has shown, the regions that are most underdeveloped and that seem today the most feudal

> ... are the ones which had the closest ties to the metropolis in the past. They are the regions which were the greatest exporters of primary products to and the biggest sources of capital for the world metropolis and were abandoned by the metropolis when for one reason or another business fell off. This hypothesis also contradicts the generally held

thesis that the source of a region's underdevelopment is its isolation and its pre-capitalist institutions.

Frank further explains that this is illustrated by

> ... the former super-satellite development and present ultra-underdevelopment of the once sugar-exporting West Indies, Northeastern Brazil, the ex-mining districts of Minas Gerais in Brazil, highland Peru, and Bolivia, and the central Mexican states of Guanajuato, Zacatecas, and others whose names were made world famous centuries ago by their silver. There surely are no major regions in Latin America which are today more cursed by underdevelopment and poverty; yet all of these regions, like Bengal in India, once provided the life blood of mercantile and industrial capitalist development in the metropolis. These regions' participation in the development of the world capitalist system gave them, already in their golden age, the typical structure of underdevelopment of a capitalist export economy. When the market for their sugar or the wealth of their mines disappeared and the metropolis abandoned them to their own devices, the already existing economic, political, and social structure of these regions prohibited autonomous generation of economic development and left them no alternative but to turn in upon themselves and to degenerate into the ultra-underdevelopment we find there today.

Despite the claims of the Rostowian theories of underdevelopment popular in the United States, the main cause of underdevelopment is control of the economy by a small percentage of the population, Frank's lumpen-bourgeoisie, which has strong connections with international capital and close affinity to the values, tastes and forms of consumption typical in the developed countries. It is this group which establishes and determines the pattern of production and consumption in underdeveloped societies, and which moulds a pattern of production and consumption that is not conducive to, nor is it aimed at, the overall development of those societies.

An example of the power of the lumpen-bourgeoisie can be seen in the automobile industry. Prebisch (42) has commented:

> What happened in the automobile industry was instructive. Not only did several countries attempt to do the same thing, but there was also an extraordinary proliferation of uneconomic plants in one country. In addition to Argentina and Brazil, countries which at present have real production, there are four other countries—Colombia, Mexico, Chile, and Venezuela—which maintain assembly plants and are preparing to begin production. The total Latin American market for passenger vehicles—estimated at little more than 300,000 units annually—has to be divided among nearly 40 present and potential manufacturers, while each of the principal European manufacturers delivers 250,000 to 500,000 units to the market annually.

It has been estimated that the annual value of automobile production in Argentina in the middle-1960s could in five years double the country's road network and

> ... that a much more complete system of public transportation could be provided if only a part of this same amount were invested in buses and trucks instead of in private cars for the affluent minority (43).

Also, that

> ... costs of both "foreign" and national investment in an industry like the automobile industry lead to greater underdevelopment. They result in underutilization of national resources, improper use of resources which might have been more adequately employed in promoting self-sustaining economic development, deepening inequalities in the distribution of national income, and the creation by these industries of vested economic, social, and political interests which are committed to continuing policies of

underdevelopment. All this has an unfavorable effect on other existing industries and on the national economy as a whole (18, p. 111).

Thus the consumption patterns of the lumpen-bourgeoisie and the middle class, stimulated by a "value system" aimed at producing a consumer society with Western, middle class standards of living (which would come about in the last stage of the Rostowian process of development), divert capital from potential investment. It should be added that in Latin America the lumpen-bourgeoisie and middle class make up only between 15 per cent and 20 per cent of the population (44), and the majority of the people, who are not of lumpen-bourgeoisie and middle class level, do not fully participate in the consumer society. In a similar manner to that observed by Marcuse (45) in developed societies, the majority of the population is made to aspire to "more," where "more" is always unattainable.

Let me state here that I group the middle class with the lumpen-bourgeoisie because, in agreement with an increasing number of social critics, I believe that economically the middle class functions as a dependent group to the lumpen-bourgeoisie. In this respect, a UN-ECLA report (46) states that "the middle class in Latin America . . . improved their social status by coming to terms with the oligarchy." Indeed, throughout the underdeveloped countries, as Kolko (47) has also shown for the U.S., when the income of the middle class rises, it increases at the expense of the large masses of poor and near poor, not at the expense of the lumpen-bourgeoisie (21, p. 39).

The pattern of consumption of the lumpen-bourgeoisie and middle class, meant to benefit a limited percentage of the population, can also be seen in the distribution of health resources. Accordingly, the distribution of health resources follows an inverse relationship to the need for them. This maldistribution, by type of care, by regions, by social class and by the type of financing, is determined by those same parameters that define the evident socioeconomic underdevelopment, which I examined in the preceding sections.

THE PREVALENT PATTERNS OF CONSUMPTION: IMBALANCE BY TYPE OF CARE

The use made by the population of Colombia of the available health services, according to the 1965-1966 health manpower survey previously mentioned (3), was such that for a period of two weeks, out of each group of 1,000 people, 387 of whom were defined as sick, 63 were under the care of an ambulatory physician and 2 under hospital care (24, p. 143). Comparing this distribution of need and utilization of health services, very likely similar in most Latin American countries, with the actual consumption of resources as measured by expenditures in several countries, shown in Table 1, we see that the pattern of public consumption of the Colombian health peso is such that the two hospital patients consume approximately 30 per cent of the health peso in the public sector and the 63 ambulatory patients about 60 per cent (with all types of curative services taking up around 91.2 per cent of the peso). In comparison, environmental services (including operating and capital expenditures), only consume 8 per cent of the Colombian health peso in that sector (48). When the private consumption is added to the public one, the percentage of overall consumption for environmental services is even lower, being between 4.4 per cent and 5 per cent. The situation is similar in other Latin American countries.

Table 1

Estimated health expenditures of the public health sector in medical care and water and sewerage supply per capita and by percentages of total health expenditures[a] [b]

Country	Year	Medical Care[c]		Water and Sewerage		Total	
		Per Capita Expenditures (U.S.$)[d]	Per cent[d]	Per Capita Expenditures (U.S.$)[d]	Per cent[d]	Per Capita Expenditures (U.S.$)[d]	Per cent[d]
Colombia	1970	8.5	91.2	0.82	8.8	9.32	100
Nicaragua	1969	14.6	94.4	0.86	5.6	15.46	100
Peru	1969	10.6	94.2	0.65	5.8	11.25	100
El Salvador	1970	6.1	94.4	0.36	5.6	6.46	100
Venezuela	1970	38.6	95.6	1.79	4.4	40.39	100

[a] Source, reference 48.

[b] If instead of considering only expenditures of public sector on medical care, we consider estimations of total expenditures in medical care (public sector plus private sector), the percentages of expenditures in water and sewerage would be as follows: Colombia, 4.4-6 per cent; Peru, 1.5-4.7 per cent; El Salvador, 0.2-2.1 per cent; and Venezuela, 4-23 per cent.

[c] Data on distribution of expenditures in medical care between primary, secondary, and tertiary care are available only for Chile (*Study of Human Resources.* Chilean Ministry of Public Health, Santiago, 1970), and are partially available for Peru (Hall, T. *Study of Human Resources.* Johns Hopkins Press, Baltimore, 1971). Extracted from these sources are the following data on medical services expenditures: Chile (1968), ambulatory, 13.4 per cent; dental, 17.9 per cent; laboratory, 4.3 per cent; hospitalization, 9.4 per cent; and pharmaceutical, 55 per cent. In Peru (1964), 29 per cent of expenditures were for pharmaceutical costs.

[d] Source, *Annual Report of the Director, 1971.* Pan American Health Organization, Washington, D.C., 1971. From the total amount invested between January 1961-December 1970, an annual mean of investments has been obtained, and from this, per capita expenditures have been calculated.

If we look at the type of morbidity prevalent in the surveyed population (i.e. infectious diseases and malnutrition) and at the comparative effectiveness of the different health activities for combating this morbidity, it would seem that environmental health services and preventive personal health services should be given far higher priority than curative services, and particularly the hospital services. In spite of this, the production of human resources, through the medical education imported from developed societies, serves to perpetuate this hospital-oriented, curative medicine approach which only strengthens the maldistribution of resources according to type of care by replicating the consumption of health resources prevalent in developed societies (49).

Imbalance in consumption by type of health care is also apparent in the distribution of health manpower according to specialties. Table 2 shows the percentage distribution of physicians, by specialty, for the United States and for three Latin American countries.

The distribution of specialties is very similar in both the developing and the developed countries represented here. Actually, in twelve Latin American countries, surgery represents the top specialty by percentage of physicians, with pediatrics and public health being the lowest categories. It should be obvious that there is an oversupply of the former specialty, and—in countries with 48 per cent of their population under 15 years of age and morbidity mainly caused by environmental and nutritional deficiencies—an undersupply of the latter specialties.

The orientation toward a hospital-based, curative medicine pattern of consumption seen in developed societies is replicated, through the medical education and the structure

Table 2

Percentage distribution of physicians by some specialties[a]

Country	Year	General Practice	Public Health	Surgery	Pediatrics
Argentina	1969	8.9	—	26.7	8.6
Ecuador	1970	45.8	—	17.8	8.4
Paraguay	1971	8.2	0.7	15.2	8.0
United States	1970	17.8	0.8	20.0	6.0

[a] Source, *Health Manpower in the Americas*. Department of Human Resources, Pan American Health Organization, Washington, D.C., 1973.

of health services, in underdeveloped countries, because the means of production and consumption in the health sector are controlled by the lumpen-bourgeoisie, which desires the same type of care (with the "latest" in medical care) given to the people in developed lands. Due to the emigration of physicians from developing to developed societies described earlier, this pattern of production of human resources also benefits consumers in the metropolis.

It is also worth noting that the patterns of production and consumption in the metropolis or developed societies also are not aimed at meeting the needs of the majority of their population. As Bettelheim (50) indicates, the pattern of economic and social production and consumption of developing countries, and the consequent economic and social dependency, concerns only the bourgeoisie of both types of societies, and does not benefit the majority of the population in either. This can be clearly seen in the distribution of human health resources by type of health care. Indeed, Table 2 shows a distribution of resources unfavorable to the pattern of need in both societies. Also, it should be noted that the decapitalization of human resources in the underdeveloped country does not necessarily benefit the majority of the population in the developed nation. In fact, as Stevens and Vermeulen (37) have shown, most immigrant physicians in the United States tend to concentrate in already overserved areas and very few practice in the underserved areas of that country.

This pattern of consumption by type of care, in both developing and developed countries, is characterized by the broadening of choice for the few, and the narrowing of choice for the many. Actually, as the prestigious Chilean economist de Ahumada (51) has indicated, each dollar spent in Latin America on highly specialized hospital services costs a hundred lives. Had each dollar been spent on providing safe drinking water and in supplying food to the population, a hundred lives could have been saved. However hyperbolic Ahumada's statement may sound, it nevertheless provides a devastating critique of the pattern of investment in most developing countries.

REGIONAL IMBALANCE

The important political and economic influence the city based lumpen-bourgeoisie has on the distribution of resources also means that most of the human health resources are centered on the poor country's "enclave" of the market foreign-oriented economy. Thus, although most of the economic production is in the non-enclave areas, the agricultural

Table 3

Distribution of population and number of physicians per 10,000
inhabitants in some Latin American countries[a]

Country	Year[c]	Physicians Per 10,000	Localities Less Than 20,000 Population		Localities 20,000-99,999 Population		Localities More Than 100,000 Population[b]	
			Physicians Per 10,000	Per cent of Population	Physicians Per 10,000	Per cent of Population	Physicians Per 10,000	Per cent of Population
Colombia	1970 (1964)	5.4	0.78	63.9	2.10	9.5	15.1	26.6
Nicaragua	1971 (1969)	4.5	1.37	72.6	11.2	8.6	13.8	18.8
Peru[d]	1969 (1961)	5.2	(1.6)	76.0	(1.6)	16.8	14.5	7.2
El Salvador	1969	2.3	2.64	81.1	6.2	5.1	11.1	13.3

[a] Source, reference 48. Data taken from *Quadrennial Projections, 1971*. Pan American Health Organization, Washington, D.C., 1971.

[b] Includes national capitals: Bogotá (1967), 13.7 physicians per 10,000 people; Managua (1971), 13.8 physicians per 10,000 people. In 1969, El Salvador had only two cities over 100,000 inhabitants, the capital, San Salvador, being one of these.

[c] Figures in parentheses refer to the census years in which the listed population distributions were determined.

[d] Figures for physicians per 10,000 people in Peru are for localities with less than 100,000 inhabitants.

and extraction sectors, the consumption of services, including human health resources, is urban and is primarily in the underdeveloped country's capital.

Table 3 compares the distribution of human health resources by community size in different countries and shows that those resources are concentrated not in the small communities, where most of the people live, but in the large cities and primarily in the capital.

The lumpen-bourgeoisie influences the distribution of resources by: (a) Stressing the "market model" in the distribution of resources, in the same way that it expounds a "liberal ideology" at the economic level. Resources are thus distributed according to consuming, not producing power.[9] This consumer power, as indicated before, is urban-based. (b) Influence on the means of production, i.e. urban-based medical education. As Freidson (53) has stated, "A profession attains and maintains its position by virtue of the protection and patronage of some elite segment of society which has been persuaded that there is some special value in its work." (c) Control of the social content and nature of the medical profession, due to the unavailability and inaccessibility to the majority of the population of university education (24, p. 200); and (d) control of the highly centralized, urban-based State organs, whereby the public sector, controlled by the different branches of the State,[10] is basically meant to support the private and social security sectors.

THE CONSEQUENCES OF THE ENCLAVE THEORY IN THE HEALTH SECTOR

Private and social security sectors take care of considerable parts of the urban-based lumpen-bourgeoisie and middle classes, with the public sector taking care of the majority of the population, either the lumpen-proletariat in the urban areas or the peasantry in the rural areas, which together constitute 70 per cent of the Latin American population (44). This distribution of resources seems to reflect the dual economy theory of Rostow. Indeed, you will recall, within the Rostowian theory, that the third or take-off stage was Rostow's stage for the change from a primitive or traditional society to a consumer-oriented society. This take-off takes place through investment (primarily in the industrial sector) in the underdeveloped countries. In this process of development the country moves toward the features of the developed countries, predicting for the developing countries a future similar to that of the wealthy ones. Within this interpretation, the industrial sector is the dynamic factor in the Latin American economy. As Roemer (55) says,

> . . . the economic development of a country depends upon industrialization. Even the improvement of agriculture depends largely on the production of farm machinery, transport, fertilizer, and other items requiring industrial processes. Thus, it is reasonable for a developing country to give priority in health resource allocation to its industrial workers. A skilled industrial worker represents a social investment; that is, the attainment of the skill ordinarily requires long training and experience.

As a result of this human investment theory, the investment of resources should be based on the industrial sector. Roemer continues:

[9] For an excellent analysis of the parameters that define the market model, see reference 52.

[10] The State includes the following institutions: the government, the administration, the military and police, the judicial branch, and the parliamentary assemblies, all of whose interrelationships determine the form of the state system (54).

Thus, it seems to me that in countries of all types—industrialized and developing, capitalist and socialist—the social insurance mechanism is virtually an inevitable stage in the political and economic process of attaining effective distribution of personal health services to a total population. In the course of this evolution there may well be temporary inequities, favoring certain social groups as compared with others, but this is in the very nature of social progress. It is realistically not a great price to pay for the advantages of stability, planning, the achievement of a higher priority for health, and all the other advantages of the social insurance approach discussed earlier.

This interpretation, however, does not correspond to the dynamics of the development currently observable in Latin America. Actually, as UN-ECLA (56) has shown, the industrial sector is not a dynamic factor in the Latin American economy.

Industry has ceased to be a driving force in the Latin American economy; instead, it has simply become one of the number of sectors with no special power to galvanize the others.

As indicated before (and also as pointed out by UN-ECLA, Frank, and very many others), the pattern of investments in this sector is aimed at sustaining the consumer goods industry rather than establishing a force for economic development. The control of that investment by the lumpen-bourgeoisie and its foreign counterparts optimizes the pattern of investments that diverts capital from actual development purposes. Also, and as Frank (18, p. 119) notes, the same productive processes and structures which promote underdevelopment also produce high incomes for the Latin American bourgeoisie. The industrial sector then is controlled by and functions for the lumpen-bourgeoisie and its foreign counterparts, not for the benefit of the development of the whole of the individual country. Furthermore, even though this sector served as a stimulant for development in North America and Europe, it is not a dynamic sector in Latin America because, unlike those two continents, the Latin American continent lacks a great internal demand that can sustain its industrial sector. The difference between Latin America and those other areas is that in North America and in Europe industrialization did not precede, but followed, profound structural changes and reforms, primarily in agriculture, which determined an internal demand that sustained the process of industrialization. As Feder (57), a consultant to UN-ECLA and UN-FAO, has pointed out, the main obstacle to industrialization and development in Latin America is the system of land ownership, and the lack of meaningful land reform which could create such an internal demand.

Because of its lack of dynamism, the industrial sector has remained stagnant, and it employed the same percentage of the labor force (14 per cent) from 1950 to 1969. In addition, and reflecting this stagnation, social security coverage for the middle sectors—professionals, white and blue collar workers—has remained rather constant in the last decade, and has exhibited very slow, if any, expansion. Table 4 shows the percentage of population covered by social security in various countries, in different time periods. Actually, all the increase in Latin American social security coverage has concerned the services sector (primarily the group comprising government employees), which has been the fastest growing sector in Latin America. In 1969, 43 per cent of the labor force was in services (18, p. 52).

It is therefore highly questionable whether, as long as the pattern of control in those sectors remains the same, the industrial (and services) sector can be the dynamic multiplier it has been assumed to be. Because of the small percentage of the population involved, the expenditures per capita in the social security sector and within social

Table 4

Percentage of population in social security[a]

Country	Year		
	1966	1968	1970
Colombia	6.21	6.22	6.21
Peru	8.90	8.90	9.00
El Salvador	4.80	4.90	4.90

[a] Source, Inter-America Institute of Social Security, Mexico City, 1973.

security in the health services, are proportionately very high indeed. Table 5 shows the expenditures per capita in the three sectors in different countries, underlining the social priorities in those societies.

Private and social security cover not more than 25 per cent of the population while consuming over 60 per cent of all health expenditures, while 70 per cent of the population consumes under 40 per cent of all expenditures (48). Since 80 per cent of all expenditures are for human resources, one could postulate that the majority of human resources follows an equal maldistribution pattern.

This distribution of resources in the health sector parallels the distribution of other resources in the tertiary and secondary sectors of the economy. Thus, social security covers a small group, the "aristocratic" portion of the labor force, and this is a group that, although not the most dynamic in the overall development, is needed to sustain the industries and services of the consumer-oriented lumpen-bourgeoisie and their foreign counterparts. In addition, not unlike the use made of the social security mechanism in developed societies, social security in Latin America has been used to try to integrate (and some may say coopt) sectors of the labor force into the "market-urban based" economy (58).

CONCLUSION

The highly skewed distribution of human health resources in Latin America is a symptom of the maldistribution of resources in the different sectors of the economy, a maldistribution that, as postulated in this article, is due to the economic and cultural dependency of Latin American countries and to the control of the distribution of economic and social resources (including health resources) in those countries by a national lumpen-bourgeoisie with links with foreign counterparts.

If the analyses reflected in this paper are accurate, the implications for Latin America would be quite substantial. It can be postulated that it would be unhistorical to expect that changes towards equity can occur in the present distribution of resources, within and outside the health sector, without changing the economic and cultural dependency and the control by the defined social classes of the mechanism of control and distribution of those resources.

Indeed, in Latin America today, it would be inaccurate to expect a more equitable distribution of human health resources within a highly inequitable distribution of all resources, because of the highly skewed distribution of the mechanism of economic and

Table 5

Estimated per capita expenditures by sector in selected Latin American countries[a][b]

Country	Year	Government		Social Security		Private	
		Population	Per Capita Expenditures	Population	Per Capita Expenditures	Population	Per Capita Expenditures
		%	U.S. $	%	U.S. $	%	U.S. $
Chile[c]	1968	78.6	22.80	–	–	10.8	±100
Colombia[d]	1970	85.0	9.14	6.0	27.27	9.0	≥100
Peru[e]	1969	73.3	8.14	8.8	52.76	12.0	≥100
El Salvador[f]	1970	84.2	5.23	4.8	35.51	11.0	≥100

[a] Source, reference 48.

[b] Studies of private expenditures have only been carried out in Chile. We have estimated that the per capita expenditures in the other Latin American countries are at least equal to the Chilean figures since every country has a greater percentage of beds in the private sector. For Peru in 1964, the public sector accounted for 76 per cent of the total health expenditures (Hall, T. *Health and Manpower in Chile*. Johns Hopkins Press, Baltimore, 1971). If we assume that in 1969, 24 per cent of the expenditures were still in the private sector, this would give a per capita expenditure of U.S. $88.37 for the beneficiaries of the private sector.

[c] Source, *Study of Human Resources*, Chilean Ministry of Public Health, Santiago, 1970. Chile has had a national health service since 1952, accounting for 75 per cent of outpatient visits and 91 per cent of hospitalizations in the country. We have considered as beneficiaries the 78.6 per cent of the population who appeared to belong to the group having a per capita income below .59 SV (vital salary). We have assumed the 10.8 per cent of the population belonging to the group having a per capita income above 1.0 SV to be the beneficiaries in the private sector.

[d] Source, *Quadrennial Projections: Colombia, 1971*, Pan American Health Organization, Washington, D.C., 1971. Social Security includes the groups of Instituto Colombiano de Seguros Sociales and Caza Nacional de Prevision. According to the study on health manpower and medical education in Colombia (see reference 3), the per capita expenditures for general population in 1961-1965 were 6-10 times lower than the per capita expenditures of the "special population," which included social security for workers and employees and health services of the military forces.

[e] Source, *Quadrennial Projections: Peru, 1971*, Pan American Health Organization, Washington, D.C., 1971. In Peru, 22 per cent of the total population lacks any type of health service. The 73.3 per cent figure for the government sector includes this 22 per cent. Social Security includes the systems for both workers and employees.

[f] Source, *Quadrennial Projections: El Salvador, 1971*, Pan American Health Organization, Washington, D.C., 1971. Social Security refers to the group of the Instituto Salvadoreno de Seguridad Social.

33

political control. As King (59) and I, myself (60), have both indicated, Cuba shows that in the world of underdevelopment an egalitarian society is required in order to achieve an equitable distribution of human health resources. To achieve it, the two parameters of underdevelopment (a) economic and cultural dependency and (b) economic and political control by the lumpen-bourgeoisie and its foreign counterparts, have to be redefined and discontinued.

Again, if my analysis of the underdevelopment of human health resources is accurate, it would seem that the political institutionalized channels currently controlled by these groups are not adequate nor sufficient to stimulate the redistribution of resources (inside and outside the health sector) in most of Latin America.

It is apparent that the institutionalization of the distribution of power and control in the mechanism of distribution of resources, inside as well as outside the health sector, is a profound, almost insurmountable, obstacle to the equitable distribution of human health resources. Meanwhile, as Myrdal (61) has said, the institutionalization of that power means that:

> In the Latin American situation gross violence is . . . exerted all the time, mostly against poor people to keep them suppressed. The whole economic and social order . . . must rightly be seen as "institutionalized violence."

And when the disenfranchised majority rebels against that institutionalized violence, as happened in Cuba, almost universal revulsion is expressed by the organs of communication (which are controlled by the groups that also control those structures). As Moore (62) has pointed out:

> The way nearly all history has been written imposes an overwhelming bias against revolutionary violence . . . . the use of force by the oppressed against their former masters has been the object of nearly universal condemnation. Meanwhile the day-to-day repression of "normal" society hovers dimly in the background of most history books.

And, meanwhile, the institutionalized violence continues. And when the privileges of the lumpen-bourgeoisie and its international counterparts and corresponding middle classes are threatened, the implied violence in those institutional structures appears explicit, as the sad event of this morning in Chile shows, with the brute use of the armed forces. (This paper was presented on September 11, 1973, a sad day for Latin America when a military junta deposed the Popular Unity Government of Chile.)

Nevertheless, the persistence of that distribution of power, the main cause of the present maldistribution of resources within and outside the health sector, cannot be considered as insurmountable. Indeed, a stimulus and cause for the dissolution of that obstacle will certainly be the increasing awareness of the disenfranchised majorities of alternative patterns for the distribution of those resources and alternative strategies for determining change.

Acknowledgments. This work was supported in part by grants from the National Center for Health Services Research and Development (5R01 HS 00110 and 5T01 HS 00112) and from the National Institutes of Health, U.S. Department of Health, Education, and Welfare (5D04 AH 00076). I am indebted to Christopher George and Renate Wilson for editing this paper, and to Kathy Kelly for preparing the manuscript.

REFERENCES

1. Myrdal, G. Diplomacy by terminology, Appendix I. In *Asian Drama*, Vol. 3, p. 1839. Pantheon Books, New York, 1968.
2. Ruderman, A. P. Book Review of Bryant, J. *Health and the Developing World*. In *Int. J. Health Serv.* 1(3): 293-303, 1971.
3. Social Science and Health Planning: Culture, Disease and Health Services in Colombia. Special Issue of *Milbank Mem. Fund Q.* 46(2, Part 2), 1968.
4. Kuznets, S. Quantitative aspects of the economic growth of nations. *Economic Development and Cultural Change* 11(2, Part 2), January 1963.
5. Birnbaum, N. *Toward a Critical Sociology*. Oxford University Press, New York, 1971.
6. Mills, C. W. *Sociology and Pragmatism: The Higher Learning in America*. Oxford University Press, New York, 1966.
7. Bell, D. *End of Ideology*. The Free Press, New York, 1960.
8. Blackburn, R., editor. *Ideology in Social Science*. John M. Fontana, New York, 1972.
9. Barkhuus, A., and Vargas, R. *Socio-Economic Planning in Latin America*. Pan American Health Organization, Washington, D.C., 1971 (mimeographed).
10. Parsons, T. *Structure and Process in Modern Societies*. The Free Press, New York, 1960.
11. Hoselitz, B. F. *Sociological Factors in Economic Development*. The Free Press, New York, 1960.
12. Frank, A. G. Sociology of development and underdevelopment of sociology. In Cockroft, J. D., Frank, A. G., and Johnson, D. L. *Dependence and Underdevelopment: Latin America's Political Economy*, pp. 321-397. Doubleday and Company, New York, 1972.
13. Kahn, H., and Weiner, A. J. The next 33 years. *Daedalus* pp. 705-732, Summer 1967.
14. Russett, B. *Comparado de Indicadores Sociales y Politicos*. Euramerica, S.A., 1968.
15. Mussaff, H. *The 1975-85 National Health Plan of the U.A.R.* United Arab Republic, Ministry of Health, Cairo, 1972 (mimeographed).
16. Rostow, W. W. *The Stages of Economic Growth*. Cambridge University Press, Cambridge, 1962.
17. Rostow, W. W. *The Stages of Economic Growth*, pp. 4, 7, 39. Cambridge University Press, Cambridge, 1962. Quoted in Frank, A. G. *Latin America: Underdevelopment or Revolution*, p. 40. Monthly Review Press, New York and London, 1969.
18. Frank, A. G. *Lumpenbourgeoisie + Lumpendevelopment: Dependence, Class, and Politics in Latin America*. Monthly Review Press, New York and London, 1973.
19. Baran, P. *The Longer-View: Essays Towards a Critique of Political Economy*. Monthly Review Press, New York and London, 1969.
20. Griffin, K. *Underdevelopment in Spanish America*. The MIT Press, Cambridge, Massachusetts, 1969.
21. Frank, A. G. *Latin America: Underdevelopment or Revolution*. Monthly Review Press, New York and London, 1969.
22. UNESCO Report. Cited in *New York Times*, p. 4, June 14, 1973.
23. UNESCO Report. Cited in Myrdal, G., *The Challenge of World Poverty*. Pantheon Books, New York, 1970.
24. Garcia, C. *La Educación Médica en la America Latina*. Pan American Health Organization, Washington, D.C., 1973.
25. McKeown, T. A historical appraisal of the medical task. In McLachlan, G., and McKeown, T. *Medical History and Medical Care*. Oxford University Press, New York, 1971.
26. Navarro, V. Report of a Visit to Cali. Department of Medical Care and Hospitals, School of Hygiene and Public Health, The Johns Hopkins University, 1970 (mimeographed).
27. Fucaraccio, A. Birth control and the argument of saving and investment. *Int. J. Health Serv.* 3(2): 133-144, 1973.
28. Illich, I. Outwitting the "developed" nations. In *National Health Care*, edited by R. H. Elling, pp. 263-276. Aldine Atherton, Inc., Chicago, 1971.
29. Technology and Development for Whom? *Bulletin of the Scientists and Engineers for Social Action* July 1973.
30. Navarro, V. Report of a Visit to the Planning Office of the Colombian Government. Department of Medical Care and Hospitals, School of Hygiene and Public Health, The Johns Hopkins University, 1970 (mimeographed).
31. International Development Bank. *Socio-Economic Progress in Latin America*, Eighth Annual Report. World Bank, Washington, D.C., 1968.
32. Foreign Ministries of Latin America, Declaration. Viña del Mar, Chile, 1969.
33. *Newsweek* June 23, 1969.
34. *New York Times Magazine* p. 79, September 16, 1973.

35. Williams, K. N., and Lockett, B. A. Migration of Foreign Physicians to the United States. Paper presented at the Pan American Conference on Health Manpower Planning, Ottawa, Canada, September 10-14, 1973 (mimeographed).
36. Ozlak, O., and Caputo, D. The Migration of Medical Personnel from Latin America to the United States: Toward an Alternative Interpretation. Paper presented at the Pan American Conference on Health Manpower Planning, Ottawa, Canada, September 10-14, 1973 (mimeographed).
37. Stevens, R., and Vermeulen, T. *Foreign Trained Physicians and American Medicine*. U.S. Department of Health, Education, and Welfare Publication No. (NIH)73-325. U.S. Government Printing Office, Washington, D.C., 1973.
38. U.S. Foreign Assistance Program, Annual Report to Congress, 1971. U.S. Government Printing Office, Washington, D.C., 1971.
39. Basin, M. Science, Technology and the People of Latin America. Unpublished paper, 1972.
40. United Nations Economic Council for Latin America. *Economic Survey of Latin America, 1968. Part I, Some Aspects of the Latin American Economy Towards the End of the 1960's*, p. 71. E/CN.12/825. United Nations, New York, 1968. Quoted in Frank, A. G. *Lumpenbourgeoisie + Lumpendevelopment: Dependence, Class, and Politics in Latin America*, p. 103. Monthly Review Press, New York and London, 1973.
41. United Nations Economic Council for Latin America. *Mobilization of Internal Resources*, p. 64. E/CN.12/827. United Nations, New York, 1970. Quoted in Frank, A. G. *Lumpenbourgeoisie + Lumpendevelopment: Dependence, Class, and Politics in Latin America*, p. 104. Monthly Review Press, New York and London, 1973.
42. Prebisch, R. *Latin American Integration*. Fondo de Cultura Económica. Mexico City, 1969 (in Spanish).
43. Peña, M. Industrialization and the national bourgeoisie. *Fichas* June 1965.
44. Petras, J. *Politics and Social Structure in Latin America*. Monthly Review Press, New York and London, 1970.
45. Marcuse, H. Repressive tolerance. In *A Critique of Pure Tolerance*, edited by R. P. Wolff, B. Moore, and H. Marcuse, pp. 81-123. Beacon Press, Boston, 1965.
46. United Nations Economic Council for Latin America. *Social Change and Social Development Policy in Latin America*, p. 79. E/CN.12/826. United Nations, New York, 1970. Quoted in Frank, A. G. *Lumpenbourgeoisie + Lumpendevelopment: Dependence, Class, and Politics in Latin America*, p. 134. Monthly Review Press, New York and London, 1973.
47. Kolko, G. *Wealth and Power in America*. Praeger Publishers, New York, 1968.
48. Navarro, V. An Analysis of Cost and Expenditures in Latin America for the Period 1965-1970. Unpublished manuscript.
49. Anderson, O. W. *Health Care: Can There Be Equity?* John Wiley and Sons, New York, 1973.
50. Bettelheim, C. Reply to A. Emmanuel, Appendix I. In Emmanuel, A. *Unequal Exchange; A Study of the Imperialism of Trade*, pp. 271-322. Monthly Review Press, New York and London, 1972.
51. de Ahumada, J. Quoted in Illich, I. Outwitting the "developed" nations. In *National Health Care*, edited by R. H. Elling, p. 266. Aldine·Atherton, Inc., Chicago, 1971.
52. Godelier, M. *Rationality and Irrationality in Economics*. Monthly Review Press, New York and London, 1973.
53. Freidson, E. *Professional Dominance: The Social Structure of Medical Care*. Atherton Press, New York, 1970.
54. Miliband, R. *The State in Capitalist Society: An Analysis of the System of Power*. Weidenfeld and Nicolson, London, 1970.
55. Roemer, M. Social security for medical care: Is it justified in developing countries? *Int. J. Health Serv.* 1(4): 354-361, 1971.
56. United Nations Economic Council for Latin America. *Industrial Development in Latin America*, p. 10. E/CN.12/830. United Nations, New York, 1970. Quoted in Frank, A. G. *Lumpenbourgeoisie + Lumpendevelopment: Dependence, Class, and Politics in Latin America*, p. 93. Monthly Review Press, New York and London, 1973.
57. Feder, E. *The Rape of the Peasantry: Latin America's Landholding System*. Anchor Books, Doubleday and Company, New York, 1971.
58. Rimlinger, G. V. *Welfare Policy and Industrialization in Europe, America, and Russia*. John Wiley and Sons, Inc., New York, 1971.
59. King, M. Reply to Book Review by A. P. Ruderman of Bryant, J. *Health and the Developing World*. In *Int. J. Health Serv.* 1(4): 415-416, 1971.
60. Navarro, V. Health services in Cuba: An initial appraisal. *N. Engl. J. Med.* 287: 954-959, 1972.
61. Myrdal, G. *The Challenge of World Poverty*, pp. 483-484. Pantheon Books, New York, 1970.
62. Moore, B. *Social Origins of Dictatorship and Democracy: Lord and Peasant in the Making of the Modern World*. Beacon Press, Boston, 1966.

CHAPTER 2

Human Rights, Health, and Capital Accumulation in the Third World

Michel Chossudovsky

This study examines the relationship between state violence and the pattern of capital accumulation in the Third World. More specifically, we are concerned with the incidence of institutionalized repression on the articulation and development of the low-wage industrial enclave. *Poverty politics* and *economic repression* have become the instrumental modus operandi of capitalist expansion in the periphery of the world economy. The repressive authoritarian peripheral State increasingly constitutes the means for enforcing the intensive exploitation of labor in Third World industrial enclaves and commercial agriculture.

Political repression and state violence constitute the means for enforcing sub-subsistence wage levels in the industrial export sector through the elimination of trade unions, the curtailment of political parties, and the suppression of organized political opposition.

While the rhetoric of American foreign diplomacy stresses human rights, the actual practice of imperial state policy has been more forcefully directed toward the consolidation of politically repressive and authoritarian military regimes throughout the Third World. The rhetorical concern for human rights provides American foreign diplomacy with an ideological weapon which elegantly mystifies the role of political repression in supporting the expansion of capitalism in the periphery. While liberal rhetoric is geared toward "achieving a more just and humane international order," organized repression and the curtailment of human rights increasingly constitute the "external economies" which support foreign investment and the internationalization of capital to the periphery.

The relationship between organized repression and capital accumulation has evolved in parallel with the shifts in the international division of labor in the postwar years. Increasingly, the peripheral labor process has moved toward the development of low-technology transformation industries which incorporate homogeneous unqualified Third World labor power hired at a wage rate more than ten times lower than in center capitalist countries.

While the development of center capitalism has evolved toward "the Welfare State" and the framework of so-called "liberal sociodemocracy," the *"peripheral State"* is generally characterized by nondemocratic and politically repressive forms of government. This *bipolarity* in the state structure between center and periphery is functionally related to the international division of labor and the unity of production and circulation on a world level.

Under center capitalism, the programs and policies of the center Welfare State (namely, education, training of qualified labor, health and social security, etc.) constitute an input of "human capital" into the labor process. Moreover, welfare programs in industrialized countries activate the process of circulation by sustaining and maintaining high levels of consumer demand and purchasing power.

In underdeveloped countries, the peripheral State supports the requirements of the low-wage economy. The distribution and allocation of state expenditure, the underlying vacuum in the social sectors, the important allocations to military expenditure and *repressive technology* are functionally related to the requirements of the peripheral labor process.

In view of the existence in the periphery of an "excess supply" or "reserve army" of unqualified labor power, the requirements of maintenance, upkeep, and training of human labor power are at a minimum. On the other hand, the process of *freezing wages below subsistence* requires the support of institutionalized repression and heavy expenditures on the instruments and equipment of repression.

CAPITAL ACCUMULATION AND THE LOW-WAGE ECONOMY

The structure of peripheral capital accumulation and its related policies of *economic repression* have a direct influence on real purchasing power and hence on the health status of the population. Capital accumulation in the periphery is based on underconsumption and low wages. Wages—invariably contained through repressive methods—constitute the objective labor costs for transnational corporations investing in the Third World. At the same time, underconsumption in the domestic market releases output to be sold and realized in the world market. Low standards of living and poverty are at the same time an instrumental "input" into peripheral capitalist production (i.e. low wages and poverty imply low labor costs) as well as a consequence or an "output" of that process.

The consolidation of the low-wage enclave under repressive Pinochet-Marcos style regimes significantly reduces the internal demand for food. While Argentina, for instance, had in the postwar period the highest level of food consumption (and food production) in the South American subcontinent, the process of impoverishment which took place after the March 1976 military coup constituted the means for reorienting the Argentinian agricultural sector more forcefully toward export markets. Whereas underconsumption reduces the internal demand for food, thereby creating the appropriate supply conditions for export, the freeze on agricultural wages constitutes the required "cost incentive" for the development of agricultural and agro-industrial exports.

A low food intake, therefore, serves a twofold purpose. First, it means cheaper "nontraditional industrial exports" (i.e. the cost of maintenance of labor power is lower); second, the reduction in internal food consumption allows a reallocation of land use patterns, thereby favoring the parallel consolidation of agro and agro-industrial export crops. Underconsumption in food and undernourishment constitute the necessary ingredients for the development of a commercial export-oriented agriculture.

Institutionalized state violence in one form or another has supported the process of capitalist expansion from the very beginning of the colonial mercantile period. "Legitimized" repression by the colonial administration was firmly integrated into the political network of the imperial State. The development of mineral extraction and the cash-crop economy in the 19th century in West Africa, for instance, required a more cohesive political structure and the development of a full-fledged colonial administrative apparatus. Bagchi (1) describes British imperial rule in India as based on plunder—plunder presumably taking on different institutional forms but always requiring the political and repressive apparatus of the imperial State.

According to Lenin (2),

> The non-economic superstructure which grows on the basis of finance capital, its politics and its ideology, stimulates the striving for colonial conquest. "Finance capital does not want liberty, it wants domination."

The exercise of state violence historically has therefore taken on different forms. During the colonial period, the imperial and peripheral State apparati are formally integrated. The colonial administration is an appendage of the national State structure of the metropolis. Decolonization and the transition to national statehood has meant the formal separation of the imperial (national) and peripheral State structures and the development of new institutional mechanisms which serve the purpose of integrating the political superstructure of center and periphery.

The imperial State structure is characterized by the national institutions of the imperial State (i.e. foreign affairs, intelligence, foreign aid, defense) and the international entities of what might be called *"the imperial State network."* These include international institutions such as the Organization of American States, the North

Atlantic Treaty Organization, the World Bank, and the Organisation for Economic Co-operation and Development (OECD). These institutions belong to an interstate network which integrates the peripheral State with the state structure of center capitalist countries.

We may speak of areas of jurisdiction. The imperial State network regulates through juridico-political and institutional mechanisms the functioning of the international economy. In this regard, the international economic and political entities of the imperial State network developed (in the postwar years) in parallel with the changes occurring in the process and structure of world capitalism. Imperial international economic policy—which is partly implemented through the various economic entities of the imperial State network (World Bank, the International Monetary Fund (IMF), OECD)—is essentially oriented toward devising the economic and institutional support mechanisms which sustain the internationalization of capital. In the economic sphere, the imperial State network is essentially concerned with (a) the regulation of trade and of the international monetary system; and (b) the monitoring of capital flows and "foreign aid" between center and periphery. Capital flows by the World Bank, for instance, are directed toward infrastructural investment projects in the periphery which constitute "external economies" for private foreign investment. The IMF has played an important role in monitoring the national economic policy of the peripheral State. IMF missions have invariably recommended "austerity measures" which often make the country more attractive to foreign investment. The *intellectual technology* which characterizes IMF mission reports is designed toward a "programmed recession" in the internal wage goods market brought about through a freeze on wages and salaries. These measures are usually accompanied by devaluations (of the local currency) and economic and financial measures which "strengthen" the export sector.

IMF package economic proposals can often only be implemented through politically repressive methods. Invariably, their "successful" adoption requires the support and endorsement of the repressive apparatus of the peripheral State.

Regulation in the political sphere (by the imperial State network) pertains to defense agreements and military aid (including the training of military personnel, intelligence, and national security), as well as to institutional arrangements and exchange in such areas as science, technology, and education.

With regard to arms sales, while much of the weaponry provided by the United States to client Third World military regimes is theoretically intended "to help these countries defend themselves against external attacks," an examination of U.S. arms exports suggests that a large portion is in fact designed for internal repression (3):

> U.S. government records show that U.S. agencies and corporations are providing arms, equipment, training and technical support to the police and para-military forces more directly involved in torture, assassination and incarceration of civilian dissidents. . . . Rather than standing in detached judgement over the spread of repression abroad, the United States stands at the supply end of a pipeline of repressive technology extending to many of the Third World authoritarian governments.[1]

---

[1] Klare (3) points out that "recent arm export deliveries [by the United States] have included armored cars, tear gas, riot guns, counter insurgency planes and other weapons unsuitable for anything else other than internal security."

The peripheral State has a *theoretical* monopoly of "legitimized" violence within the boundaries of the peripheral nation-State. In other words, political repression is conducted internally by the national police and military apparatus. The role of the imperial State in internal police operations remains latent and in the background as long as the peripheral client State has a more or less uncontested monopoly of violence. Thus, the relative autonomy of the national client State. Under these conditions, the activities of the imperial State will be limited to the training of police, military and para-police personnel, "advisory" functions relating to "internal national security" of the client State, and so forth.

The various repressive entities of the client State, however, are invariably integrated into the military and decision-making apparatus of the imperial State. This operates through several channels: the training of officers (e.g. high-ranking Latin American officers are trained in Panama and the United States), military aid, defense agreements, international consultations of chiefs of staff, and the existence of military bases of the imperial State in a number of client Third World countries.

The intervention of the imperial State becomes "active" when the monopoly of violence and underlying institutional framework of the client State are threatened, e.g. the intervention of the United States in the Dominican Republic and the dispatching of French and Moroccan troops to Zaïre in support of Mobutu in 1977-1978.

The Political Economy of State Violence

Repression by the capitalist State does not, in principle, operate *directly* on the labor process. The wage labor system (in its pure form) is only possible if state violence is not directly exercised on the labor process. There is, therefore, a fundamental distinction between the social relations of capitalist production, where the wage-laborer enters into a contract *without compulsion,* and, for instance, a system of forced labor. In the latter case, "legitimized violence" is exercised directly on the labor process, whereas in the former case state violence is applied to "enforce" the wage contract, which has been given prior legitimacy by a set of legal, institutional, and political rules pertaining to the mechanics of wage determination, the length of the working day, and the right to strike.

The labor process, therefore, is regulated *indirectly* by the juridico-political and institutional mechanisms of the State. These regulations—once they are *legitimized* by the State in terms of a body of legal and institutional norms—imply a de facto legitimization of police repression which "enforces" these legal and institutional norms.

There is a coherent relationship between institutionalized repression by the peripheral State and the conduct of economic policy. Conventional political repression, the curtailment of civil liberties, and the recess of political parties are intimately related to a parallel process of *economic repression* which consists in:

- Curtailing (and/or eliminating) trade unions, and replacing them by corporate institutions controlled by the State. Wages are often determined centrally by the State; economic policy is geared to: (a) "freezing wages and freeing prices"; and (b) the liberalization of trade and foreign investment. These measures are implemented according to homogeneous economic criteria. Liberalization and austerity measures are often monitored by the International Monetary Fund.

- In Latin America, liberalization measures have invariably contributed to a "programmed recession" in the internal wage goods sector.

THE INTERNATIONAL DIVISION OF LABOR

The international division of labor has taken on a new structure which is a consequence of the particular form whereby the peripheral economy is integrated into the industrial matrix of center capitalist countries. Whereas imperialism in its early phase until World War II was largely based on the exploitation, depletion and/or nonrenewal of natural agricultural and mineral resources, the advanced contemporary phase is increasingly characterized by the development of so-called "nontraditional exports" and transformation industries which use unqualified labor. The postwar period is characterized by an acceleration in capital exports to the periphery by major industrial nations. While petroleum and mineral extraction still receives a large proportion of international investment, the structure and sectoral breakdown of this investment are in the process of changing in favor of manufacturing industry, agro-industry, and commercial agriculture (4).

The international division of labor no longer relates to the geographical location of commodity production. It relates more specifically to the nature of the labor process. The development of transnational corporations in the postwar period has contributed to the internationalization of capital through the dispersion of the productive activities of multinational consortia on a world level. A transnational operating on the basis of cost minimization will therefore shift its productive activities in accordance with the disparities in the wage level structure between center and periphery. The available evidence suggests that the cost of labor power in the industrial enclave of the periphery is on average one-tenth of the average wage in the center. In 1973, the average hourly wage for 15 selected peripheral industrial enclaves was in the neighborhood of U.S. 40 cents whereas the average wage in the United States was in excess of $4.00 (see Table 1).

The published official figures tend to overestimate the real wage situation in the countries analyzed and do not exhibit, except in a few cases, the process of impoverishment and economic repression following the establishment of a repressive military regime. The minimum wage is substantially below the published average wage. The concept may vary from one country to another. Generally, it tends to include the salaried labor force in the so-called "modern" sector, including, in many cases, white-collar workers. The figures suggested in Table 1, while not necessarily representative of the overall tendencies in real wages, give us an idea of the *order of magnitude* of the cost of labor power for a multinational investing in the periphery (expressed in U.S. dollars). It is on the basis of these figures that we can analyze the cost structure of transnationals and the process of internationalization of capital. For the year 1975, this cost varies from a low of U.S. 12 cents an hour in Chile to U.S. 23 cents in the Philippines, U.S. 42 cents in South Korea, U.S. 53 cents in Taiwan, and U.S. 58 cents in Hong Kong and Singapore.

The official statistics—which are often deliberately biased or falsified—exhibit the fall in real wages which followed the establishment of a repressive military regime only in a few cases, i.e. Chile (1973), Argentina (1976), and the Dominican Republic (1965). In the case of Brazil, the *official* index reflects the tendencies in industrial wages in the more organized sectors of the Saõ Paulo urban labor force. The deterioration in the level of real wages and the process of economic repression are best illustrated in relation to the underlying tendencies in the minimum wage.

According to the compiled statistics, the cost of an hour of industrial labor power in the periphery has increased in real terms (constant 1963 U.S. dollars) in most of the South Asian countries with the exception of the Philippines, where it has declined by 35 percent (from 20 cents in 1965 to 13 cents in 1975, constant 1963 U.S. dollars). For the Philippines, Taiwan, South Korea, and Thailand the structure of labor costs (for a multinational) is practically identical, varying from an average for the period of U.S. 15 cents (expressed in 1963 constant dollars) in Thailand, to U.S. 16 cents in the Philippines, and U.S. 17 cents in South Korea and Taiwan. In Singapore and Hong Kong, it was U.S. 27 cents (1963 constant dollars) for the average of the period.

Inflation often is a means for implementing a programmed decline in industrial wages. Consumer prices in Chile in the month after the 1973 military coup were, *according to official falsified statistics,* in the neighborhood of 88 percent. In Argentina in the month after the 1976 military coup, the official price index increased by 34 percent.

In Argentina the fall in the real industrial wage which followed the 1976 military coup was of the order of 50 percent (5). In Chile after the 1973 military coup, real purchasing power declined by 60 percent in the first few months of the Pinochet regime and by more than 80 percent after 1 year. These shifts in purchasing power obviously imply important changes in the structure of income distribution. In Chile, for instance, at least 25 percent of total income has been transferred from the lower- and middle-income groups to the upper 5 percent income bracket. The upper 5 percent income bracket controls more than 50 percent of total income (6, 7).

In Brazil, the minimum wage has fallen by more than 50 percent since 1964 (8). According to the Departamento de Informaçao e Estudos Estadisticos Socio-Economicos, a worker receiving the minimum wage in 1972 would have to work over 132 hours to purchase the monthly minimum food bundle as opposed to 87 hours in December 1965. The fall in purchasing power has tended to be accompanied by de facto increases in the length of the working day (an 8-hour working day is insufficient to meet the costs of subsistence). In the metallurgical industry in Saõ Paulo, the working week has been extended to 66 hours.

Qualification/Dequalification of the Labor Process

The international division of labor involves a bipolar tendency towards *qualification/dequalification* of the labor force between the metropolis and the periphery of the world economy (9, 10). Capitalist development in the periphery is based on the reproduction of a homogeneous and unskilled labor power with little or no investment

Table 1

Cost for 1 hour of labor power in current and constant U.S. dollars, various countries, 1965-1976[a]

Country	1965	1966	1967	1968	1969	1970	1971	1972	1973	1974	1975	1976
Argentina												
Nominal	.37	.38	.35	.36	.40	.41	.45	.66	1.16	1.49	.33	—
Constant	.36	.36	.32	.32	.33	.32	.34	.48	.80	.92	.19	—
Brazil												
Nominal	.23	.37	.38	.35	.41	.46	.51	.63	—	—	—	—
Constant	.22	.35	.35	.31	.34	.36	.38	.46	—	—	—	—
Chile												
Nominal	—	.37	.36	.36	.38	.45	.49	.52	.10	.13	.12	—
Constant	—	.35	.33	.32	.32	.35	.37	.38	.07	.08	.07	—
Dominican Republic												
Nominal	.40	.38	.31	.34	.39	.38	.41	.41	.39	.45	—	—
Constant	.39	.36	.28	.30	.34	.30	.31	.30	.27	.28	—	—
Guatemala												
Nominal	.37	.38	.40	.41	.43	.43	.43	.43	.43	.44	—	—
Constant	.36	.36	.37	.36	.36	.34	.32	.31	.30	.27	—	—
Peru												
Nominal	.35	.38	—	.32	.36	.39	.41	.51	.63	.78	.80	—
Constant	.34	.36	—	.28	.30	.31	.31	.37	.43	.48	.45	—
Hong Kong												
Nominal	.21	.22	.22	.23	.26	.30	.37	.42	.52	.57	.58	.59
Constant	.20	.21	.20	.20	.22	.24	.28	.31	.36	.35	.33	.32
Korea, South												
Nominal	.09	.10	.12	.15	.19	.23	.24	.26	.29	.33	.42	.56
Constant	.09	.09	.11	.13	.16	.18	.20	.19	.20	.20	.24	.30
Morocco												
Nominal	.17	.17	.17	.17	.17	.16	.20	.20	.27	.53	—	—
Constant	.16	.16	.16	.15	.14	.13	.15	.15	.19	.33	—	—

Philippines												
Nominal	.21	.23	.24	.24	.25	.17	.20	.21	.23	.23	.23	—
Constant	.20	.22	.22	.21	.21	.13	.15	.15	.16	.14	.13	—
Singapore												
Nominal	.30	.29	.31	.31	.29	.29	.31	.34	.43	.54	.58	—
Constant	.29	.27	.28	.27	.24	.23	.23	.25	.29	.33	.33	—
Taiwan												
Nominal	.16	.17	.20	.22	.22	.24	.28	.30	.33	.45	.53	—
Constant	.16	.16	.18	.19	.17	.19	.21	.22	.23	.28	.30	—
Thailand												
Nominal	.18	.15	.16	.17	.18	.17	.21	—	—	—	—	—
Constant	.17	.14	.15	.15	.15	.14	.16	—	—	—	—	—
Average nominal	.25	.28	.27	.28	.30	.31	.35	.41	.43	.54	.45	
Average constant	.245	.260	.245	.245	.252	.247	.262	.297	.30	.332	.225	
Nominal U.S. $	2.61	2.72	2.83	3.01	3.19	3.36	3.56	3.81	4.07	—	—	

[a] Source, International Labor Office.

in "human capital." While accumulation in center capitalist countries is tending toward a high content of "human capital" and a sustained development of high-technology industries, capitalist development in the Third World increasingly orients itself toward *hardware* transformation industries. The technology utilized is not, however, of an inferior variety. Labor productivity depends entirely on the nature of the labor process and technology rather than on the level of qualification of labor.

The Nonrenewal of Human Labor Power

Depletion of nonrenewable as well as renewable natural resources has accompanied the development of imperial monopoly capital. The *nonrenewal of peripheral human labor power* corresponds to an advanced phase in the development of world capitalism which is associated with the growth of the low-wage industrial and agro-industrial enclaves.

The development of the low-wage enclave is invariably sustained through the maintenance of a surplus population or reserve army of unemployed. The supply of unqualified labor power is generally abundant and, therefore, the "costs of maintenance and upkeep" of human labor will be less demanding. We would suggest that the reproductive process in both peripheral industry and commercial agriculture leads to the *"nonrenewal and depletion"* of human labor power. Real wages in terms of the necessities of life are insufficient to meet the requirements of subsistence of the laborer and his family.

The *nonrenewal* of human labor power proceeds until the process of *depletion* of labor power sets in and puts an upward pressure on the wage rate. The high organic composition of capital in the enclave industrial sector controlled by monopoly capital tends, however, to limit the demand for labor, thereby counteracting the upward pressure on wages. Moreover, the elimination of trade unions, the curtailment of collective bargaining, as well as the consolidation of traditional techniques of political repression by the State become the means for implementing and enforcing an industrial wage rate substantially below subsistence.

HUMAN CAPITAL FORMATION, REPRODUCTION OF LABOR POWER AND THE ORGANIC COMPOSITION OF LABOR

We now turn our attention to the relationship between the low-wage economy and the allocation of the state financial surplus in support of capital accumulation. Particular emphasis will be given to analyzing the role of the so-called social sectors and health in particular in the maintenance and upkeep of human labor power.

Health and educational services are both a part of *social consumption* as well as a component of *social capital*. As social capital, state expenditures in health, education, social security, housing, etc. are incorporated into variable capital in terms of what conventional economists entitle "investment in man." These inputs, which originate in government social services, increase what might be designated *"the organic composition of labor."* Investment in health and education has an effect on the productivity of labor power. More specifically, it determines the "quality of labor power." The *"organic composition of labor"* refers to the *quality composition* of variable capital, i.e. the value of qualified labor in relation to total social capital.

In fact it may be difficult to separate state investments which are directed toward the maintenance and upkeep of human labor from those which have a direct influence on productivity. What is relevant, however, is to ascertain the influence of these investments on the cost structure of production and on the division between necessary and surplus labor time. In this respect, financial returns in health and education are measured in relation to the cumulative impact on surplus value over the productive lifetime of human labor power.[2]

Investment in Health

Programs in health in the Third World are hardly ever a social objective *sui generis* (except perhaps as a rhetorical-normative objective of development planning). The social and economic functions of health programs are intimately related to the organic structure of the peripheral State and the mechanics whereby the State allocates its financial surplus in support of capitalist production in the private sector. Invariably, state health programs (as well as institutions) in the Third World are socially stratified. Access to health is restricted and "socially rationed." The institutional make-up of the health sector (and hence the distribution of health services) is divided along class lines (11). The large majorities of poor urban and rural workers, of unemployed and unskilled labor receive little or no health services while the bulk of conventional curative (and preventive) health is directed toward: (a) a small privileged minority; and (b) specific programs linked to the maintenance and reproduction of professional, skilled, and white-collar labor, i.e. what might be loosely designated as the "Third World middle classes." These programs often fall under a small social security plan financed by contributions from the State, the employer, and the employee.

In other words, the health sector serves essentially two purposes:

- Insofar as the recipients belong to an unproductive high-income "elite" class, health and education programs endorse and support the "social reproduction" of that class. In this context, expenditures in the social sectors serve the purpose of "social cohesiveness" in consolidating an elite minority which identifies with the interests of imperial monopoly capital. These expenditures are a part of social consumption received by an "unproductive" so-called "elite" class.
- The maintenance and upkeep of human labor power through government health programs. As we pointed out earlier, the *"social investment"* component of these social services in the peripheral economy is of limited importance in view of the nature of the labor process (i.e. the low organic composition of labor).

---

[2]The measuring of financial returns in health and education has been written on extensively in the neoclassical literature on human capital. The underlying analysis has been applied by the World Bank and other donor institutions in the evaluation of the "social" costs and benefits of health and educational projects in the Third World.

Human Capital Formation and the International Division of Labor

Our foregoing results would suggest that the bipolarity (i.e. qualification/dequalification) in the structure of the international division of labor is conducive to bipolarity in the processes of human capital formation and "maintenance" of human labor power between center and periphery. In rich industrialized countries, the emphasis on high-technology industries implies a higher "maintenance cost" of labor power in terms of education, manpower training, low-cost housing, socialized health programs, and social security. We would argue that the various social programs of the "Welfare State" in advanced capitalist countries are intimately connected with the nature of the center labor process.

Nondepletion and *renewal* of human labor power through the center Welfare State not only are related to the requirements of qualified labor for production (increasingly oriented toward high-technology software industry with a high content of research and development, technological innovation, etc.) but also the programs of the Welfare State activate the process of circulation. High standards of living and the Welfare State constitute the means for maintaining a high rate of surplus absorption, thereby "counteracting" the tendency toward underconsumption and economic stagnation in center capitalist countries.

We would suggest that there is a functional dichotomy in the unity of production and circulation on a world level. What is produced in the periphery is almost entirely realized, i.e. sold, in the center (i.e. purchasing power in the periphery is restricted to a small privileged minority). While the tendency toward economic stagnation in center capitalist countries and the decline in the rate of profit in the postwar period have implied a slowdown in investment in center capitalist countries—particularly in the low-technology hardware industries which are transferred to the periphery—high levels of consumption, high wages, and the various programs of the Welfare State, while adversely affecting the rate of profit, play an important role on a world level in the realization of surplus value.

BIPOLARITY AND THE STRUCTURE OF THE STATE

While center capitalist countries have a well-developed police and internal security apparatus, state violence and police repression in advanced countries in the postwar period have remained latent and in the background, manifested only in periods of crisis. This does not mean that the center capitalist State is not potentially violent.

The institutional make-up of the Western capitalist State, involving the so-called "free interplay" of political parties in a "pluralistic" political spectrum, is related to the processes of both accumulation and circulation. If the Western democratic process were to be seriously undermined, the repercussions on the economic system would be far-reaching. High levels of consumer demand in the West require, in a sense, the maintenance of the institutions of the Western sociodemocratic Welfare State. These institutions, as we mentioned earlier, constitute a safeguard against underconsumption as well as an instrument for the "maintenance and reproduction" of center labor power through state programs in health, social welfare, education, and so forth.

In the periphery, on the other hand, both the nature of the labor process (i.e. based on unqualified labor) and the relative abundance of human labor power at low cost do not generally require the support and endorsement of government welfare programs. On the contrary, the activities of the peripheral State in the social sectors in fact contribute to the *nonrenewal* of human labor power.

While the center capitalist State hinges on *welfare* (i.e. the Welfare State), the peripheral State is based on *nonwelfare*. Nonwelfare and *the programming of poverty* operate in several related ways. First, through the allocation of the state financial surplus among competing public expenditure programs. The peripheral State will generally orient its spending toward physical *"material external economies"* such as port facilities, roads, etc. rather than toward *"human external economies"* (e.g. health and education). The tendency is exactly the opposite in the center (Welfare) State.

Moreover, what might be designated as "nonwelfare policies" are more forcefully realized through expenditures on the instruments and equipment for internal repression. Military equipment and *repressive technology* constitute a productive "external economy" which reduces "the political risk factor" for foreign investment by ensuring "stable and harmonious" labor relations. In view of its influence on labor costs, investment in repressive technology constitutes an "input" into capital accumulation.

Illustrations of the relationship between organized repression and the labor process are given below for selected countries.

Argentina. In Argentina a new Law (*Ley de Contrato de Trabajo*) regulating labor contracts was introduced in 1976 "so as to protect the principle of equity and avoid situations which generate abuse between labor and management." Cost of living adjustment clauses were removed from the new legislation. The right to strike has been suppressed. Wages are determined centrally by executive decree and employers are prohibited to grant unilateral wage increases (5).

Brazil. In Brazil wage readjustments are determined by the CNPS (National Wage Police Council). Strikes are forbidden in industries of "national interest." According to Institutional Act No. 5, an "unlawful strike" becomes a political crime (8). The Brazilian government, while denying the application of torture and political repression, has explicitly justified the *State of Exception* and the provisions of national security as necessary requirements for sustained economic growth (8, p. 27):

> The area of work legislation in Brazil is completely dominated by the Doctrine of National Security. The right to strike is forbidden, real unions are dissolved, and those which are tolerated are placed under the direct control of the regime and the military authorities who appoint delegates. . . .

Chile. In Chile after the 1973 military coup, trade unions were disbanded and wage and salary increases were regulated by decree law (*decreto ley*) enacted centrally by the military Junta (6).

Indonesia. In Indonesia, according to the Presidential Decree on the Eradication of Subversive Activities (12), anyone who "disturbs, retards or disrupts industry, production, distribution, commerce, cooperatives or transport conducted by the government . . . shall be convicted of engaging in subversive activities."

Iran. In Iran, trade unions are illegal and labor unrest is violently repressed. Iran is one of the few countries (with Indonesia) for which official data on industrial wages are not available (13).

The Philippines. In the Philippines, according to Presidential Decree No. 823,

> All forms of strikes, picketings and lockouts are strictly prohibited in vital industries. . . . For the purposes of this Decree the term "strike" shall comprise not only concerted work stoppages, but also slowdowns, mass leaves, sitdowns, attempts to damage, destroy or sabotage plant, equipment and facilities and *similar activities* [italics added] (14).

Taiwan. In Taiwan, capital punishment applies inter alia to "strikes by workers which disrupt public order" (15).

CONCLUDING REMARKS

In this article we have argued that:

1. Peripheral capital accumulation receives the support of the state repressive apparatus. Political repression has a direct influence on labor costs by keeping real wages under tight institutional control.
2. The State, through the allocation of its financial surplus, supports peripheral capital accumulation in terms of large outlays on repressive technology and military equipment used for internal repression. These outlays, together with other material infrastructural investment (e.g. roads, port facilities, industrial infrastructure, etc.), constitute external economies for foreign investment.
3. Investment on repressive technology and material infrastructural investment both have an influence on the relationship between necessary and surplus labor time.
4. In view of the nature of the peripheral labor process based on an abundant supply of unqualified human labor power, state investments in "human capital formation" and in the "maintenance and upkeep of human labor power" are minimal. This explains the vacuum in the social sectors. The latter, together with the low-wage structure, contributes to the nonrenewal of human labor power.

The nonrenewal of labor and the *programming of poverty* have a pervasive influence on the *state of health* of the population. The latter (which is reflected by various indicators of mortality and morbidity) may be regarded as the *state* which results from a particular pattern of social consumption. The various components of social consumption, which include both goods and services purchased in the market as well as government services (health and education), may be regarded as *flow variables* (i.e. consumption per unit of time) which have a cumulative effect on the educational and health status of the population (7, Ch. 1; 16) For instance, food consumption (i.e. the intake of nutrients) is a flow variable which has a cumulative effect on the incidence of malnutrition (undernourishment is a *flow* variable whereas nutrition is a *state* variable). Low educational achievement and illiteracy is the *state* which results from a *flow* (or *nonflow*) of educational services. More generally, education and health together with the other (market) components of social consumption are *flows* which have an influence on the *health and educational status* of the population.

This study has only made cursory and indirect reference to human rights *stricto sensu*. The corollary of our analysis, however, pertains in a very direct way to human rights, human rights not as a *moral issue* but as a *structural dimension* of capital accumulation on a world level. The *respect for* or *violation of* human rights is intimately related to the bipolarity in the international division of labor. The denial of human rights in the Third World is invariably associated with an economically repressive labor process.

The liberal humanist critic of repression in the Third World wants, in the words of Bukharin, "to eliminate dark imperialism, leaving intact the sunny sides of the capitalist order." While liberal humanist rhetoric may rally world public opinion, it serves no useful purpose in the scientific analysis of human rights and of economic and political repression. The actual practice of peripheral capitalism is in fact the exact antithesis of the "*spirit of Anglo-Saxon liberalism.*" The latter, however, constitutes the ideological cornerstone upon which an apology of the "less sunny sides of capitalism" is embodied into Western foreign diplomacy as well as into the intellectual formalizations of "official" Western scholarship.

REFERENCES

1. Bagchi, A. K. Foreign capital and economic development in India. In *Imperialism and Revolution in South Asia,* edited by K. Gough and H. P. Sharma. Monthly Review Press, New York, 1973.
2. Lenin, V. I. *Imperialism,* p. 84. International Publishers, New York, 1939.
3. Klare, M. *Supplying Repression,* p. 8. Field Foundation, New York, 1977.
4. Palloix, C. *L'internationalisation du capital,* p. 69. François Maspéro, Paris, 1976.
5. Chossudovsky, M. Legitimized violence and economic policy in Argentina. *Economic and Political Weekly* 12(16): 631, 1977.
6. Chossudovsky, M. Hacia el nuevo modelo economico chileno: Inflacion y redistribucion del ingreso. *El Trimestre Economico,* Vol. 42, No. 166, 1975.
7. Chossudovsky, M. Chicago economics, Chilean style. *Monthly Review,* Vol. 26, No. 11, 1975.
8. Weil, J-L., et al. The Repressive State. *Brazilian Studies,* Collection Documents Vol. III, No. 2. Latin American Research Unit, Toronto.
9. Poulantzas, N. *La crise des dictatures,* p. 15. François Maspéro, Paris, 1975.
10. Poulantzas, N. *Les classes sociales dans le capitalisme aujourd'hui.* Editions du Seuil, Paris, 1974.
11. Chossudovsky, M. *La Miseria en Venezuela,* Ch. 4. Vadell Editores, Valencia, 1977.
12. *Indonesia:* An Amnesty International Report, p.123. Amnesty International, London, 1977.
13. *Amnesty International Briefing Iran,* p. 2. Amnesty International, London, 1976.
14. Report of an *Amnesty International Mission to The Republic of the Philippines.* Amnesty International, London, 1976.
15. *Amnesty International Briefing Taiwan.* Amnesty International, London, 1976.
16. Drewnowski, J. *The Level of Living Index.* United Nations Research Institute for Social Development, Geneva, 1969.

The Library
Saint Francis College
Fort Wayne, Indiana 46808

CHAPTER 3

The Economic and Political Determinants of Human (Including Health) Rights

Vicente Navarro

"oh love,
they keep telling me that I have the right to sing,
but they took away my guitar;
they keep telling me that I have the right to love,
but they killed my child;
they keep telling me that I have the right to shop in the market,
but they took away my land;

oh love,
but they also keep telling me that I should not shout, hate or steal;
these, I should not do."

translated from an old Spanish folk song

This paper is based on a presentation at the symposium on "Human Rights in the New International Economic Order: The American Perspective," sponsored by the Council on Global Affairs and the Yale Association of International Law, Yale School of Law, Yale University, April 16, 1977.

INTRODUCTION: THE REDISCOVERY OF HUMAN RIGHTS IN AMERICA

The American system of power is in crisis. And that crisis is apparent in all spheres of our economic and political lives. While the economic news in the daily press hits us with constant references to unemployment, underemployment, inflation, stagnation, and other items of an equally disquieting nature, the political news carries a continuous message of concern about what a recent *New York Times* editorial called "the current crisis of trust of the people towards their political institutions." That crisis of trust, however, is not new or sudden. It crests a wave of distrust and disenchantment with our political institutions that has been increasing rather than declining for some time now. This situation was well reflected in a recent Harris Poll survey of public attitudes towards government conducted for a U.S. Congressional committee, which indicated that (1):

> ... the most striking verdict rendered [in the survey] by the American people—and disputed by their leaders—is a negative one. A majority of Americans display a degree of alienation and discontent [with government].... Those citizens who thought something was "deeply wrong" with their country had become a national majority. ... And for the first time in the ten years of opinion sampling by the Harris Survey, the growing trend of public opinion toward disenchantment with government swept more than half of all Americans with it.

Many events show such political alienation. A recent and meaningful instance was the lowest turnout for a presidential election in recent history, when barely over half of those eligible voted (2), prompting James Reston of the *New York Times* to write that "the real scandal of this election ... [has been] the indifference and even cynicism of so many of the American people." Let me add that the political alienation is reflected not only in a feeling of mistrust towards the political institutions but also in an anti-establishment mood that does not escape the notice of the establishment's centers of power. Both major presidential candidates, for example, and particularly Carter, ran the last presidential campaign with anti-establishment slogans, stressing the need "to give the government back to the people" in order to regain the people's confidence in what are supposed to be, at least in theory, their institutions. And since the election, one of the present Administration's main emphases has been—via the attendance of Carter and his Cabinet at town council meetings, the Carter telethon, and informal TV fireside chats in the evening—to convince the American people that this is indeed a People's Government.

Accompanying this new image of power has been the stress on the need for a new leadership and a new morality to be provided by the U.S. government, a leadership, incidentally, that is supposed to be asserted nationally and internationally. One strategy for winning that battle for the hearts and minds of our citizens, and for regaining their trust, has been to show the inherent superiority of our system over any other possible alternative. This emphasis on the moral superiority of our system is particularly evident in the international scene. Indeed, at a moment when alternative ideologies are proliferating throughout the world, and at a time when the western capitalist world is on the retreat, there is perceived to be a need, in the words of the former U.S. ambassador to the U.N.—today Senator Moynihan—to pass from the defensive to the offensive, and to establish the moral superiority of our system over all others (3). And in that ideological struggle and campaign, being carried out nationally and internationally, the general features assumed to be in existence in our system are abstracted as an ideal type, and are compared or contrasted with the features of other societies, particularly with regard to those other societies which have chosen patterns of development that are alleged to negate what are assumed to be the primary features of our political system, i.e. *the existence of human rights.*

Consequently, a great rekindling of debate on the nature of human rights as a determinant of policy, primarily international policy, is taking place. And all voices are being called upon to propagate, debate and discuss the concern about human rights, a concern that is presented as the new trademark of the present Administration. Today's conference here, in an established center of law, the Yale School of Law, is a partial and component response to that call.

With this interpretation of the conference's purpose in mind, let me then present an alternative and a minority view of the concern usually presented about human rights—my remarks concerning not only the whats, hows and wheres of human rights, but, equally importantly, the whys of that assumed concern for human rights. Why are significant voices of our political establishment raising that concern today? The first thing to be noticed is that most of the concern, debate and promotion of human rights, presented by conservative and liberal authors and commentators alike, is limited to its civil and political dimensions, i.e. civil and political rights as defined by the U.N. Universal Declaration of Human Rights of 1948. (For a detailed presentation and discussion of that Declaration, see Appendix B in reference 4.) And of those civil and political rights, the ones most frequently—almost exclusively—mentioned are the right to life and the right to freedom of organization and of opinion. These rights to life and liberty are the rights that supposedly characterize our system. Both the executive and the legislative branches of our government are on record for upholding the United States' dedication to human rights—as defined above—rights to life and liberty as the standards of morality in our international and national policies (5).

It is worth stressing, however, that in this strong emphasis by the established center of power in the U.S., there is no attention to or mention of the other dimensions—the social and economic ones—of human rights, also defined and included in that Universal Declaration. The rights to work, fair wages, health, education and social security that are, among others, expressed in the articles of that Declaration, are usually never even mentioned in this newly discovered concern about human rights. Actually, it is characteristic of the current presentation on human rights—as typified also by the majority of presentations in this panel[1] —that:

1. those civil and political rights, defined as rights to life and liberty, exist in this United States of ours;
2. those civil and political rights can be secured independently of the achievement of the socioeconomic rights; and

[1] Members of the panel: Eugene Rostow, Professor of International Law, Yale School of Law; Gerome Sheskack, Chairman of the International Council of the Rights of Man; Roselyn Higgins, Professor, London School of Economics; Charles Runyan, Human Rights Division, U.S. State Department; and Vicente Navarro, Professor, Johns Hopkins University.

3. human rights, as interpreted in actual debate in the U.S., i.e. the rights to life and to freedom of organization and of opinion, have a universal interpretation, valid in all types of societies and in all forms of economies.

In summary, these are the main assumptions made in present debate about human rights, and they establish the parameters on which basis that discussion takes place. It is the intention of this presentation to question all of the above assumptions and to postulate that:

1. civil and political rights are *highly restricted* in the U.S.;
2. those rights are *further restricted* in the U.S. when analyzed in their social and economic dimensions;
3. civil and political rights are *not independent of* but rather *intrinsically related and dependent on* the existence of socioeconomic rights;
4. the definition of the nature and extension of human rights in their civil, political, social and economic dimensions is *not universal,* but rather depends on the pattern of economic and political power relations particular to each society; and
5. the pattern of power relations in our society and our western system of power, based on the right to individual property and its concomitant class structure and relations, is *incompatible* with the full realization of human rights in their economic, social, political, and civil dimensions.

Due to the central importance of point 5 in explaining points 1, 2, 3, and 4, let me now expand on that point. But first, let me stress that I will have to be necessarily brief and thus will have to limit myself to the mere presentation of paradigms, and leave the burden of proof for each one to a more extensive bibliography, quoted in the text. Here, I limit myself to the presentation of those paradigms, leaving it up to the listener now and to the reader afterwards to see whether my explanation has an internal consistency and whether it helps him or her to explain our realities better than more accepted ones.

RIGHT TO PROPERTY, POLITICAL POWER, AND THE STATE, AND THEIR IMPLICATIONS IN HUMAN RIGHTS

The American Constitution established the right to individual private property and assigned to the state[2] the responsibility of safeguarding that right. This right to property determines and safeguards a concomitant class structure whereby very few— the members of the corporate class—own, control and possess most of the wealth and the means to produce it, i.e. the means of production, and where the many do not control or own much; they—the majority of Americans—own only their capacity to work—their labor power—that they sell. Indeed, contrary to the mythology that we are a people's owning society, the value of private property owned by most Americans is very limited indeed. And, for the most part, the type of property owned by the

---

[2] The term "state" includes the executive and legislative branches of government as well as the state apparatus, i.e. the administrative bureaucracy, the judiciary, the army, and the police. It is important to clarify that the state is far more than the mere aggregate of those institutions. Rather, it also includes the set of relationships between and among those institutions and with other ones that it guides and directs.

majority is property of consumer goods used for private enjoyment. But the greatest portion and most important type of property—the property of the means to produce those consumer goods—is owned by an extremely small percentage of the population. Less than 2 percent of the population, for example—the members of the corporate class and the top echelons of the upper middle class—owns at least 80 percent of all corporate stocks (the most important type of income-producing wealth) (6). In summary, under capitalism, the few control Capital and the many sell their Labor. And Capital and Labor exist in a situation of dominance of the latter by the former, a situation which is perpetuated by the responsibility of the state to safeguard the right to property. As Sweezy (7) has eloquently indicated:

> Property confers upon its owners freedom from labor and the disposal over the labor of others, and this is the essence of all social domination whatever form it may assume. It follows that the protection of property is fundamentally the assurance of social domination to owners over non-owners. And this, in turn, is precisely what is meant by class domination, which it is the primary function of the state to uphold.

Indeed, assigning to the state and to its institutions the "mere" right to protect property is in theory and practice to assure the nature of class domination. As Engels indicated, to assure the right to private property is to assure the domination of one class—the non-owners—by another—the owners. Thus, to say that it is a primary function of the state to protect private property is equivalent to saying that the state is an instrument of class domination (8). Actually, this was said and recognized by none other than Adam Smith, when, in his book, *The Wealth of Nations,* he wrote (9):

> Civil government, so far as it is instituted for the security of property, is in reality instituted for the defense of the rich against the poor, or of those who have some property against those who have none at all.

And it is that function of the state, to protect the right to property and the class relations which that right determines, that gives it its capitalist character. (For a further explanation of this point, see reference 10.) Indeed, what establishes the state, including its government, as capitalist is not so much its composition, i.e. that members of the capitalist class predominate in the main organs of the state (e.g. from 1889 to 1961, over 60 percent of the U.S. Cabinet were businessmen),[3] but, more importantly, its functions which determine (a) that they give primacy not to the interests of specific capitalist groups, but to the interests of the capitalist economy as a whole, where the private ownership of the means of production is assured and its sanctity considered to be above the interests of specific groups, and (b) that when a conflict appears between what are considered to be the needs of the economy and other needs such as an increase in the satisfaction of human needs, the former tends to take priority over the latter. And those policies respond to the need perceived by governments that the economy, upon whose health we are all supposedly dependent, has to be straightened out before "we can think of other matters." And it is this behavior, and not the specific motivation of individuals or manipulation of groups, which establishes those policies as capitalist policies.

---

[3] There is a detailed and extensive bibliography on the class composition and dominance of the organs of the state in the U.S. For a presentation and review of that bibliography, see "Social Class, Political Power and the State," Section III in reference 11.

I am aware, of course, of present mythology that indicates that ours is a "mixed economy." But ours is a society where by far the largest and most important economic activities are still dominated by private ownership and enterprise. This is why, agreeing with Miliband, I find that to speak of a mixed economy is to attribute a special and quite misleading meaning to the notion of mixture (12). In the U.S. and other capitalist societies, the state owns no more than a subsidiary part of the means of production, and, for the most part, state intervention in the economic sphere (including nationalization of economic activities) is aimed at strengthening rather than weakening the private sector. The U.S. society is a capitalist society in which the owners and controllers of the means of production have an overwhelming dominance over the organs of the state. Here again, I am also, of course, aware that this interpretation of the state and political power is contrary to prevalent pluralistic interpretations of the state as a neutral and independent set of institutions. Indeed, according to these interpretations, our societies have neither dominant classes nor dominant groups or elites. Rather, there exist competing blocks of interests, with no one having a dominant control over the state, which is assumed to be an independent entity.

In that explanation of our societies, power is thought to be diffuse, with different competing blocks balancing each other and themselves, and with no particular group or interest being able to weigh too heavily upon the state. It is believed, furthermore, that it is this very competition among interests, supervised and arbitrated by the state, that provides the prime guarantee against the concentration of power. A system is thus created that offers the possibility for all active and legitimate groups in the population to get organized and, ultimately, to make themselves heard at any crucial stage in the decision-making process. And this "being heard" takes place primarily through a parliamentary system in which a plurality of ideas is openly exchanged, complementary to the free allocation of resources that occurs in the marketplace and following, for the most part, the rules of laissez-faire. It is, of course, recognized that the system is far from perfect. But, in any case, our society is considered to have already achieved a model of democracy in light of which the notion of "ruling class" or even "power elite" is ludicrous, completely irrelevant, and of concern only to ideologues.

The main weakness of such paradigms, however, is not so much their postulate that competition exists, but, more importantly, their unmindfulness that such competition is continuously and consistently skewed in favor of some groups and against others. Indeed, as Schattschneider (13) has indicated:

> the flaw in the pluralist heaven is that the heavenly chorus sings with a very special accent ... the system is askew, loaded, and unbalanced in favor of a fraction of a minority.

As the power elite theorists have empirically shown, the different organs of the state are heavily influenced, and in some instances dominated, by specific power groups. In that respect, the pluralists' failure to recognize the consistent dominance of our state organs by specific groups is certainly not shared by the majority of the U.S. population, who believe, for example, that both political parties are in favor of big business and that America's major corporations dominate and determine the behavior of our public officials and of the different branches of the state (14).

The members of those power groups are, for the most part, components of the dominant classes—primarily capitalist but also upper middle class—and, when they are considered in a systemic and not just sectorial fashion, they are found to possess a high degree of cohesion and solidarity, with a common interest and a common purpose far transcending their specific differences and disagreements. And one of those common purposes and interests is their support of the *right to own property*.

Let me stress here that the overwhelming dominance of the capitalist class—or, in popular parlance, big business—in the organs of the state, including government, is not tantamount to actual control. There is competition between Capital and Labor realized in the area of class struggle, and defeats of capitalist interests are possible. After all, David did overcome Goliath, but, as Miliband indicates, the point of the story was that David was smaller than Goliath and that the odds were heavily against him (12). So, it is this set of class power relations that defines the rights of the citizen in society. The individual's rights, in summary, will depend on what class position he or she holds within our class society. Henry Ford and the assembly line worker of his factory have different rights, given by the class to which they belong. And the meaning of those rights is not only quite different but also in opposition and conflict. Indeed, none other than Abraham Lincoln once said:

> We all declare for liberty; but in using the same word we do not all mean the same thing. With some the word liberty may mean for each to do as he pleases with himself, and the product of his labor; while with others the same word may mean for some men to do as they please with other men, and the product of other men's labor. Here are two, not only different, but incompatible things, called by the same name, liberty. And it follows that each of the things is, by the respective parties, called by two different and incompatible names—liberty and tyranny.
> The shepherd drives the wolf from the sheep's throat, for which the sheep thanks the shepherd as his liberator, while the wolf denounces him for the same act, as the destroyer of liberty. . . . Plainly the sheep and the wolf are not agreed upon the definition of the word liberty (quoted in reference 15).

Within this introduction, describing the nature of class power relations in the U.S., let me now focus and further elaborate on the interpretation and definition of those rights under capitalism.

CIVIL RIGHTS UNDER U.S. CAPITALISM

The most frequently mentioned civil and political rights in American debate are the right to life, the right to freedom of organization, and the right of expression of opinion. Let me try to analyze very sketchily the realization of those rights in this U.S. of ours, particularly in the light of the previous discussion in which I have stressed the different degrees of power that Capital has vis-à-vis Labor in our society.

Let us start with the right to life. Here, it is worth stressing, as Raphael (16) has rightly indicated, that this right assumes not only the right to life but also the right to protection against physical or quasi-physical injury, harm, or suffering which is inflicted on someone against his or her will. The ultimate in such harm is, of course, killing someone. But the right to life in a capitalist system clearly conflicts with the right to private property, which gives to Capital the right to control the process of production intended, not to optimize workers' welfare and insure protection of life, but rather to optimize the process of capital accumulation. Because of the dominant influence that Capital has over the organs of the state, the rights to life and freedom from harm are made dependent on and secondary to the rights of Capital to pursue capital accumulation. Actually, the overwhelming amount of legislation that exists in our society to protect private property contrasts quite dramatically with the meager and obviously insufficient legislation to protect the workers against loss of life and harm at the workplace (17). And the dimensions of that harm are enormous. Four million workers contract occupational diseases every year, with as many as 100,000 deaths every year (18; also quoted in 19), while the number of on-the-job injuries exceeds 20 million per year and the number of deaths in work-related accidents reaches approximately 28,500 (20). And most of this death, harm, and disease is preventable.

Actually, the dramatic dimensions of this harm at the workplace are there for all to see. These appalling conditions are even worse for some types of occupations, such as coal mining. On the average, one miner is killed every other day in the U.S. coal mines (21). And 4,000 miners die every year from black lung disease, with one out of every five working miners being a victim of black lung (22). This is a tragic picture of the dramatic and overwhelming violations of the right to life of our working population, daily perpetuated for the glory and benefit of Capital. And very little is being done to correct such violation of human rights. And this is, no doubt, due to the overwhelming influence of Capital over the organs of the state. As indicated in a memorandum published by the Senate Watergate Committee, a Nixon official promised to the business community that "no highly controversial standards (i.e. cotton, dust, etc.) will be proposed by the Occupational Safety and Health Agency (OSHA) during the coming four years of the Nixon Administration" (23). And the records of the Ford and Carter Administrations are not much better either. The legislation to protect the worker's life and safety is extremely meager. This reality is clearly shown in this quote by A. Miller, President of the United Mine Workers of America (24):

> If a factory worker drives his car recklessly and cripples a factory owner, the worker loses his license to drive, receives a heavy fine, and may spend some time in jail. But, if a factory owner runs his business recklessly and cripples 500 workers with mercury poisoning, he rarely loses his license to do business, and never goes to jail. He may not even have to pay a fine.

Actually, after three years of operation of OSHA, only two firms have been convicted of criminal violations, and the average fine for OSHA violations has been twenty-five dollars (25). And the expressed concern by the Carter Administration that the normative functions of OSHA should not impair the functioning of the economy shows a similar set of priorities, i.e. life and safety have to be subject to a most important aim, to assure the unalterability of the process of capital accumulation. There is, in summary, a clear violation of the rights to life and freedom from harm of many and large sectors of our working population—a violation of human rights met by a deafening silence in both our legislative chambers and our media.

Here, in this context of violation of human rights, it is worth stressing the definition of violence in our society. If someone stabs and kills another person, it will be defined as an act of violence. But, if someone—an employer—perpetuates death and disease because of lack of protection of his workers against harm, this action is not considered to be *violent*. The rationale for that distinction is that the employer does not personally harm anyone, and, moreover, that he does not intend harm to the worker. Due to the prominence of the two arguments, let me further elaborate on each of them. Regarding the former, that the employer does not harm directly or personally, one must stress that the argument of impersonality as an excuse for crimes of violence was rightly dismissed in the trial of the mass murderer Eichmann in Jerusalem in 1961. The fact that Eichmann was a personable, likeable music lover, and personally unable to kill even an insect, was of *no consequence* to the definition of him as a mass murderer. The point of that judgment was that his actions, however impersonal, led to death and harm for masses of people (26). In that respect, it is worth stressing that, as Priestland (27) has indicated, most incidences of violence and violations of the right to life in the 20th century have been and continue to be impersonal. Indeed, as Barnet has also attested concerning violence in the 20th century, "those who plan, do not kill. And those who do kill, do not plan" (27, p. 80).

The other argument usually made against defining the employer's actions as violent is that the employer is *not aiming directly at the worker with the intention of causing harm*. In other words, he does not intend to kill or maim. But, as the Nuremberg judges rightly indicated, by taking an action involving a risk tantamount to near certainty that people will be killed and injured, the act must be regarded as an act of violence, regardless of the aims of the perpetrators (28, 29). Coming back to our example, many employers—coal mine owners and managers, for example—know that the absence of safety in the coal mines is highly likely to cause death and injury. In summary, then, whether or not the employers, or class of employers, do not *personally* inflict harm or death on others, or whether or not they do not *intend* to kill or injure, does not excuse their actions as nonviolent. They are indeed violent if, as a result of their actions, death and harm are likely to be and are being inflicted on their employees or workers. Consequently, it is correct to define as violent that set of class relations that puts property and the right to accumulate property over the right to life and freedom from harm, however *impersonal, indirect,* and *unintentional* those relations may be. And it is equally correct to define those economic and political institutions that sustain and replicate that set of power relations that violate the right to life and freedom from harm (established in Article 3 of the Human Declarations Charter) as violent institutions. Here, let me add a further note: while much is being said, usually with revulsion, about the individual, personal violence, not much is being said about the inherent violence of our institutions which sustain and replicate a pattern of violence that affects and harms many of our working populations.

POLITICAL RIGHTS UNDER U.S. CAPITALISM

In the previous section, I have tried to show how the control of the process of work by the few, and the overwhelming influence that they have over the organs of the state, seriously and even dramatically impairs the civil rights of the many. The overwhelming influence that big business has over the state organs is particularly accentuated here in the U.S., where there is no political arm of labor that could balance it. And that overwhelming influence by the property owners and managers of wealth—big business—over our political institutions explains the exclusion from political competition of those ideologies and those parties that question the set of class, power, and property relations in our society. Gerson (30), for example, has shown the practical impossibility for parties of the Left, parties that question the right to private property, to have any chance in the overall electoral process. The electoral and legislative processes practically exclude from political competition parties different from the two major parties—Republican and Democrat—each committed to the survival and strengthening of the capitalist system. Actually, the exclusion of alternative, anti-capitalist, anti-property voices finds its strongest expression in their actual physical repression. The physical repression of the Black Panthers, and the Communist and Socialist Parties, among others, is the subject of general knowledge and even accept-ance among the corporate-controlled media. Infiltration, sabotage, and even physical eradication of the Left are part of the normal political behavior of the American system (31, 32). The whole furor about Watergate and the use of such tactics by an over-zealous President Nixon was not because of the novelty of political repression, which has been taking place all the time against the left-wing parties, but rather because it took place against an "accepted" party, the Democratic Party.

But, far more important than physical repression is the ideological and cultural repression of the Left, aimed at excluding the presentation of alternatives to the American people. Indeed, the U.S. is a clear—almost asphyxiatingly clear—example of the accuracy of Marx's dictums that "the ideas of the ruling class are in every time the ruling ideas," and that the reason for this is that the (33):

> class which is the ruling material force in society, is at the same time its ruling intel-lectual force. The class which has the means of material production at its disposal, has control at the same time over the means of mental production, so that thereby, generally speaking, the ideas of those who lack the means of mental production are subject of it.

This situation determines what Gramsci called the "hegemony" of the dominant class in civil society, defining hegemony as (34):

> an order in which a certain way of life and thought is dominant, in which one concept of reality is diffused throughout society in all its institutional and private manifestations, informing with its spirit all taste, morality, customs, religious and political principles, and all social relations, particularly in their intellectual and moral connotations.

Let me stress here that this dominance does not require a prohibition of opposite views, but rather—and more effectively—that the ideological competition be so unequal as to give a crushing advantage to one side over the other. And it is that crush-ing inequality that profoundly constrains the political rights to both organization and expression of opinion stated in the Declaration of Human Rights. In that respect, there is an overwhelming hegemony of business in the value-generating systems of the U.S. One of those systems, the mass media, is in the private domain and is controlled not only by business, but by big business, with a rapidly increasing concentration of ownership in the press, magazines, book publishing, broadcasting, cinemas, theaters, radio, television, and all other instruments of culture (35-37; for a review of the bibliography, see reference 38). As the Commission on Freedom of the Press indicated, "the owners and managers of the press determine which persons, which facts, which version of the facts, and which ideas shall reach the public" (15). And all these corporate-controlled media foster a climate of conformity to the business values, not by total suppression of dissent, but by the

> presentation of ideas which falls outside the consensus as curious heresies or even more effectively, by treating them as irrelevant eccentricities, which serious and reasonable people may dismiss as of no consequence (12, p. 238).

This overwhelming dominance over the value-generating system by corporate class values appears also, of course, in the schools and universities, whose primary function is to replicate the ideology functional to the actual system of power relations. Indeed, a primary function of schools in America is to teach the superiority of American capitalism and the free enterprise system over any other system, to the exclusion of any alternative ideology (39). At the present time, for example, most states have laws, passed by their business-controlled legislatures, instructing the schools to teach the dangers of Communist and Socialist ideologies (40). Organizations such as the American Bar Association, National Education Association, and the American Association of School Administrators, have all passed resolutions encouraging schools to teach the evils of those ideologies, and they have even resolved that it is perfectly legitimate for schools to fire any Communists on their staffs. And, of course, the American Federation of Teachers, not to be outdone, has found that membership in the Communist Party was incompatible with membership in its union (41).

A similar, although not identical situation, appears in academia. As Professor Galbraith (42) has indicated, higher education is attuned to the needs of the private enterprise system. In colleges and universities, students are taught to understand the world in ways calculated to diminish, rather than enhance, their propensity to change it. Consequently, views challenging the set of class power relations in our society are excluded as not meriting serious analysis and debate. Actually, such exclusion of views is usually done more subtly than in the school system. It is usually presented under the ideological tenet that the holders of such unorthodox views are unacceptable deviants from the pattern of academic excellence demanded and required from all scholars. As Marx indicated, "the thinkers of the [ruling] class (its active, conceptive ideologists, who make the perfecting of the illusion of the class about itself their chief source of livelihood)," maintain that illusion by presenting "its interest as the common interest of all members of society, put in an ideal form; it [the ruling class] will give its ideas the form of universality, and represent them as the only rational, universally valid ones" (33, p. 40). Consequently, there exists a climate of suspicion, if not hostility, towards certain positions of intellectual political unorthodoxy that are dismissed as being subjects only for ideologues, positions that are put aside not as a result of prejudice—God forbid!—but rather because of doubts as to the supposed ideologues' scholarship and objectivity. The overwhelming and indisputable ideological discrimination against Marxist scholars in the academic centers of the U.S. is indeed a consequence of the dominance of bourgeois ideology in those centers, a dominance that is dictated by the function of those universities, i.e. to replicate the ideological relations of the capitalist system (43).

In summary, in these two sections dealing with civil and political rights, I have tried to show how the right to property, assumed and granted by the state, perpetuates a pattern of class relations whereby the few—the owners and controllers of the means and process of production—have a hegemony in all spheres of the civil and political lives of the many, limiting and constraining most profoundly and seriously Americans' civil and political rights. It conditions a class bias in the interpretation and extension of those rights, a bias in favor of the owners and managers of Capital and its servants, and against the rights of the majority of the U.S. population—the working and lower middle classes.

This class hegemony over our institutions also explains the very serious limitations that U.S. capitalism imposes on the socioeconomic rights of Americans. Let us now focus on those.

SOCIOECONOMIC RIGHTS UNDER U.S. CAPITALISM

As I indicated before, most of the discussion of human rights in the U.S. has focused on the civil and political rights assumed to be existent in the U.S. The notes that I presented before indicate a *class bias* in the interpretation and extension of these civil and political rights. But the Declaration of Human Rights of the United Nations also includes—and in a prominent place at that—socioeconomic rights as part of human rights. Among the most prominent are the rights to work and receive a fair wage, the right to security and retirement, and the right to health and education (44). Actually, a quick analysis of the situation in the U.S. regarding each of those rights may, at least partially, explain why we are met with a deafening silence regarding those socioeconomic rights. Indeed, the U.S. does not compare favorably at all, in those components of human rights, with the majority of other countries, including other capitalist developed countries, in which, for the most part, these rights fare much better.

Regarding the right to work, for example, the U.S. is the capitalist developed country with the highest unemployment rate (8.5 percent in 1975), totaling over 7.5 million people. Similarly, regarding the right to fair wages, the workers who, in spite of working full time, do not receive adequate income to provide a decent standard of living, total 7 million workers, or approximately 7.5 percent of the U.S. labor force. Actually, Professor Gordon, adding with the unemployed the discouraged workers (able people who would like to work but have given up the hope of finding it), the involuntary part-time workers, and the low-paid workers, has found that over one-third of the U.S. labor force is underemployed or unemployed and underpaid, and, thus, has had its human rights to work and a fair wage violated (45). Here again, we find a clear incompatibility between full employment and fair wages and the nature of the capitalist system. Capitalism needs a reserve army of idle and unemployed workers to establish a sense of both insecurity and discipline in the labor force. Let me add, incidentally, that this unemployment is not only in violation of the socioeconomic rights of the unemployed, but also of their civil rights, such as the right to life and freedom from harm. Indeed, unemployment causes, and is responsible for, much harm and damage. As indicated by a recent Congressional Report, every increase of unemployment by 1.4 percent determines 51,570 deaths (more than all casualties of Vietnam put together), including 1,540 suicides and 1,740 homicides; and leads to 7,660 state prison admissions, 5,520 state mental institution admissions, and many other types of harm, disease, and unease (46).

Similarly, in other areas, such as health and education, the U.S. is the only one among developed capitalist countries which has not yet accepted that the access to comprehensive health care is a human right. And even regarding education—usually considered a human right in the U.S.—none other than President Johnson indicated that, in 1965, over one quarter of the Americans—54 million—had not finished high school (15, p. 47). And to finish with this quick sketch of the status of the socioeconomic rights of our American people, let me finally say that our system of social security is among the least developed in the western capitalist world. And this underdevelopment of social security is very much a result, again, of the overwhelming political dominance of Capital and the political weakness of our laboring population. (For further discussion of this point, see references 47 and 48.)

THE ASSUMED INDEPENDENCE OF THE TWO TYPES OF RIGHTS

As indicated before, the current focus on civil and political rights as the primary components of human rights assumes their autonomy, if not independence from, the socioeconomic rights. Actually, these two types of rights are considered to be two separate types of rights that are frequently in conflict. It is generally assumed that the civil and political rights to life and freedom imply a *negative* obligation upon others, an obligation not to interfere with one's own exercise of those rights. On the other hand, the other rights—the socioeconomic rights—are assumed to place a *positive* obligation on others, i.e. something has to be done if they are to be secured for their recipients. These perceptions have led to the interpretation that those two types of rights may not only be different, but actually may be in conflict. Indeed, to provide the *security* guaranteed by the second type of rights, there may be a need to limit the *liberty* guaranteed by the former type of rights. As one theoretician of that interpretation has indicated (49),

> the promulgation of socioeconomic rights has brought them into conflict with civil and political rights, for the planning and control essential to the former impinge on some of the freedom of choice and action that had seemed defensible under the latter.

In a less elegant but more direct fashion, this was said by the then presidential candidate, Carter, when, in a radio broadcast, he indicated that a primary difference between the socialist countries and us—the U.S.—was that they have chosen security over liberty, while we—in the capitalist countries—prefer to emphasize liberty and opportunity over security (50).

But those interpretations of human rights that assume a dichotomy and even conflict between civil and political rights on the one hand, and socioeconomic rights on the other, are erroneous both empirically and historically. Indeed, to state the debate in terms of a choice between liberty and security is to avoid the issue of liberty for whom and for what. The analysis presented in the first part of this paper shows that the liberty held by the few who control Capital constrains and violates both the liberty and security of the many. The civil and political rights to vote and choose among political alternatives, for example, are dramatically reduced by the limited alternatives available to the population as a result of big business' control over the media and dominance over the organs of the state. And the civil rights to life and to freedom from harm are denied when the rights to employment and fair wages are—as they are under capitalism—denied. Rather than conflict, then, we must recognize that the full realization of civil and political rights cannot be realized in the absence of the fulfillment of socioeconomic rights. As Tawney (51) has indicated:

> political rights afford a safeguard and significance to civil rights . . . economic and social rights provide means essential to the exercise of political rights.

Actually, none other than President Roosevelt saw that dependency when, in his message to Congress back on January 11, 1944, he indicated that "necessitous men are not free men." Although he should also have included women, this dictum makes the point quite clear, i.e. that civil and political rights are not in conflict, but rather require the full realization of socioeconomic rights. And as I have indicated and tried to show in this article, capitalism, the social formation in existence in the U.S. today, denies the possibility of the full realization of either type of human rights.

CAPITALISM AS AN INTERNATIONAL SYSTEM AND ITS IMPLICATIONS IN HUMAN RIGHTS

The search for profits, the primary motor for capital accumulation under capitalism, does not stop at or respect national boundaries. And in that search for profits, the particular means through which the profits are gained are (1) the extension of markets, (2) the acquisition of raw materials, and (3) the exploitation of new sources of cheap labor. And in that search, the top monopolistic enterprises of the U.S. take the leading role in the internationalization of Capital. Capitalism thus becomes a set of international relations that are dominated by the giant corporations of a few countries, primarily American corporations (52).[4] In the process of expansion and internationalization, the owners and managers of the top corporations, who already have a dominant influence on the economic and political life of the U.S., increasingly come to dominate the economic and even political lives of other nations. In Chile, before Allende's government, multinational corporations (the majority from the U.S.) controlled more than 51 percent of all manufacturing; and, in each of the seven key industries of the economy, one to three firms controlled at least 51 percent of the production. In Mexico, global corporations control 100 percent of the rubber, electrical machinery, and transportation industries; and in Brazil, global corporations own 100 percent of the automobile and tire production, while their share of machinery was 67 percent in 1971 and, of electrical equipment, 68 percent for the same year (53), etc., etc. That international expansion of those U.S. corporations is of vital importance to their strength and dominance. U.S. firms' profits earned abroad, for example, represented 30 percent of the total American corporate profits in 1974 (54), and this figure is continually increasing. And the top 298 U.S.-based global corporations earn 40 percent of their entire net profit overseas, with their rate of profit from abroad being much higher than their domestic rate. Actually, this rate of profit for these global corporations is even higher in the underdeveloped world, resulting in a huge net outflow of capital from those countries back to the U.S. American corporations,

[4]Of the top one hundred multinational corporations, 65 are based in the U.S., 11 in the United Kingdom, 18 in other Common Market countries, and 5 in Japan.

for example, made direct investments in the Latin American continent of U.S.$3.8 billion during the period 1950-1965, while extracting $11.3 billion, for a net flow of $7.5 billion back to the U.S. (55). Indeed, this and other information confirms the conclusion of the Declaration of Foreign Ministries of Latin America in 1969 that (56):

> the sums taken out of Latin American countries are several times higher than the amounts invested. The Latin American capital is being reduced. The profits on investments grow and multiply, not in Latin America, but abroad.

It is that situation that classifies the pattern of international capitalist relations as a pillage of the Third World (57). Actually, contrary to what is said by the defenders of that international order, the diffusion of capital does not go from developed to developing countries, but rather from developing to developed ones. As Frank (58) has noted, the largest part of the capital:

> which the developed countries own in the underdeveloped world was never from the former to the latter at all, but was, on the contrary acquired by the developed countries in the now underdeveloped ones.

And much of this flow of capital goes back to the U.S. corporations. As Sherman (52), after reviewing all pertinent information, concludes: (a) the rate of profit of U.S. investments abroad is several times higher in the less developed than in the advanced capitalist countries; and (b) the less developed countries make a very considerable contribution to U.S. capital accumulation.

And that flow of capital, from developing countries to developed ones, requires an international political order that sustains and replicates the dominance of the international economic order by the major sectors of Capital in developed capitalist countries, and especially by the major sectors of Capital in the U.S. Indeed, the internationalization of Capital is a process that does not take place in a political vacuum. Capital requires direct protection, and the institutions through which it operates must be protected. Thus, the expansion of the areas of operation of Capital is always associated with an expansion of the political influence of the state with which that Capital is associated. Translated into the realm of foreign policy, the task of the capitalist state is to facilitate and protect the international business activities of its nationals. And this is done by assuring—by all strategies of domination—the commitment of the affected and dependent countries to a free enterprise system, where the *right of International Capital to own private property supersedes all other rights, including the human ones.* The purpose for exporting democracy and freedom as standards of American foreign policy has meant in most cases the imposition of the right of American Capital to own, dominate, and control many of the economies that are supposedly beneficiaries of that freedom. The meaning of this truth is expressed quite clearly in the words of former Secretary of the Treasury, William Simon, after his visit to Pinochet's Chile (59):

> The present Chilean regime is clearly in the best interest of the world compared with the Marxist regime of Allende. Chile has been the leader of democratic societies of Latin America, and they could not tolerate the kind of repression Allende brought. It had also taken an economic dimension. So now we are trying to move Chile back to freedom.

"Back to freedom," of course, meant (a) freedom for the U.S. corporations to regain the control of the Chilean economy that they began to lose during Allende's government, and (b) a violent change from a democratic Allende regime to a military regime that has been described as the bloodiest and most repressive regime in today's world and the main violator of human rights today (60). Here again, we can see that, as Abraham Lincoln said, the meaning of liberty and freedom is indeed different for owners of capital—the managers and owners of capital and its political servants—than for the non-owners of capital—the majority of Chileans. Their respective definitions of freedom are not only different, but in conflict. Indeed, the freedom of the few to control and manage capital has been, is, and will be incompatible with the human rights of the many—human rights defined in all their civil, political, social, and economic dimensions.

THE EXPORTATION OF REPRESSION: THE ABOLITION OF HUMAN RIGHTS AT THE INTERNATIONAL LEVEL

A primary role of the federal government of the U.S., in both the 19th and 20th centuries, has been to make the world safe for capitalism in general, and for American capitalism in particular. And that role has taken place in many forms, including (a) military intervention, (b) strengthening the apparatus of order, (c) covert operations and direct intervention, and (d) control of international agencies of legitimation, credit, and lending. Due to the importance of each in the violation of human rights in the countries subject to U.S. intervention, let me focus on each.

American Military Interventionist Policies

Contrary to what is believed by many Americans, Vietnam was nothing new. American intervention abroad in defense of American property and American interests was and is a very typical feature of American diplomacy. From 1789 to the outbreak of World War II, for example, American troops—without authorization from Congress—were sent to foreign countries 145 times (61). All of these interventions were police actions in situations of unrest that represented a threat to specific American capitalist interests. Whenever an outbreak of nationalist revolutionary activity occurred (Argentina, 1833; Peru, 1835; Argentina, 1852; Nicaragua, 1853; Uruguay, 1855, 1858; Colombia, 1860; Panama, 1865, 1885; Hawaii, 1889; Chile, 1891; Nicaragua, 1894); or a state of insurrection such as a serious riot with political overtones (Panama, 1856; Uruguay, 1868; Colombia, 1868; Haiti, 1891; Nicaragua, 1899); or a civil war in which the United States had an interest (China, 1854, 1855; Japan, 1868; Samoa, 1888; Brazil, 1894); or a coup or an attempted coup (Nicaragua, 1857; Samoa, 1899), American troops intervened. And in all those 19th-century interventions, American troops changed the nature of the political events by favoring those sides that supported U.S. interests. Regarding the 20th century, a similar history and rationale appeared. Maybe the best testimony is the one provided by someone who should know quite well, i.e. a leader of those troops, Marine Major-General S. D. Butler (quoted in 62):

I spent thirty-three years and four months in active service as a member of our country's most agile military force—the Marine Corps. I served in all commissioned ranks from a second lieutenant to major-general. And during that period I spent most of my time being a high-class muscle man for Big Business, for Wall Street, and for the bankers. In short, I was a racketeer for capitalism. . . .

Thus I helped make Mexico and especially Tampico safe for American oil interests in 1914. I helped make Haiti and Cuba a decent place for the National City Bank boys to collect revenues in. . . . I helped purify Nicaragua for the international banking house of Brown Brothers in 1909-1912. I brought light to the Dominican Republic for American sugar interests in 1916. I helped make Honduras "right" for American fruit companies in 1903. In China in 1927 I helped to see to it that Standard Oil went its way unmolested.

During those years I had, as the boys in the back room would say, a swell racket. I was rewarded with honors, medals, promotion. Looking back on it, I feel I might have given Al Capone a few hints. The best *he* could do was operate his racket in three city districts. We Marines operated on three *continents*.

Had Major-General Butler lived longer, he would have mentioned, among other instances, Iran in 1953, Guatemala in 1954, the Dominican Republic in 1965, and, of course, Indochina in 1966. Let me clarify here, that those interventions had as their purposes not only the preservation of accessibility to markets and raw materials, but, equally importantly, the maintenance of the power relations by which no country could leave the capitalist system and no country could change the rules of international capitalism. As McEwan (63) has indicated:

What is at stake in Vietnam is not just a geographic area but a set of rules, a system. A capitalist government will and must go all out to protect that set of rules. In part, this is a tactical issue: failure to protect the system in Vietnam would lead to further and more effective threats against the system elsewhere. The "domino" argument is a very real one. One need only look at the impact of the Cuban Revolution in Latin America or the impact of the Russian and Chinese Revolutions throughout the world to perceive the implications of a victory for the socialist forces in Vietnam.

The difference between the intervention in Vietnam and previous interventions was that its objective, to keep that country safe for capitalism, failed, and that that lengthy struggle created a resistance by the American people, making it the most unpopular war in American history. The recent policy of non-military intervention by U.S. forces in Angola and Zaire cannot be explained without the recent history of Vietnam.

Strengthening the Apparatus of Order

Increasingly more important than the direct mode of military intervention is, and will be, the *threat* of military intervention and/or the provision of assistance to the military and other agencies of order, such as the police, which are responsible for the maintenance of property relations in those countries that favor the interests of American Capital (64).[5] Actually, such assistance frequently has taken the form of encouraging the direct seizure of power when forces with an anti-capitalist or anti-U.S.

---

[5] According to Edward Korry, the U.S. ambassador to Chile, President Johnson ordered, as part of the successful campaign to overthrow the leftist government of Joao Goulart, the assembly of a task force of naval and airborne units to intervene in Brazil's internal affairs. A few weeks afterwards, Goulart was overthrown.

Capital tone or program have threatened those interests. As a recent article in the *Washington Post* indicated, all military juntas in Latin America, violators of all types of human rights of the majority of Latin American populations, have counted on the encouragement, support, and acquiescence of the U.S. government and the U.S. corporations involved in those countries (65-67). But, while much has been written about the by now well-known support given by the U.S. government to the military in many parts of the globe, not so much is known or written about the support to police and other agencies of order. An agency that took a prominent role in that assistance was the Office of Public Safety of the Agency for International Development, whose aims were, in the words of Bell, Director of AID in 1965, the creation and maintenance of an atmosphere of law and order under civil concepts and controls, by which the U.S. interests could be promoted and protected (quoted in 68). The meaning of those U.S. interests appears quite clearly when one sees where the assistance went, i.e. to countries where American multinationals were threatened by hostile forces and needed protection, i.e. Southeast Asia, Brazil, the Dominican Republic, Venezuela, Colombia, Guatemala, Zaire, and Liberia. The nature of that support appears quite clear when one reads that the police assistance to Venezuela went to suppress labor agitation at Goodyear and Gulf; to the Dominican Republic to suppress labor agitation at the Western plantations; and to Liberia to actually pay for the training and salaries of the private security police of Firestone Rubber (68).

Covert Operations and Direct Intervention
in Political Affairs of Other Countries

The direct intervention of state agencies such as the Central Intelligence Agency, along with the cooperation of private corporations such as ITT, Anaconda, and others in the downfall of Allende's government, is even a matter of Congressional record. But, as the U.S. Ambassador to Chile at the time of Allende's downfall, Edward Korry, has indicated, these practices were not new or the result of Nixon policies. They were a continuation of a long and well-established tradition of active participation by agencies of the U.S. government and multinational corporations in covert interventions in the doings and undoings of other governments. As Korry indicates, Nixon was just following the steps that had been previously taken by Kennedy and Johnson to support, by all means of covert activities, the interests of multinational corporations in Chile (and many other countries) and to stop—also by all means—the increased power of the Left in these countries. Actually, it is worth noting that Korry mentions that Cyrus Vance, the current Secretary of State in the Carter Administration, who is now supposed to carry the human rights message around the world, was knowledgeable about and a participant in those policies when serving in previous administrations. As Korry's testimony (64) concludes, there is an

> old boys network—of say, Mr. Geneen, Mr. McCone, Mr. Helms, the brothers Bundy, Mr. Rockefeller, and even Mr. Vance . . . [which is] designed to be self-serving, self-perpetuating, and self-protective . . . [and which] gave us Vietnam in the 1960's, assassination plots and the dark legacies of all manner of covert operations.

It is wrong, however, to assume those covert actions are a mere result of an "old boys network." They are part and parcel of the strategy of U.S. foreign diplomacy aimed at saving the world for the exercise of freedom, i.e. the freedom of capital to accumulate at whatever cost—as in today's Chile—that freedom may require. In fact, the reading of Korry's testimony—a most informative one—shows (a) how the federal foreign affairs establishment and the multinational corporations are interlinked, and (b) how the primary purpose of the former is to optimize the interests of the latter.

Control of International Agencies of Legitimation, and of Credit and Lending

The corporate-controlled foreign establishment of the U.S. government has been dominant in the creation of most international agencies and an international order by which those who do not accept or submit to that order—like Cuba—are defined as outlaws, subject to repression and punishment, such as economic blockade. This exclusion and blockade are made possible by U.S. dominance of those international institutions, such as the World Bank and the Latin American Development Bank, that are used to exercise the pressure necessary to defend the interests of the free enterprise system in which the U.S. is dominant. One instance, Chile, shows this situation quite clearly. The total assistance by those two institutions to Chile declined from $75 million (in loans) to $12 million in the first year of Allende's government (1971), and further to $2.1 million in the second year (1972), consistent with a policy of economic blockade that the corporate-controlled federal foreign establishment had declared against Allende's government. It is interesting to note that the arguments given by these international lending institutions were presented not as political but as economic, i.e. that the policies of the Allende government, from 1971 to 1973, aimed at the nationalization of most of the monopolistic and oligopolistic industries (many of which were U.S.-controlled) and at a profound change in the income distribution and popular consumption, were considered to be "unorthodox" for those institutions.

Allende's policies, which had a substantial impact in expanding and optimizing the socioeconomic rights of large sectors of the population, were considered by those international institutions to be in conflict with the sacred and ubiquitous right of private capital accumulation by U.S. Capital. And the meaning of "economic orthodoxy" appeared quite clearly when, after the coup, the Junta denationalized most of the public property and once again made Chile safe for multinational corporations; and those agencies immediately increased their loans to a most impressive $110 million for the first year of the Junta and $90.8 million for the second year. The Junta was following the "pattern of orthodoxy" of reinstating the dominance of the private sector with drastic reductions of government spending, with cuts in public expenditures for health services from 1933 thousand pesos in 1972 (Allende's), for example, to 851 thousand pesos in 1976 (Pinochet's), with full freedom for prices to rise, and with full prohibition for labor unions to strike and operate (69).

That freedom for Capital has indeed meant a most brutal violation not only of the civil and political rights, but also of the socioeconomic rights of the majority of Chileans. According to even the official Junta and International Monetary Fund figures, in 1976, a quarter of the population (2.5 million people) had no income at all, unemployment was estimated to be 22 percent (during Allende, it was 3.1 percent), and a phenomenon of mass hunger and starvation existed unknown in the recent history of Chile (70). Actually, in that battle between property owners and non-property owners, it is quite clear whose side the Junta was on. In 1972, during Allende's government, employees and workers—the non-owners—received 62.9 percent of the national income, while the property sector received 37.1 percent. By 1974, the share of wage earners had already been reduced to 38.2 percent, while that of property owners had increased to 61.8 percent (71). The consequences represented by those figures are enormous and impossible to present as mere figures. A picture of hunger, starvation, torture, harm, desperation, and death is the result of the orthodox policies perpetuated by the centers of international economic order, and they require a most brutal political repression to sustain and maintain them. Chile has clearly shown what Brazil and many other countries had already shown, that *the interests of International Capital and of the international and national political institutions that sustain it are incompatible with the realization of human rights.*

In summary, I have tried to show how capitalism and its international dimension, imperialism, are incompatible with the realization of human rights, both nationally and abroad. Let me add that this denial of human rights is a consequence of the logic of capitalism, not the result of the specific malevolence of individuals or groups. To consider that the consistent denial of human rights that U.S. foreign policy has implied for many inhabitants of the world is a result of the immorality of its leaders, is to have a religious, but not a political and economic, understanding of the forces that move history. It is the dynamic of the capitalist system that explains why some of the most repressive governments in the world, such as Iran, Chile, Saudi Arabia, South Korea, South Africa, and most Latin American governments, are also in areas where U.S. foreign capital is dominant or heavily influential. To consider the repressive policies of those governments as the result of the specific sadism or malevolence of their leaders, is to have a rather limited understanding of the economic and political determinants of human rights and denial of them. *The political repression in those regimes is required and needed to sustain an economic system whereby the few (including U.S. corporate interests) control much, and the many (the masses of those countries) control very little.* Here, it is worth stressing a further note. While much is being said—and, for the most part, with universal revulsion—by the corporate-controlled media against revolutionary violence—the force exercised by the oppressed against their oppressors—not much is being said about the inherent violence of our institutions that sustain and replicate a pattern of violence. As Moore (72) has noted:

> The way nearly all history has been written imposes an overwhelming bias against revolutionary violence . . . the use of force by the oppressed against their former masters has been the object of nearly universal condemnation. Meanwhile the day-to-day repression of "normal" society hovers dimly in the background of most history books.

CONCLUDING REMARKS

Having explained the incompatibility between capitalism and human rights, let me now finish by postulating why the centers of the establishment—or at least elements of it—have raised that issue.

First, as indicated at the beginning of this article, is the need perceived by the centers of power to express and demonstrate to the increasingly disenchanted American public a new morality in the leadership of the country, and to emphasize that repressive and regressive policies are things of the past, mistakes maybe, but, for the most part, a mere result of the actions of specific individuals. The denial of human rights at home and abroad is considered to be primarily the result of individual misjudgments, mistakes, or sins, but certainly not the result and logic of our capitalist system. Indeed, in all those explanations, it is emphasized that our system is morally superior to all others, and very much superior to socialist systems whose increasing attraction to other peoples is increasingly feared. Thus, it is worth realizing that most of the space dedicated to human rights, in the context of our administration's concern and in media presentations, deals with the rights of dissidents in the Soviet Union. And here let me add that I count my voice among those that protest repression in the Soviet Union, or in any other country, for that matter. But as some people have begun to notice, there is a clear selectivity in this concern for human rights (73). Countries considered vital to our national interests are exempt from those criticisms or concerns. But, the question has to be raised: in whose interests are those "national interests"? Certainly not those of the majority of the people living under repressive regimes. And not, I postulate, the interests of the American public. Rather, that concern is expressed in the interests of American Capital whose value has to be saved. It is not in the interest of the average American, nor of his or her security, to have U.S. foreign diplomacy support the most repressive regimes in today's world. As Marx indicated, it is always the custom of the bourgeoisie to define its own interests as human and universal (33). But this article shows that the interests of the bourgeoisie or Capital— or in popular parlance, big business—are not the same as the interests of the majority of people, either at home or abroad. Actually, these interests not only are different, but are in conflict. Using Lincoln's dictum, *the liberty of the few means the tyranny for the many,* i.e. freedom for Capital means the denial of human rights for the majority of Americans and the peoples of the capitalist underdeveloped world.

This note, then, ends my presentation. Needless to say, I am aware that it is in conflict with prevalent explanations of our realities, well represented in today's debate. A minority view, perhaps, but not an Unamerican one. None other than that great American, Mark Twain (74), already said, back in 1886:

> Who are the oppressors? The few: the capitalists, and a handful of other overseers and superintendents. Who are the oppressed? The many; the nations of the earth; the workers; they that make the bread that the soft-handed and idle eat.
>
> Why is it right that there is not a finer division of spoil around? Because laws and constitutions have ordered otherwise. . . . Then it follows that they do not have the same but contrary rights.

It has been my intention to show that what Mark Twain said then is still very much applicable today, as well. It is for the reader to judge.

REFERENCES

1. Committee on Government Operations, United States Senate. *Confidence and Concern: Citizens View American Government. A Survey of Public Attitudes,* Part I. U.S. Government Printing Office, Washington, D.C., 1973.

2. Analysis of last election. *New York Times,* November 23, 1976.
3. Pat Moynihan declarations to the United Nations. *New York Times,* p. 12, December 24, 1976.
4. Cranston, M. *What Are Human Rights?* Bodley Head, London, 1973.
5. Carter's address at the United Nations. *New York Times,* March 18, 1977.
6. Lampman, R. J. *The Share of Top Wealth-Holders in National Wealth, 1922-1956.* Princeton University Press, Princeton, N.J., 1956.
7. Sweezy, P. *The Theory of Capitalist Development.* Monthly Review Press, New York, 1942.
8. Engels, F. *Origin of the Family, Private Property and the State.* International Publishers, New York, 1942.
9. Smith, A. *An Inquiry into the Nature and Causes of the Wealth of Nations.* Clarendon Press, London, 1976.
10. Poulantzas, N. *Classes in Contemporary Capitalism.* New Left Review Editions, London, 1975.
11. Navarro, V. *Medicine Under Capitalism.* Neale Watson Academic Publications, Inc., New York, 1976.
12. Miliband, R. *The State in Capitalist Society.* Weidenfeld and Nicolson, London, 1969.
13. Schattschneider, E. E. *The Semi-Sovereign People: A Realistic View of Democracy in America.* Holt, Rinehart and Winston, New York, 1960.
14. The Hart survey, American public opinion and economic democracy. In *Own Your Own Job,* by J. Rifkin, Basic Books, New York, 1977.
15. Huberman, L., and Sweezy, P. M. *Introduction to Socialism,* p. 77. Monthly Review Press, New York, 1968.
16. Raphael, D. D., editor. *Political Theory and the Rights of Man.* Macmillan, London, 1967.
17. Navarro, V. The underdevelopment of health of working America: Causes, consequences and possible solutions. *Am. J. Public Health* 66(6): 538, 1976.
18. Discher, D. P., et al. *Pilot Study for Development of an Occupational Disease Surveillance Method,* pp. 75-162. National Institute for Occupational Safety and Health, U.S. Department of Health, Education, and Welfare. U.S. Government Printing Office, Washington, D.C., 1975.
19. Burnham, D. Ford termed cool to 3 key agencies. *New York Times,* pp. 1 and 26, January 16, 1976.
20. Gordon, J. B., Ackman, A., and Brooks, M. L. *Industrial Safety Statistics: A Re-examination.* A Critical Report Prepared for the U.S. Department of Labor. Praeger Publishers, New York, 1971.
21. Personal communication. Research Unit, United Mine Workers of America, Washington, D.C., 1975.
22. Shoub, E. B. *Overview of Coal Miners' Health Findings, Sixth Annual Institute on Coal Mining Health, Safety and Research.* Virginia Polytechnic Institute and State University, Blacksburg, Va., August 27, 1975.
23. Burnham, D. Nader group says Labor Department lagged on health rules to spur gifts. *New York Times,* July 16, 1974.
24. Miller, A. The wages of neglect: Death and disease in the American work place. *Am. J. Public Health* 65(11): 1217-1220, 1975.
25. *Wall Street Journal,* August 9, 1974.
26. Arendt, H. *Eichmann in Jerusalem,* p. 19. Viking Press, New York, 1963.
27. Priestland, G. *The Future of Violence,* pp. 19 and 139. Transatlantic Arts, Inc., Levittown, N.Y., 1975.
28. *Trials of War Criminals Before the Nuremberg Military Tribunals Under Control Council Law 11.* U.S. Government Printing Office, Washington, D.C., 1950.
29. Arblaster, A. What is violence? In *The Socialist Register,* edited by R. Miliband and J. Saville, pp. 224-249. Merlin Press, London, 1975.
30. Gerson, S. W. To put a red on the ballot, cross a "legal mine field." *New York Times,* p. 23, July 17, 1976.
31. Wolfe, A. *The Seamy Side of Democracy: Repression in America.* David McKay Company, Inc., New York, 1973.
32. Davis, A. *If They Come in the Morning: Voices of the Resistance.* The Third Press, New York, 1971.
33. Marx, K. The German ideology. In *Selected Works,* Vol. 1, p. 47. Lawrence and Wishart, London, 1962.
34. Gramsci, A. *Prison Notebooks.* International Publishers, New York, 1971.
35. Schiller, L. H. *The Mind Managers.* Beacon Press, Boston, 1973.

36. Schiller, L. H. *Mass Communications and American Empire.* Beacon Press, Boston, 1971.
37. Servan-Schreiber, J. L. *The Power to Inform. Media: The Business of Information.* McGraw-Hill Book Company, Inc., New York, 1974.
38. *Marxism and the Mass Media: Towards a Basic Bibliography.* International Mass Media Research Center, Bagnolet, France, 1976.
39. Havighurst, R. J., and Neugarten, B. L. *Society and Education,* p. 146. Allyn and Bacon, Boston, 1957.
40. Zelman, A. *Teaching "About Communism" in American Public Schools,* p. 43. Humanities Press, Atlantic Highlands, N.J., 1965.
41. American Federation of Teachers, Commission on Educational Reconstruction. Teachers and Communism. Reprinted in *American Teacher,* 33, 1948.
42. Galbraith, J. K. *The New Industrial State,* pp. 370-371. Houghton Mifflin Company, Boston, 1967.
43. Smith, D. N. *Who Rules the Universities?* Monthly Review Press, New York, 1974.
44. Watson, D. Welfare rights and human rights. *Journal of Social Policy* 6(part I): 31-46, 1977.
45. Employment Editorial. In *Problems of Political Economy,* edited by D. Gordon, p. 70. Lexington Books, Lexington, Mass., 1977.
46. Brenner, M. H. *Estimating the Social Costs of National Economic Policy: Implications for Mental and Physical Health, and Criminal Aggression.* Joint Economic Committee, Congress of the United States, 94th Congress, October 26, 1976. U.S. Government Printing Office, Washington, D.C., 1976.
47. Rimlinger, G. V. *Welfare Policy and Industrialization in Europe, America and Russia.* John Wiley and Sons, Inc., New York, 1971.
48. Wilensky, H. L. *The Welfare State and Equality.* University of California Press, Berkeley, 1975.
49. McKeown, R. Human rights in the world today. *Human Rights. Comments and Interpretation.* United Nations Educational, Scientific, and Cultural Organization, 1949.
50. Interview with Carter. WBJC-FM, Baltimore, March 1976.
51. Tawney, R. H. *The Acquisitive Society.* Methuen, London, 1973.
52. Sherman, H. J. *Stagflation,* p. 222. Harper and Row, New York, 1976.
53. Barnet, R., and Muller, R. *Global Reach,* p. 147. Simon and Schuster, New York, 1974.
54. Muller, R. Global corporations and national stabilization policy. *Journal of Economic Issues* 9: 183, June 1975.
55. U.S. Department of Commerce. *United States Business Investments in Foreign Countries,* p. 85. U.S. Government Printing Office, Washington, D.C., 1970.
56. Declaration, Foreign Ministries of Latin America, Viña del Mar, Chile, 1969.
57. Jalée, P. *The Pillage of the Third World.* Monthly Review Press, New York, 1968.
58. Frank, A. G. *Latin America: Underdevelopment or Revolution,* p. 21. Monthly Review Press, New York, 1970.
59. William Simon's declarations. *The Saturday Evening Post,* October 1976.
60. Commission on Human Rights. Study of Reported Violations of Human Rights in Chile, with Particular Reference to Torture and Other Cruel, Inhuman, or Degrading Treatment or Punishment. United Nations, February 10, 1977.
61. *Congressional Record.* 91st Congress, First Session, Vol. 115, Part 3, pp. 16 and 840-843, June 1969.
62. Butler, S. D. *Common Sense,* November 1935. As quoted in *Cuba: Anatomy of a Revolution,* by L. Huberman and P. Sweezy. Monthly Review Press, New York, 1960.
63. MacEwan, A. Capitalist expansion, ideology and intervention. In *The Capitalist System, A Radical Analysis of American Society,* edited by R. Edwards, M. Reich, and T. Weisskopf, p. 417. Prentice-Hall, Englewood Cliffs, N.J., 1972.
64. Testimony of Edward Korry. Congressional Committee on Foreign Relations, December 1976.
65. Military juntas in Latin America. *Washington Post,* April 12, 1977.
66. The U.S. Military Apparatus (handbook). North American Congress on Latin America, Washington, D.C., August 1972.
67. U.S. Training Programs for Foreign Military Personnel: The Pentagon's Protégés. *Latin America & Empire Report,* Vol. X, No. 1. North American Congress on Latin America, Washington, D.C., January 1976.
68. Stork, J. World cop. *Hard Times,* 85, August 1970.
69. Chile's Chronic Economic Crisis: 1976 and Beyond. *International Policy Report,* Vol. II, No. 2. Center for International Policy, Washington, D.C., September 1976.

70. Frank, A. G. *Economic Genocide in Chile*. Spokesman Books, Nottingham, U.K., 1976.
71. Letelier, O. *Chile: Economic "Freedom" and Political Repression*, p. 14. Spokesman Books, Nottingham, U.K., 1976.
72. Moore, B. *Social Origins of Dictatorship and Democracy: Lord and Peasant in the Making of the Modern World*. Beacon Press, Boston, 1966.
73. Ajami, F. Human rights: Sermons or substance (editorial). *The Nation,* p. 389, April 2, 1977.
74. Twain, M. *Sayings of Famous Americans.* Beacon Press, Boston, 1976.

CHAPTER 4

Drought and Dependence in the Sahel
Nicole Ball

If it is for just a year: sow seeds,
If it is for ten years: plant trees,
If for a hundred years: educate your people.

Kuan-Tzu, IVth/IIIrd Centuries B.C.

Previously ignored by most of the world, the Sahel zone of West Africa became the focus of public attention, if only temporarily, when famine threatened in 1973. Journalists and representatives of humanitarian groups descended in droves upon the region which, until 1960, was part of French-controlled West Africa. Relatively large amounts of aid (for the Sahel), primarily food aid, flowed into the drought-stricken countries of Senegal, Upper Volta, Niger, Mali, Chad, and Mauritania. As one observer remarked somewhat cynically, "The Sahel was *in*" (1).

But by the time the Sahel drought/famine was "discovered," the crisis was half a decade old for many of the area's inhabitants. The rains had begun to fail in 1968, and in that year Senegal, Mali, and Niger requested emergency food aid from the United States for about 1 million people. Between 1968 and 1971, the U.S. contributed the bulk of the emergency food aid received by the Sahelian countries, $13 million of a total $16 million (2).

Despite the need for this aid, foreign aid officials and local governments did not seem to appreciate or did not wish to understand the seriousness of the situation. It wasn't until the fall of 1972 that Food and Agriculture Organization (FAO) field representatives began to warn that disaster was likely to occur. By that time, of course, disaster was already a reality for thousands of farmers and herders in West Africa, as cattle died and crops withered or refused to grow altogether, in some cases for the second or third year in succession (2, pp. 11-20).

Reports from the region tended to center around the threat of widespread starvation. There is no doubt that food was in very short supply. Between November 1973 and July 1975, an estimated 887 million metric tons of food aid were shipped to Chad, Mali, Niger, Upper Volta, Mauritania, and Senegal by various donors (3). However, concentration on drought-period food deficits tends to obscure the extent of chronic food shortages within the region.

Even before the drought began in 1968, Sahelian countries had to import a considerable amount of their food requirements (Table 1). The reasons for this are several. Chief among them are the orientation of local agriculture toward cash crop production and the decline in soil productivity due to reduced fallowing and, in some cases, reduced manuring, as well as to the extension of food crop production into more marginal soils.

Some analysts have questioned the causal relationship between drought and famine which has been so widely assumed by government and international agency officials and the media. They have sought the roots of famine in the socioeconomic and political relationships obtaining in the drought-stricken region. One of the earliest studies along these lines was *Qui se nourrit de la famine en Afrique?* by the French collective, Comité Information Sahel (4). As a result of this and other work, there is now a greater understanding, at least among academics and some relief/development workers, of the essentially nonnatural basis of famines.

Table 1

Food imports[a] as percentage of total imports in five West African countries, selected years[b]

Country	1965	1967	1969	1970	1974
Mali	19.5 (20.4)[c]	14.3 (20.5)	15.6 (30.8)	28.6 (37.2)	36.0 (37.3)
Mauritania	8.5 (—)[d]	17.0 (—)	21.6 (—)	23.2 (—)	22.0 (—)
Niger	8.6 (11.5)	14.3 (12.8)	1.7 (10.5)	12.0 (9.9)	12.0 (—)
Senegal	36.3 (37.3)	36.3 (37.2)	32.0 (33.1)	27.1 (27.9)	25.0 (—)
Upper Volta	22.4 (20.9)	23.4 (22.3)	18.5 (17.5)	18.3 (17.4)	19.0 (—)

[a] Commercial imports, not including food aid.
[b] Sources, reference 4, pp. 133, 136, 142, 143; reference 29, pp. 54, 75.
[c] Figures in parentheses from Comité Information Sahel (4); others from Berg (29). Comité Information Sahel figures for Niger include beverages and tobacco. All figures from Berg exclude beverages. It is not clear why the figures for Mali differ so widely for 1967, 1969, and 1970.
[d] Dashes signify data not available.

At the same time, the Comité largely restricted itself to a discussion of the famine. Although it pointed out that certain practices were leading to erosion and soil infertility, the Comité did not systematically examine the nonnatural causes of the drought and tended to treat the drought as a purely natural phenomenon (4, p. 16). It can be shown that the same socioeconomic and political imbalances responsible for the creation of famine can and do create drought disasters. This article will extend the analysis used by the Comité to an examination of the causes of drought. It will draw its information from the present and past history of Mali, Niger, Mauritania, and, to a lesser extent, Upper Volta and Senegal. Chad will not be discussed at all. The focus of the article will be on the ways in which socially and politically exploitative systems contribute to or cause ecological degradation and destruction.

DROUGHT-AS-DISASTER

As ordinarily defined, a drought is a prolonged period of rain deprivation. However, many years of subnormal rainfall need not engender disaster. Many countries, primarily industrialized ones, suffer several years of low rainfall without serious disruption of either their ecology or their economy. Other countries, such as India, Bangladesh, or those in the Sahel zone of West Africa, experience partial or even total breakdowns as a result of reduced rainfall. The problem thus becomes one of discovering why some countries are capable of protecting their natural environment and their population against the excesses of natural phenomena while others are not.

A drought, like any other "natural" disaster, arises out of a combination of environmental, economic, social, and political factors. The interplay of these factors creates the "conditions for disaster," i.e. determines to what extent a system will be disrupted by new and/or suddenly intensified stresses. In cases where the system has been undermined to the point where a breakdown becomes inevitable, it is often a natural phenomenon, too little rainfall in the case of drought, which provides the unacceptable stress. This apparent link between the natural phenomenon and the breakdown causes the ensuing catastrophe to be characterized as a "natural" disaster. Such a definition encourages analysts to overlook the economic, social, and political problems which generate or exacerbate ecological instability.

"Natural" disaster appears to be increasingly a problem of Third World countries. A 1972 United Nations report demonstrates that 89 percent of the "natural" disasters which have been recorded between 1919 and 1972, and for which international assistance has been provided, have occurred in areas now described as the Third World. Furthermore, 91 percent of these Third World disasters have occurred since 1950 (5).

It is likely that these figures understate the number of disasters afflicting the non-industrialized regions prior to 1950. Before World War II, the mechanisms for collecting and distributing relief aid internationally were limited. Events now treated as international disasters were previously considered local problems. Furthermore, most areas that are currently major recipients of international relief were, until the 1950s and 1960s, colonial territories. Aid given under these circumstances was minimal. Even where the colonial government arranged for the provision of some relief aid (generally rice imported from Indochina for French West Africa), these disasters did not enter into international statistics.

Third World countries did not begin to be afflicted by "natural" disasters only after independence was granted. West African chronicles, for example, reveal that during the 16th century in the Niger Bend (present-day Mali), only 5 years were disrupted by epidemics, none of which seem to have been particularly severe. Following the collapse of the Songhai Empire in 1591 and resulting at least in part from the ensuing economic and political chaos, the Niger Bend region suffered from no less than 34 years of severe famine, drought, epidemics, and insect plagues in the 17th and 18th centuries. After 1643, famine never completely disappeared (6). During the colonial period in the late 19th century to 1960, this pattern of chronic food shortage and susceptibility to natural disruptions interspersed with major breakdowns continued (7).

Viewed historically, the inability to control the impact of natural phenomena seems to result from the lack of indigenous control within a region. Here it is important to emphasize that indigenous control is not necessarily equivalent to political independence. Politically independent states can be economically dependent upon external forces, and it is the degree of freedom in the economic sphere which should be seen as the determining factor. Within this framework, the problems currently confronting most Third World governments, particularly those under consideration here, with regard to the control of natural phenomena suggest that the "natural" disaster is linked to the process of underdevelopment and the condition of economic dependency.

DROUGHT AND UNDERDEVELOPMENT

Drought in Africa is a symptom of the underdevelopment, and only incidentally one of its causes. An analysis of the interaction between drought and underdevelopment should center around (a) the operation of the international economic system; and (b) the impact of the international economic system on the stability of Third World ecosystems.

Although the exploitation of populations and ecosystems did not begin with the first contacts between Europe and West Africa, many of the problems currently afflicting the five countries under discussion here (Mali, Niger, Senegal, Upper Volta, and Mauritania) do have their roots in the precolonial and colonial periods. In the following sections we will survey some of the more important features of colonial policy which have been carried over into the postcolonial period and show how these have affected the ecology of the region.

THE INTERNATIONAL ECONOMIC SYSTEM

The economic systems of West Africa have become progressively enmeshed with those of the dominant Western countries. In most cases, the process began several hundred years ago as European traders began to deal with coastal areas of the African continent. Slaves were initially the most important item traded. This extraction of manpower laid the basis for the subsequent loss of political and economic autonomy for most West Africans. As European traders began to extract raw materials as well as slaves from the continent, and to supply Africans with cheap, mass-produced goods from Europe (cloth, alcohol, firearms, hardware and other small manufactures), West African economies were tied more closely to those of the metropolitan centers and indigenous economic development was thwarted.

The imposition of direct colonial rule in French West Africa did not lead to the large-scale export of capital from France.

> The export of raw materials and the import of manufactured goods remained characteristic of the economies of the colonised countries under the imperialist colonial system as it had been in the preceding period. But it was the export of capital to these countries that was to assume a decisive character. The monopolies which put their capital into agriculture and mining played the essential role; commerce was subordinate to production, not the other way around as in the first colonial age.
>
> West and Central Africa under French domination seem to have been an exception in this sense; here, as before, the economy was dominated by the commercial companies, and trade was fitted into the imperialist context. The legal monopoly of the older companies was replaced by the *de facto* monopoly of the financial oligarchy. Here, too, it was exported capital that controlled the economy, but its chosen domain was the import and export trade, and not production. As a consequence, the volume of invested capital remained very small (7, p. 159).

By the 1940s, trade in French West Africa was controlled by fewer than twelve companies. Three of them, Compagnie Française de l'Afrique occidentale, Société commerciale de l'Ouest Africain, and Unilever, controlled between 50 and 90 percent of certain products, notably, but by no means exclusively, rice, flour, and sugar (7, p. 167).

The Role of Colonial Taxation

Taxation was one of the most important tools used by the French to direct the economic activities of West Africans. A head tax was imposed on the sedentary population, while nomadic herders were required to pay the *zekkat,* a tax on each adult animal owned. The *zekkat* was computed as one-fortieth of the market value of each animal as assessed by French officials. It varied from animal to animal and from region to region. Other taxes were levied on butchers, merchants, exports, and imports (for consumption by the indigenous population). Taxation was designed to fulfil two primary objectives.

The first objective was to make the French colonies self-supporting.

> The principles governing the financial relations between France and her colonies were laid down in Article 33 of the Finance Act of 13 April 1900. They embodied a system of financial autonomy; the colonies were to cover the expenditure made by France on their territories. All civil expenditure and the upkeep of the gendarmerie were to be covered by the colonial budgets. The army did not depend on the local budgets, but came under the national defence budget; however, its maintenance in the colony was charged to the colonial budgets (7, pp. 341-342).

In most cases in French West Africa, prior to 1929 at least, taxation did cover colonial expenditure and surpluses were often recorded. They were held in the colonial reserve for less successful years and to give witness to the financial ability of the Governor.

> . . . each governor felt bound to demonstrate his good management by the growth of the reserve funds; since economic expansion caused the budgets to show a regular surplus up to the time of the crisis, the reserve funds were barely touched and continued to grow regularly (7, p. 343).

The second objective of French taxation policy was to introduce West Africa to the money economy and to integrate its population into a commercialized system of production and consumption. In this case, taxation worked in tandem with the sale of European goods. Imports of European goods virtually destroyed indigenous industries such as blacksmithing and weaving, and caused the decline of caravanning—an important source of income (especially in drought years) for some pastoralists.

The primary source of funds for the peasantry which would enable it to fulfil its tax obligations and purchase necessities was the sale of raw materials to foreign companies. Those crops which were useful to French industry, primarily groundnuts and cotton in West Africa, were promoted, while food crops were not. The importance of these export crops to French industry was underlined by the use of force on uncooperative peasants. Fields were destroyed and villages razed for the failure to raise or deliver specified crops. Very low prices were paid to the producer for the items thus obtained. Under these conditions, the accumulation of capital in the hands of Africans was extremely difficult.

> The traditional trade was integrated by imperialism. Political and military control guaranteed and consolidated the monopoly of the commercial companies and the level of their profits. The weakness of production, and consequently of sales resulting from insignificant investment in production, was compensated for by the rise of profit margins. Commerce extracted more than surplus produce; it took part of the produce required for natural growth, and reduced the producer to penury. This presented an obstacle to all forms of accumulation, or any kind of technical progress (7, pp. 159-160).

The Importance of the Livestock Sector

The French administrators considered livestock the main resource of Sudan (now Mali), Niger, and Mauritania. They wanted to benefit from the trade in animals through the collection of export, the *zekkat,* and other animal-related taxes. They also anticipated that the colonies' herds would provide meat for consumption by European administrators and settlers, and, eventually, the educated African elite. Less success was recorded in the livestock sector than with cash crops. Herders traditionally raised animals for their milk and hides, as drought insurance, and for the social status they conferred upon their owners. The provisioning of local or regional meat markets was not of significant importance.

The French administration, nonetheless, persisted in its view of livestock as a form of capital from which financial resources for the colonies could be derived. One French official described the *zekkat* as a "sort of tax on capital" which "corresponds much better than the personal tax to modern ideas of fiscal justice" (8). Because of the need to pay the *zekkat,* herders did begin to increase their sales. However, they tended to sell only as many animals as necessary to meet tax requirements and to obtain necessities, the purchase of which increasingly required cash.

Traditional attitudes toward animals were, however, only one of the obstacles facing increased commercialization in the livestock sector. Although some infrastructural improvements were made, primarily after World War II, offtake facilities remained seriously underdeveloped. To make matters worse for the French tax collector, the export taxes levied on cattle merchants resulted in "illegal" or "uncontrolled" exports. The situation was well summarized by a Veterinary Service official in Sudan (9):

> Every year we lose considerable income not only because cattle die en route due to inadequate organization, but also through uncollected taxes and especially because of the suspicions about our animals in importing countries, suspicions which have made them close the Guinea border permanently and occasionally the borders of the English colonies. . . . It is more necessary than before 1. that cattle export trails be equipped, 2. that exit posts be created, 3. that all cattle exported be vaccinated, as we have done for some time for the Ivory Coast.[1]

Despite frequent warnings of this nature, a coordinated development program for the livestock sector of French West Africa was never instituted. It was the herders, of course, not the French, who suffered from this state of affairs. Not only did they have to sell at least some animals each year under poor marketing conditions, but they rarely received adequate remuneration for these sales. Animal prices were not consistently high, and herders were often at the mercy of middlemen. As in the case of the peasantry, capital accumulation was extremely difficult and, in the absence of reasonable alternatives, herders continued to keep what profits they made in the form of livestock.

The Nature of Colonial Expenditure

The French colonial system in West Africa reduced the resources available to the indigenous population both directly, through taxation, and indirectly, through the imposition of an exploitative economic system. Although taxes were used to finance some investment within the colonies, the nature of these investments added little to the economic well-being of the region or its inhabitants. Most colonial expenditure was used to support the colonial administration, the army, the police, and the prisons, and to subsidize French concerns operating in the colonies (7, 10).

Some investment in roads and railways was made, but intra-African trade was not stimulated. Transportation lines ran between inland centers and the coast and were primarily designed to provide better access to the population by the military and the police (as a control mechanism) and by French traders and companies (as a means of

---

[1] Author's translation. Since the original of this source is found only in the French National Archives, it might be useful to reproduce the original wording: *"Nous perdons chaque année des sommes importantes non seulement par le bétail qui meurt en route faute d'une organisation sommaire, mais aussi par les taux non perçues et surtout par la suspicion qui est née dans les pays importateurs à l'égard de nos animaux et qui leur a fait fermer définitivement les frontières de la Guinée et périodiquement celles des colonies anglaises . . . Il est nécessaire plus qu'avant encore 1. que les routes d'exportation soient équipées, 2. que les postes de sortie soient créés, 3. que tout le bétail exporté soit vacciné; ainsi que nous le faisons depuis quelque temps pour la Côte d'Ivoire."*

tapping the economic wealth of the region) (7, 11, 12). As a result, even today, "it is frequently cheaper for country A to import from overseas industries rather than obtain the same production from the infant industry of neighbor or near neighbor" (13).

At independence (1958 for Senegal, 1960 for the others), several of the former French colonies were left with virtually no infrastructure and no economic base from which to work. In part, this was a direct result of a preference for Senegal as an investment site. French private capital set up some 250 light industries in Senegal before 1960, mostly in the Cape Verde peninsula. Because of the desire for a good profit margin, the sorts of industries set up tended to be those where cheap labor provided an important price advantage and those in which transport costs from extra-African sources would have been prohibitive. The former included canning, sugar processing, matches, textiles, brewing; the latter, cement, oil manufacturing, packing (14). Until decolonization, these factories supplied the rest of French West Africa with their products. Thus, there was no great urgency, from the European point of view, to establish others in more remote areas of the region, although some industrial investment did take place outside Senegal prior to 1960. Between 1948 and 1955, almost all of the private investment made in French West Africa went into the Cape Verde industries (14, p. xii).

Because Senegal was the earliest groundnut-producing area and because it was chosen as the major port center, the country had received, by independence, the most in terms of long-term public investment of the five countries under consideration. The transport sector was particularly well developed; roads, a railway, the port of Dakar, were all designed to facilitate the movement of produce from the agricultural regions to Europe. The rice project, Richard Toll, near the Mauritanian border, was also the object of considerable investment. Unfortunately, output lagged behind expectations and imports of rice continued to rise in the post-World War II period (15).

Niger, Mauritania, Mali, and Upper Volta were left less well-off. Niger did not have at independence in 1960 (nor has it today) a rail network (12, p. 24). One of the largest states in Africa, it had, nearly 15 years after independence, just over 4000 miles of road, of which 300 miles were paved (16). In 1942, Siconiger, a company that produces groundnut oil, was set up at Maradi. It remains the most important oil-producing company in Niger (17).

In Mauritania, investments have centered around the mining sector. Investments in mining began in the 1950s, with funds for MIFERMA, the iron-ore company, derived partly from French state and partly from foreign sources. However, it is open to conjecture how much the mining industry has benefited the majority of Mauritanians (18, 19). For example, at the end of 1968, there were some 8800 people privately employed in Mauritania, about half of whom were in the mining industry (20). Some two-thirds of the privately employed were Mauritanians, but they received only about one-third of the wage/salary bill. Furthermore, although MIFERMA increased its output per man by 40 percent between 1964 and 1972 (1500 tons to 2100 tons), it gave its wage earners no increase in pay (19, p. 99). Finally, about 90 percent of the population is engaged either in herding or in agriculture and is virtually untouched by the situation in the mining enclave.

Upper Volta was attached to the Ivory Coast between 1932 and 1947. Its primary role was and continues to be that of labor reserve for the Ivory Coast. It is manpower from Upper Volta that has worked the plantations and, increasingly, the industries of the Ivory Coast. Its own economy is extremely underdeveloped. The railroad that links Ouagadougou to the sea was completed in 1934. But even in the early 1970s, "The poverty of infrastructure creates an obstacle to the development of any industry which could reasonably compete with the industries of the Ivory Coast" (14, p. 143). And so, the manpower drain continues.

As for Mali, it had no industry to speak of in 1960 (21). The main investments were the Office du Niger, some roads, and the Kayes-Bamako railway. Despite the huge financial outlays required by the Office du Niger, it provided very little employment for Malians, who, for the most part, were not eager to relocate themselves in the project (22). The roads and railway system benefited groundnut and cotton exporters, but little, if any, attention was given to the improvement of production techniques (23).

In the Malian livestock sector, attention was focused on vaccinating cattle while marketing mechanisms and range management were largely ignored. The French did establish various livestock research stations (sheep farms at Nioro, Nara, Gao, El Oualadji; a farm school at El Oualadji; a cattle farm at Sotuba). But very little of the work they did there had, in the end, much relevance to local herders, particularly nomadic herders. And, partly because of chronic staff shortages, the little that was useful was not widely disseminated.

Probably the most successful aspect of the work done by these stations was the local production of vaccine. Even that had unanticipated, harmful side-effects when introduced in isolation from range management and improved marketing facilities. The pastoral hydrology section of the Veterinary Service was not set up until 1948. Like the vaccination service, its work exacerbated the problem it was intended to solve.

A considerable amount of time was spent in attempting to improve local breeds of sheep, goats, cattle, and chickens by crossing them with imported (generally European) breeds. The distribution of "improved" animals was limited. In general, it was found that the European breeds did not survive well in West Africa. Nonetheless, work continued along these lines.

Similarly, experiments with fodder production tended to concentrate on the improvement of local grains through cross-breeding with imported (generally North American and southern African) varieties. Again, these experiments were not very successful. Veterinary Service reports noted, from time to time, that it might be more productive to concentrate on improving local fodder crops without the introduction of foreign strains. Unfortunately, this sort of experiment does not seem to have been widely attempted (24-26).

Such experiments were entered into colonial records as investments in the livestock sector. And it was this sort of expenditure that the Inspector General of Livestock in French West Africa referred to when he described the *zekkat* as "the counterpart of the free aid given to the livestock sector in the form of sanitary protection[,] pastoral hydraulic works [, and] animal husbandry activities" (27).[2]

---

[2] Author's translation. Again, this source resides in the French National Archives and the French original reads: ". . . *la contrepartie de l'assistance donnée gratuitement à l'élevage sous forme de—protection sanitaire—travaux d'hydraulique pastorale—action zootechnique.*"

Current Trends

A movement away from France, the former exploiter, has enabled West African governments to claim that links with the past are being cut. Agreements with other Western European governments, the U.S., United Nations agencies, and even with Soviet bloc countries and China have encouraged the notion that some form of change is occurring within the region. That, however, is largely an illusion.

The economies of the five countries under discussion continue to be externally directed, in both senses of the term. There is virtually no local capacity to save. Between 1960 and 1970, local saving came to about 1 percent of gross domestic product (GDP) for West Africa as a whole. During the same period, investment was largely financed by foreign capital: Senegal, 81 percent; Mali, 78 percent; Mauritania, 78 percent; Upper Volta, 72 percent; and Niger, 72 percent (14, p. 270). At the same time, the export of primary products (ores and agricultural produce) dominated, and continues to dominate, the economies of these countries. In fact, in each of the five countries, one or two commodities have accounted for over 50 percent of export earnings since independence. Mining exports are gaining in importance, but agricultural products and livestock continue to predominate, as can be seen from Table 2.

The reliance on the agricultural sector is both a symptom of the underdeveloped and dependent state of the Sahelian countries and a major contributing factor to their continued underdevelopment and dependence. Prices for agricultural crops and livestock tend to be low and to fluctuate so that the benefits of higher prices are not maintained. Table 3 shows the changes in the prices paid to producers for major agricultural cash crops.

In the agricultural sector in general, although credit facilities, cooperatives (mainly for marketing), and the use of machinery and animal traction have been introduced, particularly for the production of export crops, the result has more often been peasant indebtedness and increased social differentiation rather than increased productivity and technical progress. The Comité Information Sahel has found that, whereas ground-nuts were previously raised in Senegal to purchase food and other necessities to the benefit of the trading companies, they are now used to pay off debts incurred through the purchase of the means of production (seeds, fertilizer, equipment) to the benefit of the state and wealthier farmers (4, pp. 71-77).

It is becoming increasingly possible for one person to acquire fairly large amounts of land, even in societies where the alienation of land was previously unknown. For example, although much land continues to be held communally in Mali, by the mid-1960s some 25 percent of the peasantry lived in conditions of semi-serfdom (28). In many cases, the most recent drought has accelerated this process (4, p. 229). Very often, it is members of the administration (civil and military) and traders who amass large private holdings.

Traders have been particularly adept at acquiring land by forcing peasants into indebtedness. They purchase crops at low prices at harvest time when the peasant most needs cash and later, when the peasant's food stocks run low, sell grain (some-times the peasant's own grain) at high prices. The 1968-1973 drought only increased the opportunities for this form of exploitation. The Comité Information Sahel has documented this process at least partially for Upper Volta, Niger, and Mali. They

Table 2

Selected exports as percentage of total export in five West African countries, various years[a]

Country and Commodity	1964	1968	1970	1972
Senegal				
Value total exports (billion CFA francs)	37.4	45.0	48.8	64.7
(equivalent in million U.S. dollars)	(151.5)	(181.0)	(176.0)	(252.0)
% Groundnuts	77.8	71.9	48.3	52.9
% Phosphates	6.4	5.8	7.4	7.1
% Groundnuts and phosphates	84.2	77.7	55.7	60.0
Mali				
Value total exports (billion Malian francs)[b]	–	9.0	19.2	22.7
(equivalent in million U.S. dollars)	–	(18.1)	(34.7)	(44.2)
% Cotton: seeds and fiber	–	35.0	30.0	33.0
% Groundnuts: decorticated, shelled and oil	–	11.0	14.0	19.0
% Livestock	–	28.8	29.6	24.2
% Livestock, groundnuts, and cotton	–	74.8	73.6	76.2
Mauritania				
Value total exports (billion Mauritanian ouguiyas)	2.8	3.7	5.4	5.4[b]
(equivalent in million U.S. dollars)	(11.3)	(14.9)	(19.5)	(21.0)
% Iron ore[c]	75.0	86.5	79.6	75.0
% Livestock[d]	7.1	5.4	5.5	3.7
% Iron ore and livestock	82.1	91.9	85.1	78.7
Niger				
Value total exports (billion CFA francs)[b]	4.7	7.1	8.8	13.7
(equivalent in million U.S. dollars)	(19.0)	(28.6)	(31.5)	(53.0)
% Groundnuts	68.1	69.0	64.8	45.9
% Livestock	–	12.7	15.9	16.1
% Uranium concentrates[e]	–	–	–	17.5
% Groundnuts, livestock, and uranium	68.1	81.7	80.7	79.5
Upper Volta				
Value total exports (billion CFA francs)[b]	3.3	5.3	5.1	5.1
(equivalent in million U.S. dollars)	(13.3)	(21.4)	(18.4)	(19.1)
% Livestock	55.5	47.7	31.2	48.7
% Cotton: seeds and fiber	5.2	18.8	29.4	21.4
% Livestock and cotton	60.7	66.5	60.6	70.1

[a] Sources, reference 4, pp. 130, 132, 135, 140, 143; reference 29, Annex B, Table III, pp. 182-186. Sources for exchange rates for 1964, *UN Statistical Yearbook 1968,* Table 192, p. 595; for 1968, 1970, and 1972, *UN Statistical Yearbook 1975,* Table 194, p. 704.

[b] Figures for recorded exports only. Unofficial exports, especially of livestock, are considerable, if difficult to quantify.

[c] Comité Information Sahel percentages (4) differ from Berg's (29) since they are a percentage of recorded exports only: 1964, 68 percent; 1968, 84 percent; 1970, 84 percent.

[d] While the number of cattle exported rose substantially between 1964 and 1972, at least partly in response to the drought, the annual value of animals exported remained nearly constant at 0.2-0.3 billion Mauritanian ouguiyas.

[e] By, 1973, uranium accounted for 39.1 percent of recorded exports.

Table 3

Index of farmer incomes from main cash crops in four West African countries, 1967-1975 (1967-1969 = 100)[a]

Country[b]	1967/ 68	1968/ 69	1969/ 70	1970/ 71	1971/ 72	1972/ 73	1973/ 74	1974/ 75
Mali	102	98	143	204	235	198	53	269
Niger	103	97	97	86	96	84	34	114
Senegal	113	87	84	69	137	87	104	267
Upper Volta	80	120	125	96	109	136	133	169

[a] Source, reference 29, Table 46, pp. 124-126.
[b] The main cash crop for Mali was cotton; for Niger, Senegal, and Upper Volta, cotton and groundnuts.

have demonstrated that the speculation on food during the drought could not have occurred without, at the very least, governmental acquiescence. In some cases, government officials were actively involved (4, pp. 202-212, 224-229, 249-250).

Cattle and fish merchants are perhaps the most successful group of traders. It is reported that efforts made during the 1960s to improve the health of Mauritanian livestock have also improved the financial situation of at least some herders (29). Nonetheless, among the wealthiest Mauritanians are the meat merchants who take livestock to Dakar (14, p. 77). Toward the end of the colonial period, Malians began to reenter the livestock and fish trades as demand for these commodities began to increase in the coastal states. They eventually formed the core of a small but dynamic bourgeoisie (14, pp. 131-133). At the same time, the Malian livestock traders are known to exploit the herders they deal with (28, p. 12).

Of course, not all herders are exploited. Some take their animals south themselves and avoid being cheated by middlemen. Just as there are wealthy, middle-class, and poor peasants, some herders are wealthier than others. On the whole, however, herders are not in a very favorable position, since as a group they are frequently discriminated against at the government level. A bias against pastoralists exists in most Sahelian countries. It derives in part from ancient antagonisms between nomads and agriculturalists, and in part from the belief that pastoralists resist integration into the prevailing economic and social system. As a result, the situation of herders in general has improved only marginally since 1960. Table 4 shows that, with the exception of Senegal, the share of the livestock sector in Sahelian budgets has declined on average 35 percent in the decade following independence.

THE DESTRUCTION OF THIRD WORLD ECOSYSTEMS

Prior to 1968-1973, the drought of 1912-1915 was accepted as the driest period during the last 70 years in the Sahelian countries. Now, the 1968-1973 drought is recognized as being at least as severe as the one of 1912-1915. However, it has proven very difficult to make comparisons between the two drought periods in all geographical regions. The reason for this is simple—a lack of data. While precipitation records

Table 4

Livestock budgets of five West African states as percentage of national budgets, various years[a]

Country and Years	National Budgets[b]	% Share of National Budgets	Budgets of Livestock Services[b]			% Share Personnel	% Share Material
			Total	Personnel	Material		
Upper Volta							
1960	6,044,700	1.43	86,673	62,176	24,497	71.73	28.37
1970	9,756,861	1.31	134,403	115,348	19,055	85.82	14.18
1973	13,000,000	0.98	128,200	110,000	18,200	83.36	12.64
Mali							
1960	6,798,590	2.67	181,750	150,890	30,860	82.82	17.18
1970	23,351,250	1.08	252,006	109,006	143,000	43.25	56.75
1973	25,760,000	1.15	296,848[c]	129,686	167,162	43.68	56.32
Mauritania							
1960	2,993,057	4.21	126,000	55,696	70,304	44.20	55.80
1970	8,257,000	1.97	163,100	80,300	82,800	49.23	50.77
1973	12,108,000	1.81	200,090	96,390	123,700	43.80	56.20
Niger							
1960	6,000,000	3.00	181,000	109,000	72,000	60.22	39.78
1970	12,573,000	1.95	245,840	136,760	109,080	55.62	44.38
1973	13,267,610	2.11	280,600	156,500	124,100	55.77	44.23
Senegal							
1960	20,806,767	0.95	197,859	119,264	78,595	60.27	39.73
1970	42,508,000	0.95	404,353	330,660	73,687	81.77	18.23
1973	47,000,000	1.11	523,955[d]	390,495	133,460	74.52	25.48

[a] Source, reference 46.
[b] All figures are in millions of CFA francs, except for Mali, where, since 1970, budgets have been expressed in millions of Malian francs.
[c] Includes research credits for the IER, the nursing school, and the national laboratory for veterinary research.
[d] Does not include research and higher education.

for parts of Senegal go back over 100 years, only a dozen stations in other parts of West Africa reported regularly prior to World War II. One French meteorological expert believes that it is impossible to state categorically that 1968-1973 was drier than 1912-1915 on the basis of existing rainfall data (30). John Caldwell, the Australian demographer, points out that many older people in the Sahel believe that 1913 was the driest year, and he says that there is "some evidence" (which he does not relate) that 1913 was drier than the early 1970s in the savannah farming areas but perhaps not in the Sahel zone proper (31). The data presented in Table 5 demonstrate the difficulty in arriving at definite conclusions.

There is general agreement, however, that the recent drought affected a larger area than any other serious drought in this century. The data in Table 5 show that for coastal areas in Senegal (e.g. Dakar) and some areas south of the 700-millimeter isohyet (e.g. Ouagadougou) the most recent drought was the driest period of this century. Nonetheless, in the Sahel zone proper,[3] where two out of three stations consistently reported the 1910s as drier than 1968-1973, considerable dislocations occurred in the 1970s. (It should be remembered that throughout the drought zone, local variations in rainfall occurred and that any statement about precipitation trends will have its exceptions.) Of all the groups in the drought-stricken area, it was the Sahelian herders who suffered the most.

One observer has pointed out that there were fewer animals and people in the

Table 5

Driest periods during 20th century in Sahelian countries, 2-year, 5-year, and 10-year rainfall averages[a]

Station and Country	2 Consecutive Years		5 Consecutive Years		10 Consecutive Years	
	mm	yrs	mm	yrs	mm	yrs
Dakar (Senegal)	242	71/72	334	68/72	460	63/72
Saint-Louis (Senegal)	147	13/14	255	68/72	314	63/72
Ségou (Mali)	516	71/72	592	68/72	630	40/49
Timbuktu (Mali)[b]	107	65/66	144	38/42	164	63/72
Ouagadougou (Upper Volta)	505	12/13	580	10/14	669	07/16
Niamey (Niger)[b]	319	14/15	383	12/16	(443)[c]	10/19
Zinder (Niger)[b]	222	12/13	305	11/15	(394)	10/19

[a] Source, reference 30, Table VI, p. 28.
[b] Denotes station in the Sahel zone.
[c] Figures in parentheses are estimates.

[3] The five countries discussed here are generally termed "Sahel" countries because they lie in part in a geographical zone to the south of the Sahara known as the Sahel. The boundaries of the zone have been defined in terms of vegetation, rainfall, and geography by various authors. Here we will say that the Sahel zone proper is where 100-400 millimeters of rain fall annually. The area where 400-600 millimeters of rain fall annually is the Sudano-Sahelian zone, but some writers include that in their definition of the Sahel zone (see, for example, reference 14, p. 3).

1910s to suffer the harmful effects of drought (30, p. 12). The point to be made here is that not only were there more animals and people in the late 1960s who were likely to suffer or die, but also that expanding populations have put considerable pressure on fragile ecosystems, making them more vulnerable to breakdown.

To focus on the population issue per se, however, would be to miss the crucial connection. To explain why the impact of the 1968-1973 drought was so much wider than that of the one in the 1910s, it is necessary to look at the existing social and economic relations within the region. Attempts to integrate African economies into the economic system of the industrialized countries have, in a number of cases, led to a progressive deterioration of African ecosystems, increasing their vulnerability to drought. A semi-arid region, such as the Sahel zone of West Africa, where the ecological equilibrium is dynamic and easily disrupted, is most vulnerable. The population question, along with the rainfall data, is an important, but not the only, element in the equation.

Agricultural Zones

In West Africa, the need to produce ever-increasing amounts of export crops led to an intensification of production in the more populated areas (near the coast and around large towns), and to the expansion of farming into areas with poorer soils and less regular and less abundant rainfall than the older agricultural regions. High levels of rainfall during the 1950s and 1960s encouraged this northward movement of peasants into lands previously devoted to herding. The unusually good weather conditions of this period helped to obscure the dangers inherent in this strategy:

> Cultivation in marginal areas during periods of higher than normal rainfall is especially dangerous and perhaps the main cause of desertification against which it may be necessary to take preventive action. When dry years follow years of relative plenty, ploughed soil or soil from which the sparse cover of natural plants has been eliminated by cultivation is at the mercy of winds. The fine clays and silts are carried away as dust, and the sand drifts into dunes. The effect is likely to be irreversible except at great cost (32).

Several other factors have contributed to the trend toward intensification. A reduction in the agricultural labor force—resulting from the requisitioning of men for forced labor and for army service (both prior to World War II) and from migration to European-owned plantations, urban areas, or Western Europe to increase family incomes—has led to difficulties in clearing new or fallowed land. The increasing sedentarization of formerly shifting cultivators, partly as a result of the creation of permanent amenities, such as schools and wells, has caused land in some areas to be used more regularly than in the past.

Fallowing, the traditional means of restoring some fertility to the soil, has been curtailed, particularly in the more populous areas. This has become a significant problem in the old coastal groundnut-producing regions, such as Senegal. In some cases, the loss of fertility has led to wind and rain erosion, and to the subsequent deterioration of the soil. Examples of this phenomenon exist in cotton-growing regions, particularly Chad, and around large towns, especially Zinder in southern

Niger (31, p. 46). The tendency to invade fallow land is greatest following a period of drought, and it can be expected that even greater soil degradation will occur as a result of the most recent drought if other methods of protecting the soil and increasing its fertility are not quickly introduced. The clearing of land for agricultural purposes and deforestation resulting from the need for firewood and timber have contributed to erosion and, again, are particularly noticeable around large towns (12, p. 8; 32, pp. 40-41; 33-35). According to one observer (33, p. 10),

> In Ouagadougou, Upper Volta, so intensive has the deforestation been that virtually all the timber stands within 70 kilometers of the city have been completely exhausted.

The opportunities for guarding against these harmful practices have been limited. The emphasis, in both the colonial and the postcolonial periods, has been on increasing production of export crops, not on conservation. Even the postindependence expansion of credit has not generalized the use of fertilizer. Many areas continue to depend on migrating herds to provide nutrients for the soil, but these arrangements have sometimes broken down as farmers move into the dry season grazing reserves of herders. These breakdowns have intensified as a result of the 1968-1973 drought and can only have a negative impact on the ecology of the Sahel in the absence of alternative methods of regulating land use and of fertilization.

Pastoral Zones

In the pastoral areas, overgrazing has been induced, to a large extent, by the alteration of the pastoral environment by external forces. Pastoral economies have been shaped by the need to exist within an essentially hostile environment. The level of technology in a pastoral society is low, and its means of manipulating its natural environment are limited. This does not mean, however, that pastoralists are at the mercy of natural forces. An extensive knowledge of the soil, plant life, and water resources of the Sahel has been built up over centuries. Methods designed to mitigate the harmful effects of climatic changes have included migrations of varying lengths, changes in herd composition, controlled reproduction of animals, and caravanning.

Attempts, first by the French and later by independent African governments, to integrate the Sahelian livestock sector into a commercialized economic system have worked to negate the impact of some of these traditional means of combatting drought.

The freedom of movement of pastoralists has been progressively curtailed, first by the creation of colonial boundaries and the introduction of the *laissez-passer*, and subsequently by the definition of international borders. The northward movement of peasants has further reduced grazing land. Of particular importance have been restrictions on the use of river-flooded land, increasingly used for irrigated farming, which had provided important dry season grazing reserves.

Technical innovations in pastoral areas, generally after 1950, have disrupted the animal-water-fodder balance and must bear a major portion of the blame for overgrazing. New wells and bore-holes provided assured and continuous water supplies for herds, and encouraged the growth of animal populations. Relative overpopulation, both of human beings and of animals, has been stimulated by improved medical health and veterinary services. Although herd sizes may not have increased substantially, the human population did, due primarily to improved health services. More people were thus available to own animals. This, in turn, led to a greater number of animals grazing the region.

Improvements in offtake and marketing facilities lagged behind changes in water and health services. But most important, no serious attempt at range management was made at any point in the 20th century. In fact, official encouragement of irrigated agriculture along river banks, the installation of wells and bore-holes, and restrictions on herders' movements have combined to break down the very systems of pasture division, constructed and implemented by pastoralists themselves, that had been designed to minimize both overgrazing and conflict between pastoral groups.

As in the case of peasant-based agriculture, a northward movement in the 1950s and 1960s took place among herders. Good weather conditions and the installation of permanent water points in northern grazing regions encouraged the use of more marginal land. Pastures which had been previously used as seasonal grazing were submitted to more continuous use. As in the case of the agricultural sector, these changes were ecologically viable only as long as rainfall continued at the higher level. But even under these good climatic conditions, deterioration was evident. Overgrazing around permanent water sources is documented from the early 1960s during a period when rainfall was particularly high (12, pp. 9-11). As the level of rainfall declined, particularly at the beginning of the 1970s, the process of range deterioration accelerated.

The degradation of pasture land has been documented by a number of experts and, according to Anders Rapp (34), in the Sahel zone it is characterized by the development of *brousses tigrées* or "striped bush." These formations, strips of vegetation divided by degraded soil, occur where wind and rain erosion denude the slopes of small ridges covered by plants which are drought-resistant but which offer very little protection in the dry season. The soil washed or blown down the slopes of these ridges forms an impermeable layer of clay and silt which reduces water infiltration. This, in turn, eventually kills the woody plants. In the end, it is only the depressions between the ridges which are vegetated due to the concentration of runoff water. Such formations are reportedly widespread in both the Sahelian and Sudan zones (34, pp. 44-45).

As the northern grazing lands deteriorated during the 1968-1973 drought, herders moved south. They often discovered that former grazing reserves had become agricultural plots. In some cases, farmers had abandoned the land because of the drought, but its value to the herds was severely diminished by wind erosion or by overgrazing by other herds. In other cases, the land was under irrigation or otherwise off-limits to nomadic herders. Some farmers, however, whose crops withered for lack of rain, did allow herds to graze the stubble. A number of West African governments, eager to protect their own herds, restricted the entry and the freedom of movement of pastoralists who were not their own nationals. Most animal deaths during the drought were due to starvation, not lack of water.

PROPOSALS FOR THE FUTURE

The problems of ecological degradation currently facing the Sahel zone of West Africa can be seen to arise in large part from the implementation of policies designed primarily to obtain immediate financial and material benefits for essentially non-producing groups, both domestic and foreign. Such investments as have been made have been localized and little attention has been paid to their potentially harmful social and ecological impact. The tendency to adopt this sort of strategy results from production for profit rather than for the well-being of the community as a whole. The rational exploitation of natural resources over the long term in this situation is accorded low priority because it is difficult to place a monetary value on the protection of range land or the conservation of water, while a ton of groundnuts or a piece of machinery has a definite price.

The Improvement of Livestock Production

The policy of the French colonial administration and, subsequently, of independent West African governments, toward the livestock sector typifies this sort of attitude. The French colonial government lamented the lack of commercialization within the livestock sector, as well as the poor quality and low numbers of animals produced. As one means of stimulating commercialization, cattle taxes were imposed. This solution had the double benefit of providing income for the colonial government (and subsequently African governments), while avoiding both excessive outlays on adequate offtake facilities (e.g. roads, railways, well-provisioned cattle trails, and markets) and guaranteed remuneration for herders. To some extent, the taxation policy was successful. Herders did have to sell some animals each year to pay taxes. But the lack of an efficient marketing system and the variability of cattle prices gave herders little incentive to produce for the market to the extent anticipated by the French.

To improve quality and quantity of livestock, the colonial administration made some investments in permanent water sources and inoculation programs. International financing has been responsible for similar projects in the postindependence period. Both the colonial administration and West African governments appear to have ignored warnings from the colonial Veterinary Service and other groups that unless range management were pursued in conjunction with these other improvements, severe ecological degradation was likely to occur.

As a result of the 1968-1973 drought, more attention is being given to the question of range management. Some observers think that ecological deterioration is too far advanced for the continued use of the Sahel as a grazing area (36). For others, including some private companies and national and international development agencies, the vision of the Sahel as a major cattle-producing area still exists. The U.S. Agency for International Development (USAID), for example, considers that "The semiarid areas immediately south of the Sahara are the most critically abused range-land areas of Africa, yet their potential for livestock production is substantial" (11, p. 39). Estimating that demand for meat in West African coastal states will double by 1980, AID maintains that the Sahel "will remain the major cattle production area" (11, p. 41).

The need for an integrated livestock development program—having as its core careful management of range lands—is recognized. With such a program, the agencies involved believe, a prosperous and ecologically sound system of livestock production can be initiated and maintained. However, as USAID has noted, "there is as yet little agreement among donor agencies and governments on the specific principles and modalities of instituting range management policies and practices" (11, p. 47).[4] While donors and potential recipients talk, their good intentions run the risk of being undercut.

Private capital and donor agencies are already financing investment in the livestock sector. These groups include the World Bank, the European Economic Community, FAO, USAID, Fonds d'Aide et de Coopération (FAC), the Canadian and West German governments, a number of French and American companies, and Nestlés. The sorts of projects they are funding include fattening and reproduction ranches (Niger, Mauritania, Senegal, Upper Volta, and Mali), a milk factory in Senegal (Nestlés), and tanneries and abattoirs in all countries. Infrastructure improvements associated with some of these projects include well improvement and expansion, health programs, firebreaks, livestock markets, and some training for infrastructure upkeep and for extension services (4, pp. 165-169; 38).

Some of these programs will undoubtedly benefit pastoralists, but the problem of providing mobile herders with amenities and financial security remains difficult. Some agencies, notably USAID, recognize the need to improve the economic condition of herders, but just how they expect that improvement to occur is left vague (11, pp. 37-54).

Furthermore, in the absence of a coordinated, long-term plan for the management of the Sahelian environment, these isolated interventions could well have the same sort of negative impact as their predecessors. Some ranching projects are being set up by private capital. There is no guarantee that private capital will protect the resources within its own control (see the section on "ecological drawbacks" below). And there is certainly no reason for it to be concerned about the general situation in the Sahel or the impact its operations might have on independent herders. The French-owned Ekrafane ranch in Niger is a case in point.

The Agro-Industrial Connection

In the agricultural sector, as long as profits could be made without large capital and material inputs, peasant-based agriculture continued to be the dominant form of production. However, the recent drought has suggested that the ecological limits of peasant-based production under the current system have been reached. Foreign interests seem to have decided that only a large-scale injection of capital into that sector, along with the transformation of production, will secure a reasonable level of profits and raw materials (39).

---

[4] For additional discussion concerning livestock development programs, see Van Dyne (37).

Such an approach, it should be noted, is not incompatible with increased emphasis on food crops. In fact, a number of international and national aid agencies are promoting the notion of self-sufficiency in foodstuffs. It is anticipated that the growth of internal food markets will help transfer resources from urban to rural areas and will contribute to the fight against famine. Greater wealth in rural areas would mean, of course, that the farmer would be better able to purchase largely foreign-produced farming inputs (seeds, fertilizers, machinery, and the like).

It is also expected that the number of people engaged in agricultural production will decline. A growing number of people, including pastoralists deprived of land through ranch enclosures, would thus be available for work in industry (4, pp. 127-170). But such investment as is being made in industry is largely in the processing of primary products. As the Senegalese Foreign Ministry noted in 1973 (4, p. 166):

> . . . most of the large industrial projects under study or in progress are related to the processing of agricultural products, milk industries, meat, fish, rice projects, the extension of the capacity of certain oil factories. . . . In other sectors, projects are less numerous.

Economic Drawbacks

These developments are disturbing for a number of reasons. A large part of the production of existing or projected market-gardening schemes is destined for export to Western Europe, North America, Japan, and urban areas in Ghana, Nigeria, and the Ivory Coast, although post-1973 increases in air and sea freight have made exporting outside Africa somewhat less attractive. Such schemes include Bud-Senegal; an International Bank for Reconstruction and Development-financed farm in Mauritania; a farm in Upper Volta (Tomentente) partly financed by capital from the Ivory Coast; and a French private investment farm in Niger (4, p. 169; 40).

Once the quality of beef raised is such to enable it to enter non-African markets, it can be expected that this commodity too will be exported in large quantities. This latter is admittedly a long-term project and, until it can be realized, the Ivory Coast, Ghana, Togo, Benin, Nigeria, and, to a lesser extent, Cameroon, Guinea, Senegal, and Zaire, are expected to make increasing demands on livestock production in the Sahel (11, p. 40). The choices of whether and of how much to export will rest primarily with those who have financial control over the concerns, not the West African producers and consumers. The profits from sales, whether to foreign or domestic markets, will largely bypass the producers as well.

Investment in the industrial sector can be expected to expand. However, the nature of the investment to date (generally light industry and, as noted above, raw material-processing plants) militates against economic independence for West Africa. Despite the fact that some international donor agencies, such as the World Bank, give preference to local producers in materials procurement, the pattern of industrial development to date means that most industrial components for development projects will still have to be imported. This is as true for the inputs promoted as vital for the successful expansion of agricultural output as for those of industrial development. Furthermore, anyone employed in these industries should not expect very high wages.

To the extent that areas like West Africa are considered attractive investment sites, it is often precisely because very low wages can be paid to workers (4, pp. 127-170; 41).

Under such a system, the countries of the Sahel can be expected to maintain their dependence upon imports of industrial machinery and technology, as well as capital and, possibly, food, into the foreseeable future. The returns on private capital will largely accrue to the owners of that capital. Since capital accumulation will continue to be difficult for all but a few well-placed West African elites, external sources will continue to provide the bulk of investment funds. Balance-of-payments deficits will persist since loans from national and international agencies must be repaid. Thus, taxation on products and individuals will be diverted to the repayment of foreign debts, rather than being used to generate more development within the region. The countries of the Sahel will remain largely dependent upon France and other industrialized states for their trade and financial security. In short, indigenous development will be blocked once again.

Ecological Drawbacks

The ecological future could be equally poor. Any trend toward the consolidation of land in private hands which caused a rise in the numbers of absentee landlords and tenant-farmers would militate against conservation farming. Neither absentee landlords nor tenants are interested in making substantial land-conserving improvements; the landlord, because his interest lies in collecting the rent and reinvesting it in more rapidly profitable urban projects or in increasing his personal consumption, and the tenant, because he is not willing to improve someone else's land as long as he risks eviction or higher rents as a result. Even if the tenant wants to invest in conservation techniques, he very often does not have sufficient savings to do so since his surplus production ends up in the landlord's pocket.

There is no proof that intensive farming or grazing can be supported ecologically, even in the more fertile areas, over the long term. The farming techniques promoted thus far have been developed in countries in North America and Western Europe, where there are different soils and more regular rainfall than in the Sahel. To promote ecological viability, a strong dependence on water and fertilizers is necessary.

Fertilizers are in short supply and are costly. Their widespread application would create an additional drain on foreign exchange and would increase reliance on the industrialized countries. This would be true even if local fertilizer industries were set up to exploit West African phosphate deposits, for the technology, machinery, and capital would have to be largely imported.

The only means of guaranteeing continuous, large-scale supplies of water is to tap subterranean sources, many of which are known or thought to be nonrenewable or to recharge slowly. The example of Libya demonstrates the dangers inherent in reliance on subterranean water. In some Libyan coastal regions, the expansion of irrigated farming promoted by tapping *renewable* groundwater reserves has caused the water table to drop up to 3 meters a year (42). Many experts, believing that there is insufficient knowledge of the nature and the extent of West African groundwater reserves, caution against the massive exploitation of them until such time as complete local and regional surveys have been made.

It is debatable whether American companies interested in establishing farming enterprises in West Africa will be able to show the restraint advised by the experts. Their record in their own country has been one of apparent disregard for environmental constraints. The "mining" of the Ogallala Reservoir in the state of Colorado is a case in point. The Ogallala Reservoir is a subterranean formation covering about 9000 square miles in southeastern Colorado alone. Large farms operated by agribusiness corporations are extracting such enormous quantities of water from the Colorado portion of the Reservoir that it has been estimated that reserves will be depleted in 25 years. According to Ray (43),

> The Colorado State University Experiment Station at Fort Collins pointed out that replenishment is only about half an inch a year, and that one well pumping 500 gallons per minute would withdraw the equivalent of one-half an inch of water from under a section [640 acres] of land in less than two weeks. Many corporate farmers are withdrawing at the rate of 1,000 gallons a minute from under each quarter section [160 acres] of land!

AN ALTERNATIVE DEVELOPMENT STRATEGY

It is possible to envisage a system of production for Sahelian countries which would run less risk of disturbing the region's fragile ecosystem and which would encourage indigenous development. Such a system would be characterized by a reliance on local materials and manpower, a low priority accorded to imports of capital and goods, and an adaptation of farming and grazing practices to the known limits of the ecosystem.

Peasant-based agriculture would form the core of crop production. There is scope for the expansion of flood-retreat cultivation in many parts of West Africa. It has the benefit of familiarity for many farmers, and would entail a lower investment rate and less resettlement than industrial schemes. Simple methods of constructing weirs and embankments could be used to extend the areas exploited by irrigation as well as to utilize off-season labor to improve the agricultural infrastructure (44). The collection of surface water and the use of renewable, shallow groundwater resources would also aid the expansion of irrigation and facilitate multiple cropping.

Various groups have suggested the division of West Africa into cattle breeding and fattening areas, with the Sahel proper as the breeding ground (11, 35, 41, 45). A regular destocking of young animals from pastoralists' herds would reduce the tendency toward overgrazing while enabling maximum land exploitation in the region. Pastoralists would be guaranteed a more regular income through the operation of such a program. Coupled with a drought insurance plan, this could encourage herders to reduce herd sizes under good weather conditions, thus minimizing the risk of overgrazing in drier periods.

Some experts fear that the kind of changes necessitated by the transformation of the Sahel into a zone primarily devoted to breeding animals (*zone de naissance*) would prove unacceptable to pastoralists (11, p. 48). Others believe that if herders were actively involved in the choice and the implementation of new strategies, the changes would be accepted (41, p. 19). Within this context, the development of herders' cooperatives may provide a workable solution.

Herders' cooperatives would provide a forum both for the expression of pastoralists' needs and for the dissemination of information and services to herders. The division of range land among groups and the implementation of grazing rotation schedules could be undertaken and enforced by cooperatives. They could also organize labor for infrastructure construction projects and help to determine priorities in this area. Cooperatives might also operate animal insurance programs, banking, and, possibly, credit facilities (41, p. 19; 46). In these ways, the economic and ecological security of herders and the environment would be promoted.

In the wetter areas to the south of the Sahel, peasant-based animal-fattening schemes would be combined with the farming of agricultural produce. Mixed-farming would help to improve soil fertility and reduce the likelihood of erosion in these areas. It would also require less capital investment than industrial fattening schemes, and would help to modernize peasant holdings and to diversify peasant activities. It would also provide an excellent use for agricultural by-products. Family income would also be raised in this way (45).

Fodder production could also be undertaken in the less arid zones. If animal production is to be increased, meat quality improved, and herders' security in time of drought guaranteed, fodder production is essential. The emphasis on production for export during the colonial and postcolonial periods has meant that inadequate attention has been paid to both food and fodder crops. Just as the priorities and attitudes of governments and producers alike must change if livestock production is to be pursued profitably and in an ecologically sound manner, a shift is required in the agricultural sector.

A considerable amount of land currently devoted to cash crops must be turned over to the production of food and fodder crops. It has been suggested that the construction and repair of earthen dams would increase the area available for cultivation of these crops. At the same time, storage facilities must be constructed in all parts of West Africa (12, p. 17). Again, off-season labor of peasants and pastoralists could be mobilized for these purposes.

The improvement of the livestock sector and the expansion of mixed-farming into the less arid zones faces a number of other difficulties. The lack of transportation as well as the existence of animal pests in the less arid zones are two primary problems which must be overcome.

It may prove possible to lessen the transport problem, in the short- to medium-term at least, by the adoption of a three-tiered system of animal production such as that suggested by Van Dyne (37). Three overlapping geographical regions (arid/semiarid, semiarid/semihumid, semihumid/humid) would concentrate on different aspects of livestock rearing and crop production. Initially, animals could be moved through each stage by trekking. Fodder and food crops would move south to north, making use, at first, of what road and rail transport currently exists. Part of the surplus resulting from animal sales could be used to gradually extend the transport system, making the transport of animals possible (37, pp. 42-43).

The operation of such a system makes the eradication of animal pests in the more humid areas a top priority. Some internationally funded programs toward this end are already in progress. As land is freed for use by humans and animals, livestock raising in the north can be progressively integrated with animal and crop production in the south.

Obviously, rapid progress cannot be made everywhere and at once. Nonetheless, this is the sort of program which must be considered if the countries of the Sahel are to be able to feed themselves with the minimum of ecological disequilibrium and if independent, self-sustaining economic development is to occur. This sort of program has a further advantage. Parts of it, particularly those infrastructure projects which can be undertaken by off-season labor, can be started immediately without the necessity of waiting for funding organizations to approve proposals.

CONCLUSIONS

The notion that human activity is an important cause of ecological deterioration, particularly in fragile ecosystems, is not a new one. In 1935, Lowdermilk (47) wrote,

> . . . so devastating seems the occupation of man that, with a few striking exceptions, a desert or near-desert condition is often associated with his long habitation of a region. . . . The operation of mankind's exploitative and destructive activities is often decisive in zones of delicate balance between soil formation and destruction, between rain absorption and rapid run-off.

At about the same time, Stebbing (48, 49) was writing of the dangers facing West Africa from overcultivation and overgrazing of marginal lands.

At the end of the 1930s, Jacks and Whyte (50) made a "world survey of soil erosion." They documented case after case of poor land management, both in colonial territories and in politically autonomous states. Although their purpose was not to prove that the misuse of land arises out of certain social and economic conditions, a number of their examples give witness to the importance of these factors.

In discussing the advanced erosion evident in the Kikuyu and Kavirondo Reserves in Kenya, they pointed out that erosion had become a problem only since the arrival of Europeans. A number of specific erosion-inducing factors were cited. These included the cultivation of steep hillsides, the concentration of too many animals in too small an area, and the desire (or need?) to grow cash crops, several of which, notably maize and cotton, are known to be especially destructive of soil fertility (50, pp. 62-63). Clearly, it was certain colonial policies, the creation of "native reserves" and the promotion of cash crop production, which were at the root of this misuse of land.

A more explicit statement of the relationship between ecological degradation and an exploitative socioeconomic system was made by Kellogg (51) in 1941:

> Soil erosion is an important symptom of bad relationship between people and the soil. . . . Civilization can hardly be said to have declined from soil exhaustion—soil exhaustion is more a result of the decay of the people, of the civilization.

The Dust Bowl in the U.S. mid-West during the 1930s was just as much a product of that "bad relationship" as are any number of ecological breakdowns facing people throughout the world today. As a result of the Dust Bowl, a number of conservation methods were introduced and their use expanded over the next few decades. Many experts have predicted that the mid-West will never suffer another Dust Bowl. However, a report presented to the U.S. Senate in 1975 (52) indicated that the higher wheat prices of the early 1970s had led a growing number of farmers to ignore such basic conservation methods as fallowing, cultivating land of substandard fertility, and strip-cropping in order to put as much land under production as possible. Now, it is by no means certain that widespread soil destruction will not occur once again.

Stryker (23) has reported that, at about the beginning of the 1970s, the demand from coastal states for cattle from Mali, Mauritania, and Upper Volta (and probably also Niger) had begun to exceed the supply, causing animal prices to rise. Stating that the "substantial growth" of other West African countries (such as Senegal, the Ivory Coast, and Ghana) was based on the production of one or more primary products in which those countries had a "comparative advantage," Stryker suggested that Mali (and by implication the other major livestock-producing countries in West Africa) develop the livestock sector to take full advantage of this excess demand for meat (23, pp. 451, 455).

However, it can be shown that the "substantial growth" of Senegal, Ghana, and the Ivory Coast is largely illusory (14, pp. 3-75, 155-166, 170-186, 191-195). It is in fact precisely this sort of "development" that has ensured the economic and ecological impoverishment of the region and its inhabitants. Greater efforts to squeeze more and more out of both the people and the soil will only hasten the day when neither will have the strength to produce anything further.

It might be argued that many of the elements outlined in the section on "alternatives" above are to be found in the development programs of international and national donor agencies and that the participation of foreign private capital is not necessarily at odds with the implementation of an ecologically sound economic policy.

It should be remembered, however, that money borrowed must be repaid, and with interest. It makes sense to use local manpower and resources whenever possible, for surplus production can be turned into further investment, rather than used for debt repayment.

Private capital invests in order to make a profit. It prefers to invest in enterprises or sectors in which the returns are highest. These sectors are not necessarily those which will provide the greatest benefits to the majority of the population. Even where investment is in a sector that could generate income for other developmental purposes, the people and their governments generally receive only a limited amount of the financial benefits or are unable to direct the investment of profits. The mining industries in Mauritania and Niger provide excellent examples of this problem (14, p. 137; 19). Local governments may also be unable or unwilling to channel investment in a more socially productive direction.

In general, the previous reliance on foreign capital and know-how and on imported development strategies has only brought ecological degradation and economic marginalization to the majority of the Sahel's population. Industrialized capitalist countries have succeeded in maintaining their own ecologically wasteful economic systems through the extraction of financial and material resources from Third World countries (and, increasingly, Soviet bloc states). Those at the bottom of the dependency heap inevitably pay for environmental degradation both in their own territories and in the metropolitan countries. The most recent drought in the Sahel and the decline in world food stocks have provided foreign interests with a rationale for the further transformation of production methods in West Africa. The record of previous foreign interventions in the region suggests that environmental protection will take, at best, second place to the pursuit of profits and of economic stability for the industrialized Western governments.

REFERENCES

1. De Young, K. Selling the Sahel. *The Washington Monthly*, p. 33, September 1975.
2. Sheets, H., and Morris, R. *Disaster in the Desert: Failures of International Relief in the West African Drought*, pp. 11-13. Carnegie Endowment for International Peace, Washington, D.C., 1974.
3. *Special Report to the Congress on the Drought Situation in Sub-Sahara Africa*, p. 15. Bureau for Africa, U.S. Agency for International Development, Washington, D.C., June 1975.
4. Comité Information Sahel. *Qui se nourrit de la famine en Afrique? le dossier politique de la faim au Sahel*. Maspero, Paris, 1974.
5. Stanissis, P. C. *Disaster Analysis*. United Nations Disaster Relief Office, Geneva, September 1972.
6. Cissoko, S-M. Famines et épidemies à Tombouctou et dans la Boucle du Niger du XVIe au XVIIIe siècle. *Bulletin de l'Institut Fondamental d'Afrique Noire*, Series B: Sciences Humaines 20(3): July 1968.
7. Suret-Canale, J. *French Colonialism in Tropical Africa, 1900-1945*, translated by T. Gottheiner. C. Hurst and Company, London, 1971.
8. Rapport No. 98. Ministère des Colonies, Inspection des Colonies, Mission de 1922-1923 de M. Kair, Inspecteur Général des Colonies, Bamako, May 25, 1923.
9. Rapport Annuel. Afrique Occidentale Française, Soudan, Service Zootechnique et des Epizooties, Bamako, 1930.
10. Rapports Annuels. Gouvernement Général de l'Afrique Française, Gouvernement du Soudan Français, Affaires Politiques, Bamako, 1923-1927, 1929-1932 and 1934.
11. *Development Assistance Program, 1976-1980, Central-West African Region—Volume I: Overview and Program Conclusions (Sections I and II)*, p. 61. U.S. Agency for International Development, Washington, D.C., November 1975.
12. Glantz, M. Value of a Reliable Long Range Climate Forecast for the Sahel: A Preliminary Assessment, p. 24. National Center for Atmospheric Research, Boulder, Col., May 15, 1976 (mimeographed).
13. Howe, J. The future of surface transport in Africa. *African Affairs*, p. 315, July 1975.
14. Amin, S. *Neo-Colonialism in West Africa*, translated by F. McDonagh, pp. 16-17. Monthly Review Press, New York, 1973.
15. Suret-Canale, J. *Afrique Noire de la Colonisation aux Indépendances, 1945-1960 I*, p. 204. Editions Sociales, Paris, 1972.
16. DuBois, V. D. *The Drought in Niger—Part I: The Physical and Economic Consequences*. American Universities Field Staff, New York, July 1974.
17. *Niger 1971-1972: Dossier d'information économique*, p. 35. Secrétariat d'Etat aux Affaires Etrangères Chargé de la Coopération, Paris, 1973.
18. El Mauritanyi, H. *"L'Indépendance" . . . Néo-Coloniale*, pp. 93-94, 155-162. Editions des Six Continents, Paris, 1974.
19. Bonte, P. Multinational companies and national development: MIFERMA and Mauritania. *Review of African Political Economy* No. 2: 89-109, January-April 1975.
20. Westebbe, R. M. *The Economy of Mauritania*, p. 48. Special Studies in International Economics and Development. Praeger, New York, 1971.
21. *Mali, 1972-1973: Dossier d'information économique*, p. 10. Secrétariat d'Etat aux Affaires Etrangères Chargé de la Coopération, Paris, 1974.
22. De Wilde, J. C. *Experiences with Agricultural Development in Tropical Africa—Volume I: The Synthesis*, pp. 71-77. Johns Hopkins Press, Baltimore, 1967.
23. Stryker, J. D. The Malian cattle industry: Opportunity and dilemma. *Journal of Modern African Studies* 12(3): 443, 1974.

24. Rapports Annuels. Gouvernement Général de l'Afrique Occidentale de l'Ouest, Service Zootechnique et des Epizooties, Bamako, 1923-1928, 1930-1933.
25. Rapports Annuels. Gouvernement Général de l'Afrique Occidentale de l'Ouest, Service de l'Elevage et des Industries Annexes, Bamako, 1944, 1948.
26. Rapports Annuels. Gouvernement Général de l'Afrique Occidentale de l'Ouest, Service de l'Elevage et des Industries Animales, Centre Fédéral de Recherches Zootechnique, Bamako, 1952-1955, 1958.
27. Feunteun, L. M. L'Elevage en AOF: Développement-Amélioration, Programme d'Equipement. Paris, 1955.
28. Amin, S. Trois expériences africaines de développement: Le Mali, la Guinée et le Ghana, p. 11. Presses Universitaires de France, Etudes "Tiers Monde," Paris, 1965.
29. Berg, E. The Recent Economic Evolution of the Sahel, p. 13. Center for Research on Economic Development, University of Michigan, June 1, 1975 (mimeographed).
30. Sircoulon, J. Les Données Climatiques et Hydrologiques de la Sécheresse en Afrique de L'Ouest Sahélienne, p. 11. Secretariat for International Ecology, Sweden (SIES), Stockholm, 1974.
31. Caldwell, J. C. The Sahelian Drought and Its Demographic Implications, OLC Paper No. 8, pp. 19-20. American Council on Education, Washington, D.C., December 1975.
32. Grove, A. T. Desertification in the African environment. In Drought in Africa, edited by D. Dalby and R. J. Harrison Church, p. 41. School of Oriental and African Studies, London, 1973.
33. DuBois, V. D. The Drought in West Africa—Part I: Evolution, Causes and Physical Consequences, pp. 9-10. American Universities Field Staff, New York, 1973.
34. Rapp, A. A Review of Desertization in Africa—Water, Vegetation and Man, pp. 48-49. Secretariat for International Ecology, Sweden (SIES), Stockholm, 1974.
35. Report on the Sahelian Zone: A Survey of the Problems of the Sahelian Zone with a View to Drawing up a Long Term Strategy and a Programme for Protection, Restoration and Development. Swedish International Development Agency/Food and Agricultural Organization, Rome, 1974.
36. Campbell, D. Drought could be a blessing in disguise. Financial Times, July 9, 1975.
37. Van Dyne, G. M. Preliminary conclusions regarding long-term development strategies in relation to environmental management in the Sahel. In International Development Strategies for the Sahel, Report of October 1974 Conference at Bellagio, pp. 38-50. Rockefeller Foundation, New York, May 1975.
38. International Development Association and International Bank for Reconstruction and Development fact sheets on projects funded in West Africa, 1968-1975.
39. Meillassoux, C. Development or exploitation: Is the Sahel famine good business? Review of African Political Economy No. 1: 27-33, 1974.
40. Meunier, R. L'Aide d'urgence et les Nouveaux Projets de Développement. In Sécheresses et Famines du Sahel I, edited by Jean Copans, p. 128. Maspero, Paris, 1975.
41. International Development Strategies for the Sahel, Report of October 1974 Conference at Bellagio, p. 22. Rockefeller Foundation, New York, May 1975.
42. Allen, J. A. Reports by session chairmen: Climate and water resources. In Drought in Africa, edited by D. Dalby and R. J. Harrison Church, p. 15. School of Oriental and African Studies, London, 1973.
43. Ray, V. K. Pumping the Ogallala Reservoir. In The People's Land: A Reader on Land Reform in the United States, edited by Peter Barnes, p. 121. Rodale Press Book Division, Emmaus, Pa., 1975.
44. Harrison Church, R. J. The development of the water resources of the dry zone of West Africa. In Drought in Africa, edited by D. Dalby and R. J. Harrison Church, pp. 62-66. School of Oriental and African Studies, London, 1973.
45. Boeckh, E. Etudes sur la situation actuelle de l'élevage dans les pays du Sahel et des mesures de sauvegarde à envisager. European Development Fund, Brussels, 1974.
46. Memorandum from Jeremy Swift, University of Sussex, to N. Ball on proposal for herders' cooperatives in Somalia.
47. Lowdermilk, W. C. Man-made deserts. Pacific Affairs 8(4): 409, 1935.
48. Stebbing, E. P. The threat of the Sahara. Journal of the Royal African Society, Vol. 36, 1937.
49. Stebbing, E. P. The encroaching Sahara: The threat to the West African colonies. Geographical Journal 85: 506-524, 1935.

50. Jacks, G. V., and Whyte, R. O. *Vanishing Lands: A World Survey of Soil Erosion.* Doubleday, Doran & Company, Inc., New York, 1939.
51. Kellogg, C. *The Soils that Support Us,* p. 303. Macmillan Company, New York, 1941.
52. Council for Agricultural Science and Technology. *Conservation of the Land, and the Use of Waste Materials for Man's Benefit.* Prepared for the Committee on Agriculture and Forestry, United States Senate, March 25, 1975. In *Losing Ground: Environmental Stress and World Food Prospects,* by Erik P. Eckholm, p. 9. W. W. Norton and Company, Inc., New York, 1976.

PART 2

U.S. Foundations, U.S. Foreign Policy and International Health

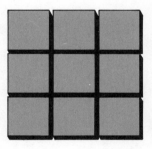

Foreign Intervention in Medical Education: A Case Study of the Rockefeller Foundation's Involvement in a Thai Medical School

Peter J. Donaldson

Strong professional groups are considered key elements in the modernization efforts of less-developed societies. Vast amounts of money are spent by developing countries themselves as well as by developed countries and various international donor groups in support of the training of professionals from the developing world.[1] There is, however, a growing body of evidence which suggests that the modernizing contributions of the professions have been less than expected or hoped for, in part because of the apparent inappropriateness of much professional training and the allegiance of many professionals in the developing world to role models derived from the experience of professionals in the advanced, industrialized nations of the West (2). Many of the frequently heard complaints about the "westernization" of indigenous professionals are grounded in the belief that Third World professionals have little understanding of or ability to serve their own societies because of their socialization to alien models of professional work.

The role of developed countries, international agencies, and philanthropic organizations in promoting the patterns of professional orientation found in the developing world is often mentioned but rarely examined in detail. Despite the fact that a great deal of criticism has been voiced against the influence of foreign agencies and person-

---

[1] As one example, in 1974 Thailand received approximately 4.3 million dollars of foreign assistance for professional development. This represented about 13 percent of all foreign technical assistance (1).

nel on the development of indigenous professional competence, very little is known about the precise role foreigners play in the evolution of the professions in the Third World.

The medical profession provides an especially important example of both the influential role of foreigners in professional development and the problems that result from the failure of professional training to fit the needs of less-developed societies. Throughout the developing world the role of foreign agencies in the development of medical education and health care has been extremely important. Nearly everywhere foreign influences have helped shape the character of health care delivery. However, although the issues of health and illness are central to the development plans of most Third World countries, the majority of people in the developing world do not have access to adequate health care. Health services are concentrated in the largest metropolitan areas, and there is a trend toward specialized, hospital-based practice which is widely regarded as inappropriate to the medical needs of the developing world (3).

Numerous analysts have attributed the difficulty most developing countries have in providing adequate health services to the "westernization" of medical education and health care. Bryant (3, p. xi), for example, notes that a major cause of the "pitifully limited benefits reaching the majority of the people" is the fact that "patterns of medical care and education of health personnel are copied closely from Western countries. . . ." Lathem (4) believes the problems result from developing countries having "imported a system of medical care, and medical education, developed elsewhere: in Western industrialized societies. . . ."

Among the many organizations providing support for medical and health activities in the developing world, the Rockefeller Foundation has played an exceptionally significant role. The Foundation's campaigns against hookworm disease, yellow fever, and malaria are well known (5). The Foundation has also had an important influence on medical education and the development of health professionals. It helped found the first school of public health in the United States and has supported numerous other schools of public health, as well as state health departments, medical schools, and individual medical researchers. Through its funding of full-time clinical departments at Johns Hopkins, the Foundation contributed to the change in the character of American medical education in the early decades of this century. The Rockefeller Foundation has supported medical and health work in North and South America, Europe, Africa, and Asia (6). Because of its scope and obvious impact, the program of the Rockefeller Foundation provides an important example of the role of foreign agencies in the development of the medical profession in the Third World.

Among the countries in which the Rockefeller Foundation has provided assistance, Thailand offers a particularly valuable case study.[2] In part, this is true because Thailand has never been colonized. Thus, it is possible to consider the program of the Rockefeller Foundation without the confounding influence of a colonial rule or heritage. More important, the Rockefeller Foundation has played a central role in the

[2] The name Siam was officially changed to Thailand in 1939. I use Thailand throughout except when quoting from a document of the earlier period. Likewise "Thai" is used in preference to "Siamese."

history of medicine in Thailand. The Foundation's first representative arrived in 1917. Beginning in 1923, the Foundation helped reorganize what was then Thailand's only medical school. This school served as the model for medical education in the country until the early 1960s (7).

In the remainder of this paper, the Rockefeller Foundation's program of assistance to medical education in Thailand will be examined in an attempt to analyze various aspects of the process of foreign intervention in Third World professional development. In addition, some consequences of this process will be reviewed.

THE BACKGROUND

The roots of the present Thai system of modern health care are in the work of American missionary physicians beginning early in the nineteenth century. The best known of these early medical missionaries was Dan Beach Bradley, who arrived in Bangkok in 1835. Bradley is credited with introducing surgery, aseptic obstetrical methods, and vaccination against smallpox in Thailand (8). He also helped during several of the periodic epidemics of cholera that struck Bangkok. However, he died in 1873, before the epidemic of 1882 which encouraged the Thai King to establish a permanent hospital, in contrast to the temporary facilities previously used during cholera outbreaks. The first hospital, named Siriraj after a Thai prince who died as a child and built in part from the wood of his crematorium, was opened in 1888.

A medical school was opened at Siriraj Hospital in 1889. By 1918 the medical course was six years long, but, nevertheless, dismally inadequate according to all accounts. Several attempts were made to upgrade the school. However, it was not until the advent of the Rockefeller Foundation that significant changes took place (9, 10).

The system of medical care that developed in Thailand from these foundations has been sharply criticized in recent years. The appropriateness of current medical education, the maldistribution of physicians in the capital and larger urban areas, and the problems most Thai doctors apparently have in interacting with a rural, poorly educated, peasant clientele are among the most frequently mentioned problems. Senior Thai Ministry of Public Health officials (11) claim these problems are "due to the application of outdated methods copied from the developed countries. . . ."

The problems of providing adequate health care in Thailand are similar to those in other developing countries. In Thailand, as elsewhere,

> The usual approach thus far has been to focus on training highly skilled medical doctors and building hospitals—two central components of the Western health system. The effect of this approach . . . has been to provide relatively high quality health care for a small urban elite, while depriving most of the population of health services altogether (12).

Although nearly all the commentators have concluded that Thailand and other developing countries eagerly took over Western models of medical education and health care, as yet, no one has analyzed the process by which these Western standards were adopted.

THE ROCKEFELLER FOUNDATION AT SIRIRAJ HOSPITAL

The Rockefeller Foundation program at Siriraj Hospital represents the first substantial foreign influence on professional development in Thailand. Indeed, one Thai scholar dates the beginning of foreign aid to Thailand from the start of the Rockefeller program (13). The Foundation's program was initiated after a member of the Foundation's field staff working on a hookworm campaign in Thailand notified his New York office of local interest in improving medical education (14).[3] Following visits by Rockefeller officials to Thailand and additional meetings in Europe between officers of the Foundation and the Thai Prince Mahidol,[4] who was assigned by his government to negotiate with the Foundation, a formal request for assistance was sent to the Rockefeller Foundation on August 16, 1922 by the Thai Minister of Education. On December 9, 1922, the Rockefeller Board of Trustees officially agreed to assist the school at Siriraj (15).

The Thai, the staff of the Rockefeller Foundation, and the local and expatriate doctors then at work in Bangkok were agreed on the type of medical education best suited to the needs of Thailand. As Richard M. Pearce (16), Director of the Rockefeller Foundation's Division of Medical Education, described the situation after a visit to Thailand in 1921:

> The only solution appears to be in developing two types of school. A class "A" school with proper entrance requirements and a thorough training to supply a small annual number of well qualified Medical Practitioners who will act as leaders in important positions ... [and] a practical school receiving men with moderate entrance requirements, and giving two or three years training in the more elementary practical aspects of Medicine. ...

Among the other reports proposing a "Standard B School" were those of Dr. M. E. Barnes (17), a representative of the International Health Board in Thailand, and Dr. M. Carthew (18), a British physician serving as an adviser to the Thai Department of Health.

Pearce's report made it clear that the Rockefeller Foundation "should be concerned financially or otherwise only with the high grade school for the preparation of properly qualified physicians receiving a degree." To ensure that the school it would support met the standards the Rockefeller Foundation thought appropriate, Pearce (16, p. 55) noted that while

> Nominal control of the higher school should rest with the Siamese ... a Dean or Director, or a Committee approved by the [Rockefeller Foundation], should have authority in regard to character of courses, type of examinations, passing qualifica-

---

[3] See the Appendix for a discussion of sources used in this research.

[4] Prince Mahidol of Songkla was one of several Thai princes who had important roles in the development of medicine in Thailand. The prince, properly referred to in the third person as Prince Mahidol, signed all of his correspondence with the Rockefeller Foundation "Mahidol Songkla." Thus, I refer to "Prince Mahidol," but use "Songkla" for citation. The same convention is used with other Thai who likewise are properly referred to by their first names.

tions, and eventually of graduation, with the power of vetoing any action that might be inimical to the development of a good system of Medical Education.[5]

The Thai government agreed to the conditions laid down by the Rockefeller Foundation, including giving authority "to one of the temporary American teachers" as proposed by Pearce (20). The conditions under which the Rockefeller Foundation would assist the medical school at Siriraj were spelled out in a letter from Pearce to Dhatmasakti Montri, Thai Minister of Education (21). Among other things, the Thai government agreed to provide a salary increase to graduates of the new medical program entering the government service, reorganize the university with which the medical school was affiliated to provide a better premedical program, establish six chairs in the basic and clinical sciences, and transfer all medical course work to Siriraj. Pearce's letter also mentions a "shorter, simpler course" and suggests that it "could be given in the medical school utilizing all its facilities." The Minister's reply does not bring up the question of the short course. Neither was the short course covered in the early letters or memos of Prince Mahidol who was responsible for the original negotiations with the Foundation.

With approval of the program given by the Foundation's Board of Trustees and the Thai government moving to fulfil its obligations under the agreement, the concern of the Rockefeller staff was directed toward specific aspects of the cooperation. The main problem was finding professors to fill the six chairs the Foundation had agreed to help support at the medical school (22).

It soon became apparent, however, that enthusiasm for the Rockefeller program was not universal among the Thai. When W. S. Carter visited Bangkok in May 1923 on behalf of the Foundation, the Under-Secretary of the Ministry of Education told him that "smaller communities cannot afford to support the highest type of man . . . a lower type should be provided . . . men who have had less training. . . ." (23). Carter told the Under-Secretary that "it would be impossible to conduct two different types of training simultaneously . . . such an effort would only result in weakening the higher course and lowering its standards" (23). Carter's visit was an important one. Eight years later he would remember (24) the opposition first encountered in 1923 "to the establishment of the present school . . . on the ground that a lower type of training for larger numbers is needed to supply a sufficient number of practitioners for the medical needs of Siam."

Dr. Aller G. Ellis, the Division of Medical Education's representative in Thailand, arrived in Bangkok on October 10, 1923. Two days later he met with Dr. Carthew, who told Ellis, "the school as planned is not needed." On the sixteenth Ellis talked with Prince Sakol, then Assistant Director General of the Department of Public

---

[5] Later in the period of cooperation the Foundation's officers would "explain their position, [their] desire to avoid all appearance of controlling the situation. . . ." (19). The granting of authority was, at least in the early stages, acceptable to the Thai. Barnes (14) reports he was told "unofficially" by the Under-Secretary of the Ministry of Education that the government "would let the Foundation have practically any amount of control they desired if only the Foundation would come and help at this time."

Health. Ellis found the Prince "very pessimistic about the medical school." Prince Sakol thought the graduates of the school would not be very useful and wanted instead to train sanitary inspectors and other lower-level health workers. Ellis (25) rejected Sakol's suggestion on the grounds that graduates of such courses "would go into the country and pose as graduates of the [medical] school."

Prince Mahidol's ideas during this period were reported to Pearce in two letters. In August 1923 the Prince wrote (26), "It will take some time to reorganize the medical school itself, and I do not think it possible to take up the problem of a training school for health officers at the same time." In December the Prince wrote (27),

> It is ... not unlikely that we shall have to make a compromise of running another school of lower standing, which I would suggest to call a School for Health Officers. This school, if at all necessary, should be run absolutely separate from the Medical School and the graduates should not be qualified practitioners in medicine, but certified health inspectors. ... In no case should the standard of the Medical School proper be lowered.

The years from 1924 to 1928 were uneventful in terms of the controversy over medical education. The Rockefeller professors arrived, new buildings were constructed, and the medical school began to function in a more or less routine manner. W. S. Carter visited Bangkok in September 1926 and again early in 1928. His reports provide an overview of the situation during this period (28, 29). Among other reasons for a lack of interest in the program at the medical school may have been the preoccupation of senior Thai officials and members of the royal family with other issues. According to Batson (30), "... the end of the Sixth Reign [1925] found the administration in disorder, the monarchy in disrepute, and the state finances deeply in the red" (see also reference 31).

Prince Sakol, however, did not change his mind about the appropriateness of the program at the school. During a trip to Europe in the summer of 1928, the Prince, by now Director General of the Public Health Department, visited the Rockefeller Foundation's Paris office. In a meeting with the Foundation's officers the Prince criticized medical education policy in Thailand. His complaints were reported in a memo on the meeting (32): "present plans [are] on too high a level; a half dozen graduates a year will make little impression ... Siam now needs [a] large number of reasonably competent men for a state medical and public health service combined...." (In a long paper written for the Far Eastern Association of Tropical Medicine, Prince Sakol laid out his objections in detail (33).)

In April 1929, Ellis (34) wrote to New York outlining the need for further Rockefeller Foundation assistance. He said, in part, that "the officials of the Siamese government, meaning our Minister and other high officials, including the King, greatly desire the cooperation of the [Rockefeller Foundation] for at least a few years beyond 1931." Ellis added, "one external condition that, in the opinion of some, will develop is that the Public Health Department will endeavor to gain control of the school to put in force their old idea of training large numbers of short time men. ... As long as the [Rockefeller Foundation] is here this will not be done apparently." In 1930 the Foundation extended its support of the visiting professors for one year, less than the Thai and Ellis had hoped for. Ellis was "disappointed" and, according to him, so was the Minister of Education (35, 36). The following year Ellis left on furlough to America.

Before leaving for the States, Ellis (37) wrote to Prince Sakol presenting his views on the future of medicine in Thailand. Ellis was especially concerned about "untrained practitioners, especially the second grade of the modern group in medicine," who, he thought, would "exploit" modern medicine. (Second-grade doctors were mainly older practitioners who had acceptable, but non-university training, typically received in the army or at a hospital.) Ellis suggested that Prince Sakol "remember that those in the second grade have had no real training in the fundamental subjects of medicine, namely, anatomy, physiology, chemistry and pathology, without which no one is competent to make diagnosis of disease—and efficient treatment can follow correct diagnosis only." Ellis (37) told the Prince that

> This crying need for doctors . . . is . . . a theory rather than a fact . . . [The] fact is that modern medicine has yet to be "sold" to the great majority of people. . . . The problem now . . . is not to turn out hundreds of doctors yearly; it is how best to use the ones that are turned out in "selling" modern medicine to the people of the interior.

Ellis (37) went on to propose a way

> by which the practice of medicine would be extended gradually, surely . . . to all parts of your country. . . . In the largest or most accessible town in each [administrative] circle, build a small hospital. . . . Staff this with at least two trained physicians. . . . An outpatient clinic should be conducted. . . . As rapidly as finances permit and general conditions warrant, smaller hospitals in radiating lines from the first are to be established. . . . Later . . . still others can be placed until eventually all the people in Siam are within a reasonable distance from a hospital. . . .

Ellis developed this plan in more detail in a short monograph (38) published in 1932. At that time, he said ". . . modern medicine means hospitals. . . . [H]ospitals are the unit with which to begin, not to end" the development of medical service.

When Ellis reached New York he met several times with Foundation officials to discuss the program in Bangkok. Considerable opposition to the Rockefeller effort had developed in Bangkok, in large part because of the report of Harvard sociologist Carle Zimmerman (39), who conducted a large scale research project on social and economic conditions in rural Thailand during 1930 and 1931.

Zimmerman's report (39) concluded that

> the Siamese country people cannot participate in the benefits of Western or "scientific" medicine . . . unless a new system of distribution of medical treatment is evolved. It is not suggested that the present system is wrong. It is just not sufficient. . . . Siam needs all the good doctors it can get. But in addition, something else is needed—a country system. . . . It may be called the Junior Doctor System.

Zimmerman's "junior doctor" system called for a reduction in the time spent in training, an emphasis on the treatment of "simple diseases," and a system of supervision and referral by "provincial medical officers and by the regional hospital doctors."

The Thai were also continuing to question the wisdom of the Rockefeller plans. On a visit to New York, Prince Thavara Chayant, Surgeon General of the Thai Navy, "spoke of the lack of medical assistance in his own service and wondered if there were not some means by which, while an adequate supply of medical men were under training, these services could be helped by men with less training. . . ." (40). Prince Mahidol himself may have had second thoughts about training for a lower grade of practitioner. Correspondence between Heiser and Barnes (41) mentions a letter from Prince Mahidol to Pearce "which contains a suggestion on his part to establish a school of health officers which might produce a sort of low grade doctor." Prince Mahidol's original letter cannot be found and thus we must rely on Heiser's interpretation of the Prince's position on this matter.

The Rockefeller Foundation's opposition to a lower grade of medical education was very evident during the meetings Ellis had in New York. Carter (24) told Ellis that "as the result of Prince Sakol's position and activities one of the conditions of the [new] grant . . . was that the Siamese were to continue after the period of co-operation, the same standards of medical education that had been established during the period of co-operation by the [Rockefeller Foundation]." An interoffice memo (42) was even more direct: "The last appropriation made by the [Rockefeller Foundation] to the Bangkok School was made on the express condition that no lower grade of practitioner be considered by the School."

While Ellis was in New York a conference "was called . . . to consider the adverse reports made . . . by various Siamese authorities. The complaint is that although [the] Government has made large sums available, the school does not turn out enough doctors to furnish even the needs of the Government" (43).[6] Ellis argued that the small number of graduates was due to (45) "deficient educational training in the secondary schools" and not the program at the medical school. Also discussed at the conference were various proposals for a "low standard course in medicine to meet immediate needs." All of these were "strongly opposed" by those at the meeting (43). However, according to one participant in the conference (43) the question remained unanswered "as to whether it is better to abandon to charlatans or other unqualified persons the thousands who urgently need treatment, or to give them partially qualified aid." The question was answered in a handwritten note added to the conference memo by Alan Gregg, who had recently been promoted to Director of the Foundation's Medical Sciences Division (formerly the Division of Medical Education). Gregg stated, "It is better for us to protect one school of the best calibre obtainable than to imply a direct immediate and impossibly extensive obligation for thousands of suffering Siamese" (43).

Ellis thus returned to Bangkok with Gregg's approval "to protect one school." Shortly after his return, he wrote to Carter that there was "now considerable agitation for second-class [medicine] in addition or even instead of" first-class medicine (46). Among those Ellis mentions as agitating for "second-class medicine" are some of the most important names in the history of medicine in Thailand: Prince Thavara was said to favor "a large supply of poorly trained men." Prince Rangsit wanted junior

[6] The Thai and the Rockefeller Foundation had each contributed nearly $800,000 to the development of Siriraj during the period of cooperation. There had been approximately 70 graduates by 1931 (44).

doctors. And Luang Ayurabaed, according to Ellis, "favors taking in larger numbers and letting the flunks practice under certificates." Carter (47) replied on behalf of the Foundation, enclosing earlier correspondence between Pearce and the Minister of Education (20, 21), and suggested that Ellis "may wish to call the present Minister's attention to the understanding. . . ." He added, "The obligation is one of honor. . . ."

In September 1932 Ellis (48) wrote to Carter, "I have been making a drive on the Zimmerman 'Junior Doctor' plan. . . ." Ellis' "drive" included a letter to *The Siam Observer* (49), a local English language newspaper, in which he concluded, "it is quite beyond comprehension that qualified physicians can conscientiously recommend the Zimmerman plan for adoption by a government." Carter (50) also found no evidence to support the need for a shorter course and referred to the "nonsense . . . used as propaganda by Sakol in favor of the lower grade of medical training."

In spite of Ellis' efforts, by late October the Rockefeller program was under attack in the local press (51). *The Daily Mail* (52), published in English and Thai, came out in a series of editorials against the Rockefeller plan for advancing medical care and endorsed the Zimmerman plan. In December, the paper began publishing letters from missionary doctors in support of Zimmerman's proposal for training junior doctors (53).

Two other proposals for a short course in medicine were offered, one by Dr. E. C. Cort (54), a missionary physician working in northern Thailand, and another favored by Phya Damrong (55), Director of Chulalongkorn Hospital in Bangkok. Carter (56), after reviewing the Cort proposal, wrote to Ellis, "If a lower type of medical training is . . . established . . . it will undo all the constructive work that you and your colleagues have accomplished." However, for the first time, Carter suggests the possibility of supporting a short course for training "health assistants" who "would be practically public health nurses, with a little more instruction in what to do in emergencies, the recognition of common diseases, and the administration of such drugs as quinine, etc."

Ellis (57), however, saw the plan for exactly what it was and reacted accordingly: "the health assistants are something of the type that Prince Sakol has been talking about for years. . . . I am not in favor of turning these out by the hundreds until there are definite stations manned by graduate physicians. . . ." Ellis (58) concluded that a short course for a lower-grade practitioner "would set back real medicine in Siam irretrievably." Ellis (38) rejected the Cort plan in part because he thought that students could not be trained "to treat only malaria, hookworm, dysentery, and a few other so-called simple diseases." Carter (59) wrote back that although he was concerned that "sufficient emphasis has not been placed on public health" at the medical school, he hoped that Ellis might be successful in his efforts to persuade the Minister and other government officials to keep the single high standard of medical education.[7]

---

[7] Carter's views on public health at Siriraj may have been influenced by those of John B. Grant, a Rockefeller professor at Peking Union Medical College. Grant visited Thailand in February 1933 and wrote a very critical report noting, among other things, that "The [Rockefeller Foundation] has brought out visiting professors for everything except the field in which the largest number of graduates are to go on the day of graduation! . . . . Four full time pathologists—no full time public health man and fifty percent of the graduates going immediately into public health" (60).

Ellis was not successful. Early in 1934 the Thai Prime Minister promised the National Assembly he would "bring about an agreement . . . to cooperate in acquiring as many Junior Doctors as possible to send out into the interior" (61). Carter (62) noted that this development was "most discouraging." But there was little the Rockefeller Foundation could do.

The last grant to Siriraj Hospital Medical School had been made in 1930. The visiting professors were no longer supported by the Rockefeller Foundation. The school and medical education policy were, for better or worse, in the hands of the Thai. The Foundation's interest had turned elsewhere and it had little leverage in Thailand.

Ellis stayed on in the Thai government service after the Rockefeller program ended. He fought the junior doctor proposal, as did his colleagues on the medical school faculty and the medical school graduates. However, the advocates of the junior doctor plan, who argued "If you can't wear silk, wear cotton," prevailed. A course for junior doctors, or "doctor's helpers" as they were called in Thai, was started in 1935 (63-65). The "Act for the Control of the Practice of the Art of Healing" (66), passed the following year, licensed "second class practitioners in the modern art of healing."

THE ROCKEFELLER FOUNDATION AND MEDICAL EDUCATION

The Rockefeller Foundation's medical education policy in Thailand was not unique. Pearce rejected a request for assistance in training lower-grade health workers in Fiji, noting that the Foundation was "not prepared to enter into any program which would give less training than that required to practice in this country" (quoted in 6, p. 118). A similar policy of nothing but the best was followed in the Foundation's largest overseas medical education project, Peking Union Medical College (6, p. 116; 67).

At present, it appears that the model of medical education supported by the Rockefeller Foundation has failed both in the United States and, much more so, throughout the developing world. Those fortunate enough to have access to a hospital will generally receive first-rate care. However, medical schools and hospitals, and their graduates and staffs, assume little or no responsibility for the well-being of the people in the community as a whole (68). Even Allan Gregg, who took over the Division of Medical Education after Pearce's death, became convinced that the result of the Foundation's work was " 'exquisite care' for a small segment of the population and neglect of the rest" (quoted in 69).

Two important questions are raised by the experience of the Rockefeller Foundation in Thailand. First, why did the Thai government cooperate with the Foundation, especially after the publication of Zimmerman's report and the tremendous increase in criticism of the prevailing policy of medical education? And second, why didn't the Thai medical system develop into a more appropriate vehicle for serving the health needs of the Thai people, given the early use of paramedics of a type now widely advocated as a remedy for the medical care problems of developing countries (70, 71) and recommended by the Rockefeller Foundation itself for Thailand in 1965 (72)?

The answer to the first question provides considerable insight into the role of foreign organizations in the development of Third World professions. The answer to the second suggests the limitations of professionals and their foreign supporters in the process of modernization.

FOREIGN INTERVENTION AND PROFESSIONAL DEVELOPMENT

The history of medical education in Thailand, in particular the long delay between the first suggestion of a school for lower-grade practitioners in 1921 and the school's actual opening in 1935, is worth examining because it illustrates a sociological process that is typical of those situations in which foreign organizations intervene in the development of the professions in the Third World. The experience of the Rockefeller Foundation in Thailand depended at least as much on the structure of social relations between donor and recipient as it did on the participants in the program or the times.

The Rockefeller Foundation program in Thailand was started because the Foundation and members of the Thai royal family shared a common set of social values and interests. Both were concerned with the modernization of medical education and health care in Thailand. Staff of the Rockefeller Foundation had been interested in medical education in Thailand for several years before the Thai formally requested the Foundation's assistance (73). For its part, the Thai government had made several attempts to improve the medical school on its own before inviting the Rockefeller Foundation to cooperate in the effort (21). Thus, in the early stages of the cooperation there was a strong consensus that medical education and health care ought to be improved.

In addition, the Rockefeller Foundation needed situations like Thailand's to justify its philanthropic status while Thailand needed an organization like the Foundation to assist with its development. The relationship was thus reciprocal but unequal. The Rockefeller Foundation was the powerful partner and when the conflict arose over the program at Siriraj it was therefore able to greatly influence the Thai to adopt its model of medical education.

The Foundation's power was derived from its control of large amounts of capital and personnel resources, as well as from its central position in the dissemination of ideas about medical education and health care during the 1920s and '30s (74). Thailand and other recipients of Rockefeller aid had the power to legitimate the Foundation's activities, which they did by accepting assistance. Recipients, of course, could refuse funds. If done collectively such action would have had a major effect on the Foundation's programs. However, the absence of the possibility of meaningful collective action meant that an individual recipient was in fact left with the choice of taking what was offered or receiving nothing.

When the consensus over medical education broke down, the Rockefeller Foundation used its power to influence the development of medicine in Thailand. For example, the Foundation maintained control over its grants, even after the funds had been officially given to the Thai, and it used this control as leverage in the attempt to introduce the model of medical education it considered most appropriate. Richard M. Pearce (75), the Director of the Division of Medical Education early in the period of cooperation, reminded the Foundation's Bangkok representative of this fact in 1924:

> There is one point for you to keep in mind and that is although the money has been allocated to Siam and the appropriation rests in a Siamese bank, it cannot be utilized without your approval. In fact a check cannot be drawn except over your signature. I know you are using this fact to influence the situation wisely. . . .

Two social structural conditions seem to explain the role of foreign agencies in the evolution of the professions in the developing world, and in particular the international diffusion of Western professional role models. These conditions are (a) values shared between the foreigners who intervene and the ruling class of the developing country in which they intervene, and (b) the competitive advantage foreigners have in the marketing of professional models. The typical error in the interpretation of the evolution of the professions in the Third World is an overemphasis on the extent to which developing countries "imitate" or "import" alien professional models. Thus, it is worth stressing that the usual situation is one in which foreign agencies and their personnel apply considerable pressure on Third World countries to develop and maintain professionals patterned after Western models.

The particular historical period in which the Rockefeller program at Siriraj took place helps to explain the Thai interest in high-quality medical education and the Foundation's reaction to Thai proposals for an alternative approach to medical education. The Rockefeller Foundation staff reacted the way they did, in part, because they considered the Thai a "primitive" (76), "backward people" (77), who "lack initiative" and were "incapable . . . of reorganizing their medical school" (23). The policy suggestions of such people as the Thai in the complex field of medical education were thus not to be judged on an equal basis with those of the Foundation staff.

The Foundation's insistence on supporting only the highest quality of medical education was based in part on the famous Flexner Report (78) of 1910 on American medical education and on the developments that surrounded its publication. Flexner's Report led to the closing of numerous medical schools in the United States and an increased emphasis on scientific quality and specialized medical practice in those schools that remained opened. These developments were supported by the Rockefeller Foundation and its sister organization, the General Education Board (69, p. 55).

Outside the United States the influence of the Flexner Report was less significant. Ten years after the Report, Pearce (16), it will be recalled, recommended that the Thai open a "class B" school of the type that surely would have been closed in the United States as a result of Flexner's study. The Foundation's support of only the highest standard of medical education was based, in the developing world, on the experience of its International Health Board and Sanitary Commission. The Division of Medical Education was created in 1919 largely because the work of the International Health Board led those involved to conclude that public health activities in a country would never be sufficient without well trained indigenous physicians (74, 79).

It is also important to recall that the Rockefeller Foundation program was started during the period of American history when a variety of social conditions were first defined as "social problems" amenable to treatment from specialized professionals. Ellis, Pearce, Carter, and the other Rockefeller Foundation staff shared a world view that fit well with the Thai hierarchically ordered patron-client culture. Both the Americans and Thai felt that the people would benefit if they put their trust in "exceptional fellow-countrymen" (80). The Thai citizenry trusted the royal family and the royal family trusted the Rockefeller Foundation. The Foundation's staff clearly saw itself as "exceptional" in the fields of health and medical education.

Well before the 1920s, Thailand's rulers, for their part, had considered modernization along Western lines to be an important defense against colonization. During the 1920s, concern about the health of the Thai people became especially important because of a large increase in Chinese immigration and fears about the "depopulation" of Thailand (33, 39, 81). Moreover, the tradition of influential foreign advisers in the government service was well established by the time the Rockefeller Foundation arrived (82).

Another factor which doubtless prevented some Thai from acting on their misgivings about the Rockefeller Foundation was Prince Mahidol's support of both the Foundation and its representative, Dr. Ellis (83). Prince Mahidol was a Harvard-trained medical doctor, a senior member of the Thai royal family, half-brother to the two Kings who reigned during the period 1910-1935 and, after 1925, himself potentially heir to the throne. Because he had received degrees in both public health and medicine from Harvard University and had also practiced in his own country, he could speak with authority on health care and medical education. Probably many of those inclined to protest against the Rockefeller program were discouraged, at least in part, by the feeling that medical education and health were Prince Mahidol's affair.

After Prince Mahidol's death in 1929, one of the tactics used by Ellis and other Rockefeller Foundation staff members during the conflict over the junior doctor issue was to say, "Prince Mahidol would have wanted it this way" (15). Prince Mahidol was the most important patron of and biggest contributor to the development of Siriraj hospital and medical school (84). However, his position on junior doctors and the various short course plans is not clear. Like the Rockefeller Foundation staff with whom he negotiated the original agreement, Prince Mahidol apparently saw a shorter training course coming later (27). He brought up the matter in 1924 but his position, although seemingly in favor of a short course for health officers, is not completely clear (41, 85).

Thus, while the Prince supported Ellis and the Foundation, there is no clear evidence of his opinion at the time of his death in September 1929. Two points are, however, relevant: First, his own interest was in public health, and, second, the fact that his scholarly work was in the area of public health and infectious diseases (86). He had even mentioned to Ellis his interest in becoming a professor of public health at the medical school (87). It should also be noted that the only medical practice Prince Mahidol had in Thailand was at a well established missionary hospital in a rural area of northern Thailand. Thus, while Prince Mahidol's thinking on the junior doctor issue is not clear, I think it unreasonable to conclude that he would have completely rejected short-course plans.

Thailand's economic position during the period of cooperation also inhibited the development of alternative approaches to medical education. Batson (30) notes that among the ruling class ". . . the economic situation stands out as perhaps the major concern of the period 1925-1932. . . ." Although the economic difficulties improved somewhat between 1927 and 1930, a lack of planning meant that there were no clear investment priorities, and the unexpected budget surpluses were not spent on medicine or health.

Finally, it is important to understand that the Thai were less likely than other peoples to object to the Rockefeller program because they had been trained by the social order to accept the largess of a patron and turn it to the use of their dependents (88). The King who reigned during most of the period of Rockefeller assistance to Siriraj once approved a program sponsored by Thailand's Christian missionary groups on the grounds that it would be a mistake to hurt the feelings of well meaning foreigners (89). Such sentiments also affected the Thai response to the Foundation's effort.

In summary, the Western professional role for doctors became dominant in Thailand, at first because the Thai thought it valuable and, when they became less sure of its value, because of the force of the Rockefeller Foundation behind the idea at a time when Thailand was especially open to Western models and Westerners were especially aggressive in advocating them.

MEDICAL PROFESSIONALS AND THE DEVELOPMENT OF MEDICAL CARE

A second question raised by the Rockefeller experience in Thailand and the Thai response to the Foundation's program concerns the subsequent development of the medical profession and health care services. If by the late 1930s Thailand had both a quality medical school and a network of health auxiliaries, why did the system of medical care develop into its present form which is so widely regarded as unsatisfactory?

A full answer, considering both the historical and the sociological determinants of the present system, is beyond the scope of this paper. A great deal more has to be learned about the role of the early "junior doctors," including their part in the post-World War II malaria campaigns which did result in substantial reductions in mortality (90, 91). The very complex problem of the impact of modern medicine and its practitioners at all levels on changes in aggregate morbidity and mortality would also have to be examined in detail. Moreover, the use of various traditional healers and of paraprofessionals also needs to be studied (92). It is, however, possible to say something about the failure of medical professionals to provide a system of care appropriate to Thai society, a system centered in the rural areas and directed primarily toward the rural population.

Thailand's medical profession did not emerge as the result of a gradual differentiation of professional roles from premodern or traditional Thai society (93). The differentiation of modern medical professionals from the group of traditional healers occurred as a result of the development of Siriraj hospital and medical school under Rockefeller Foundation auspices. During the early stages of the development of the medical profession, the status and privileges of the doctor's role were granted by the monarchy. Western-type medical practice existed because of the support provided by a few key members of the Thai royal family. Since the overthrow of the absolute monarchy in 1932, the status and privileges of the professional role have been granted by the military-aristocratic ruling class. Doctors have become medical technocrats, co-opted by the bureaucratic and military regimes that have ruled Thailand.

During the early stages of the Rockefeller Foundation program, which were the last years of Thailand's absolute monarchy, the professional role was directed toward social change. At present, professionals are among the main stabilizing elements in Thai society (94). At the same time, because the monarchy was a service-oriented institution, and the state bureaucracy is not, the clients of those in power have changed from the people at large to the ruling class itself (95, 96).

As with all of the products of development, professionals in general and doctors in particular have great symbolic importance for a developing country. A key issue in judging the impact of professionals in the modernization process is how they are manipulated as symbols by those in power. The extent to which foreign agencies and their personnel can influence professional development is determined to a considerable degree by the nature of the relationship between professionals and the ruling class and the social role that the ruling class endorses for its country's professionals. Thai doctors are concentrated in metropolitan areas not only because of their socialization to a professional role first introduced by the Rockefeller Foundation but also, and more importantly, because the Thai elite have not encouraged doctors to move from the metropolitan areas or to curtail their specialized, hospital-based practices.

The importance of this ideological component is well illustrated by the Chinese medical care system. Many of the doctors currently in charge of China's health care system, which has received so much attention for its apparent success in bringing adequate care to the people, are graduates of the Rockefeller Foundation's most important overseas medical education project, Peking Union Medical College.

THE ROCKEFELLER FOUNDATION PROGRAM IN THAILAND IN THE 1960s

Much of the preceding would run the risk of being of interest primarily as an exercise in historical sociology were it not for the fact that not only in health but in many other fields as well the same approaches used a half-century ago are still employed to "assist" developing nations. Unfortunately, the sort of material that is available for the early Rockefeller Foundation program is either not available for other projects or cannot be cited in international scholarly publications.

The Rockefeller Foundation itself began another assistance program at a second Thai medical school at Ramathibodi Hospital in 1963. A Foundation report (72) prepared at the time the program was beginning is characterized by a change of heart on the issue of a short course for lower-level medical practitioners. Six possible alternatives were given for improving the availability of medical care, among them a "diploma" course of "say two years," the graduates of which could "be utilized within proscribed conditions in public service, especially in rural areas. . . ." Another alternative, one which would please Prince Sakol and Professor Zimmerman, was to "train a straightforward medical assistant who is concerned primarily with the sick individual, and to train such an auxiliary directly toward these needs. . . ." It was felt that "a course of between 2 and 3 years should prove adequate" in order for the medical assistants to be sufficiently trained to provide this care.

The report summed up the need for a short-course type of worker by noting: "The present situation is that quantitative demands need to be met as well as qualitative and this dual requirement can only be realized by delegating to a person other than a physician responsibility for treatment of some of the more simple ills" (72, p. 25).

Given this background, the Rockefeller Foundation did not, as one might think reasonable, support a program to train medical assistants. Instead, the Foundation concentrated on the development of a graduate program in the life sciences. The development of the life sciences program followed almost exactly the approach used at Siriraj. The Rockefeller Foundation was invited by the Thai government to help build a graduate program. The Foundation agreed. The Rockefeller Foundation representative was appointed Associate Dean of the Mahidol University Faculty of Science. Six new departments were established, those in anatomy, biochemistry, microbiology, pharmacology, physiology, and pathobiology. Visiting professors were recruited from American universities to head the newly formed departments. Additional American scientists served in departmental staff positions. The faculty graduated its first Ph.D.s in 1973 and plans "progressively more emphasis" on Ph.D.-level training (97).

In addition to the graduate students in the life sciences there are an equal number of medical students in the program obtaining preclinical training before entering the University's Faculty of Medicine for clinical work. The life sciences program, then, was designed for and serves as part of the system of medical education. The program represents a continuation of the Rockefeller Foundation's interest in specialized professional development. Like the Foundation's program at Siriraj, its latest efforts to improve medical education are viewed with considerable misgiving by at least some Thai (11, 98, 99). The Foundation is able to continue its work for the same reasons it was successful in reorganizing Siriraj Hospital Medical School. Influential Thai have accepted the view that modernization requires increasing professionalization. Moreover, the Rockefeller Foundation remains an important and powerful international agency, especially in the fields of health and medical education.

The Rockefeller Foundation's experience in Thailand is, in my judgment, typical of what happens in most large scale assistance programs involving substantial foreign intervention in professional development. The shortcoming of these programs is not that they create the inequality associated with professional services throughout the developing world but that they so neatly serve those who maintain it.

Acknowledgments—I would like to thank Jeanie and Marie Curtin for their help in obtaining material from the Rockefeller Foundation Archives. I am also grateful to the following people for their valuable comments on an earlier draft of this paper: Benjamin Batson, Michael Cook, Sidney Goldstein, Chitt Hemachudha, Peter

Kunstadter, Jajaval Osthanond, Warren Robinson, Allan Rosenfield, Manasvi Unhanand, Joe Wray, Charas Yamarat, and Srisavangvong Yugala.

APPENDIX

The period of the early Rockefeller Foundation involvement in Thai medical education has not been covered in depth by historians. In large measure this is because the common interpretation is that "the history of Thailand between the death of King Chulalongkorn in 1910 and the outbreak of World War II in 1941 is essentially the political working out of the social consequences of the reforms of Chulalongkorn's reign" (100). Thus, both Thai and foreign scholars have concentrated on the period up to 1910 and, more recently, on the overthrow of the absolute monarchy in June 1932. While some work is currently under way, no substantial social history of the type that would be useful in this research is, as yet, available (see reference 100, p. 485, for a short bibliography of the most important references in Thai and Western languages).

There is not much material available on medicine in Thailand during the 1920s and '30s. Moreover, the work that has been done tends to be fugitive. It proved difficult to locate several sources either in Thailand or overseas. There is only a minimum amount of material in Thailand's National Archives, and most of what can be found appears to be of little importance. The available documents consist mainly of correspondence about sending Thai students abroad on Rockefeller Foundation fellowships.

It is perhaps useful to note that letters from Thai officials to the Rockefeller Foundation were probably written only in English. There is no evidence that a duplicate set of correspondence, memos, or reports exist in Thai. The extent to which English was used as a means of communication by the Thai royalty is discussed briefly by Chakrabongse (31, p. 271).

It is more difficult to make a reasonable judgment regarding the evidence collected from the Rockefeller Foundation Archives. I have no doubt that the history of the Rockefeller Foundation program in Thailand in the period 1923 to 1935 is as reported here. However, it is true that I have surveyed only a sample of the items available at the Foundation Archives.

Two sampling problems are worth noting. First, although I reviewed a large amount of material I clearly did not cover everything. For example, W. S. Carter is cited frequently in this report. I looked at all of Carter's letters, reports, memos, and the like which were filed under "Chulalongkorn," "Siriraj Hospital," and "Siam." However, I did not systematically review Carter's correspondence or reports on other programs or on general Foundation policy. This was typical of my approach. Second, I have used only items found in archives. Some program correspondence, probably including some of the most important material, was sent as personal mail to an individual's home. Gregg wrote of communication with Pearce which included "being able to write him at his home . . . about such items as did not belong in the record of the organization. Pearce warned me not to go too far with this privilege, but I can say it came in very handy" (quoted in reference 79, p. 101). Ellis (75) also employed this privilege. How often and with regard to what issues is not known.

REFERENCES

1. *Eleventh Compendium of Technical Assistance to Thailand.* Development Assistance Group for Thailand, Bangkok, 1974.
2. Evers, H. D., and Regan, D. Specialization and Involvement: The Modernizing Role of Doctors in Malaysia and Indonesia. Working Paper No. 16, Department of Sociology, University of Singapore, 1973.
3. Bryant, J. *Health & the Developing World.* Cornell University Press, Ithaca, N.Y., 1969.
4. Lathem, W. Introduction in *Community Medicine: Teaching, Research and Health Care,* edited by W. Lathem and A. Newberry, p. 5. Appleton-Century-Crofts, New York, 1970.
5. Williams, G. *The Plague Killers.* Charles Scribner's Sons, New York, 1969.
6. Fosdick, R. *The Story of the Rockefeller Foundation.* Harper and Brothers, New York, 1952.
7. *Public Health in Thailand,* p. 25. Ministry of Public Health, Bangkok, 1971.
8. Lord, D. C. *Mo Bradley and Thailand,* pp. 85-90. W. B. Eerdmans Company, Grand Rapids, Mich., 1969.
9. Mendelson, R. W. *I Lost a King,* p. 139. Vantage Press, New York, 1964.
10. Graham, W. A. *Siam,* Vol. 1, p. 254. Alexander Morning Ltd., The De La Mare Press, London, 1924.
11. The Country's Public Health Problems, Especially in Personnel and Proposals for a Development Policy to Solve Public Health Problems, p. 5. Unpublished paper, Ministry of Public Health, Bangkok, 1973.
12. Rich, W. *Smaller Families Through Social and Economic Progress,* pp. 25-26. Monograph No. 7, Overseas Development Council, Washington, D. C., 1973.
13. Ariyapruchya, S. Sources of Aid and International Relations of Thailand, pp. 3-4. Paper presented at a seminar on Foreign Aid to Thailand in the 1980s, Chiengmai, Thailand, June 1974.
14. Barnes, M. E. Letter to W. Rose, August 3, 1921. Rockefeller Foundation Archives, Record Group 1, Series 617A, Chulalongkorn University (hereafter cited as RF617A).
15. Ellis, A. G. The service to medicine in Siam rendered by H. R. H. Prince Mahidol of Songkla, M.D. In *Chumnum Phraniphont le Botkhawan Charlem Phrakiat, Somdej Prarachabida Chao Fa Mahidol Adulyadet, Krom Luang Songkla Nakharin,* pp. 330-331. Prabida Haeng Karnphaet Phaen Bachuban Khong Thai, Khana Phaetsart le Siriraj Phayabal, 1965 (B.E. 2508).
16. Pearce, R. M. Report on Medical Education in Siam, pp. 45-46. RF617A, November 1921.
17. Barnes, M. E. Confidential Report on Medical Education. RF617A, September 30, 1921.
18. Carthew, M. A Plea for the Registration of Medical Practitioners in Siam. Included as Exhibit 2 in Pearce, R. M. Report on Medical Education in Siam. RF617A, November 1921.
19. Pearce, R. M. Diary Notes. Meeting with Prince Mahidol Songkla; luncheon conference with GEV [George E. Vincent] and RSG [Roger S. Greene]. RF617A, March 24, 1927.
20. Montri, D. Letter to R. M. Pearce. RF617A, August 16, 1922.
21. Pearce, R. M. Letter to D. Montri. RF617A, January 23, 1922.
22. Pearce, R. M. Letter to A. G. Ellis. RF617A, December 8, 1923.
23. Carter, W. S. Report on the Medical School in Bangkok, Based upon a Visit, May 1-4, 1923. RF617A, 1923.
24. Carter, W. S. Diary Notes. RF617A, August 18-19, 1931.
25. Ellis, A. G. Chronological Review of Events in Bangkok. RF617A, 1923.
26. Songkla, M. Letter to R. M. Pearce. RF617A, August 12, 1923.
27. Songkla, M. Letter to R. M. Pearce. RF617A, December 10, 1923.
28. Carter, W. S. Letter to R. M. Pearce. RF617A, October 3, 1926.
29. Carter, W. S. Memorandum of Conference on January 25, 1928, between H. E. Phya Baisal, Under-Secretary, Phya Bhaiata, Dean of the Faculty of Arts and Sciences, Dr. A. G. Ellis, and W. S. Carter. RF617A, January 25, 1928.
30. Batson, B. *Siam's Political Future: Documents from the End of the Absolute Monarchy,* p. 3. Data Paper No. 96, Cornell University, Southeast Asia Program, Department of Asian Studies, July 1974.
31. Chakrabongse, C. *Lords of Life: A History of the Kings of Thailand,* pp. 268-317. Alvin Redman, London, 1960.
32. Memo to FFR [Frederick F. Russell], interview of GEV [George E. Vincent], SMG [Selskar M. Gunn], and Prince Sakol of Siam, in Paris, July 8, 1928. RF617A, 1928.

33. Varavam, S. [Prince Sakol]. *Public Health and Medical Service in Siam: General and Medical Features,* pp. 185-244. Far Eastern Association of Tropical Medicine, Executive Committee of the Eighth Congress, editors. Bangkok Times Press, Bangkok, 1930.
34. Ellis, A. G. Letter to R. M. Pearce. RF617A, April 18, 1929.
35. Carter, W. S. Letter to A. G. Ellis. RF617A, September 15, 1930.
36. Ellis, A. G. Letter to W. S. Carter. RF617A, October 16, 1930.
37. Ellis, A. G. Letter to S. Varavam. RF617A, March 30, 1931.
38. Ellis, A. G. *Medical Education and Practice,* p. 14. Bangkok Times Press, Bangkok, 1932.
39. Zimmerman, C. *Siam: Rural Economic Survey, 1930-31,* pp. 239-242. Bangkok Times Press, Bangkok, 1931.
40. O'Connor, F. W. Letter to W. S. Carter. RF617A, September 9, 1931.
41. Heiser, V. G. Letter to M. E. Barnes. Record Group 5, Series 617, International Health Board, February 1, 1924.
42. FFR [Frederick F. Russell]. Memo to VGH [Victor G. Heiser]. RF617A, April 24, 1931.
43. Heiser, V. G. Memorandum on Medical Sciences Conference on Siam. RF617A, September 10, 1931.
44. *Vejnisit B.E. 2482.* Karn Pim Thai, Bangkok, 1941 (B.E. 2484).
45. Carter, W. S. Diary Notes. RF617A, September 10, 1931.
46. Ellis, A. G. Letter to W. S. Carter. RF617A, January 27, 1932.
47. Carter, W. S. Letter to A. G. Ellis, RF617A, May 9, 1932.
48. Ellis, A. G. Letter to W. S. Carter. RF617A, September 8, 1932.
49. *The Siam Observer,* September 5, 1932.
50. Carter, W. S. Letter to A. G. Ellis. RF617A, September 12, 1932.
51. Ellis, A. G. Letter to W. S. Carter. RF617A, October 26, 1932.
52. *The Daily Mail,* October 21-25, 1932.
53. Ellis, A. G. Letter to W. S. Carter. RF617A, December 6, 1932.
54. Cort, E. C. Suggested Scheme for Providing Medical Care for the Rural Population of Siam. Version available in Rockefeller Foundation Archives.
55. Schapiro, L. Letter to V. G. Heiser. RF617A, October 8, 1931.
56. Carter, W. S. Memo to A. G. Ellis. RF617A, April 19, 1933.
57. Ellis, A. G. Letter to W. S. Carter. RF617A, October 16, 1933.
58. Ellis, A. G. Letter to E. C. Cort. RF617A, undated (around September 1933).
59. Carter, W. S. Letter to A. G. Ellis. RF617A, March 5, 1934.
60. Grant, J. B. Diary Notes on Trip to Philippines, Java, Malay, Singapore, Siam and India. Record Group 9, Series 600, pp. 141-142. Rockefeller Foundation Archives, 1933.
61. *The Bangkok Times,* January 16, 1934.
62. Carter, W. S. Letter to A. G. Ellis, RF617A, April 30, 1934.
63. Personal communication from Charas Yamarat, 1975.
64. Landon, K. P. *Siam in Transition,* pp. 128-129. University of Chicago Press, Chicago, 1939.
65. Ministry of Public Health. *Commemoration of the Fifteenth Anniversary of the Ministry of Public Health: 1942-1957,* pp. 303-305. Udom Press, Bangkok, 1957.
66. Penal Code of Thailand, Section 306, 1936 (B.E. 2499).
67. China Medical Commission of the Rockefeller Foundation. *Medicine in China,* p. 81. Rockefeller Foundation, New York, 1914.
68. Ebert, R. H. The medical school. In *Life and Death in Medicine,* p. 105. W. H. Freeman, San Francisco, 1973.
69. Nielson, W. A. *The Big Foundations,* p. 61. Columbia University Press, New York, 1972.
70. King, M., editor. *Medical Care in Developing Countries.* Oxford University Press, London, 1966.
71. *Training and Utilization of Village Health Workers.* Working Document HMD/74.5. World Health Organization, Geneva, 1974.
72. Report to Thailand on Health Services, Health Personnel, and Health Education. Rockefeller Foundation, New York, 1965.
73. Barnes, M. E. Letter to V. G. Heiser. Record Group 5, Series 617. International Health Board, August 3, 1921.
74. Gregg, A. The work of the Rockefeller Foundation in medical education and the medical sciences, 1920 to 1929 inclusive, under the direction of Richard Mills Pearce, M.D. *The Rockefeller Foundation Quarterly Bulletin,* Vol. 5, No. 2, 1931.
75. Pearce, R. M. Letter to A. G. Ellis. RF617A, June 18, 1924.

76. Heiser, V. G. Letter to F. F. Russell. Record Group 5, Series 617. International Health Board, January 26, 1926.
77. Carter, W. S. Memo to R. M. Pearce. RF617A, August 26, 1923.
78. Flexner, A. *Medical Education in the United States and Canada.* Bulletin No. 4, The Carnegie Foundation, New York, 1910.
79. Penfield, W. *The Difficult Art of Giving: The Epic of Alan Gregg,* p. 143. Little Brown, Boston, 1967.
80. Kunitz, S. J. Professionalism and social control in the Progressive Era: The case of the Flexner Report. *Social Problems* 22(1): 25, October 1974.
81. Skinner, G. W. *Chinese Society in Thailand: An Analytical History.* Cornell University Press, Ithaca, N.Y., 1957.
82. Numnonda, T. The first American advisers in Thailand. *Journal of the Siam Society* 62: 2, July 1974.
83. Songkla, M. Letter to R. M. Pearce. RF617A, May 14, 1927.
84. Carter, W. S. Letter to A. G. Ellis. RF617A, January 18, 1930.
85. Heiser, V. G. Letter to M. E. Barnes. Record Group 5, Series 617. International Health Board, August 12, 1923.
86. McGavran, E., and Songkla, M. Diphyllobothrium latum in Massachusetts. *JAMA* 90: 1607-1608, May 19, 1928.
87. Ellis, A. G. Diary Notes. RF617A, January 26 and March 31, 1924.
88. Hanks, L. M. Another Vietnam? American aid is damaging Thai society. In *America and the Asian Revolutions,* edited by R. J. Lifton, p. 129. Aldine Publishing Company, Chicago, 1970.
89. Minutes of a Cabinet Meeting on July 9, 1929. National Archives of Thailand, Seventh Reign, Ministry of Foreign Affairs 35/21.
90. Saibua, S. Foreign Aid to Thailand, pp. 13-14. Paper presented at a seminar on Foreign Aid to Thailand in the 1980s, Chiengmai, Thailand, June 1974.
91. *Public Health Statistics,* p. 168. Ministry of Public Health, Division of Vital Statistics, Bangkok, 1971.
92. Riley, J. N., and Sermsri, S. The Variegated Thai Medical System as a Context for Birth Control Services. Working Paper No. 6, Institute for Population and Social Research, Mahidol University, Bangkok, June 1974.
93. Evers, H. D. Group conflict and class formation in South-East Asia. In *Modernization in South-East Asia,* edited by H. D. Evers, p. 113. Oxford University Press, London, 1973.
94. Evers, H. D. The Role of Professionals in Social and Political Change, pp. 20-22. Working Paper No. 24, Department of Sociology, University of Singapore, 1974.
95. Riggs, F. W. *Thailand: The Modernization of a Bureaucratic Policy,* p. 349. East West Center Press, Honolulu, 1966.
96. Nairn, R. *International Aid to Thailand: The New Colonialism?,* p. 101. Yale University Press, New Haven, Conn., 1966.
97. Dinning, J. S. University development in Thailand: A program in the life sciences. *J. Med. Educ.* 49: 767, August 1974.
98. Benchakarn, V. Teaching Population and Family Planning in a School of Health Professions, p. 3. Paper prepared for a symposium, Southeast Addresses Its Health Problems, Bangkok, October 28-November 1, 1974.
99. Harinasuta, C. The need for clinical assistants in Thailand. *Lancet* pp. 1298-1300, June 9, 1973.
100. Steinberg, D., Wyatt, D. K., Small, J. R. W., Woodside, A., Roff, W. R., and Chandler, D. P. *In Search of Southeast Asia: A Modern History,* p. 313. Oxford University Press, Kuala Lumpur, 1971.

CHAPTER 6

Nutrition, Development, and Foreign Aid: A Case Study of U.S. Directed Health Care in a Colombian Plantation Zone
Michael Taussig

This paper is an attempt to assess the effects of U.S. health care projects in an area of the Third World where U.S. interests have a considerable stake in supporting many of the basic causes of disease and malnutrition.

The need to make this assessment and phrase it in this way was forced upon me in 1971, when, as an anthropologist and medical doctor, I was working in the south of the Cauca Valley in Colombia with peasants and landless laborers who were arrested by the police for trying to invade and reclaim land appropriated by expanding sugar plantations.[1] What made this particular invasion more worrisome to the authorities and large landowners than the several preceding ones was that (a) it coincided with a wave of invasions in many other parts of Colombia, and (b) for the first time in forty years, peasants were organized nationally into a militant left wing union. Shortly thereafter, U.S.-sponsored health and peasant development programs were initiated in the area, largely channeled through the nearby Rockefeller-funded University of Valle in the city of Cali. In 1974 a half-million-dollar U.S. Agency for International Development (USAID) malnutrition project was added, led by Rockefeller personnel and ex-trainees under the auspices of the Community Systems Foundation (CSF), a private consulting firm informally attached to the University of Michigan. In this food-rich area where the expansion of intensive large-scale farming has driven the bulk of the peasantry off the land in recent years, 50 percent of the children six years and under are said to be suffering from malnutrition (1).

[1] Between 1970 and 1971, my field research was funded by the Institute for Latin American Studies at the University of London and the Foreign Area Fellowship Program. Six months of research in 1972 were financed from my own savings, and another eighteen months in 1975–1976 were funded by the School of Graduate Studies at the University of Michigan, the Wenner-Gren Foundation, and the National Science Foundation.

On the basis of its research into the causes of this malnutrition, the CSF's solution has been to improve dietary composition by getting the poor to eat more of the crops that the remaining small landowners normally sell on the open market. In the Candelaria area near Cali, where a basically Rockefeller-funded team has been at work since the late 1950s (when massive strikes, occupations, and marches were being launched by plantation workers), overpopulation was seen as the heart of the problem, and birth control the main measure chosen to resolve it. The existing state system of medical care was used because in this way the political problems associated with birth control could be minimized and "because the medicine man effect of the MD allows an entree into the community which is unequalled" (2).

On the other hand, local peasant leaders seek the solution in a land reform which would redistribute income and power through a system of small farming collectives in place of the mono-cropping estates. The heartfelt land hunger of the peasants and landless laborers makes them deeply cynical about the plans for their welfare being imposed by the Colombian government with the aid of U.S. organizations which do not even touch on the land tenure question. But then, monopoly control of the land is essential to the burgeoning agribusinesses—not merely as acreage for their crops, but also as a way of forcing the previously independent small farmers into wage labor in the estates.

THE COMMUNITY SYSTEMS FOUNDATION

Established in 1963 as a non-profit Michigan corporation, CSF describes itself as "dedicated to improving humankind through scientific research and direct assistance to communities in helping them to improve themselves" (3). Its core personnel are senior professors from the University of Michigan, Ann Arbor, who also use their graduate students in CSF's new-found role in nutrition and health, such as in the project entitled "Community Experiments for the Reduction of Malnourishment in Colombia." With U.S.$363,000 from USAID, channeled through an offshoot of the University of Valle known as the Foundation for Higher Education (FES), this project aims at nothing less than developing a universal strategy for assessing communities' nutritional status, thereby promoting self-help strategies to overcome the problem. Giving much emphasis to community learning, the project has received another $260,000 from USAID for this purpose alone.

While it remains to be seen to what extent the poor can help themselves, the CSF has set a good example in self-help by gaining contracts from USAID to apply its methods to Chile[2] and possibly Zaire, with other Third World countries such as

[2]The Chile intervention demands a future analysis of its own. Briefly, this $9 million project (involving the CSF and other groups) is necessitated by the inability of the prevailing economic measures and system to distribute the food that is, according to a USAID paper (AID-DLC/P-2079, 1975), potentially available in sufficient quantities to feed all the people. During the period of the Allende government, the U.S. suspended all food credits under the PL 480 (Title 1) program and food supplies became a major problem, helping to bring down the government. On the other hand, since the Central Intelligence Agency-abetted coup, U.S. food aid to Chile has amounted to 85 percent of all PL 480 allocations to Latin America (4). Because the anti-inflation policies of Milton Friedman ensure that the bulk of the population lacks the purchasing power to acquire food, even this aid is inadequate, and nutrition science is necessary to devise what amounts to rationing schemes that will allow the Pinochet dictatorship some stability, in place of a government which could organize the more equal and ample distribution of food.

Thailand—countries crucial to U.S. foreign policy—in the offing. The Department of Nutrition at the Massachusetts Institute of Technology is said to be trying to insert itself into CSF's Cauca Valley project so as to train students, and the Colombian government is using the techniques developed by CSF's research in the Cauca Valley as the basis for the first phase of its national nutrition plan—the PAN (Plan de Alimentación y Nutrición).

Housed in the University of Valle's medical school in a building adjoining that of the Rockefeller offices and those of the International Center for Medical Research and Training (Tulane University), the CSF project is under the direction of a medical graduate from Valle whose postgraduate U.S. studies were sponsored by Rockefeller, and a U.S. systems engineer from the University of Michigan who has been part of the Rockefeller academic staff in Cali for many years. The community whose malnutrition CSF is working on has also been the subject of a health-oriented peasant development project by the CIMDER group (Centro de Investigaciones Multidisciplinarias en Desarrollo Rural), also operating out of the medical school. Funded mainly by the International Development Research Center of Canada, CIMDER is also headed by an ex-Rockefeller Scholar, a graduate from Valle's medical school.

CSF's "philosophy" owes much to current progressive trends on U.S. campuses. Its planning theory is described as one "in which planning, implementation, and management are integrated as a learning process" (3), and learning through doing, as opposed to formal learning, is the chosen mode. This is fused with an emphasis on self-help, and local and personal self-sufficiency based on intermediate technology. Women's liberation finds a place in CSF's latest reports and grant proposals, because by means of its nutrition teaching, "CSF's equipping women with a highly potent [sic] form of knowledge in one of the few areas excepted from traditional Latin machismo dominance may well become an engine of change—a means for women to win more respect and through it, a more equal position" (5).

Where self-help, self-sufficiency, learning through doing, and intermediate technology, not to mention women's liberation, are insufficient to the task of overcoming malnutrition and poverty in the Third World, then CSF has recourse to rather grander cosmologies and methodologies such as Darwinism and systems theory. As it has been expressed in one CSF paper, "The Malnourished as Nutrition Planners: Self-Help Concept Summary" (5):

> If CSF strategy is simple, its philosophical underpinnings are likewise clear—and clearly derivative. Its roots lie inextricably embedded in Darwinism. CSF is trying to compress a behavioral version of adaptive selection into a very short time frame. It seeks to produce life-enhancing habit patterns harnessing the scientific method to functional adaptation. Only local stimuli are used to speed the process, for they alone can produce modifications tailored to immediate conditions. In essence, CSF methodology is a behavioral analogue of the evolutionary process of natural selection. Through artificially-induced bombardments of local stimuli, community habit patterns are shifted to produce permanent, functional adaptations to local conditions.

The emphasis on "only local stimuli" contradicts CSF's very presence. The aim of having the poor adapt—permanently—to local conditions rather than changing those conditions is the key to understanding CSF's presence, especially when it is realized just how oppressive those conditions are.

THE AREA AND ITS PATTERN OF DEVELOPMENT

The community whose malnutrition provides CSF with its grant lies in the semi-tropical rural area of Villa Rica on the southern rim of the Cauca Valley. It is composed of very poor, semiproletarianized Afro-American peasants whose main source of income derives from their work on the vast sugar plantations and large commercial farms that occupy most of this fertile land. While workers' income is so low that malnutrition is a major problem, the profits of the sugar plantations are very high: 26 percent for plantations with mills and 54 percent for those without, between the years 1970-1974, expressed as annual net income over costs (6). The wages of middle-level administrators (invariably whites) are around 10 times those of the field hands (invariably blacks), while U.S. technicians in the mills receive some 100 times more. The mills discharge their effluent into the rivers, the main supply of water to the rural slum towns which house the major part of the population, and all sources of drinking water are fearfully contaminated with fecal bacteria according to repeated surveys by competent bacteriologists. Infestation by hookworm (in 50 percent of the population), *Entamoeba histolytica* (25 percent), *Strongyloides* (20 percent), and *Ascaris* (70 percent) abounds, for in addition to the pollution of potable water, there are practically no adequate sewage facilities and people commonly go barefoot.

Political tension and crime are very high. As in much of Colombia (which formally speaking is a democracy), official "States of Emergency" are more often in force than not, which means that military law prevails most of the time, preventing, for example, popular assembly and group meetings. The owners of the large estates, such as the two sugar plantations closest to Villa Rica, rarely travel without armed escorts for fear of kidnapping, and top-level administrators have their high-powered jeeps fitted with two-way radios for the same reason, connecting them to the *Defensa Civil* in Cali. The plantation workers' trade union organization is nowhere weaker than in this area, and salesmen for John Deere claim that the rate of sabotage of mill machinery and field equipment is higher here than in any other part of the Valley.

The plantations and large farms are all owned by Colombians, but U.S. and World Bank loans have provided much of the capital (6). For the Valley as a whole, sugar production on large estates increased 1.5 times between 1950 and 1960, and doubled between 1960-1974 to reach 853,460 metric tons per annum, 128,000 of which were exported—mainly to the U.S.—after Colombia acquired part of the sugar quota that had been Cuba's prior to the revolution and subsequent U.S. embargo (6). Between 1958 and 1970, the area planted in seasonal cash crops on large farms increased around five times (7). In the Villa Rica (Norte del Cauca) area, four sugar plantations owned by four individual families produced 2,000 tons of sugar in 1938, 13,220 in 1963, and 91,750 in 1969 (8). Government censuses show that while some 80 percent of the cultivated land is owned by four sugar plantations and a few large farms, 90 percent of the holdings are less than ten hectares and land is becoming increasingly concentrated into fewer owners. The majority of holdings are so small that their peasant owners are forced to work on the large estates. My own census in 1971 indicated that 30 percent of households in the Villa Rica jurisdiction are landless, while another 50 percent have less than the two hectares necessary for subsistence (9).

Neither peasant land scarcity nor peasant poverty can be blamed on the "social malady" of the population explosion, an explanation the Rockefeller doctors on the nearby Candelaria project (10, 11) would offer, but rather stem from a quite different malady: that of the social explosion unleashed by the development of large-scale capitalist agriculture. Land tax records show that while the modal size of peasant holdings decreased 15 times between 1933 and 1967, the population no more than doubled. State archives in Popayan, together with peasant oral history (9), provide ample testimony as to the violent struggles for land between peasants and large landowners that have occurred from the second decade of this century onwards, accentuated greatly by the development of sugar plantations in the 1930s and again in the early 1950s, when the infamous Colombian "Violencia" was at its peak.

Following the abolition of slavery in 1851, the ex-slaves and their descendants developed a flourishing subsistence economy on illegally occupied land, while their old masters struggled desperately to little avail to tie them to the failing estates as day laborers or tenant farmers. Land was plentiful, labor was scarce, and there were practically no market outlets. Reports during the second half of the 19th century (12-14) indicate that the black peasants were raising large surpluses of plantains and cocoa in addition to some livestock raising. Indeed, because these peasants could so easily subsist, in the opinion of the late-19th-century observer, Evaristo García (14), they were loath to work for the large landowners. For this reason, he says, there were few functioning haciendas until the opening decades of the 20th century, and the private correspondence of the Arboleda family, the largest landowners of the region, supports this claim in full (9).

With the end to the civil wars of the 19th century and the formation of a centralized and dictatorial state machine, U.S. investors felt secure in making loans to Colombia, which went mainly into the building of infrastructure. These loans were larger than those given to any other Latin American country between 1913 and 1928 (15), and much of this U.S. capital entered the Cauca Valley. With the opening of the Valley to the world markets, via the railway to the Pacific and the canal through Panama (both completed in 1914), the stage was set for the take-off in capitalist agriculture on large holdings. Land values soared, and peasants in the Villa Rica area were forcibly removed to make way for cattle raising in the 1920s and sugar cane cultivation shortly thereafter. Direct force, flooding of plots, and aerial spraying of herbicides formed the main measures used until recently, when the government and USAID encouraged the peasants to adopt a modified "green revolution" in lieu of the promised land reform; under this program, the process of depeasantization and proletarianization has almost been completed.

This "green revolution," which was funded by USAID and administered by the government's agricultural extension service (ICA—Instituto Colombiano Agropecuario), meant the uprooting of the peasants' traditional crop mix of cocoa, coffee, plantains, and fruit trees, and its replacement by an expensive, mechanized, open-field system of mono-cultivation of soya, beans, or corn. This has astronomically increased peasant indebtedness, virtually eliminated the local subsistence base of plantains, and accelerated the rate of land loss by poor peasants. In the Agua Azul neighborhood of the Villa Rica area, for example, a third of the land that was in peasant control in 1972 had passed to the sugar plantations by 1976.

Practically all labor on large holdings is paid by piece rate, which, as is well known, allows employers the opportunity to exploit workers more intensively than if a time-rate system is in force. Furthermore, around 33 percent of the work force on the plantations, and nearly all that on the large farms, is recruited and supervised by independent labor contractors. These contractors not only pay even lower rates than the plantations themselves, but are able to avoid paying all or most of the legally obligatory social security and medical benefits. This contracting system has been adopted so as to lower labor costs, weaken the rural trade union movement (which was very militant in the Cauca Valley in the early 1960s), and ensure an elastic supply of labor to meet the continual variations in demand.

Whenever possible, the contractors prefer to use female and child labor. They say that "women are tamer than men." They have to be, because the burden of child care and feeding is falling increasingly on women as a result of the decomposition of the extended and nuclear family structure, and the working mother is highly conscious of the hungry children left at home, awaiting their rice at nightfall. Breast-feeding diminishes for the same reason.

The Comparative Efficiency of Farming Systems

It certainly cannot be claimed that the development of large-scale agriculture in this area has improved the general standard of living. In fact, such development has meant a growing rupture between agriculture and nutrition.

Contrary to all the propaganda of the large landowners, it is by no means clear that large-scale farming signifies a more efficient use of land, labor, energy, or capital than does peasant farming, even though yields are generally higher on the large farms due to the capital- and energy-intensive nature of their inputs. "Efficiency" can be computed in many different ways, but, as Table 1 shows, the sugar plantations supply fewer jobs per hectare, with less cash return per hectare to the worker (and the owner), and demand far greater human energy output per day than occurs on peasant farms, traditional style or modern.[3]

Traditional-style peasant farming in this area is some six times more efficient than that of the sugar plantations, in terms of the energy yielded in food, compared with the energy input required to produce that food.[4]

---

[3] Data on traditional-style peasant farming come from my continuous nine months' monitoring of four plots every two weeks in 1971. Data on modern-style peasant farming come from similar on-the-spot fieldwork in six plots in 1972 and 1976. Data on plantations come from Fedesarrollo (6), and from personal interviews with plantation personnel. Labor energy expenditures (7.4 kcal/minute) for plantation workers were calculated by Spurr et al. (16, p. 992), using respirometry techniques on local cane cutters and loaders, while those for peasant labor were indirectly calculated from tables in references 17-19. An alternative lower assessment for plantation workers by Spurr et al. was ignored as this was derived from methods conflicting with and not comparable with those used in references 17-19.

[4] Sugar plantation energy efficiency is calculated only on the basis of its three main energy inputs (and therefore has been overestimated): (a) human labor, 197,000 kcal/ton of sugar; (b) electricity, 112,000 kcal/ton; (c) fuel oil, 452,000 kcal/ton. Traditional-style peasant farming energy efficiency is calculated only on the energy input-output ratio involved directly with cocoa production, assuming a low average yield of 290 kg/interplanted hectare, as determined by fieldwork. Household tasks such as drawing water were not included as energy inputs. The ratios came to 5:1 for sugar plantations, as compared with 30:1 for peasant cocoa farming.

Table 1

Comparison of income, land use, and labor energy output
between traditional and modern peasant farmers and plantation workers
in Cauca Valley, Colombia, 1970–1976

| | Peasant Farmer on 2-Hectare Plot | | Plantation Worker |
	Traditional	Modern	
Annual net income (1971)	$10,000	$ 8,000	$10,000
No. hectares/worker	1.0-2.0	1.0-2.0	3.2
Labor days required/year	105	243	275
Individual's labor energy output/working day (kcal)	1,700	1,700	3,500
Individual's labor energy output/year (kcal)	173,000	415,000	804,000

Furthermore, even though peasant yields per hectare of modern-style crops (such as soya) are only around half those of the large-scale farmers growing the same crops, peasants' production costs are so much lower that their return on capital invested— their "capital efficiency"—is the same as or higher than that of the large farmers (depending on whether or not one includes the peasant landowner's own labor as a cost). This is just as true when we compare peasant profit rates on the new crops with those of the sugar plantations.[5]

Thus, large-scale farming is not inherently more "efficient" than peasant farming— efficiency being defined in terms of output over input, in currency or in calories. What the large-scale system achieves over peasant farming is capital accumulation, and it does this because (a) peasant farming on small plots devours its profits in living expenses and (b) peasants have shown worldwide, and especially in this Cauca Valley situation, that they will not be coerced into providing a surplus over which they have no control. The infamous "backward sloping supply curve of labor" is a notorious concern of the plantation owners in the Valley, and the only way to overcome its more drastic consequences is to deprive peasants of their means of production, thus forcing them into wage labor.

Conversely, this curve also exhibits "forward sloping" characteristics, so peasants with land less than subsistence size will redouble their efforts to make that land pay. This is part of the reason why their economic performance is, on many criteria, superior to that of the capitalists. So long as a substantial proportion of the plantations' and large farms' labor force is composed of workers who own or share in small plots, the costs to the capitalist farming sector of maintaining and reproducing wage labor are lower than they would be if capitalist farming had to meet such costs on its own. For not only does the workers' self-provisioning cover part of those costs, but, as

---

[5] If we were to make the comparison with the traditional peasant mode of production, then the difference in favor of the peasantry would be infinitely higher than that of the agribusiness since capital inputs in the former are negligible (especially if one discounts the peasant landowner's own labor as a capital cost).

stated above, they put their capital to work on their own farms in a more efficient manner than do the capitalist farmers. This means that the rate of profit accruing to the large landowners is greater than if they had a work force without some (but less than sufficient) independent means of subsistence, since *pari passu* their wage bill would be higher.

If they were to function as designed, the government's new national nutrition program and CSF's model local one would interlock with this mechanism for maintaining low-level costs for the maintenance and reproduction of wage labor, ensuring high-level profits for the large landowners.

Lower-class people are well aware that wage labor on the plantations is an enormous energy drain in comparison with peasant labor. They fetishize the cane as a plant "which dries one up," and say that the work, which they detest, makes one thin and prematurely old. "On the coast we have food but no money," mourn the immigrant cane cutters who have left the jungles of the Pacific coast. "Here we have money but no food!" or "I would rather be fat without money than old and skinny with money" is how local peasant laborers and peasant landowners put the issue. But when their land shrinks below subsistence size, then they are forced to intensify their labor and energy output by going to work on the plantation.

Malnutrition is widespread. Some 50 percent of children are said by the CSF to be malnourished, using the Gómez scale. From CSF's data on nutrient deficits (imperfect as they are), it appears that the nutritional balance which must be achieved by working adults is done so at the expense of pregnant women and children. It is impossible to prove conclusively that people are eating less now than before the latest phase of plantation development, but fieldwork impressions since 1970 and indirect statistical information (such as that on livestock slaughtering) support the locals' *adamant* claim that this is indeed the case.

What is certain, and what has been so totally ignored by the health professionals, is that the evolution of the means and relations of production, carried through by force and with inputs from USAID and the World Bank, has greatly increased the intensity of labor, the food requirements per worker, and the cost of maintaining nutritional balance, while delivering a generous surplus of labor energy to the large landowners. At the same time, the peasantry has lost its capacity for self-support, and the region has lost its plantain subsistence base.

THE COMMUNITY SYSTEMS FOUNDATION'S ANALYSIS AND SOLUTION

Given the history of land struggles and the oppressive nature of existing economic conditions and class relationships, it is with wild disbelief that one reads the full description that CSF presents of the Villa Rica area—a description which faithfully mirrors its entire approach to these questions. Not only is there not a single word on the land tenure situation, let alone of its development and implications for income and nutrition, but CSF seems to obscure such issues and not simply ignore them. According to a CSF report,

It [Villa Rica] is a rural area with a population of approximately 10,000. Nearly 90% of the inhabitants are engaged in agriculture. Major crops include: sugar cane, coffee, cocoa, soya, plantain, maize, and beans. Nearly 95% of the cultivated crops are sold (1, p. II-14).

The language of the project's first-year report (1) leaves little doubt as to the self-assurance with which its authors regard their methods: "Like most good diagnostic procedures, ours is based on a theory of the *underlying causes* of the problem" (1, p. I-3, emphasis added). In addition, the authors regard their diagnosis as "complete."

The theory of the "underlying causes" is a prize-winning example of pseudo-scientific formulation. Named the "Nutrient Flow Theory," it states, without any hint of embarrassment, the tautology that the level of malnutrition is the difference between nutrient requirements and their availability. And nutrient availability is conceptualized not in terms of the social class system, but as

> . . . determined by the complex process by which food is produced, distributed, and consumed. Nutrient flow theory describes the losses which occur at various stages of the process, for example, during harvest, storage, transport, processing, unequal allocation among [peasant] families and non-optimal allocation within families, seasonality and preparation (1, p. I-3).

The actual diagnosis consisted of taking some of the above-mentioned CIMDER data and measuring a sample of children to assess nutritional status by weight and height, together with surveys of food purchasing and consumption by household and household member; peasant crop yields were also used in the diagnosis.

The conclusion reached was that 50 percent of the children under six years were malnourished, and that, in effect, this community of poor peasants and day laborers was misusing its resources. If the community would only retain 7 percent of its soya production, and each household would consume two-thirds pound of soya each and every day, then they would close the "protein gap"; if they would only consume 8 percent of the calories that they sold, then they would close the "calorie gap." The only snag, as far as CSF is concerned, is that people don't like to eat soya, which they consider as a pure cash crop to be sold to the rich for their livestock and oil-processing plants. But then, this merely serves to reinforce the drift of the analysis itself: that attitudes and nutrition education are the key.

Gaps in the Analysis

However, there are many other and far more serious queries raised by this disarmingly simple "solution," and these queries strike at the heart of the social issues and positivism underlying its genesis. Even at the technical level—at which, with its systems engineers, nutritionists, MDs, statisticians, and computers, the operation is meant to excel and thereby justify its role as impartial authority on the nutrition problem—there are grave defects imposed by the logic of the overall situation. In the first place, the project's peasant production figures are incorrect. The soya solution, for example, rests on wildly exaggerated claims as to the proportion of peasants cultivating it (70 percent as compared with the true figure of around 30 percent) and as to the implied amount produced. Peasant production surveys require infinitely more patience, care, and trust than anybody but peasants themselves seems to realize. Certainly in this case, with its large variety of different crops and cropping schedules, its changing land use and credit opportunities, its convoluted rental patterns, its informally organized inputs and outputs based on face-to-face social relationships, and, above all, with its deep divisions between peasants and the middle-class local or foreign researchers, there can be no reliable results unless lengthy and rewarding participation is involved—by peasants in the research process as much as by researchers in the peasants' daily lives. Neither of these has occurred nor is likely to occur, because the peasants perceive no rewards (especially when they are told to eat soya), and the researchers cannot adopt an egalitarian "science for the people" approach which really means precisely that and not just good intentions.

Moreover, there is a misplaced and mishandled emphasis on quantification, as though this in itself guarantees scientific knowledge. There are very profound inadequacies in relying solely, as this project does, on weight and height as accurate and meaningful indices of nutritional status. And this is vastly accentuated in this case as there is no indication that whatever such figures mean, they are only relative, and that the unstated basis for "normal" is that of upper-class urban children in highland and genetically distinct Bogotá. The calorie and protein "gaps" are similarly paraded as hard scientific fact against which no layperson could argue. In reality, there is little justification for dividing calories off from protein, and furthermore, these "gaps" are assessed with reference to the unreliably excessive Food and Agriculture Organization/ World Health Organization Required Daily Allowances. Added to this, CSF has made no attempt to gauge the energy requirements of its subjects, which in the case of plantation workers and chronically ill and parasite-ridden people, i.e. most of the locals, are bound to be exceptionally high. So much for "science." The room for bias, conscious or unconscious, is therefore very great, and guesswork and unstated assumptions must intrude in crucial ways. The general direction of the results that eventuate does little to dispel the thesis that researchers tied to cash incentives may, on occasions, find it in their interest, wittingly or unwittingly, to exaggerate the degree of malnutrition, while simultaneously downplaying the role of vested powers in either causing it or blocking its most obvious solution.

The glaringly simple truism that people must remain in energy balance or die seems to have escaped nutritionists who report astronomical "energy gaps" like that of the CSF. The more appropriate question for Villa Rica's nutritional problems is not the supremely difficult one of the precise prevalence of malnourishment, but the more qualitative question: How do these people maintain energy balance in a food and income situation that is progressively tightening with the development of agribusiness? The rough sketch of an answer is that they do so by having to increase vastly their energy expenditure (which further increases their food needs), and in so doing, deliver a sizable fraction of that increase to the large landowners, free, in the form of surplus value which can be expressed in cash or in energy units and amounts to anything between 25 percent (cane cutters and loaders) and 50 percent (contracted labor in the large farms) of their labor time. If one chooses to talk in terms of "energy gaps" and total systems, then here is where one could very fruitfully begin. The real malnutrition that results from this, such as that of young children and pregnant women, is due to the fact that the chief breadwinner must, according to the laws of thermodynamics, remain in balance. Even so, that balance is probably, in most cases, in a no-man's land between physiological and pathological alteration of metabolic pathways. The consequences of the overall situation are such that there is a steady decrease in height and weight over generations (which is not the same as genuine malnutrition), such that Villa Rica children are becoming progressively smaller than those of the Bogotá upper class.

The attempt to measure meticulously malnutrition and poverty, when it is patently obvious to everyone that the scale of deprivation is colossal, amounts to the most cruel fetishism of scientific method and displays a total misconception of the issues at stake—a misconception which conditions the purely technical defects. For it is absurd to say that the causes, indeed, the "underlying causes," of malnutrition have been diagnosed when no mention is made of the political system which determines food production and distribution.

The only *cause* we find in CSF's analysis is really a socially determined *effect*: that the institution referred to as the "community" is selling what it might be better off eating. One might just as well add that everyone would be better off eating what the large landowners insist on selling and exporting!

And what is this "community" that the researchers posit in place of an exploited social class? It corresponds faithfully to what Eric Wolf (20) has called an "*open* community," typical offspring of plantation organization in particular and commercialized agriculture in general. As atomized internally as it is exposed to the harsh winds of the national economy externally, such a community is sadly bereft of communality. The small amount of peasant land remaining is very unequally divided into private property plots; 30 percent of the population is in fact landless, while another 50 percent lacks the two hectares necessary for subsistence. There are no community-wide organizations which draw the support of the people. The government-imposed Communal Action Committees are led by the wealthy few for their own benefit. Festive labor parties and reciprocal labor exchanges died away in the 1920s, to be replaced by wage labor almost as much within households as between them, and the flow of migrants into and out of the area adds to the general flux whose only stability lies in the currents of individual self-defense and greed that follow the cash nexus. Given this, and that only two-thirds of the community owns land, and that less than half of the land-owning peasants cultivate soya (although the CSF inaccurately states that 70 percent do so), it becomes obvious that we are not dealing with a case in which the "community" would have to withhold "its" soya production from the market. Rather, market mechanisms would have to be used to transfer the soya from the cultivators to the rest of the community.

In accord with the same ideological drift which induces them to fetishize the community as an organically meshed totality of mutual aid, separable from the society in general and the plantation sphere in particular, the researchers ignore the harsh facts of economic history which make most peasants the world over turn increasingly to cash cropping at the expense of autarky. The pious appeal to turn the clock back—that *all* the community has to do is withhold production destined for the market—flies in the face of all that is known concerning peasant economies, even if it sits well with the rise of commune-consciousness among the middle classes of the industrialized world. Wrenched out of context as an isolated calculation, it makes good sense to eat one's product if the protein value is greater than the cash gain. But then, how does the peasant compare these two dissimilar entities and how does protein gain compare with the stark necessity for cash which confronts these people at every turn? To withhold 7 percent of soya production (accepting CSF's soya production figures, which are way too high) means a substantial financial burden when it is realized that the farmer gets income from soya only twice a year at harvest time. At a yield of one ton per hectare, the peasant producer grosses around 8000 pesos and nets around 4500. Withholding 7 percent of production would lower that net by 560 pesos or 12.5 percent, and it is most unlikely that any peasant is going to allow the six-month lump income to suffer that.

Moreover, the growing social stratification and pauperization of the peasantry are heightened by the recent government- and USAID-imposed innovation of soya cultivation—the very solution that CSF has hit upon to solve the "protein gap"! In brief, protein production has augmented the protein gap, and more such production is likely to make that gap yawn.

Feeding Human Capital

Soya is considered to be food not for people but for the livestock of the rich, because that is how it was introduced in Colombia. As the locals bitterly note, the animals of the rich are better fed and better nourished than they, and this also appears to have been true of their slave ancestors (9, p. 22; 21). The apparently humane concern with improving the nutrition of the poor becomes tainted with the same bestiality as livestock and slave breeding if that concern is not subject to the economic and political liberation of the people concerned. The flood of writing in development economics referring to human "*capital*," steadfastly followed in the Colombian government's national nutrition plan (22, 23), as well as the frequent argument by public health planners and the World Bank that medicine and nutrition are vital to the improvement of a society's labor force, all bear the same imprint.

Even so, this appeal to the self-interest of large employers and the rationality of capital misses the point that the tendency in the Third World, as exemplified in this Colombian case, is to pay workers by piece rate, i.e. per product, and not for time worked. Workers' productivity is thus of little or no consequence to profits as long as there are plenty of workers around, and the concentration of land into fewer owners, with the displacement of peasants from the land, ensures that this is the case.

Learning through Doing

Working under the assumption that malnourished people are more ignorant than powerless, not only must people be taught to like soya, but, through participation in the project itself, they will adopt a new mentality allowing them more of a chance to get along in the world. But, as Dwyer and Mayer (24) have stated: "There is . . . overwhelming evidence that such economic factors as price and income have at least equal importance [as nutrition and health education], if not much greater influence."

The Community Systems Foundation informs us that there is no satisfactory theory of community learning (1), and so, with the help of professors at the University of Michigan's School of Education, the Foundation has invented its own. Contextualized within an attractive Deweyesque format stressing learning through doing, its essential "norms for enquiry" include "a disposition to be skeptical about assertions of fact, even when they are uttered by authorities such as teachers" and "a willingness to convert ideas to action quickly" (1, p. I-6). By taking part in the diagnostic studies on the "causes" of malnutrition, the community members will "also begin to grasp the learning process which underlies it" (1, p. I-7). In other words, participatory education along the lines laid out by liberal and radical thinkers such as Dewey and Paul Goodman will, in this context, amount to participatory delusion, since the CSF diagnostic procedure systematically diverts attention from the underlying causes of malnutrition. Furthermore, the economic and political situation of the poor is hardly one in which they could, as CSF says they could, "convert ideas into action, quickly." And the same applies with equal force to the other progressive ideas touted by CSF, e.g. women's liberation, self-help, self-sufficiency, and intermediate technology. Do not CSF's own limitations suggest how limited the options for meaningful action are? But in that case, why and how did CSF ever get the action it has?

ECONOMIC AND HEALTH PLANNING TRENDS IN RURAL COLOMBIA

While modernization of agriculture in Colombia over the past twenty years has resulted in enormous increases in yield and production from large holdings, it has been of little or no benefit to the bulk of the population who live in the countryside—some 45 percent of the Colombian people, whose income is declining relative to that of the large landowners and who are probably worse off, absolutely, today than they were forty years ago (25, 26). Peasant production has remained virtually stagnant since 1950, peasants' land area has slightly decreased, and the size of the underemployed rural proletariat has vastly increased (25). The 10 percent average annual growth rate in production on large commercial farms over the same period owes much to a "green revolution" in which World Bank loans and generous government subsidies have played a large part. The role of the Rockefeller Foundation, with the later assistance of certain U.S. agricultural colleges such as Nebraska and Michigan State, has been important in this pattern of development. It has closely influenced the development of Colombian agronomy since 1941 when it set up the government's agricultural extension service (now ICA), encouraging its orientation toward the capital- and energy-intensive production of new, often exportable, and more profitable crops such as sorghum, cotton, sugar, soya, irrigated rice, and sesame.

This has meant a decrease in the per capita availability of lower-class staples, which could be cultivated on the land now occupied by the new crops. The average annual rate of growth in food production between 1950 and 1970 was 3.3 percent, which was slightly higher than the rate of population growth. However, disaggregation reveals that there has been a decrease in the per capita production of peasant-produced and lower-class consumer foods such as cassava, plantains, beans, panela, corn, and potatoes (25, 27, 28). The conditions have been well-laid for malnutrition and development to go hand in hand. A striking example of this is provided by the fact that one million tons of animal food concentrates are produced annually for animal protein which the majority of the population can rarely afford (29).

The instigator and chief processor of animal concentrates in Colombia is the U.S. multinational, Ralston Purina, on whose board sits Earl Butz, the former U.S. Secretary of Agriculture, as well as the Secretary whom he replaced. Ralston Purina is credited with the introduction of sorghum as an animal-destined crop in Colombia, which, like the other components of the concentrates, occupies land that could be used for the direct feeding of human beings. There was no sorghum cultivated in Colombia as of 1950. In 1960, 14,000 hectares were planted, in 1970 it occupied 77,000 hectares, and in 1975 it covered 134,000 hectares of prime agricultural land (30). The Cauca Valley is the main region for sorghum, producing 37 percent of the national total; 11 percent of its best soil is devoted to sorghum production (31). The government's institute of agronomy (ICA) and Ralston Purina are actively investigating and promoting new strains. George (32) cites Ralston Purina's penetration of the Colombian market as a good example of how U.S. agribusiness is able to acquire government financial cooperation (in this case, that of USAID and of the Colombian government) in establishing itself in a supposedly risky venture, and is then able to acquire the government's interest when profits are assured.

According to 1973 government statistics (33), at least 50 percent of the population lacks the purchasing power required for adequate nutrition even though there are more food calories currently available in the country than are needed to cover nutritional needs. (The report does not mention protein.) Needless to say, decline in real wages since then has greatly aggravated this problem, and it is now patently obvious that the free market system is unable to satisfy the food needs of over half the country.

Reluctant to effect the sweeping social changes necessary for more equal distribution, which most say would require a massive land reform (26), yet at the same time fearful of the growing social polarization, the government and the World Bank are pressing for a battery of state welfare programs, very much including medical and nutritional care for the rural poor. With loans from the World Bank, USAID, and other international development organizations, this package (known as the DRI—Programa de Desarrollo Rural Integrado— and the PAN—Plan de Alimentación y Nutrición) follows the policy laid down in recent World Bank Sector Policy Papers on Health and on Rural Development. Whereas before it was said that the fruits of aid investment would trickle down from the rich to the poor, the World Bank now belatedly acknowledges that political structures prevent this, and that some aid should now go directly to the poor, especially the rural poor, without activating a land reform.

In Colombia (as elsewhere), these integrated rural development programs are to occur in discrete rural enclaves, virtually under the complete control of the international development agency involved, with an initial budget of around U.S.$400 million, aimed at covering 80,000 families—some 20 percent of the potential population. In place of a land reform, it is assumed that purely technical changes in production will increase the income of the rural poor, which combined with social services will diminish discontent and reduce rural-urban migration. Latest reports are that the lower limit for credit shall be peasants with 20 hectares, ". . . since their farms are the more viable." Even if the lower limit were reduced to 3 hectares, the lowest ever mentioned, this would still leave the majority of peasants and all of the landless without credit. Here is where the social welfare package assumes its importance, especially the health and nutrition components of which the government is making so much, and it should be noted that the CSF nutrition project has been the prime mover in establishing the methodology for the application of this nutrition aid.

The plan as a whole has been forthrightly condemned by the Colombian Peasants' Association (ANUC) as it coincides with the dismantling of the land reform program.

It also coincides with the phased withdrawal of the U.S. free food shipments under the CARE programs (PL 480, Title II), which are said to reach two million Colombians and will be terminated in 1979. In its analysis of health in Colombia, USAID expresses anxiety about this cutoff and states the urgent need to develop plans to avert it (34). In this regard, it is insightful to read the following letter from a Catholic nun to the priest responsible for CARE programs in the Villa Rica area:

> ... As the person responsible for the Mother-Child center I have to inform you that the mothers have stopped coming because we insist that they also attend literacy and sewing classes, so that they can better themselves. Fifty or so women used to come, but only for the food. They are ignorant people and are not interested in bettering themselves. . . . I propose, Monseñor, that we replace the women who refuse to come with very old and invalid people to whom we will more easily be able to teach the catechism. . . . The mothers like to receive food, but refuse to take part in bettering themselves. Awaiting the orders that you send to me as a humble servant of Christ. . . .

The connection between low income and health was statistically verified in the mid-1960s by the National Morbidity Survey (35, 36).[6] Organized by ASCOFAME (the partially Rockefeller-funded and University of Valle-inspired Colombian Association of Medical Faculties), this report indicated that malnutrition was a severe problem in Colombia. Sixty-one percent of rural children and 44 percent of urban children were thus affected. Hence, rural nutrition welfare features heavily in the government's new health plan to the extent that U.S.-style food stamps are to be administered to some 33 percent of the "at risk" fraction of the rural population. This enormous undertaking could not proceed without the pool of U.S. health professionals fortunately available to the government, and nowhere more active than in the U.S. medical enclave in Cali.

THE U.S. MEDICAL ENCLAVE IN CALI

Attached to prestigious U.S. medical schools and universities, these planners and researchers operate out of the University of Valle, a long-standing recipient of funds from the Rockefeller Foundation's University Development Program. Under this program—which also includes medical schools in Brazil, Chile, and Mexico—the Cali school has become the leading medical center in Colombia, affecting other parts of Latin America as well (38). The University's Committee of Population Investigation (CUIP) is described as having been instrumental, through its Family Planning Clinics, "in making this country a leader in Latin America in population control programs" (38, p. 66). And over the past fifteen years a plethora of interlocking U.S.-controlled health planning and research institutes have mushroomed in the Cali center, working on a wide range of projects that encompass the social as much as the health sciences.

---

[6]The only socioeconomic analysis of this vast body of data that I know of is that by Navarro (37). He concludes that the picture of health and health delivery systems that emerges from this survey is not that of an undeveloped country so much as of a dependent or neo-colonialized country, and states that attempts to "modernize" the health system reflect this status.

The Rockefeller Foundation

The Rockefeller Foundation entered Colombia as early as 1913 with its hookworm eradication program. This was largely a failure as it could not raise the support of the rural poor. Hookworm was found to be epidemic in the country below 2,000 meters altitude, its highest prevalence (93.9 percent) being among the coffee plantation laborers (39). As many of these laborers were then in open revolt, and as coffee provided the bulk of the country's foreign exchange, it was not surprising that the government was "keenly interested" in the Foundation's campaign, which by 1920 included the provision of fellowships for "promising young Colombian physicians" to study in the U.S. By 1928 Colombia had received U.S.$227,436, making it the second highest recipient (after Brazil) of Rockefeller Foundation funds in South America, and in 1932 the entire public health system was reorganized.

Having set up and continuing to influence the government's institute of agronomy from 1941, the Rockefeller Foundation increased its sway over Colombian medical practice through its patronage of the medical school of the University of Valle, beginning in 1953. In 1961 this university was the first in the world to be funded under the Foundation's new University Development Program, destined to make it "a pace setter in Latin American higher education" (40). "The universities are places of infinite hope and despair," wrote a Foundation spokesperson with reference to its new policy, "but they are the West Points where social scientists are germinated and professional standards determined" (41).

Great emphasis was given by the Foundation to elite-building and to the "changing of basic attitudes and implanting new concepts and procedures" (38, p. 60). The Foundation's pride in its achievement is indicated by John Bryant, who, in the late 1960s, reported in his influential (and Rockefeller Foundation-funded) book, *Health & the Developing World*, "Its [Valle's] faculty of medicine is young, but in vision, creativity, and leadership it is one of the world's impressive institutions" (42). In its 1970 listing of Foundation scholars and fellows receiving grants for U.S. higher education, the Rockefeller Foundation states that Colombia was second in number only to Thailand (51 as compared with 74) out of a total of 36 countries and 393 awards.[7] And of these Colombian awards, the University of Valle received the lion's share of 73 percent. The Foundation also sent U.S. academics to teach at Valle.

As early as 1963, six such U.S. academics were largely involved with the internationally famous Candelaria family planning project, one of the oldest in Latin America and currently being used as a model for other Third World countries (2). Conceived as a "pilot project" to improve the lives of the poor in an area sociologically identical to Villa Rica where CSF is now working, the project has shunned any mention of how land and politics influence poverty, instead substituting the problem of human numbers for the number of problematic human relationships and calling not for economic planning but for family planning. As a means to improve people's economic well-being, it has been declared a failure by a close observer (2), but that has not stopped the inevitable succession of further "pilot projects," such as CSF's, which issue forth in the name of its success.

[7]For an analysis of the Rockefeller Foundation's stimulation of the U.S. health care model in Thailand, see Donaldson (43).

By 1970 the Rockefeller Foundation proudly took credit for having remolded the University of Valle. If not exactly like West Point, it had increased its enrollment 2.5 times, pioneered fiscal and administrative reforms in Latin American universities, and, through its U.S.-modelled teaching programs, visiting professorships, and U.S. study grants, was in a position to offer consulting services to government, business, and industry (40). But the same development produced a strong radical-nationalist reaction against U.S. domination of higher education and research, particularly against the Rockefeller Foundation, birth control programs, and the International Center for Medical Research and Training, which was finally expelled from the university and virtually from the country. It has become physically difficult, if not impossible, for U.S. organizations to continue openly as before.

How to Cope with Nationalism: The Low Profile

This nationalism has forced a strategic shift in policy such that the Rockefeller Foundation (and the Ford Foundation) now have to channel their interests in new ways—focusing on high-technology projects such as the CIAT (Centro Internacional de Agricultura Tropical) "green revolution" center near Cali, or on specific projects that catch the public's eye as directly helping the poor. Neither aim challenges the political structure which determines the problems the projects are meant to efface. Scientific "breakthrough" is not a magic wand that can transform a poor class or country into a rich one, and the evidence at hand concerning the "green revolution," for example, indicates that somewhat the opposite is more likely to occur as long as the political system remains intact. Likewise, the focus on the problems of the poor is quite inadequate as long as the basic problem rests more with those who wield power than with those who suffer under it.

As regards the U.S. relationship with the universities, events have led to the formation or upgrading of extramural and private research groups. Operating under the Colombian flag, these groups act so as to disguise the U.S. presence while preserving its influence, thus ensuring tighter security and the promise of more efficiently applied research. In Cali this occurs under the aegis of the Foundation for Higher Education (FES). Originally established in 1964 at the direct or indirect prompting of the Rockefeller Foundation as part of its drive to better integrate the local business community with the University of Valle (38, p. 66), FES is headed by an ex-dean of Valle's medical school. In 1970, when student opposition impeded further U.S. expansion within the university, FES set up a special Department of Research and Education, which now channels practically all of the U.S. grants and research in the Cali area (extending throughout southwest Colombia) and which, in all likelihood, will soon take over the Ford Foundation's Colombian office.

Most of the research thus channeled by FES is under the direction of U.S. nationals. In 1974 FES was administering U.S.$2.4 million in some 35 projects, mainly ones dealing with health and nutrition such as the CSF/USAID project discussed above. Being at the same time a private investment company, dependent as much on the profits of local big business as on the U.S. grants it administers, FES is hardly likely to encourage research that is in any way critical of the status quo. Indeed, the thrust of its public relations is that research is to serve business as a way of overcoming social problems (44)—a concept parallel to the doctrine of USAID, so frankly spelled out in 1964 by its Deputy Director's official testimony (quoted in reference 32, pp. 70-71):

> Our basic, broadest goal is a long range political one. It is not development for the sake of sheer development. . . . An important objective is to open up the maximum opportunity for domestic private initiative and to ensure that foreign private investment, particularly from the U.S., is welcomed and well treated. . . . The AID program planning process recognizes that the program is an instrument of U.S. foreign policy.

CONCLUSION

As this paper should show, the health sciences can be recruited for these political goals in a large number of complicated and interacting ways. The basic allure of health care such as discussed in this article is that it might take the political edge off some of the outstanding social problems that the system as a whole produces, without necessitating deep changes in the system itself—changes such as have occurred in China or Cuba. Also, medicine is a specially privileged tool in that its humanitarian image allows for the penetration of forces that might otherwise be unacceptable. There is nothing new in this. Referring to the Rockefeller Foundation's Peking Union Medical College in prerevolutionary China, the British surgeon, Joshua Horn, has commented (45):

> On the surface, it seemed to many, including Chinese students and staff members, to be a purely philanthropic undertaking. In fact, it trained a generation of willing henchmen who helped America dominate China. . . . Responsible American officials themselves admitted that this type of penetration was cheaper and more effective than other forms.

But none of this means that the immediate health objectives are bound to succeed. For not only are the basic conditions underlying the disease pattern untouched, but those very same conditions promote a work situation—a research nexus of ideation and social activity—which seems more likely to stifle than promote constructive results.

Collaboration of local professionals is essential to the aim of elite-training, and without the active support of host governments the foreign projects would be seriously handicapped. As Third World nationalism grows, however, such collaboration not only becomes increasingly necessary (e.g. in order to mitigate charges of imperialism), but also becomes increasingly difficult to sustain on terms that are suitable to the U.S., and increasingly ineffective as the nationalism divides and even sabotages the work teams. Collaboration becomes a matter of trading off ambivalent loyalties in the scramble for grants, grants which are ultimately determined by the conflicts seething in the surrounding society. Yet the root causes of these conflicts can find no place in the intellectual orientation of the aid projects, as much because of government sensitivity as because of the trained incapacity or structured ignorance of the professionals and the conservatism of the imported health and social sciences.

Political interest has to be denied, and the appeal to "value-free" science to effect this is what turns it into "scientism"—a parody of positivism, quantification, and sociobiology. As failure can rarely be admitted (or proven, because the social world resists analysis in these terms), the endless leap-frogging of one "pilot project" onto another owes far more to the ambitions and political skills of the project entrepreneurs than to convincing results. To call it a whorehouse, as did one USAID consultant when speaking to me, is not much of an exaggeration.

The fact that the research and its application are constrained by the interests of the powerful, and that it is so tied to economic incentives that knowledge and creativity become market commodities like any other, adds to the erosion of scientific values and the stifling of critical thought. The inability to raise popular support for health programs severely restricts the gathering, interpretation, and application of data. The fact that *appearances* are what count—the appearance of real aid instead of self-interested aid and Machiavellian manipulation—completes this erosion, so that the projects are little more than a triple play in desperation—the desperation of the poor, the desperation of governments to act in a way that does not threaten their power, and the desperation of the local and foreign professionals for the grants and international connections by which their careers can be furthered—leaving rational social change an empty promise. Mute testimony to this mesh of negativity comes from a stanza of a poem hung on the walls of the Foundation for Higher Education office in Cali:

> We bring in consultants whose circumlocution
> Raises difficulties for every solution,
> Thus guaranteeing continued good eating
> By showing the need for another meeting.

The cynicism thus generated is as understandable as the mediocrity of the output. As the CSF's "Learning Theory" acknowledges, learning ability is a direct function of the community institutions that exist for the framing and solving of problems, and of the "norms for enquiry" that prevail. While busily attempting to change these in a peasant community, so as to stimulate a scientific and critical outlook, it is obvious that their own community institutions and norms for enquiry hinder the CSF and its kin the world over from being themselves scientific or critical. Since learning comes from doing, from one's social activity—as the CSF is also at pains to point out—can one expect much more? To continue with the above-cited verse:

> Enough of these verses, on with the mission!
> Our task is as broad as the human condition!
> Just pray God the biblical promise is true;
> The poor ye shall always have with you.

Or was Kipling more prescient as the death knoll was sounding for the British Empire?

> Take up the White Man's burden —
> The savage wars of peace —
> Fill full the mouth of famine
> And bid the sickness cease;
> And when the goal is nearest
> The end for others sought,
> Watch Sloth and heathen Folly
> Bring all your hopes to naught.

Take up the White Man's burden —
Ye dare not stoop to less
Nor call too loud on Freedom
To cloak your weariness;
By all ye cry and whisper,
By all ye leave and do,
The silent sullen people
Shall weigh your Gods on you.

Acknowledgments—I wish to acknowledge the invaluable assistance of David Stoll in helping me formulate many of the issues involved in this paper, as well as his help in gathering some of the data on the U.S. projects analyzed herein. I am also grateful to Rachel Wyon, Anna Rubbo, Tony Skillen, Sandra Zurbo, and Scott Robinson for their comments.

REFERENCES

1. Community Experiments in the Reduction of Malnourishment in Colombia: First Year Progress Report (June 30, 1974–June 30, 1975). Community Systems Foundation, Ann Arbor, Mich., 1975 (mimeographed).
2. Bertrand, W. Development and Family Planning: A Case Study of a Colombian Town. Paper presented to the Third World Congress for Rural Sociology, Baton Rouge, La., August 22-27, 1972.
3. Community Systems Foundation Brochure, Ann Arbor, Mich., 1975.
4. NACLA (North American Congress on Latin America). U.S. grain arsenal. *NACLA'S Latin American Empire Report* 9(7), 1975.
5. Eisendrath, C. The malnourished as nutrition planners: Self-help concept summary. Community Systems Foundation, Cali, Colombia, and Ann Arbor, Mich., 1976.
6. Fedesarrollo (Fundación para la Educación Superior y el Desarrollo) *Las industrias azucareras y panaleras en Colombia*, pp. 340-346, Editorial Presencia, Bogotá, 1976.
7. Plan de desarrollo agropecuario, p. 44. Corporación Autonoma Regional del Cauca, Cali, 1970 (mimeographed).
8. Asocaña (Asociación Nacional de Cultivadores de Caña de Azucar), Cali, undated.
9. Taussig, M. Rural Proletarianization: A Social and Historical Enquiry into the Commercialization of the Southern Cauca Valley, Colombia. Unpublished Ph.D. dissertation, University of London, England, 1974.
10. Wray, J., and Aguirre, A. Protein-calorie malnutrition in Candelaria, Colombia: 1. Prevalence, social and demographic causal factors. *J. Trop. Pediatr.* 15(3): 452-471, 1969.
11. *Annual Review*, pp. 115-118. Rockefeller Foundation, New York, 1963.
12. Pérez, F. *Geografía físicia i política del Estado del Cauca.* Bogotá, 1862.
13. Palau, E. *Memoria sobre el cultivo del cacao, del café, y del té.* Imp. de M. Rivas y Cia, Bogotá, 1889.
14. García, E. *El Platano en Colombia y particularmente en el Valle del Cauca.* Cali, 1898.
15. Rippy, J. F. *The Capitalists and Colombia,* p. 152. Vanguard Press, New York, 1931.
16. Spurr, G. B., Barac-Nieto, M., and Maksud, M. G. Energy expenditure cutting sugar cane. *J. Appl. Physiol.* 39(6): 990-996, 1975.
17. Durnin, J. V., and Passmore, R. *Energy, Work, and Leisure.* Heinemann Educational Books, London, 1967.
18. Cleave, J. H. Labor in the Development of African Agriculture: The Evidence from Farm Surveys. Unpublished Ph.D. dissertation, Stanford University, Stanford, Cal., 1974.
19. Norgan, N. G., Ferro-Luzi, A., and Durnin, J. V. The energy and nutrient intake and the energy expenditure of 204 New Guinean adults. *Philos. Trans. R. Soc. Lond.,* Series B 268: 309-348, 1974.
20. Wolf, E. Types of Latin American peasantry: A preliminary discussion. *American Anthropologist* 57: 452-471, 1955.

21. Chandler, D. L. Health and Slavery: A Study of Health Conditions among Negro Slaves in the Vice-Royalty of New Granada and Its Associated Slave Trade, 1600–1810. Unpublished Ph.D. dissertation, Tulane University, New Orleans, 1972.

22. Departamento Nacional de Planeación de Colombia, Bogotá. Programa de desarrollo rural integrado; esquema preliminar. *Revista de Planeación y Desarrollo* 6(2): 39-50, 1974.

23. *Para cerrar la brecha.* Departamento Nacional de Planeación de Colombia, Bogotá, 1975.

24. Dwyer, J. T., and Mayer, J. Beyond economics and nutrition: The complex basis of food policy. *Science* 188: 567, 1975.

25. Kalmonovitz, S. La agricultura en Colombia. *Boletín mensual de estadística,* Nos. 276-278, 1974.

26. Urrutia, M., and Berry, A. *La distribución del ingreso en Colombia,* Editorial Lealon, Medellín, 1975.

27. Junguito, R. El sector agropecuario y el desarrollo económico Colombiano. In *Lecturas sobre desarrollo económico Colombiano,* edited by H. Gómez Otalora and E. Wiesner Durán. Fedesarrollo, Bogotá, 1974.

28. Rico Velasco, J. Crecimiento demográfico y la disponibilidad de alimentos; el problema de la desbutrición. Paper presented to the seminar on Política Mundial de Producción y Distribución de Alimentos, Cali, November 4-6, 1976 (mimeographed).

29. *Programas ganaderos,* p. 56. Ministerio de Agricultura de Colombia, Bogotá, 1976.

30. *Programas agricolas.* Ministerio de Agricultura de Colombia, Bogotá, 1975.

31. Plan de desarrollo del Valle del Cauca: Diagnostico, p. 44. Corporación Autonoma Regional del Cauca, Cali, 1974 (mimeographed).

32. George, S. *How the Other Half Dies.* Penguin Books, Middlesex, England, 1976.

33. Ingresos, consumos, y salud. In *Boletín Mensual de Estadística,* Nos. 264-265, p. 94, Departamento Administrativo Nacional de Estadística de Colombia, Bogotá, 1973.

34. Un analisis del sector Colombiano de Salud Publica, p. 42. United States Agency for International Development, Bogotá, 1974 (mimeographed).

35. *Study on Health, Manpower and Medical Education in Colombia,* Vols. 1-3. Pan American Health Organization, 1967.

36. *Investigación nacional de morbilidad: Evidencia clínica.* Ministerio de Salud de Colombia, Bogotá, 1969.

37. Navarro, V. The underdevelopment of health or the health of underdevelopment: An analysis of the distribution of human health resources in Latin America. *Int. J. Health Serv.* 4(1): 5-27, 1974.

38. *The President's Five Year Review and Annual Report,* p. 62. Rockefeller Foundation, New York, 1968.

39. *Annual Report.* Rockefeller Foundation, New York, 1919.

40. *President's Review and Annual Report,* pp. 74-75. Rockefeller Foundation, New York, 1970.

41. Shaplen, R. Quoted in *Towards the Well Being of Mankind: Fifty Years of the Rockefeller Foundation,* edited by A. B. Tourtellot, p. 161. Doubleday, Garden City, N.Y., 1964.

42. Bryant, J. *Health & the Developing World,* p. 82. Cornell University Press, Ithaca and London, 1969.

43. Donaldson, P. J. Foreign intervention in medical education: A case study of the Rockefeller Foundation's involvement in a Thai medical school. *Int. J. Health Serv.* 6(2): 251-270, 1976.

44. *Informe 1974,* and *Informe 1975.* Fundación para la Educación Superior, Cali, 1974 and 1975.

45. Horn, J. *Away with All Pests,* p. 70. Monthly Review Press, New York, 1971.

CHAPTER 7

Community Medicine Under Imperialism: A New Medical Police?

Jaime Breilh

The middle of the 20th century marks the beginning of a period of reappearance of social issues in the medical context of capitalist countries.

The occasional occurrence of social and humanistic rhetoric in the "Hospital-Research Institute Era" has evolved into a systematic effort by the State to extend the field of institutional medical work to other strata of the "community" which has explicit social objectives that we must study to uncover their underlying aims and make sure that authentic social alternatives are established.

We will outline the conditions of capitalism that could lead us to explain the reasons why, for approximately 10 years now, national and international health plans and programs have been incorporating, with increasing financial support, forms of medical practice that have been called "social" or "community."[1]

[1] Official institutions broadly refer to "community medicine" services ("primary care," "first contact," or "simplified" medicine) as including low-cost services, principally oriented to the non-wage-earning poor who inhabit geographical areas ambiguously called communities. Their operational object is not (as in the social security programs) the worker or the bureaucrat, but the poor urban district or the rural "community," and they pretend to overcome the purely biological focus by considering cultural, political, and environmental "components." They are not directed at the specialized treatment of acute patients but at basic treatment of elementary cases and the development of low-cost administrative and preventive measures.

This is a translation of a paper presented to the Second National Seminar on Social Medicine in Mexico (Mexico D.F., 1976) as part of a research project on the economic, political, and ideological implications of community medicine. The original Spanish version was published in the *Mexican Journal of Political Science*, Vol. 84, pp. 57-81, 1977.

Our intention has been to study the structural conditions of the powerful capitalist nations and of the subordinate economies of Latin America in order to explain this change in policies and the reallocation of health investments of national and multi-national organisms, corporations, private foundations, and medical associations (e.g. the American Medical Association).

THE HISTORICAL DEVELOPMENT OF COMMUNITY MEDICINE, RISE OF A NEW FORM OF MEDICAL POLICE

To liken contemporary community medicine to the medical police which appeared in a previous phase of capitalism may seem useless, but if we trace the pattern of historical events we find certain facts that would support such a comparison. For there are certain similarities between the State's aims at power building, legitimization, and political control underlying the medical police programs of the 19th-century absolutist states and the ones that are implicit in most official health programs today.

In order to trace historically the "social" or "community" tendencies of medical practice under capitalism, we have defined the periods shown in Table 1, which outlines the basic elements of our historical working hypothesis.

The periods of historical development have relative and movable limits. However, delineation by periods is a useful resource for historical analysis not so much as a strict definition of stages but as a means of reconstructing the principal events and of identifying the most significant changes and their determinants. We have, therefore, presented the outline in Table 1 in an attempt to provide an approximate synthesis of the historical totality in which we have to find the origin and local distribution of the "community" trend.

The Appearance of a Medical Police

As Rosen (1) has demonstrated, in the countries of Western Europe, from 1779, the year of the publication of John Peter Franks' work on "Medical Police," until the beginning of the last third of the next century (i.e. approximately 1860-1875), the concept (if not the term) of "police"[2] is employed in conjunction with "medicine" to define the official forms of medical activity in Europe at this time.

In his work, *From Medical Police to Social Medicine* (1), Rosen presents extensive bibliographical evidence on a series of books and textbooks following Franks' lines of thought and published since the end of the 18th century in Europe and later in the United States. Chapter titles of the works described by Rosen suggest the conceptual and technical concerns of the majority of authors:

- Health Legislation
- Population Problems[3]
- Vital Statistics
- Mother and Child Health

[2] "Police" by definition refers to the internal organization and regulation of the State, especially in respect to factors affecting the security, well-being, prosperity, morals, and health of the public.

[3] It is important to notice that at that time the main concern was to increase population, since the productive force of man had been discovered and there was a labor deficit. Rosen quotes Hoffmann, who argues for "... the promotion of population and the need to train competent doctors for that purpose ..." (1, p. 147).

- Organization of Personnel
- Prevention and Control of Communicable Diseases
- Sanitary Education

- Household and Personal Hygiene
- Nutrition
- Occupational Hygiene
- Recreation

Rosen also mentions the fact that even though the application of the "medical police" concept extended to most of Europe, its interpretation varied in accordance with the particular economic and political conditions of the states that adopted it (1, p. 143). In the less-developed countries in which the power of the bourgeoisie was more limited, the medical police retained fully its paternalistic and autocratic nature; there the need was to legislate and extend control over society. In the more advanced capitalist nations where the bourgeoisie had acquired full dominance, there was a tendency to emphasize the operative or functional aspects of Franks' doctrine in relation to working and urbanization conditions. Let us look at these aspects in greater detail.

In less-advanced countries like Germany and Italy, the ideas and methods of "medical police" were implemented in such a way that:

> ... the concept of medical police meant a program of social action for health grounded on a primary calculation to augment the power of the state rather than to increase the welfare of the people (1, p. 155).

The inclusion of medical services as part of the process of building state power was a political necessity in these countries in the 18th century and the first half of the 19th century. They were undergoing a transitional phase, with aristocrats and capitalists struggling to obtain control of the State. Deutscher (2) explains why the absolutist monarchies in Germany and Austria, for instance, being embryonic (mercantilist) capitalist formations that were weak and subordinate to England and France, experienced the rise of a strong interventionist state which would compensate for the weakness of the bourgeoisie as a social class by penetrating the institutions and lives of the growing urban "communities" with the aim of political control.

The case of England and to a lesser extent of France is the inverse of this pattern. In these countries industrial capitalism had been consolidated by the end of the 18th century and the national integration process was achieved under the direction of the bourgeoisie; thus, administrative absolutism did not develop. This seems to be reflected in the particular forms of medical police which these countries adopted until the last decades of the 19th century.

In England and France the relative weight of the police (controlling) function was diminished and emphasis was given to sanitary measures applied to urban development and improvement of working conditions. New structural conditions required health actions which were oriented directly to the improvement of general conditions of productivity and of the environmental conditions of the cities. This new tendency ran counter to the authoritarian principles of a medical police. However, both approaches, liberal as well as absolutist, reflected the conflict of the interests of the aristocracy and the growing capitalists. During this period, the legal and administrative compulsion implicit in state support declined gradually and had to be reoriented toward productivity and the construction of the new order. Even then it retained its legitimizing and control functions.

One can infer the role of English sanitary police in that period from an analysis of

Table 1

Main historic features of central capitalism and stages of official medical practice

Period	Approximate Times	General Processes	Trends of Official Medicine
ABSOLUTISM (Transition)	14th-15th Centuries	Major feudal crisis; Consolidation of strong juridical system and bureaucracy	
FREE ENTERPRISE • Manufacture	1550-1775	Collapse of feudal agriculture; Manufacture; Initial formation of collective worker; Consolidation of bourgeois power.	MEDICAL POLICE
• Heavy industry	1775-1860	Industrial mechanization; science and technology appear as autonomous productive forces; prolonged work day (absolute surplus value) to increase productivity; intense wearing down of labor force (including females and children); Intense process of urbanization; Legislative control to organize new patterns of living and production; Social movements.	
MONOPOLISTIC • Formative period	1870-1900	Corporations, cartels, trusts; Movement to limit duration of work day; to maintain and increase productivity; a) Research on functional effi-	PERIOD OF SCIENTISM IN MEDICINE (Hospital-Research Institute Based)

Table 1 (continued)

Period	Approximate Times	General Processes	Trends of Official Medicine
		ciency of the body and fast recuperation of sick labor force; b) Technological improvement. Increase in capital composition and average volume of productive units; Consolidation of collective worker.	
● Final phase: Imperialism	1920-1950	Conquest of economic territories and markets.	
SEVERE CRISIS OF CAPITALISM	1960	Severe imperialistic crisis with significant political repercussions in Latin America. Fiscal crisis, inflation; Conditions for concentration of state power. Intensification of state intervention and control. Agricultural crisis in Third World; Massive unemployment (or subemployment); High degree of mass political conscience.	COMMUNITY MEDICINE (NEW MEDICAL POLICE)

Chapters 8, 12, and 13 of *Capital* (3), where Marx transcribes extensive portions of commission reports about occupational mortality, public health, etc., which demonstrate the State's concern with the extensive exploitation of the labor force (adults and children of both sexes) that was undermining the main resource of capitalism. In the fourth section of Chapter 13, Marx reproduces a report of a "General Dispensary of Nottingham" which shows the striking prevalence of consumptive pulmonary disease cases among 686 female textile workers aged 17 to 24 years. He presents a table with alarming figures (3, p. 567):

Proportion of Consumptive Pulmonary
Disease Cases in Female Textile Workers
Aged 17 to 24 Years, Nottingham

Year	Proportion of Cases
1852	1 out of 45
1853	1 out of 28
1854	1 out of 17
1855	1 out of 18
1856	1 out of 15
1857	1 out of 13
1858	1 out of 15
1859	1 out of 9
1860	1 out of 8
1861	1 out of 8

In the same chapter, Marx quotes a public health report which unequivocally states that it has been demonstrated that ". . . as long as the workers remain incapable of imposing themselves the sanitary justice, they will not benefit effectively by the actions of sanitary police personnel . . ." (3, p. 566).

Generally speaking, documentary evidence shows that the regulatory functions of sanitary police in the more-developed countries did not so much emphasize the promotion of state power as the means to cope with problems of population deficit, mother and child health, administrative regulation and control of communicable disease problems, and supervision of sanitary urban conditions; in general, that is, they laid the foundations for the promotion and protection of labor force productivity.

It seems that the United States experienced a development similar to that of England but with a time difference which is due to historical reasons.

This period of a "social outlook" in medicine, of the enforcement of a new order, signifies the rise in the period of manufacture (1550-1775), and its subsequent consolidation during the great industrial stage (1775-1860), of what Marx called the *"collective worker."*

The combination in the manufacturing centers of different trades, or the division of one trade into a range of specific operations, with the objective of producing one commodity, caused the transformation of independent tradesmen into a unitary cooperative working body (i.e. the collective worker) which was eventually consolidated by the unifying effect of machine-based work. The "part" worker could no longer produce any merchandise by himself; from then on, the decisive factor was the whole working collectivity operating as a socialized entity, the combination of individual capacities and techniques.

The inception of these conditions made it possible to recognize the social or collective basis of work, the social entity which could not be pictured clearly in previous stages of historical development. This was to have profound effects not only on productive forms but on the political struggle and in the ideological sphere. From then on each class, capitalists and workers, would seek to obtain different and conflicting results from work. The first group tried to increase, for its own benefit, the potential of the social entity in terms of productivity gains and was prepared for limited acceptance of "social" problems related to labor, while trying to avoid at the same time the recognition of the social origin of wealth and to keep the workers divided in familiar "atoms" that could operate as consumers of their privately owned commodities. On the other hand, workers started the long, still unfinished, struggle to reunite society's collective potential and to abolish privatization.

At the beginning of the manufacturing period there was still a persistent individual and subjective response of workers in production. There was still a margin for personal desires, individual working attitudes, and speed. In this stage there was no unifying frame or link that could operate as an objective mechanism of subordination. That is why, in the early manufacturing days, constant insubordination was reported and the State's main function was necessarily the enforcement of order.

In those days the most capable workers were generally the most obstinate and undisciplined ones. Capitalists often found themselves controlling disorder. In Marx's words:

> Order must be established one way or the other, exclaimed in 1770 the frequently quoted author of the Essay on Trade and Commerce. Order, answered like an echo 66 years later Dr. Andrew Ore: Order is badly needed in manufacture . . . (3, p. 448).

It was a stage in which a new mode of production was being organized, and capital investments by productive units had to impose new labor patterns on supposedly "free" workers; the new modes of urban life had to be regulated, and the political control of the whole process assured. The State had to push forward the new order and medicine was soon trapped in the historical need for a social police.

Poulantzas (4) describes this period as one in which we witness the ". . . formation of concepts like 'the people,' the 'nation' as constitutive principles that supposedly represented the interests of the public."

The contradictory nature of services under capitalism, their dual character, conditioned their advantages and limits for the opposing classes. Because of productive needs, the bourgeoisie had to recognize, if unwillingly, the collective linkage of workers and to provide services for them, but by retaining the social nature of the working force they accepted the unity of their opponents. The aims of production and of social well-being were opposites which both classes have tried to advance since then in an intense struggle.

At this time, we do not have available a wide range of information about the evolution of medical police in Latin America. As shown by partial evidence, the feudal or semi-feudal character of Latin American structures in colonial days, in which the fight for a bourgeois dominance had to break aristocratic resistance and imperialistic dominance, suggests that principles like Franks' must have been applied in the sanitary policies in most of the countries instead.

The Era of Scientism in Medicine and Its Crisis

The last quarter of the 19th century marked the beginning, particularly in the powerful capitalist nations, of a decline in the practice of medical police and the appearance of a different approach that we will call "scientism." There was an outburst of concern with individual biology expressed in a new understanding of man (whence the "human machinery") and in the adoption of alternative fields for medical research (i.e. pathology, pathologic anatomy, and physiology) and oriented toward curative actions dedicated to repair isolated segments of that "corporal machinery." Hygiene, therapeutics, and semiology were thus instituted as the fundamentals of official medicine.

By following the historical advance of societies like the English, we can understand the structural determinants of that change in the medical model and the decline in the level of official stimulus to the "social" or "public" approach to medicine, which lasted from the end of the 19th century until approximately 20 years ago; at that time, in the era of modern imperialism, it reappeared as national and international community programs. Let us examine some basic historical facts about these events.

The clues to understanding the substitution process which medical concepts and methods experienced since the 1870s are to be found in the historical conclusions of Marx (3, Ch. 8) and in his research on the forms of productivity and changes of duration of the work day. Marx demonstrated that until approximately 1860, the capitalist system of exploitation was based on increased work days or extensive work procedures (absolute surplus value), but later, because of trade union pressure and the inefficiency of a labor force that had been worn out by prolonged and gruelling work days, the State passed laws limiting work time which stopped the voracious growth of the length of daily work. As a result, the capitalistic compulsion to gain profit had to find some sort of compensation, and the alternative was the application of intensive forms of labor (i.e. relative surplus value extraction).[4]

The period of extremely destructive working conditions, concerned only with the control and regimentation of labor, had reached its limits and gave way to a new stage that was based on an examination of the potential of the human body and its protection; the aim was to equal previous levels of productivity in a shorter time period and to rationalize the use of the human labor force so as to repair quickly any possible injuries to workers who were becoming more scarce, more expensive, and more aware of their rights.

Let us see how Marx described this turning point in capitalist development. In relation to the previous phase of excessive work times, he states (3, Ch. 8, p. 335):

> After capital investment took centuries to extend the work day to its normal maximum and then beyond it to the natural day limit of 12 hours, a violent rate of increase was reached when great industrial activities started in the last third of the 18th century, an attack as violent and disproportionate as an avalanche. All the limits that had been established by cultural and natural patterns, by age and sex, by day and night were crushed and overlooked.

Describing the period of intensive exploitation he continues:

> As soon as the workers recovered from the violence and confusion of the production of the previous decades they started a process of resistance, which began in England, the birthplace of great industry (3, Ch. 8, p. 336).
>
> If this anti-natural extension of the work day for which capitalists strive in their desperate battle for profit increase, shortens the life of individual workers and consequently the duration of their labor force, a faster replacement of the worn out capacities will be necessary and for that reason the sum required to cover the costs of replacement will become bigger ... consequently it seems that even capitalists will be interested in a normal work day (3, Ch. 8, p. 320).

---

[4] A condensed explanation of the mechanisms of surplus value extraction discovered by Marx can be found in Sweezy's "Theory of Capitalist Development" (5).

The concern for labor protection and the development of more efficient forms of work was the point of contact in that new phase, between the demands of capitalist production and medical-scientific work.

Bauer (6) describes in detail the period in which intensive research into the functional efficiency of the human body was started. An insight into working physiology had to be obtained in order to assess the rational utilization of human energy and invent methods of fatigue reduction and time-saving movements.

Once the national basis for production had been established and the development of productive forces was sufficient, a process of territorial conquest for economic expansion was started by the beginning of the present century. This extension of economic space was mainly directed toward the tropical territories of Latin America, Africa, and Asia. The imperialist powers of Europe, and later the United States, invested huge sums of money in the development of agro-exporting units and the construction of communication arteries which often were exposed to the hazards of the jungle, including the infectious diseases. To protect technical personnel and the native labor force, and to keep the productive enterprise marching on, it was necessary to study microbial and parasitic diseases.

The advance of this huge project of colonization and the intensive production of metropolitan units required the development of research and therapeutic resources and the construction of high-technology hospital complexes and interrelated scientific institutes.

The United States soon became the main promoter of the new trend. This objective received full economic support from private enterprise, e.g. in the enormous investments of the Rockefeller Foundation to implement the recommendations of the strategic Flexner Report (7), which was financed in 1910 by the Carnegie Foundation to set out the basic lines of a development plan for "scientific" medicine.

The Crisis of Flexnerian Medicine

The Flexner Report started a movement toward the institutionalization of scientism in medicine in the United States. Like a snowball, it accelerated the pace of educational and service changes, with heavy financial backing by wealthy private corporations and the State (8).

Far from supporting Flexner's ideas for humanitarian reasons and as a compromise with the progress of medical education, the powerful corporations were establishing with clear vision the foundations for the medicine of the new monopoly capitalism.

"Scientific" medicine, as well as other superstructural resources, received priority because it represented a means of aiding the efficient reproduction of the most appreciated commodity: the labor force. For from the point of view of monopoly capital, proletarians have to be kept in optimal condition because their productivity is a basic ingredient of the capital accumulation process (the "sine qua non" survival factor in the competitive world of capitalism) which eliminates inefficient production units.

Besides, as Navarro (9) pointed out when referring to the nature of Flexnerian medicine in the United States, it was an ideology that by stressing the significance of disease as something that affected the individual, and by emphasizing individual therapeutic response, absolved the economic and political elements from all responsibility in relation to disease.

That is how, since the first decade of the present century, the United States, as the commanding country of monopolist development, became the principal and most influential locus of medical scientism.

Kelman (10) describes this transformation of U.S. medicine as the shift from an individualized trading relation based on the payment of personal fees and symbolized by the doctor's small black bag, to a system built upon the pillars of "science," a system of specialized attention to private cases which overturned the traditional forms of professional control.

The wheel was passed from the practitioners to the scientists, who rapidly gained control of the top directive bodies of the American Medical Association and through this control secured political and ideological dominance over the whole medical system. The importance of this political conquest of the professional union was that it made possible the formal linkage of the medical "scientists" with the capitalists (8, p. 589), completing a new and coherent system of medical activity subordinated to capital accumulation. This specific, mutual, and efficient relationship was based on highly technological work.

Finally, one of the most significant points explaining the rise and later the crisis of "scientific" medicine is the economic dynamics of high-complexity resources.

We explained already that the technological nature of this medicine required the development of a complex infrastructure (i.e. hospitals, medical centers, research institutes) which gradually diverted service funds to research work dependent more on the needs of productive expansion than on social benefit. It was a costly model, based on heavy financial support from corporations or the State. But we know that all of these sources operate only under rigorous cost-benefit analysis (benefit referring to positive effects of health actions on productivity and, where necessary, on legitimization of the political order).

However, the capitalist system generates its own contradictions and faces today the existence of a great mass of unemployed and subemployed labor whose protection and maintenance is not, in the strictly productive sense, a need of the system; to the contrary, it signifies an unproductive expense that threatens to diminish productive assets. But even though the logic of capitalism operates along these lines, the dominant class cannot leave unattended and uncontrolled the masses of ghetto inhabitants, the rural poor, and the families of the workers, and it is precisely this contradiction which helps us understand the operational crisis of Flexnerian medicine. It is not possible to extend coverage of costly services because that would reach the financial limits of a system in which an extremely irrational concentration of resources blocks any redistribution, and where the economic needs and ideological characteristics of decision makers (i.e. representatives of the dominant class) do not correspond to a social philosophy.

To demonstrate the present marked preoccupation with the problem of costs and extension of coverage, the following high-level commission reports from the United States and Canada can be cited as evidence:

A report by the Canadian Committee for Community Health Centres (11) speaks about the alarming increase of health system expenditures in Canada, which during 1955-1968 reached an average annual increase rate of 10.7 percent, so that by 1968 operating and capital expenses amounted to 6.6 percent of the Gross National

Product. The same document points out that by 1971 the percentage of budgetary increase in the health field had reached the 12.5 percent level and emphasizes that the rate of increase for acute hospital care cases corresponded to 14 percent. In the final part, this report gives some estimates which suggest that if contemporary rates persist, by 1981 the costs of the health system will amount to 7.4 percent of the GNP. The authors of the report say: "The question is, therefore, not how much we are investing, but what do we obtain in exchange of the invested money" (11, p. 12).

The basic conclusion of the report is that community centers offer a solution to the problem of rising costs and the need to increase the benefits of investors.

Similar problems are being discussed by United States and Western European health planners. They too are alarmed by the rapid cost increases in their systems. Statistics produced by R. Maxwell and quoted by Navarro (9, p. 56) demonstrate that, for instance, in none of those countries was less than 5.3 percent of the GNP invested during 1973 in the health area, and even so, vast proportions of the public remain without or with insufficient coverage. One can well imagine the proportions of this problem in Latin American countries, where health expenditures seldom exceed 2 percent of the GNP.

The reasons for the crisis of the Flexnerian model become evident: they are, on the one hand, increasing costs, slow and inefficient service delivery, and restricted coverage, and, on the other hand, working-class demands banging loudly on the doors of the system's institutions.

Monopoly capitalism implies a complex social division of work that is reflected in a general trend toward specialization; health services are no exception to this and that brings about costlier personnel reproduction. Capitalism permeates all spheres in its search for profit, commercializing all services and making them more expensive. Capital concentration goes together with mass proletarianization and increasing impoverishment. In general, the socialization[5] of production generates the need for more State intervention to assure private concentration of capital and power.

This is the contradictory context in which, since 1960, the "community medicine" alternative has appeared.

Community medicine is one of the few solutions that capitalism can propose for the problems of public health. It provides a means to attend to minimal levels of social demand, as well as basic conditions for the protection of previously neglected populations, without changing the social relations or significantly diminishing productive investments. To the contrary, it seems that primary care coverage extension projects are efficiently interwoven with other forms of consumer market expansion.

When we define "community medicine" as an alternative of imperialism, it must be clearly understood that we do not question the intrinsic value and potential of social medicine; what we impugn is the use of primary medicine as a strategy of low-cost service for the purpose of social conciliation and political deformation.

For if it were not for the community solution, the capitalist State would not be able to extend services to other sectors of the population, or else it would be forced to make available resources for all levels of care providing full-scale services. This alternative would imply a massive increment of state social investment and a marked

[5] Socialization in this case means that the production of goods and services depends on ever-increasing components of the labor force.

decrease of productive funds, and both contradict the structural fundamentals of bourgeois society.[6]

Social process not only has imposed growing demands on the dominant groups of the weak Latin American economies; the huge imperialist corporations also suffer from the consequences of societal contradictions. That is why, as in 1910 when the great corporations were eager to expend, by means of their dependent institutions (i.e. the private foundations such as Carnegie and Rockefeller), enormous sums for financing the Flexnerian medical reform, we now find the big hand of imperialism, through the same foundations, giving out huge grants and subsidies, this time for the "communitization" of medicine. That is the case demonstrated by the Carnegie Report of 1970 (12), equivalent in importance to community medicine to the Flexner Report of the era of "scientific" medicine. It points out certain weaknesses of the Flexnerian model, as well as the deficits "it has generated," and stresses the urgent need of an application of compensatory measures (financial, administrative, and educational) by the State and universities, with the object of achieving a de-elitification (de-Flexnerianization) of medicine.[7] It is not surprising that this proposition has received considerable financial support.

The Rockefeller Foundation has made special efforts to show concern for the "community." It has financed projects in Asia, Africa, the United States, and Latin America. In September 1968 it gave full support to a meeting of 22 key experts in Belagio, Italy in an effort to provide to this group of assiduous "social thinkers" the opportunity of preparing a conceptual framework for the "new social medicine." The result was a heavy document (13) which sums up some of the most relevant theoretical and methodological developments of bourgeois ideology programs.

There are many other examples of how community medicine is being used as a conciliatory instrument. We are considering these efforts as a particular case of social medical programs, leaving aside the analysis of experiences that have been promoted by progressive groups because we consider that the latter oppose conciliatory procedures, generate important political effects, and therefore fall in a separate category which demands a separate analysis that is not part of the present paper.

In this section we wanted to submit official community medicine programs to discussion and underline their limitations and the potential which history has placed before exploiters and exploited. Which group will be able to direct them to the benefit of its own class interests?

[6]Since the capitalist countries of Latin America expend less than 2 percent of their GNP on health, a higher-level expenditure would require (a) a bigger percentage of the state budget for health; (b) control by the State of production so that gains are rationally distributed; (c) an increase in health expenditures of working-class families; and (d) a significant increase of national income by drastic reduction of the escape of funds due to foreign investment profits. The implementation of important changes in these aspects is incompatible with the interests of the ruling class and highly improbable under present conditions.

[7]The Carnegie Report of 1970 (12), which is being implemented with strong support from private enterprise, lists as goals for 1980: (a) opening of university medical centers to the problems of service and of teaching-service integration; (b) expansion and acceleration of the training programs for all sorts of personnel (including intermediate ranks); (c) curriculum integration of basic sciences with professional subjects; (d) 50 percent increment of student matriculae, with partial priority for low-income family students and minority groups; concern for student demands; and (e) better service distribution, construction of 9 university centers for health sciences and 126 medical education centers, and a national program of sanitary services.

THE CONTEMPORARY STRUCTURE OF THE MEDICAL POLICE
AND ITS FUNCTIONS

Having looked at some of the most serious political drawbacks of community medicine, it does not appear to be so very "community" oriented, nor for that matter exclusively medical. We begin to discover its hidden aspects and implicit motives. We have managed to understand that in a class society the "community" does not exist (if we stick rigorously to its etymology, i.e. a group distinguished by common properties; essentially similar people); it appears only as a mystifying label placed on poor peasants, urban subproletarians, and the families of workers, and the ultimate intention of such community services is not to provide the people with the best possible care but to install a cheap and invisible structure of "concession" and "repression" through medicine.

Since imperialist and pro-imperialist organs cannot operate in "communities," and since their primary medical care programs reflect important class biases, we prefer to choose another name for community medicine, one that will suggest its real dimensions and evoke the hidden facets. For that reason we have decided to describe the forms of community medicine that benefit (willingly or unwillingly) the interests of the ruling classes as the "modern system of medical police." We are aware of the fact that, by doing so, we are straining at the limits of strict definitions.

It is possible to argue that it is a mistake to extend to contemporary community medicine the label of medical police, a label which corresponds to the sanitary policies of European absolutism. But our intention is to emphasize certain if limited similarities between two types of official medical activities; they share the inclusion of the social domain in a conceptual framework of health services that is directed toward the enforcement of state power and control, and both imply direct or indirect benefit for their respective stage of capitalist production.

"Modern community medicine" is not a replica of 18th century "medical police." It is a new form of police work, more subtle and refined. Instead of strong, compulsive, and explicit direction, it controls by means of surreptitious penetration and methods of persuasion. It draws on "voluntary" participation and assigns hierarchical positions to people instead of using explicit and authoritarian methods.

As mentioned before, the medical police appeared in embryonic capitalist development. It was intended to promote favorable conditions for the growth of manufacture, support the maintenance of absolutist power, enforce order, and regulate a society that was unfit for the new regime. Its basic instruments were public legislation and the police code, both clear expressions of the need to back and to enhance the birth of a new mode of production that was being consolidated on the ruins of feudalism.

Community medicine reflects, in its sophisticated methods of penetration and in the fetishism of community self-determination or participation, the capacity to manipulate and legitimize. It establishes a subtle dominance that spies upon and penetrates the people by means of a simplified medicine that generates invisible forms of repression and control and is performed in a secret manner, resembling a technique of service expansion.

To understand community medicine as an instrument of state political intervention we have to, first, analyze the objective conditions now determining state intervention; second, describe in more detail the hidden objectives of community programs; and, finally, describe the mechanisms of that intervention, emphasizing those that have more relative weight.

The structural basis for the appearance of a strong State in the monopolistic period (imperialism) was considered in a previous section. To complete this brief analysis, we must rely on Lenin's explanation of monopoly capital as summarized by Sweezy (5).

In the phase of imperialism, the process of centralization and monopoly development generates a greater degree of anarchy than was present in free enterprise capitalism. Each monopoly tries to reach its private interests, to the detriment of the whole system's stability. The State has to intervene as a moderator to arrest extreme deviations. Besides, the State has to protect minor capitalists from monopolist voracity, and for that purpose tries to take control of services and energy sources. Finally, and as part of the same tendency, the State absorbs extremely costly, risky, or low-profit activities.

This first group of arguments explains why medicine for the poor (whether proletarians or not) is absorbed by the State, and allows us to understand the search for equilibrium of official health policies, which is easy to confuse with their socializing mask. The organization of social security plans in the era of scientific medicine, and more recently low-cost compensatory medicine, compete with private medical enterprise and contribute to the conciliatory mechanisms described above because they "nationalize," to a small extent and with the least cost, the expenditures for the protection and maintenance of the labor force. They counterbalance the excessive ambitions of the medical field that drive up costs and place the humanitarian image of the State in a bad dilemma. The State tries, for this same reason, to neutralize the powerful professionals and enterprises. But due to its contradictory role, the State also acts as a source for the expansion of the drug, equipment, and other material markets.

Attempts to conquer the people's unity, power, and consciousness by mass organizations, as well as evident misery, have to be controlled by a vigorous State. This is achieved by a series of mechanisms for "concession" and "repression," and by the weakening of legislative bodies to fortify the role of the executive; community medicine (i.e. medical police) is one of the most serviceable repression-concession mechanisms.

So far we have analyzed the historical reasons why a strong, police-type State has reappeared as the institutional basis for the development of "community medicine," which has two main tasks: (a) to act as a stimulant for productivity; and (b) to provide an instrument for legitimization of the political apparatus.

Each of these functions is accomplished through certain mechanisms that must be clearly understood before we can define our strategy. Based on Lenin's arguments about State tactics, and taking into account some aspects of the previously quoted work by Navarro (9, p. 46), one can develop certain descriptions of the mechanisms implicit in community work.

Community Medicine as a Mechanism of Stimulus, Rationalization,
and Redistribution for Productivity Purposes

Here we are referring to a mode of intervention directly related to the economic sphere and designed for the process of regulating the dynamics of production. One must be careful not to confuse the external regulating function of the State in relation to production, e.g. in services like community medicine, with its direct participation in the procurement of surplus value. What we are saying is that the development of "community" work and resources does not impinge directly upon capitalist production, but only intervenes indirectly, stimulating or defending that production from the sphere of the market and of political direction.

Community Medicine as Stimulant of Productivity. This mechanism works principally as a stimulus for the consumption of therapeutic resources and other components of the infrastructure, expanding the market for relevant products of private enterprise. When operating on a rural and urban nonproletarian labor force, it increases their "functional" capacity as workers, thus increasing their efficiency. Besides, community medicine attends to elementary needs at minimal fees, making possible some savings by the poor and a reallocation of those funds in the family budget. The consequences of these measures are a modest increase in the consumption capacity of those families and family conditions more conducive to production patterns.

The World Bank clearly points in this direction when it states in one of its documents on "Health Policy" (14) that plans carried on to improve health can be considered as a profitable investment and mentions, as an example, the "great success" of a project in Indonesia to treat anquilostomiasic peasants with parentheral iron, at a cost of 43 cents per treatment, which increased productivity by 19 percent (or a cost-benefit ratio of 1 to 280).[8]

Community Medicine as a Rationalization Mechanism. This makes possible economies in State expenditure for inevitable health outlays that respond to social demand; thus, state funds can be reallocated to the productive areas. This mechanism is plausible because community-type services provide ample coverage at low cost and because they constitute the base of operations from which cheap diet substitutes or contraceptives can be distributed as a means to rationalize misery. In addition, it makes possible economies in personnel expenditures by the utilization of community resources (e.g. in Ecuador "la minga," an old Indian method of cooperation in collective building, is used to obtain free labor for sanitary projects), personnel with minimum qualifications and university students. Surprisingly, even universities and other progressive groups fall for this type of rationalization scheme without realizing

----

[8] Based on this type of logic, authors like Kerr White (in reference 13, pp. 246-250) insist on the necessity of applying as evaluation criteria for community projects the degree of function (productive functionality) that has been achieved for the individual and the community, measuring primarily the degree of transformation that is accomplished in relation to disability, discomfort, discontent, disease (perceived morbidity), and mortality. He stresses the first four criteria because they influence more clearly "productivity, functional capacity and well-being."

its possible risks and the need to guide their students and teachers so that their actions make up for the negative implications of this mechanism.

Community Medicine as a Mechanism for Redistribution. Redistributory mechanisms are already implied in some of the previous functions, but certain forms of capitalism establish formal strategies for redistribution using the legislative power of the State. Depending on political conditions and needs and on the structural characteristics of a specific social formation, "community medicine" serves as an instrument of redistribution either in favor of the people (concession) by imposing taxes on the dominant groups to finance sanitary projects, or for the benefit of the bourgeoisie (repressive developmentalism), the latter by means of public fund investment through community programs (such as the so-called "community development" programs) to improve, for instance, means of communication, or to provide funds for capitalization of projects that are then promptly transferred to capitalist control.

Community Medicine as a Method of Social Constraint and State Legitimization

In connection with the previously described mechanisms of economic regulation that contributed to the "orderly anarchy" of monopoly capitalism, "community medicine" makes possible other types of interventions consistent with its medical police function.

Community Medicine as an Alternative to an Integrated System. In the present situation of the majority of countries under imperialism, "community medicine" can be used as a small concession that helps provide minimum levels of service to demonstrate the humanitarian concerns of governments. This is the main difference between the aims of the medical police in the capitalist societies and of social medicine in a socialist formation. Under socialism, primary-level care is built upon a structure that promotes equality and health. It is offered universally as the first stage of a complete care system, and not only as a cheap and limited resource for the poor.

Community Medicine as an Ideological Mechanism. Community education programs generate and publicize substitute values for the real interests of the working classes, and thus contribute to an exclusion or distortion of the peoples' own ideas. In addition, they transmit to health personnel (frequently recruited from the same "communities") the official doctrine on social problems, the origin of diseases, and the types of action that are considered licit.[9] This reasoning is designed to conceal the structural determinants of the health-disease process. We are here faced with a complex mechanism which, like others, deserves a more detailed analysis to start the search for alternatives.

---

[9] A Canadian program reads: ". . . among the examples of personal and social sickness we find the mental disorders, drug dependence, delinquency, father-children alienation, personal violence against the established institutions of society" (11, p. 10).

Community Medicine as a Disciplinary Mechanism. This aspect is probably the least evident one. The medical bureaucratic apparatus, when penetrating into the poor urban district or rural village, is tantamount to an invisible surveillance network that penetrates the daily life of families and has a triple function: to assert the presence and hierarchical role of state representatives among the poor population; to feed back to the State's information system relevant social data by formal or informal channels; and to achieve adequate conduct of the people by means of a subtle disciplinary apparatus that operates through a reward-punishment method, sanctioning "normal" conduct that conforms to the dominant ideology.

Deutscher (2, p. 20) explains why in capitalist society the "bourgeois fiction of legal equality" creates the impression of total independence of the State and the dominant classes; for that reason bureaucracy (e.g. sanitary bureaucracy) appears like a special group whose hierarchical status is accepted as a natural form of collective life, as a result of the bureaucrat's special capacities. Once the class nature of the State is concealed, it can project itself surreptitiously, assuming different labels and taking hold of the innermost elements of social life.

In his work "Surveillance and Punishment," Foucault (15) examines the implications of that "disciplinary apparatus" which constantly but imperceptibly surveys the people. Its relative success is due to the fact that they ". . . use simple instruments: hierarchical inspection, normative sanctioning and their combination in a procedure which is specific to them: the exam."

Through those instruments, "community medicine" becomes part of the State's range of vision. It is a form of hierarchical vigilance that operates simultaneously for the fulfillment of health activities and for the consolidation of the lowest strata of a leadership system which manages, among other things, to generate a discreet form of power that substitutes for violence and brute force as normative resources. Small, indirect gratifications and sanctions build up consensus supporting a normality adapted to what are, in the long run (historical perspective), ruling-class interests.

The idea we are trying to emphasize here is that comprehension of the health-disease conditions of a group living today under a capitalist regime is based on a set of rules or normal patterns which are adapted to productivity and the needs of political dominance. Normality is established as a principle of coercion in the arrangement between health personnel and participating community much as in the instruments for measuring agreement with normality (i.e. clinical records, family records, questionnaires, group dynamic conclusions, etc.) which systematically omit the real health-disease conditions and show results which conveniently fit into the State's objectives. For instance, one of the key members of the Belagio conference (13, p. 248) argues in favor of restoring the functioning of the people and of alleviating discomfort (perceived disease). By stating it, this "expert" has summed up two of the main procedures of the medical police, mentioning later that evaluation of programs "can be extended to include other forms of social interruption associated with unemployment, conduct disturbances, delinquency and crime." (He most probably would consider nonconventional political organizations and the struggle for social rights as "disturbances" that have to be detected and turned back to the "normal" condition.)

Community Medicine as a Coercive and Repressive Mechanism. This presumes unity with the previously discussed mechanism but is expressed by more tangible actions. First, it implies the control of decision-making processes and groups. The local health team usually penetrates the least politically coherent (but nonetheless influential) organizations of the people and infiltrates them with petit-bourgeois values and State passwords. It forms parallel organizations related to minor or superficial health-disease issues that are divorced of the real interests of the people.

Second, the enforcement of special laws (e.g. sanitary codes) can signify the adoption by the health team of a directly coercive role. This is the case with the sanitary regulations (health code) concerning occupational hygiene, health education, etc. Also, in some countries, the administrative organization of the system is itself based on a marked social division of medical work. Thus, what appears as an administrative stratification is in fact a repressive structure in which the activities of the lowest-rank employees (of poor social background) are controlled from above so that their work is separated from their own class interests.

Finally, the most visible repressive mechanisms are projects like the family planning and "nutritional" programs (distribution of cheap dietary protein substitutes) which obtain enormous financial support as means of counterbalancing some of the effects of institutionalized poverty without dealing with its underlying causes. These have been associated with some of the most violent forms of medical state intervention, such as massive sterilization.

So far, we have tried to outline a methodological framework for defining the new medical police. A few comments are now in order to stress that we are not intrinsically questioning the true, technical core of primary-level services; they are indispensable, whatever the context, as a potentially rational resource of a health care system. We are criticizing the ideologically deformed and repressive practices that result from capitalist misuse of this first-stage, basic resource. Our future obligation is to always bear in mind the contradictions inherent in "community medicine," and study every concrete experience with the logic of class analysis.

Briefly, our basic argument in this paper is that the contradictions of advanced capitalism have caused the appearance of a new stage of vigorous development of "police" actions through medicine. It is indispensable to study this phenomenon rigorously in order to understand the socio-historical dynamics which could severely distort our aims, and to prepare an astute and aggressive alternative for community medicine if our desire is to participate as allies of the working people.

As a final summary, we present an outline (Appendix) that highlights the elements that, in our opinion, illustrate the contradictions of "community medicine": the *appearance* of official programs of "community medicine" and their *reality* or actual implications, which we have decided to describe as "the new medical police" under imperialism.

Appendix

"Community" medicine in the capitalist state
(primary care, first contact, simplified medicine)

APPEARANCE (Community Medicine)	*REALITY* (Medical Police)
COST-BENEFIT (SOCIAL BENEFIT) IN MEDICAL SERVICES Primary services • Social savings to achieve universal access to primary services and continuous care of minority populations; • Decrease in morbidity and disability.	COST-BENEFIT (INVESTMENT) FOR CAPITALIST PRODUCTIVITY Stimulate productivity • Investment market expansion: drugs, new equipment, and other (i.e. construction); • Increase in popular productivity and reduction of family waste on "unproductive" expenditures; reorientation of family consumption (health or non-health) to capitalist goods;

Extension of state medicine coverage (integrated system)
• Primary prevention and adequate elementary care;
 	
• First-contact services under regionalized system;
 	
• Service-teaching integration.
	Rationalization of state expenditures for productivity
	• Savings in health resources and reallocation of state funds to the productive sector:
	  a. coverage expansion with exclusively low-cost services (fictitious regionalization);
	  b. use of low or medium qualification or "ad-honorem" personnel (teachers and students) as cheap labor;
	  c. low-cost health actions as palliatives;
	  d. control of social demand (i.e. volume of population).

Income redistribution	State conciliatory moves
	  a. concessions (to the people)— i.e. taxes on the rich;
	  b. coercive dispositions (against the people), compulsory savings, or "voluntary" (free work) labor projects.

COMMUNITY WELFARE Satisfaction of health needs to promote human well-being; Community participation;	COERCIVE ACTIONS AND LEGITIMIZATION Low-cost "state humanitarian" publicity; "Satisfaction" of social pressures;

Appendix (continued)

APPEARANCE (Community Medicine)	REALITY (Medical Police)
Sanitary control and surveillance;	Formation of disciplinary and political surveillance apparatus. Diversionary organization oriented toward secondary health problems;
Multiprofessional team work;	Reproduction of general social relations;
Family planning;	Overtly repressive actions;
Health education programs.	Promotion of bourgeois or petit-bourgeois ideology.

REFERENCES

1. Rosen, G. *From Medical Police to Social Medicine: Essays on the History of Health Care.* Science History Publications, New York, 1974.
2. Deutscher, I. *Las Raices de la Burocracia.* Editorial Anagrama, Barcelona, 1970.
3. Marx, K. *El capital,* Ed. 4, libro 1, Vol. 1, capítulo XIII, p. 567. Siglo XXI Editores, Mexico, 1975.
4. Poulantzas, N. *Poder politico y clases sociales en el estado capitalista,* Ed. 11, p. 205. Siglo XXI Editores, S.A., Mexico, 1975.
5. Sweezy, P. *Teoria del desarrollo capitalista.* Fondo de Cultura Economica, Mexico, 1974.
6. Bauer, O. *Capitalismo y socialismo en la postguerra; racionalizacion, falsa racionalizacion.* Edit. Espana, Madrid, 1932.
7. Flexner, A. *Medical Education in the United States and Canada.* Carnegie Foundation for the Advancement of Teaching, Bulletin No. 4, New York, 1910.
8. Berliner, H. A larger perspective on the Flexner Report. *Int. J. Health Serv.* 5(4): 573-592, 1975.
9. Navarro, V. Social Class, Political Power and the State, and Their Implications in Health and Medicine. Johns Hopkins University, Baltimore, 1976.
10. Kelman, S. Hacia una economía política de la attención médica. *Inquiry* 8(3), 1973 (translated from English).
11. The Community Health Centre in Canada—Publication of the Canadian Health Centre Project. Community Health Centre Project Committee, 1972.
12. Report on Health Manpower Education. Carnegie Foundation for the Advancement of Teaching, New York, 1970.
13. Lathem, W., and Newberry, A. *Community Medicine, Teaching, Research and Health Care,* Ed. 1. Appleton-Century-Crofts, New York, 1970.
14. Politica sectorial de salud, Banco Mundial, Washington, D.C., 1975.
15. Foucault, M. *Vigilar y castigar.* Siglo XXI Editores S.A., Mexico, 1976.

PART 3

Critiques of Malthusian and Neo-Malthusian Population Theories and Their Political Function

CHAPTER 8

Population Growth—
A Menace to What?

Erland Hofsten

The United Nations designated 1974 as the World Population Year. Now that the year is ended, we can appraise its events and, in particular, evaluate one of the year's highlights, the World Population Conference, which was held in Bucharest in August 1974.

There was a time, only a few years ago, when numerous organizations and individuals in the Western world maintained that birth control in the less-developed countries was extremely important and that, consequently, family planning measures should be given top priority. Then-President Lyndon B. Johnson's remark that $5 spent on family planning was worth more than $100 spent on development was often quoted. The main problems were finding new and better contraceptives, distributing them efficiently, and persuading reluctant governments of the expediency of family planning.

Many of the initiators of the World Population Conference no doubt hoped that the Conference would demonstrate a final breakthrough of family planning ideas in all countries of the world and would result both in many new ideas about family planning and in vast resources to be spent on such programs.

Nothing of that sort came out of the Conference. Instead, it was admitted that family planning programs do not work in isolation. No longer was Lyndon Johnson's remark quoted approvingly. A typical change of mind was that of John D. Rockefeller III, a man who for many years had shown strong interest in family planning, e.g. through his support of the Population Council. In a lecture at Bucharest, however, he admitted that he had changed his mind and had come to the conclusion that population policy works only "within the context of general economic and social development." There were many similar statements from the Conference discussions and documents.

Insofar as it is now accepted that development is the primary factor and that family planning will work only within the context of development, the Bucharest Conference can be considered an important step forward. But will the resolutions passed in Bucharest change the world in any fundamental respects? Henceforth, will rapid development take place in all "developing" countries? It is most doubtful.

THE WORLD POPULATION PLAN OF ACTION

Among the documents adopted by the United Nations Conference, the Plan of Action is no doubt the most significant. At Bucharest it was soon discovered that the draft presented to the Conference required considerable rewriting, and at one stage of the Conference proceedings it seemed doubtful whether any plan of action would come out of the Conference at all. Consequently, a certain amount of euphoria spread among the delegates when it was finally agreed that all delegations except one (the Vatican) could accept the final version. But do the Plan's 108 odd paragraphs really contain anything of fundamental importance?

As with all other UN documents the Plan is written to please everyone. Thus, it is vague, wordy, and oblique. Moreover, it is full of contradictions. In its entirety it may not please anyone, yet everyone could selectively quote and use paragraphs in appropriate contexts.

One point made in the Plan which I consider to be of importance is the strong emphasis on the necessity for action in order to promote rapid social and economic development in the less-developed countries. The Plan states further that neocolonialism continues to be among the greatest obstacles to progress, and that woman should have the right to a complete integration in the development process. Statements of this kind are important and deserve to be quoted and receive wide circulation. However, regarding population per se, there are in fact few statements in the Plan of Action that merit attention. They are either vague or have a more or less self-evident content; for example, those paragraphs in which it is stated that mortality—and in particular infant mortality—should be further reduced.

In the documents distributed prior to the Conference, the impression was created that the main aim of the upcoming meeting was to express the opinion that the population of the world, as well as the population of most individual countries—particularly the developing countries—was growing too rapidly and that measures were needed to check this growth. Nothing of this sort can be found in the final version of the Plan of Action. It contains only vacuous phrases of the type that countries that consider their present or expected rates of population growth to be hampering their goals of promoting human welfare are invited to consider adopting a population policy. It is not even clear whether "population policy" implies reduced or promoted population growth. And who can make anything out of a paragraph which states that in many parts of the world couples have more children than they want, while in others they have less than they want?

Not all paragraphs are so obscure. It must have been somewhat difficult to reach unanimity about a paragraph in which it is stated that all countries should respect and ensure "the right of persons to determine, in a free, informed and responsible manner, the number and spacing of their children." This wording implies that family planning as a principle is accepted. Not even this is a novelty, however. In toto, nearly everything said in the Plan of Action has been said before. It is therefore impossible to maintain that the Plan of Action or any of the other documents adopted at Bucharest really imply any original thought. As a result, there has been very little discussion about the conference documents following their distribution.

This is unfortunate, because the subject matter discussed at Bucharest *is* of great importance. It is no exaggeration to say that the problem of development of the less-developed countries is the most important issue of our time, and population growth remains one of the fundamental aspects of social and economic development. In light of the importance of the issues discussed at the Conference, let us consider the topic of population growth in detail.

THE FOUR IDEOLOGIES

It seems possible to discern four different ideologies in the area of population growth: the moral, the nationalist, the neo-Malthusian, and the anti-imperialist.

According to the *moral ideology* all use of contraceptives is immoral. Sexual life is accepted only within marriage and only for the purpose of producing offspring. In marriage, the concept of "safe periods" of fertility possibly is acceptable. Sterilization and abortion are, of course, unacceptable. The fact that the Vatican was the only delegation at Bucharest that refused to accept the Plan of Action demonstrates that the moral ideology position has lost ground.

The *nationalist ideology* expresses itself in favor of a large population and, consequently, also for rapid population growth. Governments of some of the more important countries in Latin America adhere to this position, and there are also many African countries whose governments maintain that their countries ought to have much larger populations. Although it is no doubt true that there are countries that could benefit from larger populations, there is no need to take any special action in this direction; with the present reduced mortality, this will come about anyway. Furthermore, most of those countries showing an interest in a larger population have not really demonstrated the capability to take care of the population they presently have. Thus, the nationalist ideology is unacceptable.

The *neo-Malthusian arguments* are well known. Some of the more common ones include the following:

- The size of world population is (or is rapidly becoming) too large in relation to the size of the earth and its limited resources.
- The developing countries are overpopulated.
- Rapid population growth makes it impossible to achieve satisfactory social and economic progress.
- Industrially developed countries also have a population problem, and should endeavor to attain zero population growth as soon as possible.

The conclusion from these arguments is that all efforts must be concentrated on family planning programs. New and better contraceptives must be devised and be distributed in an efficient way. Sterilization and abortion must also be emphasized.

The *anti-imperialist ideology* criticizes the neo-Malthusian position. It purports that the concept of "overpopulation" is unscientific and that all such expressions as "population explosion," and "population bomb" should be avoided. It has become so popular to speak about the importance of family planning because this creates the impression that the chief reason why there is so much poverty, unemployment, large slum areas in too rapidly expanding cities, and slow economic development is because there are "too many people." But population must not be blamed for the diseases of society.

The overpopulation concept has been criticized by Karl Marx and Friedrich Engels (1-3). Their main argument was that it is impossible to speak about any generally applicable "law of population"; every historical mode of production has its population law. According to Malthus, there will always be a tendency for the population to grow more rapidly than its means of subsistence. It is correct that under the capitalist system there is capital accumulation, thanks to the surplus value derived from the labor of workers, and that this accumulation creates a relative overpopulation which becomes manifest in the form of unemployment. But it is the mode of production that must be changed; with a new mode of production the relation between population and the means of subsistence would be entirely different.

Adherents of the neo-Malthusian ideology often have spoken of the "unholy alliance" between the anti-imperialist ideology on the one hand and the moral-nationalist ideology on the other. It has been maintained that both positions imply a denial of the use of contraceptives. This is not true. The essence of the anti-imperialist ideology is that it denies the possibility to achieve anything through family planning measures. This does not imply that those who want to limit the number of their children should be denied the use of contraceptives or access to abortion or sterilization. Population control as a policy measure directed toward everyone must be sharply distinguished from the right of the individual to have access to family planning measures. Furthermore, the anti-imperialist ideology does not imply a denial that the population in a country or an area may become too large or may grow too rapidly. A relevant quotation in this connection is the following one from a letter from Engels to Karl Kautsky, the well-known Austrian Marxist, in 1881 (3, p.108):

> There is, of course, the abstract possibility that the number of people will become so great that limits have to be set to their increase. But if at some stage communist society finds itself obliged to regulate the production of human beings, . . . it will be precisely this society, and this society alone which can carry this out without difficulty.

FAMILY PLANNING IN CHINA

It is well known that contraceptives are in widespread use in the People's Republic of China, and that limiting the number of births is considered part of China's development efforts. Consequently, some information and conclusions about the population growth and the outlook on population problems in China are of considerable interest. The following is primarily based on articles written by Han Suyin, gynecologist by profession and an eminent expert on China (4, 5). Her views are supplemented by information I gathered during a visit to China in November 1974.

During the first period after liberation in 1949, the official attitude in China was in favor of rapid population growth. After a few years, however, the government reversed its position and began talking about the necessity of limiting the number of births. During the Campaign of the 100 Flowers in 1957 there was a countrywide campaign favoring family planning, but the campaign died during the Great Leap Forward movement in 1958, presumably because there was a strong resistance among the peasants, to whom the ideas of birth control were foreign. It was later admitted that the first campaign had very little effect.

The campaign that began in 1962 is still going on. The propaganda favors late marriages as well as limiting the number of births to two per family. Premarital sex and illegitimate births are virtually unknown. Pills of the Chinese type seem to be the most commonly used contraceptive, but other methods, such as intrauterine devices and condoms, are also in wide use and are freely available. Abortion and sterilization are also important factors.

In China there is an efficient system for current registration of both the resident population and the number of births. Although no comprehensive data about the total number of births for the country as a whole or for main regions have been released, data for individual cities or districts are available. They demonstrate that the campaign has been amazingly efficient. For example, in Kweilin in southern China, the present birth rate is given as 13 per 1000 of population for the city proper and 17 per 1000 for the suburban area. For Shanghai the birth rate was 39 per 1000 in 1952, 23.5 in 1962, and 6.4 in 1972. The last figure is presumably extreme. If it were typical, the Chinese would soon have to stop the campaign in order to avoid a rapid population decline and an unfavorable age distribution in the future. However, for rural areas the birth rate no doubt still remains high.

The Cultural Revolution in China has, among other things, implied that the contacts between rural and urban populations have become much more intense than before. The consequence must be that the family planning ideas have spread rapidly and have become accepted among the rural population. To illustrate this conclusion, when television people in Shanghai were asked whether they produced any programs on family planning, they answered that there was no need for such programs, because everyone was already well informed about family planning.

The Chinese arguments in favor of family planning are not that rapid population growth as such is wrong, for they claim that it is possible to achieve economic growth much more rapidly than population growth. Rather it is that because main parts of China are already so densely populated further population growth in these areas would be disadvantageous. Therefore, population growth is considered favorable in the sparsely populated areas of China. In the outlying areas of China the minority peoples especially are encouraged to give birth to more children than they now do.

There can be no doubt that the People's Republic of China has succeeded in achieving economic, social, and cultural development. Although there have been certain setbacks, the most well-known one occurring during the Great Leap Forward, when bad crops added to the difficulties, those difficulties encountered during the late 1950s are now past history, and current development is very rapid. People are employed, production has been increased, a remarkable school system for children and youth has been organized, and training and studies continue among the entire population.

The Chinese themselves maintain that China is one of the less-developed countries. This is true insofar as productive forces on the whole are not yet very highly developed. There is not much modern industry, and agriculture is to a very large extent carried out with human power, without the aid of tractors or draught-animals. But also in China one finds no signs of mass poverty, unemployment, vast slum areas in too rapidly growing cities, illiteracy, squalor, crime and prostitution—phenomena which are present everywhere in other less-developed countries.

HAVE THE IDEOLOGICAL DIFFERENCES DISAPPEARED?

Returning to the discussion of ideological differences with regard to population growth, we find that the moral-nationalist ideology no longer plays any major role, that the neo-Malthusianist ideology accepts that population programs do not work in isolation but must be combined with development programs, and that, for example, the People's Republic of China has accepted family planning as part of its development program. Does this mean that there are no more important ideological differences in the field of population? I think not. The ideological split between neo-Malthusian and anti-imperialist ideologies no doubt persists and is in reality quite sharp.

The neo-Malthusian position still implies that population growth is considered a primary issue. Social reforms are considered necessary not for their own sake, but rather in order to achieve population control. It is not recognized that much more thorough changes of society are needed than those that can be classified under the heading of social reforms. It is the distribution of economic wealth and of political and economic power that is at stake. Talk of family planning serves to hide this fact.

THE FUTURE OF THE LESS-DEVELOPED COUNTRIES

Population statistics for many countries are not satisfactory, but a UN data source (6) puts the present world population at some 4 billion people, with an annual rate of increase of about 2 per cent. The same source gives the breakdowns shown in Table 1.

Table 1

World population in 1973 and annual rate of increase[a]

Area	Population in Billions	Rate of Increase
		%
Developed countries (Europe, North America, Oceania, U.S.S.R., and Japan)	1.1	0.8
China	0.8	1.7
Other less-developed countries	2.1	2.7

[a] Source, reference 6.

With regard to the developed countries, the tendency for the increase rate is in the downward direction. If it were not for the demographic momentum, the rate of increase would be considerably lower, and in many countries a complete stop to population growth can soon be expected. Concerning China, the rate given in Table 1 is probably too high; in any case, a much lower growth rate is expected in the near future. For the other less-developed countries, the growth rate estimate of 2.7 per cent is rather low. It is known that in many of these countries the present growth rate is 3-3.5 per cent.

There are many less-developed countries that could doubtless feed a population considerably larger than their present one. It should be remembered that the total population of Africa and Latin America combined is less than 700 million, compared with 800 million for China alone. Thus, it cannot be maintained that population growth as such makes economic progress impossible to achieve. On the contrary, population growth in many cases may actually stimulate progress. Rapid population growth certainly did not hamper economic growth in the United States during the 19th and the early 20th centuries.

One should not forget, however, that there are many countries where the population is already quite dense. This is especially true in Asia, but if the present rate of increase continues, many of the now sparsely populated countries in Africa and Latin America will soon attain fairly dense populations. In the long run then, continued population increase at the present rate is out of question.

Family planning programs in most less-developed countries have largely failed. It is not difficult to understand why this is so. In order for it to be possible to encourage the individual family to accept and make use of contraceptives or for one of the spouses to undergo sterilization, the family must have the desire to limit their number of children. That this is not so has been shown in many surveys. Two recent surveys in Nigeria and Ghana showed that women considered six children the ideal family size and that many wanted an even higher number of children (7). On the basis of information collected in India, Mamdani (8) has demonstrated that in Indian villages children are considered not as an economic burden but rather as an asset.

If the usual family planning programs will not work, politicians and administrators of these programs will have to resort to coercive measures. Lately, there have been a number of reports of a tendency in this direction, e.g. in the form of experiments with contraceptives added to drinking water or salt. Sterilization festivals in some states in India were intended to function in such a way as to force people to accept sterilization. However, it was soon discovered that these had an opposite effect; people became frightened, and after the festivals it was even more difficult to encourage them to use contraceptives. As a consequence, sterilization festivals have been discontinued. Other similar measures presumably will meet a similar fate. That coercive measures are contrary to the UN principles quoted above is obvious.

The present rapid population growth in the less-developed countries is a consequence of a heavy decline in mortality and in particular in infant mortality. That it has been possible to achieve this reduction must of course be considered a success. Sooner or later a mortality decline must be followed by a fertility decline. For technical demographic reasons (the "demographic momentum"), a period of reduced mortality must be followed by a period of rapid population growth, even if the decline in fertility follows immediately upon the mortality decline.

Not long ago infant and child mortality was so high that individual families knew they must have many children, in order that at least a few would survive. Because the reduction in mortality is still new and it no doubt will take a certain amount of time before families react to this, the fact that more children survive than before may result in a wish for a reduced number of births. Whether this wish is strong enough to result in a rapidly reduced number of children or whether the reduction will be a limited one remains to be seen.

It is sometimes said that what is possible in China should be possible in other countries as well. China is even sometimes considered as a model for other less-developed countries (9).

Earlier it was stated that the Bucharest Conference implied a general acceptance of the opinion that family planning programs do not work unless they are part of a development program. To what extent, then, is there development in the "developing" countries apart from China? The sad truth is that there is very little real economic and social development. The most misleading idea of our time is that present development programs for the countries of the Third World are leading them to rapid social and economic development. Insofar as there is economic growth (and there are a number of countries for which the growth figures are satisfactory), the growth is largely absorbed by a small but rapidly growing upper class. Some people now indulge in expectation with regard to the effect of the "New International Economic Order." But if the resolution on this subject as adopted by the UN Assembly in May 1974 is examined (10), we will discover one paragraph in which it is stated that foreign investment, both public and private, from developed to developing countries, should be promoted (II/2/e). Another paragraph states that "developed countries should encourage investors to finance industrial production projects, particularly export-oriented production, in developing countries" (III/b).

There is ample evidence demonstrating the fact that private investment from developed to developing countries has resulted in a distorted economic development that does not favor the masses of the population. Instead, it aids the rise of industry that favors the upper classes and thus promotes the generation of widening class differences (11).

However, it is true that in a number of countries, or perhaps rather in limited areas of many countries, continued population growth at the present rate of increase will soon create an intolerable situation. Or rather, in order to avoid a neo-Malthusian type of argument, let us say that the present intolerable condition, because of the population growth, will affect a larger number of people.

Less rapid population growth does not guarantee any remedy; furthermore, it is unrealistic to believe in a substantial fertility decline until society has undergone a very thorough transformation. Thus, it is concluded that population growth implies a menace to the present form of society.

REFERENCES

1. Marx, K. *Capital*, Vol. 1. Lawrence & Wishart, London, 1970 (original German edition,1867).
2. Engel, F. *Outline of a Critique of Political Economy* (original German edition, 1844). Quoted in Meek, R.L. *Marx and Engels on the Population Bomb,* Ed. 2. Ramparts Press, Berkeley, California, 1971.
3. Meek, R.L. *Marx and Engels on the Population Bomb,* Ed. 2. Ramparts Press, Berkeley, California, 1971.
4. Han Suyin. Population growth and birth control in China. *The Conference Board Record,* pp. 51-57, October 1973.
5. Han Suyin. The Chinese experiment. *UNESCO Courier,* pp. 52-55, July-August 1974.
6. *Demographic Yearbook 1973.* United Nations, New York, 1974.
7. Gaisie, S. K. Determinants of Population Growth in Ghana. Unpublished Ph.D. dissertation, Australian National University, 1973.
8. Mamdani, M. *The Myth of Population Control: Family Caste and Class in an Indian Village.* Monthly Review Press, New York and London, 1972.
9. Population and Family Planning in the People's Republic of China. Pamphlet issued by the Victor Bostrom Fund and the Population Crisis Committee, Washington, D.C., 1971.
10. *Problems of Raw Materials and Development. Declaration and Program of Action.* United Nations Center for Economic and Social Information, New York, 1974.
11. Hamid, N. Alternative development strategies. *Monthly Review,* pp. 31-52, October 1974.

CHAPTER 9

An Historical Sketch of the American Population Control Movement

Bonnie Mass

THE ODYSSEY OF REVEREND MALTHUS

At the start of the 19th century, Reverend Thomas Robert Malthus predicted that, because of rapid population increase, Britain would soon suffer widespread starvation, degeneration of morality, and political turmoil. He assumed that multiplication of the impoverished, rather than an abrupt transition toward industrialization, was responsible for growing social disorder. Malthus evoked the French Revolution of 1789, where the lower classes had violently obtained "unrestrained liberties," as a lesson for the British aristocracy, maintaining that if the French example were to incite Britain's discontented lower classes, chaos was inevitable. The few pennies grudgingly handed to the urban poor had to be reduced, he believed, since charity encouraged the indigent to multiply:

> The poor-laws of England tend to depress the general condition of the poor in these two ways. Their first obvious tendency is to increase population without increasing the food for its support. A poor man may marry with little or no prospect of being able to support a family without parish assistance. . . . Secondly, the quantity of provisions consumed in work-houses upon a part of society that cannot be considered the most valuable part diminishes the shares that would otherwise belong to more industrious and more worthy members, and, thus, in the same manner, forces more to become dependent (1).

Malthus' *Essay on the Principle of Population* and his economic treatises retained a degree of popularity until the 1840s, but Britain's elite ultimately forgot the dire warnings which he had issued at the beginning of the century. The deep crisis which Malthus had originally predicted was averted, owing to such factors as continuing emigration and, particularly, expansion of industrialization and foreign trade. Whereas Malthus had foreseen shrinkage of the empire's resources as a consequence of population growth, Britain's wealth and its colonial dependencies grew throughout the 19th century.

A new generation of economists and social theorists, which included Karl Marx and Friedrich Engels, soon uncovered the falseness of Malthus' assumption that Britain's productive capacities had reached their maximum limit prior to the Napoleonic Wars. Moreover, such works as Charles Darwin's *Origin of Species* (1860) served to refute Malthus' fundamental "scientific" principle that human numbers expand geometrically while food supplies increase only arithmetically.[1]

Nonetheless, more than a century after the eclipse of Malthus' ideas, predictions of a deepening gap between human numbers and productive capacities are being made again. Despite their dubious scientific basis, views derived from Malthus nourish frequent and simplistic pleas that worldwide population planning be implemented. Population increase patterns are seldom discussed in relation to the complex interplay among social and economic conditions, and, similarly, the influence of those conditions upon neo-Malthusian trends is often ignored.

Inevitably, the question arises as to why, after protracted dormancy, Malthus' discredited principles have been revived. The question acquires particular interest with respect to 1974, which the United Nations officially termed World Population Year. Study of the "Population Establishment," or those who currently shape population control programs, can greatly aid comprehension of fears that population growth has now assumed explosive proportions. Because agencies based in the United States have occupied a leading role in population planning, this article will concentrate upon the complex political and economic motivations of those agencies and their financial sponsors.

THE ROLE OF THE EUGENICS MOVEMENT

During the first decades of the 20th century, after Malthus' views had been nearly forgotten, many "captains of industry" in the United States and other industrialized nations were strongly pro-natalist. Development of new manufacturing techniques, new products, and new markets seemed endless and nourished a belief that temporary problems related to unemployment and impoverishment could ultimately be alleviated by such phenomena as continued immigration to the Americas and to European settler colonies in Asia and Africa.

In the United States, where high demand for labor dictated an open-door policy on immigration from Europe, eugenics first emerged as a small Anglo-Saxon nativist current. Like their immediate predecessors, the social Darwinists, eugenicists defended industrial capitalism in terms of "survival of the fittest." The "unfit," or the indigent, were to be

---

[1] Readers interested in a compact collection of refutations of Malthusian "principles" by Karl Marx and Friedrich Engels may consult *Marx and Engels on the Population Bomb* (2).

weeded out and the affluent or "gifted" were to be encouraged to breed selectively so that the "human stock" could be improved.[2]

Increasingly, members of the most privileged layers of American society became interested in eugenics, especially as birth rates among Anglo-Saxon families began to decline. In his 1906 State of the Union Message, President Theodore Roosevelt evoked the dangers of "wilful sterility . . . the one sin for which the penalty is national death, race death" (4).

Two years prior to Roosevelt's speech, the wealthy industrialist Andrew Carnegie had established the first eugenics "data center," the Station for Experimental Evolution in Washington, D.C. In 1909, the Harriman dynasty created the Eugenics Record Office, which continued to exist until 1953. In 1913, on the eve of World War I, the Kellogg dynasty, in Battle Creek, Michigan, opened the well-known Race Betterment Foundation in order to lobby for a "policy of national eugenics," and, in the same year, the movement's growing popularity was indicated by establishment of the American Genetic Association, which commenced publication of the widely distributed *Journal of Heredity*.

When World War I ended, a wave of Anglo-Saxon xenophobia and anti-labor agitation swept the United States, and the eugenics movement became even stronger. Recent immigrants, many of whom had been influenced by the socialist movement in Europe or had enthusiastically joined the most active wing of the American labor movement, the Industrial Workers of the World, became a primary target of right-wing demagoguery. With the Russian Revolution of 1917 and the postwar instability of Southern and Eastern Europe, nativist agitators intensified their demands for ending the open-door policy on immigration. Similarly, in the Deep South, states were encouraged to pass laws prohibiting interracial marriage and to fortify the "Jim Crow" system of blatant discrimination against Blacks.

Works such as Madison Grant's *Passing of the Great Race* (1918), whose preface was written by the respected naturalist Henry Fairfield Osborn, popularized the "race suicide theory." Increasingly, it was argued that immigration restrictions and reduction of the numbers of the "unfit" were required for offsetting falling birth rates among Americans of Anglo-Saxon origin.

The new mood was deeply reflected in the writings and activities of Margaret Sanger, who had become famous before World War I for her advocacy of birth control as a means of liberating women from male oppression.[3] Now, she began to argue that birth control

---

[2] Useful articles on the early development of the American eugenics movement and on Margaret Sanger's close collaboration with prominent eugenicists are, respectively, Gar Allen's "A History of Eugenics in the Class Struggle" (3) and Linda Gordon's "The Politics of Population: Birth Control and the Eugenics Movement," published in *Radical America*, Volume 8, July-August 1974.

[3] Before World War I, Margaret Sanger had been actively associated with both the feminist movement and the socialist movement in the United States. In 1914, she briefly published a magazine entitled *The Woman Rebel*, whose issues included articles by the anarchist leader Emma Goldman. Mrs. Sanger's own articles at that time sharply criticized the feminist movement for its irrelevance to working-class women. In 1916, Mrs. Sanger was briefly imprisoned for having opened a birth control clinic in Brooklyn, New York. Thereafter, she sought to produce another magazine entitled *Family Limitation* in order to circumvent postal censorship, but soon decided that the term "birth control" possessed a potentially broader appeal than "family limitation." In her *Autobiography* (5), Mrs. Sanger wrote: "My idea of control was bigger, and we wanted family in it, yet family control did not sound right. We tried population control, race control, and birth rate control. Finally someone suggested 'Drop the rate.' Birth control was the answer."

could limit the number of children among the "unfit." Her own journal, the *Birth Control Review*, commenced regular publication of articles by prominent believers in eugenics, and in 1920 Mrs. Sanger herself wrote *Woman and the New Race*, a work that called for immigration restrictions.

During this period, one of Mrs. Sanger's closest collaborators, both on the *Birth Control Review* and in the American Birth Control League, was Guy Irving Burch, a director of the American Eugenics Society and a leader in the American Coalition of Patriotic Societies. Burch was also principal lobbyist for the National Committee on Federal Legislation for Birth Control, and he later established the Population Reference Bureau, which became a major supplier of eugenics and demographic data. In his opinion, support for birth control served the aim of "preventing the American people from being replaced by alien or Negro stock, whether it be by immigration or by overly high birth rates among others in this country" (6).

Burch's outlook was shared by such co-directors of the American Birth Control League as Lothrop Stoddard (7):

> But what about the inferiors? Hitherto, we have not analyzed their attitude [on birth control]. We have seen that they are incapable of either creating or furthering civilization and are not mere negative factors in civilized life; they are also positive—in an inverse, destructive sense. The inferior elements are, instinctively or consciously, the enemies of civilization. And they are its enemies not by chance, but because they are more or less uncivilizable.

Thus, increased interchange between the eugenics movement and the birth control movement of the 1920s permitted the latter to become a secondary podium for adherents of the "race suicide theory." At the Sixth International Neo-Malthusian and Birth Control Conference in New York in 1925, for example, panels on eugenics comprised a major portion of the proceedings.

During the same period, members of both movements also began to express alarm over demographic trends within the colonial world. Warren Thompson, a director of the Scripps Foundation for the Study of Population and a regular contributor to the *Birth Control Review*, visited China and other regions of the Orient and subsequently published *Danger Spots in World Population in 1929*. Thompson's concern with "population powder kegs" won international acclaim, and, during the 1930s, he and other scholars continued to warn of future perils in Asia. During the decade after World War I, the birth control movement had proved highly receptive to eugenicists' viewpoints and had abandoned its earlier promotion of birth control as a contribution to women's emancipation. Despite this transformation, however, the severe effects of the Great Depression temporarily forestalled unification of the eugenics movement and neo-Malthusianism. Whereas revival of Malthus' dire prophecies could be expected during a period of worldwide economic crisis and labor unrest, many eugenicists retained a pro-natalist outlook with regard to "superior" races living in North America and Western Europe. Because of falling birth rates in those regions, it was still not uncommon to encounter predictions consistent with the "race suicide" theory:

> What will be the result of this clash of low and high birth rate nations in the future world? In the last analysis, numbers will count.... If the people of Russia, of India, of China continue to people the earth, will they not in all probability be the dominating influence in it? (8).

> The low birth-rate nations ought to form a league . . . even though the low birth-rate
> nations control the raw materials without which industrial and military strength is
> impossible, they cannot retain this control if their populations dwindle (9).

When Depression conditions worsened and worldwide opposition to Hitler's "eugenic" faith in Aryan superiority grew, some leaders of the American eugenics movement became less sure of how to advocate their demands. On at least one occasion, Margaret Sanger indicated that the birth control movement was a superior vehicle for stimulating public interest in halting "dysgenic" trends:

> Eugenics without birth control seemed to me a house built upon sands. It could not
> stand against the furious winds of economic pressure which had buffeted into partial or
> total helplessness a tremendous proportion of the human race. The eugenicists wanted to
> shift the birth control emphasis from less children for the poor to more children for the
> rich. We went back of that and sought first to stop the multiplication of the unfit (5, p.
> 120).

Gains in the birth control movement elsewhere[4] encouraged Mrs. Sanger and her colleagues in the United States to adopt new strategies for winning public support. For example, a concerted campaign by birth control advocates during the early 1930s ultimately resulted in judicial decisions that overruled laws prohibiting distribution of contraceptives and birth control information. Concurrently, the American Birth Control League undertook campaigns to win endorsement from Protestant and Jewish leaders in order to counterbalance Catholic opposition.

Whereas the birth control movement's earlier publicity had often relied upon "pure" neo-Malthusian arguments, emphasis was now placed upon ostensible virtues of the small, planned family unit. This thematic change partially reflected recognition of a decline in American birth rates since the turn of the century, and it readily awakened interest among eugenicists who increasingly understood that the birth control movement could be utilized for checking multiplication of the "unfit." In 1940, Frederick Osborn, who later became a vice-president of the Population Council, concisely expressed the eugenicists' fear that ". . . today, resentment on the subject of hereditary classes is very near the surface" (12).

Population control's potential usefulness to schemes of economic and political oppression was most dramatically demonstrated during the 1930s in the impoverished American possession of Puerto Rico. There, the Nationalist Party was vigorously demanding independence from the United States. In 1936, while the American military

---

[4] In the British Isles, as the first three chapters of R. Symonds' and M. Carder's *The United Nations and the Population Question* (10) indicate, neo-Malthusian organizations during the 1920s and 1930s had gained a substantially broader level of support than their American counterparts. One indication of the British population control movement's popularity was its endorsement by the noted economist John Maynard Keynes, who praised Malthus' *Essay on the Principle of Population* as being "profoundly in the English tradition of humane science . . . a tradition marked by a love of truth and a most noble lucidity" (11).

Britain's domestic policies remained officially pro-natalist, but in British-ruled India the world's first government-sponsored birth control clinic was opened in 1930 in the impoverished state of Mysore. Despite Mohandas K. Gandhi's opposition to birth control, significant layers of the native elite adopted neo-Malthusian views, and, in 1935, the Congress Party established a special subcommittee to contemplate post-independence birth control programs for all parts of India (10, pp. 8-9).

undertook a campaign to crush the Nationalist Party, the Roosevelt Administration's newly appointed governor, Ernest Gruening, actively attempted to incorporate family planning within health programs of the Puerto Rican Reconstruction Administration.

Although complaints from the Catholic hierarchy in the United States temporarily compelled Gruening to abandon his efforts, the Puerto Rican legislature, in 1937, voted to authorize large-scale population control programs. The programs, which included sterilization and distribution of contraceptives, became so extensive that, in later years, American advocates of neo-Malthusianism often invoked Puerto Rico as a model that could be widely emulated. By 1949, sterilizations were being performed in 17.8 per cent of all hospital deliveries on the island, and, in one survey, 21 per cent of the women interviewed had undergone sterilization (13, 14).

Because of its broad appeal during the Depression years, the birth control movement in the United States began to undertake significant structural changes. In 1939, the Birth Control Federation of America was established to provide a centralized organizational framework for the movement, and in 1940, at the Federation's annual conference, Henry Pratt Fairchild, the former president of the American Eugenics Society, spoke glowingly of a possible merger between the eugenics and birth control movements:

> One of the outstanding features of the present conference is the practically universal acceptance of the fact that these two great movements, eugenics and birth control, have now come to such a thorough understanding and have drawn so close together as to be almost indistinguishable (15).

In 1940 and 1941 the Birth Control Federation sponsored symposia on such topics as "Race Building in a Democracy" and "Strengthening Our Population for National Defense." In 1942, its name was changed to Planned Parenthood Federation, and Margaret Sanger was designated honorary chairman of the new organization.

The merging of the birth control and eugenics movements at this point was indicated not only in Planned Parenthood's statements of purpose, but also in the composition of its leadership. The first board of directors included the former presidents of both the American Eugenics Society and the Race Betterment Conference. From such roots came a deeper and continuing commitment to prevent the impoverished from multiplying, a commitment amply demonstrated by the Population Establishment's growth and activities since 1942.

DWINDLING RESOURCES AND THE RISE OF NATIONALISM

As World War II concluded, leading American financial and industrial figures boldly dreamed of penetrating the postwar economies of Europe and the colonial world, but they comprehended events in Eastern Europe and the rise of nationalism in Asia and Africa as significant obstacles. To ambitious American policy makers, growing demands for independence from colonial rule implied such possible "dangers" as confiscation of foreign investment and limitation of access to precious raw materials and pools of cheap labor. In response to these and other challenges to American hegemony, the basic strategies of the Cold War were being formulated within the United States even as political figures throughout the world advanced the hope of an unprecedented era of peace.

At the same time, supporters of the family planning movement in the United States were quickly adapting their perspectives and activities to new international realities, including the after-effects of World War II upon food production throughout the world. In October 1946 their efforts were encouraged by the United Nations' acceptance of a joint Anglo-American proposal for a Population Commission to examine international demographic trends. Moreover, private agencies within the United States began to display increased interest in population questions (10, pp. 33-51). The Milbank Memorial Fund, which had funded the eugenics-oriented Office of Population Research in 1936, began to play a particularly prominent role. In order to foster development of a global approach to demographic issues, the Fund sponsored round-table discussion series for federal officials, economic planners, and United Nations personnel. The Fund's 1947 Conference featured a roundtable entitled "International Approaches to Problems of Underdeveloped Countries," and participants included such important United Nations officials as Ralph Bunche (Director, UN Division of Trusteeship), Henri Laugier (UN Division of Social Activities), and Sir Raphael Cilento (UN Division of Social Activities). Also among the participants were prominent American eugenicists and demographers, including Henry Pratt Fairchild (American Eugenics Society, Planned Parenthood Federation), Warren S. Thompson (Scripps Foundation), and Frank W. Notestein (Director, Office of Population Research) (16).

These private efforts were accompanied by the establishment in 1948 of the International Planned Parenthood Federation (IPPF), whose new London headquarters were donated by the English Eugenics Society. At its founding conference in Cheltenham, England, the IPPF adopted a resolution which strongly echoed Reverend Malthus:

> In view of the present world food crisis, due in part to the growing pressure of global population on food and other resources, control of population increase is one of the essential measures whereby real progress towards peace and prosperity can be made . . . (10, p. 103).

Within the United Nations, however, debate continued over demographic theories and preparation of statistical information. Accordingly, Sir Julian Huxley, Director-General of the United Nations Economic and Social Council, sounded a note of alarm in his annual report of 1948: "Somehow or other, population must be balanced against resources, or civilization will perish. War is a less inevitable threat to civilization than is population increase" (10, p. 54).

At this time, the upheavals sweeping China and other Asian nations significantly stimulated concern with "danger spots" in world population. As the peoples of Asia rebelled against mass starvation and impoverishment resulting from colonialism and backward feudal structures which American leaders hoped to maintain, vigorous efforts were made to convince the American public that international communism and "overpopulation" were fomenting disorder. For example, in the preface to the White Paper explaining the overthrow of Chiang Kai Shek in China, Secretary of State Dean Acheson wrote:

> The population of China during the eighteenth and nineteenth centuries doubled, thereby creating an unbearable pressure upon the land. The first problem which every Chinese government has had to face is that of feeding this population. So far none has succeeded. . . . In no small measure the predicament in which the National Government

finds itself today is due to its failure to provide China with enough to eat. A large part of the Chinese Communists' propaganda consists of promises that they will solve the land problem (17).

For the mass audience, similar notions were advanced by William Vogt's widely distributed *Road to Survival*, published in 1949 (18). For Vogt, "the major threat in Asia is mounting population pressure in the Soviet Union." Proposing that the United Nations make birth control programs a component of its food distribution activities, he urged that the United Nations "not ship food to keep alive ten million Indians and Chinese this year, so that fifty million may die ten years hence" (18). At IPPF's 1952 Conference in Bombay, where the world's first national family planning program had been initiated one year before, the same theme predominated, and Vogt was a principal speaker (10, pp. 102-105).

During the early 1950s, American leaders became increasingly conscious that prosperity in North America or Western Europe depended heavily upon raw materials from the impoverished or underdeveloped nations. In 1951, the President's International Development Advisory Board estimated that nearly three-quarters of the raw materials needed for military production in the United States were drawn from Asia, Africa, and Latin America. The Board warned:

> . . . it is to these countries that we must look for the bulk of any possible increase in these supplies. The loss of these materials, through aggression, would be the equivalent of a grave military setback (19).

Along with the postwar disparity between world population and food output, fears of widespread commodity shortages accelerated the revival of Malthus' long-outmoded "principles." At this point, however, implementation of large-scale population planning depended upon a significant increase in political support and financial contributions.

During the United States involvement in Korea, which was intended to halt the "spread of communism," American businessmen and political leaders became far more receptive to theories that "excess population" in underdeveloped nations was a primary factor behind popular upsurges. Faced by new challenges to the drive for American hegemony in the postwar world, policy makers now began to define population growth as a serious "threat" to global security.

THE CONQUEST OF PUBLIC OPINION

In the summer of 1952, under the sponsorship of the National Academy of Sciences, John D. Rockefeller III convened a conference of specialists in Williamsburg, Virginia, to establish an international council for population planning. When the Population Council was inaugurated in November 1952, its board of trustees included Rockefeller himself, Frank G. Boudreau of the Milbank Memorial Fund, and Frank W. Notestein of the Office of Population Research, United Nations Population Division.[5] Among the charter members of the Council were such dignitaries as Secretary of Commerce Lewis L. Strauss, Caryl P. Haskins of the Council on Foreign Relations, and General Dwight D. Eisenhower (20).

Creation of the Population Council inspired a dramatic change in the practices of major philanthropic foundations in the United States, which had previously contributed

---

[5] Frederick Osborn, formerly prominent in the eugenics movement, was chosen by Rockefeller as first vice-president of the Population Council. In 1957, he succeeded Rockefeller as its president, and from 1959 until 1968 was chairman of the executive committee (20, p. 467).

only token amounts to family planning and related fields. Between 1952 and 1958, the Population Council's own budget quadrupled, with the Rockefeller family's foundations providing a major portion of funds. Its funds were dispensed on every continent, in keeping with John D. Rockefeller III's belief that "the relationship of population to material and cultural resources of the world represents one of the most crucial and urgent problems of the day" (21).

Despite lavish support from such entities as the Rockefeller, Ford, and Mellon Foundations, the population planning movement continued to face certain obstacles during the fifties. Catholic opposition to forms of contraception other than the rhythm method remained vocal, even though Catholic leaders became increasingly tolerant of the movement's aims. Secondly, few governments had stated official support, and India was one of the few underdeveloped nations that had established a national program. Finally, the United Nations had not officially taken a supportive stance, although several of its agencies were conducting research on world population. Conquest of public opinion therefore became a fundamental goal for the emerging Population Establishment.

Between 1952 and 1954, American advocates of population planning maintained hopes that the United Nations World Population Conference, to be held in Rome in 1954, would serve to legitimate their cause. Accordingly, P. K. Whelpton, who had formerly been associated with the eugenics-oriented Scripps Foundation and had subsequently become head of the United Nations Population Division, played a vital role as chairman of the Preparatory Committee for the conference, which was intended for discussion of world demographic trends. Whelpton was aided by Frank Lorimer, a former staff member of the Milbank Fund's Office of Population Research who had become the American representative to IPPF's board of directors in 1948. Whelpton, Lorimer, and other American participants in the Rome Conference arranged for at least nine papers to be presented by American members of IPPF, and they successfully lobbied for presentation of firsthand reports by delegates from nations where family planning programs had already been established, such as India and Japan (10, pp. 82-86).

In the same year, the neo-Malthusian movement in the United States was momentarily thrown into controversy by the appearance of a brief pamphlet entitled *The Population Bomb* (22).[6] Aimed at the mass audience, *The Population Bomb* cleverly capitalized upon common fears of the mid-fifties, asserting that,

> The population bomb threatens to create an explosion as disruptive and dangerous as explosion of the atom, and with as much influence on prospects for progress or disaster, war or peace (22).

The pamphlet was sponsored by the Hugh Moore Fund, a private foundation established by the chairman of Dixie Cup Corporation. Hugh Moore, having been deeply moved by Vogt's *Road to Survival*, had concluded that population planning was a cause that should be promoted by hard-hitting modern advertising techniques rather than the semi-scholarly tone that had heretofore dominated the movement.[7] The potential of an

[6] The 1954 pamphlet, which was reprinted many times, is not to be confused with Paul Ehrlich's *The Population Bomb* (Ballantine Books, New York, 1968). Ehrlich received permission from the Hugh Moore Fund to borrow the title of the original pamphlet (23).

[7] Thomas Griessemer, the former Dixie Cup executive who wrote *The Population Bomb*, later became head of the New York offices of the International Planned Parenthood Federation. In the mid-sixties, the pamphlet's 12th edition continued to employ an aggressive, sensationalistic approach to readers: "There will be 300 million more mouths to feed in the world four years from now—most of them hungry. Hunger brings turmoil—and turmoil, as we have learned, creates the atmosphere in which the communists seek to conquer the earth" (24).

aggressive approach was soon realized by such veterans as Guy Irving Burch, a former leader of the American Eugenics Society who headed the Population Reference Bureau. At Burch's request, Moore gave lavishly to the Bureau and became chairman of its board of directors. In that capacity, Moore undertook an active fund-raising campaign and persuaded many other business leaders to make substantial financial contributions for the first time (23, pp. 1-37).

Moore's personal efforts to ensure a steady flow of funds to the population planning movement in the United States were, at this time, paralleled by expanded research and personnel training. The Ford Foundation was assuming a leading role in furnishing "seed money" for the creation of population studies centers at leading American universities, and it also became the principal financial source for biomedical research aimed at developing more effective means of contraception, such as the birth control pill.

In 1958, the Ford Foundation chose India as a target area for intensive research in demography, contraceptives, and distribution systems, thereby following in the path of the Population Council, which in 1955 had made a grant to India's Institute of Public Health for a "field study of population control in West Bengal." The Ford Foundation's 1958 grant to India, which totalled $9 million, was designed to assist the national program that had existed since 1951. Subsequently, a similar grant was provided to Pakistan so that a national program in population planning could be started (10, pp. 105, 108-109).

Despite its successes after 1952, the Population Establishment had not yet obtained firm support from federal officials and legislators in the United States. Although the Senate Committee on Foreign Relations had listened favorably in March 1957 to Vogt's pleas for large-scale oral contraceptive programs aimed at underdeveloped countries, there was still no official stance in support of birth control.

However, a dramatic change began in November 1958, when President Dwight D. Eisenhower created the Committee to Study the U.S. Military Assistance Program for a comprehensive review of U.S. foreign assistance programs. The ten-member committee included such dignitaries as General Alfred Gruenther (former Supreme Allied Commander in Europe), Admiral Arthur Radford (Head of the Joint Chiefs of Staff), and John J. McCloy (a former head of the World Bank who had become chairman of both the Chase Manhattan Bank and the Ford Foundation), and its chairman was General William H. Draper, an investment banker who had formerly served as under-secretary of the Army and United States ambassador to the North Atlantic Treaty Organization (13, pp. 36-42).

Shortly after his appointment, General Draper was approached by his personal friend, Hugh Moore, who urged scrutiny of world population trends and arranged for the committee to receive material from the Population Reference Bureau, as well as copies of Moore's *The Population Bomb*. In 1959, the final version of the "Draper Committee's" report specifically endorsed the following: (a) assistance to "developing" countries in establishing programs to check population growth; (b) increased assistance to maternal and child health programs; and (c) support for research programs on population, including research by other countries and the United Nations (13, pp. 40-42; 23, pp. 15-20).

The Draper Committee set a precedent by becoming the first official body of the United States government to call for population control measures. Although its proposals were not openly endorsed by the Eisenhower Administration, officials were privately encouraged to consider population issues more closely, and in November 1959 the Department of State released a study which concluded:

Rapid population growth may prove to be one of the greatest obstacles to economic and social progress and to maintenance of political stability in many of the less developed areas of the world (25).

APPLICATION OF STRATEGIES

The new trend represented by the Draper Committee in 1959 was soon echoed by leading members of the Population Establishment. At the May 1960 National Conference on the Population Crisis in Dallas, Texas, John D. Rockefeller III emphasized the limitations of private efforts on behalf of population planning:

> The problems of population are so great, so important, so ramified and so immediate that only government, supported and inspired by private initiative, can attack them on the scale required. It is for the citizens to convince their political leaders of the need for imaginative and courageous action—action which may sometimes mean political and economic opposition (13, p. 49).

At a 1960 memorial dinner for Margaret Sanger, another plea for government commitment was delivered by Marriner S. Eccles, the former chairman of the Federal Reserve Board who had become a trustee of the Hugh Moore Fund. Citing effects of the economic recession then occurring in the United States, Eccles urged that population restriction be considered not only abroad, but domestically:

> Our total tax load as a percentage of our national income is likely to increase unless there is a drastic reduction in our rate of population growth. Our entire concept of a healthy and happy world at peace, with pestilence and premature death eradicated, is totally unrealistic unless we recognize the severe limitations of population growth which are necessary in the United States as well as the rest of the world (23, p. 58).

Concurrently, Hugh Moore initiated a new campaign to win broader public support for population control. The World Population Emergency Campaign (WPEC) was established in 1960, with a strong orientation toward increasing the public role of the International Planned Parenthood Federation. Even more than other organizations, the WPEC was characterized by strong support from business leaders and the wealthy, due in part to the naming of Lammot du Pont Copeland (vice-president of the du Pont Corporation) and William H. Draper as its co-chairmen (23, pp. 10-14).

Following a year of high-pitched publicity efforts, the WPEC merged with the International Planned Parenthood Federation, and portions of its large "war chest" were used to finance IPPF's overseas work, including reprinting and distribution of *The Population Bomb*. As a trustee of the IPPF, Hugh Moore now turned his attention to the legislative front, hoping that, in the near future, the United States Congress could be persuaded to appropriate funds for population control domestically and internationally. At this time, Congress was particularly preoccupied by challenges to American policy from Cuba and elsewhere in Latin America and, hence, was potentially receptive to proposals for population control.

During the same period, George C. McGhee, a former member of the Draper Committee who had become Policy Planning Director of the United States Department of State, released a new document defining the ability to "control population growth" as a primary component of economic development abroad. This 1961 report recommended that the Department of State undertake such steps as appointment of a full-time population officer, encouragement of population planning within the United Nations, use of foreign aid funds to establish population planning programs in underdeveloped nations, and sponsorship of research by the newly created Agency for International Development (AID).

Establishment of the Alliance for Progress was regarded as a major innovation in foreign assistance, and neo-Malthusian goals were promptly integrated with those of the new showcase program. Its director, Teodoro Moscoso, had been responsible for population planning initiatives in Puerto Rico during the 1950s, and he stimulated AID's Latin American branch to select personnel whose qualifications and orientation would facilitate persuasion of Latin American governments. In 1964, Moscoso obtained approval from the Senate Foreign Relations Committee for the first State Department-financed efforts in Latin America, namely grants to the Pan American Health Organization and to CELADE, a United Nations-sponsored demographic research center based in Chile. Likewise, in 1964 AID and the IPPF jointly sponsored a population conference in Puerto Rico, with representation from each Latin American nation except Cuba[8] (13, pp. 84-86).

The new trend was accompanied by a notable expansion of the Population Establishment's own activities. By 1962, the Ford Foundation alone was furnishing $3 million annually for projects, and it accounted for at least one-third of the Population Council's Funding. The Ford Foundation also maintained a virtual monopoly in financing reproductive biology research, and between 1959 and 1970 it supplied at least $50 million in that field. Grants were issued not only for study of anti-ovulatory agents, but also for perfection of the intrauterine device, with much of the testing being performed in underdeveloped nations (13, pp. 14-15).

In the mere six years since Eisenhower's establishment of the Draper Committee, population planning had become an officially endorsed reality, as the United States sought a better return on its foreign assistance programs. The new outlook was strongly reflected in proposals accepted by AID's December 1, 1964, staff meeting:

> It is proposed that the full complement of assistance tools available to AID be brought to bear on the population problem. This would involve ... provision of commodity inputs (with the exception of contraceptives) ... authorizing releases of counterpart and PL-480 Loans and Grants ... provision of technical assistance. It is clear that private resources in the U.S. cannot alone cope with the demand (13, p. 93).

At the beginning of the Johnson Administration, a new level of operational efficiency had already been obtained in such vital agencies as the Department of Defense and the Agency for International Development, and struggles for national independence in Asia, Africa, and Latin America had greatly intensified. Even the much-praised "European miracle" wrought by the Marshall Plan of 1948 had begun to falter, as industrial growth rates slowed in many European countries. Within this historical context, a redoubled American effort to streamline global security and international development became inevitable, if continued capitalist expansion were to proceed unchecked.

As early as 1963, the Kennedy-appointed "Clay Commission," also known as the Committee to Strengthen the Free World, had proposed reductions of American foreign assistance expenditures. As the Johnson Administration undertook a major military effort in Southeast Asia, appeals for recognizable results from foreign assistance sharply increased. These appeals were often backed by references to the "population explosion" as a factor that was allegedly negating foreign aid's economic and political benefits.

[8] By 1964, Cuba had already begun to implement nationwide economic and social programs which were contributing solutions for demographic problems. In Cuba, means of birth control were made available within the context of broad-based programs in health and women's emancipation.

The new attitude was exemplified in 1965 by Lyndon B. Johnson's statement at the United Nations 20th anniversary ceremonies:

> Let us all in all our lands—including this land—face forthrightly the multiplying problems of our multiplying populations and seek the answers to this most profound challenge to the future of all the world. Let us act on the fact that less than five dollars invested in population control is worth a hundred dollars invested in economic growth (13, p. 90).

The same mood was also visible when the much-publicized "Great Society" programs began in the United States. By late 1965, the newly created Office of Economic Opportunity, in collaboration with Planned Parenthood, was actively establishing birth control clinics and supplying contraceptives in poor urban communities (13, pp. 91-92).

The new trend was greeted with a new publicity campaign under the aegis of the Hugh Moore Fund. The Population Crisis Committee, chaired by William H. Draper after 1965, was created in order to develop "real fire power" in Washington. In his new post, General Draper arranged special briefings for Congressmen on the latest technical advances in contraception and played a leading role during the 1965 Fulbright Committee Hearings on Foreign Aid. In his testimony, Draper warned:

> I have gradually become convinced that unless and until the population explosion now erupting in Asia, Africa, and Latin America is brought under control, our entire economic program is doomed to failure. . . . Rapid population growth is offsetting increased economic resources almost everywhere. Failure to satisfy the revolution of rising expectations is already sowing the seeds of discontent in many countries (23, p. 46).

Fearing social repercussions of the 1965-1966 famine in India and of challenges to American power in Southeast Asia, Moore, Draper, and other members of the Population Establishment began to advocate specific large-scale spending for population control by AID and other agencies. In 1965, an AID task force proposed rigorous modernization of Public Law 480, the "Food for Peace" Act. The new version of Public Law 480 included a provision for "voluntary programs" aimed at population control. Nations willing to institute family planning programs would receive additional amounts of foreign assistance to finance the programs. To this end, the Tydings amendment to Public Law 480 authorized AID to deviate from normal balance of payments restrictions by utilizing foreign currencies instead of dollars to finance other nations' family planning programs.

Concurrently, AID was inaugurating its own Office of Population under Dr. R. T. Ravenholt, so that a series of interdepartmental guidelines could be designed. During this period of transformation, AID's appropriations and expenditures for population control rose sharply, from $2.1 million for fiscal year 1965 to $45.4 million for fiscal year 1969. During the same four-year span, other forms of foreign assistance spending were reduced by 25 per cent (13, pp. 128-138). Clearly, such a phenomenal expansion of funding for population control programs marked a decisive step toward attainment of goals held by the post-World War II neo-Malthusians. At last, "real fire power in Washington" had been obtained.

Shortly after Johnson's historic statement at the UN's 20th anniversary, AID's overseas missions received instructions to inform host countries of American readiness to furnish assistance for family planning projects. In response to the increased flow of funds, the number of nations with official population programs or family planning services grew to more than 25 by late 1966.

The United Nations was soon affected by these changes in American policy. During

1966, Secretary-General U Thant circulated a statement by 12 heads of state who called upon other nations to recognize the growing importance of population planning. As a result, the General Assembly passed a landmark resolution on December 17, 1966, calling upon all bodies and agencies "to assist when requested in further developing and strengthening national and regional facilities for training, research, information, and advisory services in the field of population" (10, p. 214).[9]

Nevertheless, within individual agencies, including the World Health Organization, action remained limited on account of fears that population planning commitments would divert funds from other spheres. For example, the Director-General of WHO, Marcolino Candau, had warned in 1966 that a separate WHO family planning program would require reduction of funds for control of malaria and cholera in underdeveloped nations (10, p. 155).

The reluctance of WHO and other agencies to divert funds from ongoing projects was met by mounting pressure from population control advocates such as John D. Rockefeller III and William H. Draper. If a new separately financed body could be created, then the United Nations could be drawn into a much deeper role in population planning. In July 1967 Secretary-General U Thant established a special trust fund for population activities, open to donations from member governments and private sources. With the creation of the trust fund, there existed for the first time an international mechanism that could foster expanded action by UN agencies, member governments, and the traditional components of the Population Establishment.

CONSOLIDATION OF THE MULTILATERAL APPROACH

Despite its long-range implications, the trust fund for population activities initially faced severe limitations because of difficulties in securing contributions from a wide variety of sources. During 1967-1968, at least one-third of its funds were supplied by the Agency for International Development, and other American sources furnished a large portion of the remainder (10, pp. 188-189).

Disappointed with the trust fund's slow start, Draper concluded that additional lobbying efforts were necessary, and he approached Paul Hoffman, the former Marshall Plan administrator and Ford Foundation official who headed the United Nations Development Program (UNDP). By December 1967, Draper had successfully persuaded Hoffman that UNDP should "give quick consideration to any request from any government for an action program in the population field." Subsequently, the trust fund was transferred to UNDP and was renamed the United Nations Fund for Population Activities (UNFPA) (13, p. 207).

Assured by Draper that the United States was willing to contribute large sums to UNFPA, Hoffman sought and won approval from the United Nations Economic and Social Council (ECOSOC) for technical assistance outlays by UNDP. ECOSOC's July 1968 decision was also stimulated by a new stance on the part of the International Bank for Reconstruction and Development, or World Bank. In April 1968, World Bank president George Woods had issued a directive calling for closer scrutiny of prospective borrowers' policies on population growth (10, pp. 170-172). To this end, the World Bank group stated in 1968:

---

[9] U.N. General Assembly Resolution 2211 also states that the General Assembly is "concerned at the growing food shortage in the developing countries which is due in many cases to a decline in the production of foodstuffs relative to population growth" (10, Appendix II, p. 214).

All such activity arises out of the concern of the bank for the way in which the rapid growth of population has become a major obstacle to social and economic development in many of our member states. Family planning programs are less costly than conventional development projects and the pattern of expenditures involved is normally very different. At the same time, we are conscious of the fact that successful programs of this kind will yield very high economic returns (26).

In the final half of 1968 Robert S. McNamara succeeded Woods as president of the World Bank. In response to underdeveloped nations' growing dissatisfaction with the World Bank, McNamara created a special committee headed by Lester Pearson, former prime minister of Canada. The Pearson Committee was asked to undertake a comprehensive review of plans for the United Nations Second Development Decade, and it soon became evident that the committee would reach conclusions similar to McNamara's proposals for transforming the World Bank into a more powerful regulator of international development programs.

Under John D. Rockefeller III's chairmanship, the United Nations Association of the United States (UNA-USA) assembled a panel of experts to furnish the Pearson Committee with data and perspectives on population. The UNA-USA's Policy Panel on World Population included such veterans of the Population Establishment as Ansley Coale (Office of Population Research), Oscar Harkavy (Population Officer of the Ford Foundation), and Frank Notestein (president emeritus of the Population Council). The staff also included such officials as David E. Bell, the former budget director of AID, and John Hannah, the current AID director (13, p. 208).

Rapid changes occurring within United Nations agencies were but one indication of the victories achieved by population planning advocates since the early 1960s. From Lyndon B. Johnson's pleas for worldwide population planning as the key to "development" to AID's "War on Hunger," branches of the United States government had emerged as strong forces within a field where private entities had formerly been the sole source of funds. The much-publicized "population crisis" had become the concern not only of American foundations and government departments but of such bodies as the World Bank and the World Health Organization. Through its efforts at the end of the decade to perfect a multilateral approach, the Population Establishment was quickly developing a capacity for enforcing Malthus' "principles" on every continent.

AID SETS AN EXAMPLE

In the early months of 1969, as the Nixon Administration reorganized the Agency for International Development, the "War on Hunger" Office was renamed the Bureau for Technical Assistance, and AID's Population Office was provided with additional personnel. Meanwhile, General Draper and other members of the Population Establishment continued their efforts to convince Congressmen of the need for increased appropriations. As a result, the House and Senate Foreign Aid Committees agreed to earmark $75 million for population planning for fiscal year 1970 and $100 million for 1971 (13, pp. 165-168).

On July 18, 1969, in his "Message on Population," Richard Nixon declared that population growth was a major problem both overseas and in the United States, and recommended that a Commission on Population Growth and the American Future be established. In the message Nixon also stated:

It is our belief that the United Nations, its specialized agencies, and other international bodies should take the leadership in responding to world population growth. The United States will cooperate fully with their programs (13, pp. 169-170).

By that point, UNA-USA, under John D. Rockefeller III's guidance, had already submitted its recommendations to the United Nations, and Paul Hoffman of the United Nations Development Program had assumed management of the United Nations Fund for Population Activities. UNA-USA's Policy Panel on World Population had proposed that the UNFPA budget be expanded to $100 million and that a population commissioner be appointed by the UNDP. Likewise, the panel recommended that activities of other United Nations agencies be reduced so that UNDP could eventually become the central channel for United Nations population planning projects (13, pp. 208-209).

These proposals resembled those contained in the World Bank's Pearson Committee report, which was released in 1969 under the title *Partners in Development* (27). The report focused upon the much-publicized "Green Revolution" as an indispensable tool for raising living standards in underdeveloped countries. Seeing greater technologic inputs from industrialized nations, instead of agrarian reform, as the sole method for agricultural development within the Third World, the Pearson Committee report advocated population control programs as a necessary precondition for World Bank loans:

> Aid-givers cannot be indifferent to whether population problems receive the attention they require, and both bilateral and international agencies should press for adequate analysis of these problems and their bearing on development programs ... In particular, social policies which reduce the dependence on the family as the sole source of security would lessen the need and desire for large families (27).

At the same time, the report called for deflationary monetary policies within debt-ridden nations, more effective administration of development funds, and a changeover from bilateral to multilateral aid. The same concepts were echoed in the April 1970 report issued by the President's Task Force on International Development. This panel of experts was headed by Rudolph Peterson, then chairman of the Bank of America and presently administrator of the United Nations Development Program. The Peterson Report was particularly concerned with the flaws of bilateral foreign assistance:

> A predominantly bilateral United States program is no longer politically tenable in our relations with many developing countries, nor is it advisable in view of what other countries are doing in international development (28).

As a strategy for transforming foreign assistance programs, the Peterson Report suggested such measures as transferral of appropriations decisions to the executive branch of the United States government, increased military aid to other nations so that United States forces overseas could be reduced, and strong encouragement of European countries to bear the costs of international development programs. Finally, the report called for creation of an International Development Institute that would take over technical assistance programs, including those in the population planning sphere (13, pp. 183-185).

Governmental insistence upon massive funding increases was paralleled by the activities of such elements of the Population Establishment as the Hugh Moore Fund. During the summer of 1969, after Nelson A. Rockefeller's "Fact-Finding" mission to Latin America, the Hugh Moore Fund sponsored a series of provocative newspaper advertisements headlined "Latin American Aid Nullified by Population Explosion." A parallel series of advertisements highlighted excerpts from a recent speech by Robert S. McNamara:

My responsibilities as President of the World Bank compel me to be candid. Are we to solve this problem by famine? Are we to solve it by riot, by insurrection, by the violence that desperately starving men can be driven to? (29).

At the same time, the Hugh Moore Fund's public persuasion campaign was facilitated by the growing popularity of Paul Ehrlich's doomsday book, *The Population Bomb*, whose title had been borrowed from the Fund's original 1954 pamphlet. At the end of 1969, Moore encouraged Ehrlich to lead a new organization called Zero Population Growth, which quickly gained thousands of members in the United States (13, pp. 189-190).

Such pressures at the public level led to Congressional acceptance in March 1970 of an earlier presidential bill for creation of a population commission. By June 1970, the Commission on Population Growth and the American Future, headed by John D. Rockefeller III, had begun meeting. Other members long associated with the Population Establishment included Bernard Berelson (president of the Population Council), David Bell (former AID official and vice-president of the Ford Foundation), and Dr. Joseph Beasley (chairman of Planned Parenthood).

During the same month that it created the Rockefeller Commission, the United States Congress passed the Family Planning Services and Population Research Bill, which authorized expenditures of $382 million for the next three years. Although the bill made a minor concession to Catholic organizations by specifying that no funds were to be used for programs involving abortion, it was the first bill providing a separate funding structure for population planning inside the United States (13, p. 195).

As neo-Malthusian aims on the domestic arena steadily grew in popularity, the Population Establishment's campaign at the United Nations level continued to accelerate. William H. Draper, whom the Nixon Administration had appointed in 1969 as United States delegate to the United Nations Population Commission, undertook a whirlwind campaign to secure contributions for UNFPA. By the end of 1970, Draper had obtained more than $15 million in pledges from 24 nations, not including the United States (10, pp. 188-96; 13, pp. 210-211).

At the same time, UNFPA's future activities were assured through creation of an advisory board that included such prominent advocates of population planning as John D. Rockefeller III, B. R. Sen (former head of the Food and Agricultural Organization), and Alberto Lleras Camargo (former president of Colombia). Rafael Salas, a former cabinet member of the Philippine government, was appointed executive director of UNFPA by Paul Hoffman in 1969. At first, Hoffman and Salas concentrated upon channeling UNFPA funds to United Nations agencies, but by the end of 1971 UNFPA had established agreements to disburse $24 million in population planning funds to individual governments. In this manner, the United Nations followed a pattern defined by AID's Dr. R. T. Ravenholt in 1969:

I see AID and the UN playing essentially complementary roles in the development of family planning programs. The Agency is ahead of the UN, which will follow trails blazed by AID (13, p. 218).

The growing acceptance of population limitation as a necessity for the 1970s was exemplified by the vote of the United Nations General Assembly on December 11, 1970 designating 1974 as World Population Year in order to effect a more "dynamic population policy." The agency chosen to implement this new policy was UNFPA, which, by 1971, was directly allocating 54 per cent of its expenditures to implementation, rather than policy formulation, of population control measures. By 1973, UNFPA's yearly budget had expanded to more than $40 million, and it had funded large-scale projects in many developing countries.

More significantly, in 1969 the General Assembly accepted the Tinbergen Report, which ECOSOC had commissioned. The report suggested that, for the Second United Nations Development Decade, gross national product increase rates in the Third World be determined according to a projected annual population increase of 2.5 per cent. This figure was even lower than the 2.8 per cent rate projected by the United Nations Population Division. Hence, integration of the Tinbergen Report's demographic assumptions with international development plans marked an important ideological triumph for population control strategists (10, pp. 183-185).

TOWARD WORLD POPULATION YEAR

Although creation of new entities such as UNFPA marked a transition away from the dominant role long held by American agencies in population planning, there has been an uninterrupted increase in actual sums spent by federal and private sources in the United States. This condition corresponds to the world view expressed by the Rockefeller Commission in its final report in 1972:

> The Commission has been deeply impressed by the unprecedented size and significance of the looming problems of resources and environment on a world scale. We see the need for much greater efforts than are underway now to analyze and understand these problems, and to develop international policies and programs to deal with them. We foresee potentially grave issues of clashing interests among nations and world regions, which could have very serious effects on the United States (30).

Although the Commission's support for removal of abortion restrictions in the United States drew criticism from former President Richard Nixon, its pleas for greater population control efforts were closely heeded by both the executive and legislative branches. For 1973, AID's population budget reached an unprecedented $125 million, or nearly three times its 1969 budget. Similarly, the population budget of the Department of Health, Education, and Welfare was raised to $239 million for 1973 (31).

Rapid expansion of population planning efforts in the United States coincided with a tendency to reduce government outlays for health, both domestically and overseas. Between 1968 and 1972, for example, AID's health assistance budget had been reduced from $164 to $60 million. At the same time, AID's increased expenditures were accompanied by greater spending on the part of private entities. By 1972, the International Planned Parenthood Federation, with chapters in 79 nations, had boosted its expenditures to $26 million, while the Population Council was spending more than $17 million (30, pp. 38-43).

Whereas Latin America had been the primary target of the Population Establishment throughout the 1960s, concern now decisively shifted to Africa and Asia. Between 1969 and 1972, AID's programs in Latin America grew from $10.3 to $11.1 million, but during the same period its African and Asian programs expanded from $9.4 to $25.7 million. As a result of this aggressive expansion, AID-backed programs, by 1973, were operative in more than 70 countries, including South Vietnam (30, p. 3).

In anticipation of World Population Year, Dr. R. T. Ravenholt of the AID Office of Population defined AID's role in these terms:

A key action of AID during recent years, and a major U.S. contribution to World Population Year is the financing of contraceptives at the request of host governments for their population programs. During fiscal 1973, AID purchased 125 million monthly cycles of oral contraceptives. These will be delivered in the developing countries mainly during World Population Year (32).

For Dr. Ravenholt, both the expansion of UNFPA and the worldwide campaign linked to World Population Year (WPY) promise solutions for obstacles that AID and other American agencies have often encountered:

The WPY initiative greatly expands UN involvement and leadership in population action and brings much nearer the long-sought goal of family planning leaders in the United States and elsewhere—that of achieving a coherent world population planning movement with appropriate multilateral assistance unhampered by the limitations of aid between individual countries. The promise of this goal's attainment is greatly strengthened by the recent expansion of UNFPA's assistance resources (32, p. 6).

Since the United Nations 1970 decision to sponsor a World Population Conference in connection with World Population Year, there have been many indications that Ravenholt's hopes are not unrealistic. In preparation for the conference in Bucharest, the United Nations authorized a World Fertility Survey, new population censuses in 21 African nations, and a series of preliminary seminars conducted by international experts. In October 1972, officials from the United Nations Population Commission agreed upon five general topics for the conference agenda (33):

- Recent population trends and future prospects;
- Relations between population change and economic and social development;
- Relations between population, resources, and environment;
- Population and the family; and
- World Population Plan of Action.

Under UNFPA's direction, World Population Year activities were initiated in more than 60 nations, with at least $3 million in expenditures anticipated. Those activities, as UNFPA's *Work Plan: 1972-1975* (34) indicates, have been strongly oriented toward breaking down national or local resistance to basic premises of population planning:

An important feature of the Year will be information and education activities designed to sharpen awareness of population problems and their implications among policy-makers, community leaders, and teachers as well as the population at large. Emphasis will be on activities at the country level, involving, where appropriate, national non-governmental organizations (34).

UNFPA's current "communication and education" projects, like comparable long-term efforts by AID to encourage mass acceptance of population planning, can be weighed in relation to the multilaterally supported national programs that have existed in the Philippines since 1970. Both AID and UNFPA have been actively supporting preparation of films, posters, and booklets by the University of the Philippines' Mass Communications Institute. Through the Philippine Press Institute, journalists have been encouraged to join seminars on population planning, and, through the school system, the AID-financed Pathfinder Fund, which is a United States-based organization known primarily for testing and distribution of contraceptives, has been developing a multilevel educational program. At the *barrio* level, the Family Planning Organization of the Philippines often conducts intensive campaigns, with reliance upon specially trained "motivators" who utilize films, booklets, and person-to-person appeals (31, pp. 118-22; 35).

WORLD POPULATION CONFERENCE

On August 18, 1974, the first session of the World Population Conference in Bucharest was inaugurated by United Nations Secretary-General Kurt Waldheim, who evoked the theme of "demographic explosion." In his address, Waldheim asserted that "The problem posed by world population not only constitutes a danger, but the world's population is in danger," and personally proposed that "plans of action" be developed for cutting the world population growth rate from 2.0 to 1.7 per cent annually, in order to prevent the world's population from doubling during the next generation (36).

Waldheim's neo-Malthusian projections were also echoed by Caspar Weinberger, the United States Secretary of Health, Education, and Welfare, who urged that goals be established for reducing population increase to "replacement level" by the year 2000. In his address to the conference, Weinberger suggested that satellite technology could be applied to produce increased awareness of the population question throughout the world.[10]

As the conference proceeded, efforts to alter and, on some occasions, delete neo-Malthusian premises and goals occurred. Along with Argentina, several Latin American nations called for amendments designed to incorporate social and economic goals. At one point, the delegate of the People's Republic of China called upon the conference to "thoroughly liquidate the absurd theory of the population explosion."

In the early stages of the conference, *Oi*, an organization that was formed at the August 1971 International Youth Conference on the Human Environment, denounced the conference as a diversion from the real problems of disease, illiteracy, and unjust distribution of resources. One of its spokesmen, Dr. Yusuf Eraj, a Kenyan gynecologist, said:

> The world should be aware that 4 million people have already perished and thousands are still dying every day in the Sahelien Belt of Africa. 500 million children, according to UNICEF, are facing starvation in spite of the fact that enough food can be produced in USA, Canada, Australia, Argentina, and USSR, if only the desire was there.

To the dismay of many advocates of world population planning, the World Youth Population Conference in Bucharest, for which UNFPA had furnished $300,000, issued a final report recommending that

> ... the UN discontinue specific aid to family planning programs in underdeveloped countries and that these programs should be supported only within the context of broader economic and social development programs.

As efforts were made to win acceptance of the World Population Plan of Action, additional opposition arose within the conference's Working Group, the body in charge of drafting a plan. At the urging of Algeria's delegate, Mr. Ali Oubouzar, the Working Group voted 52-42 to delete a clause that called for making family planning information and services available throughout the world by 1985. When asked about his views, Mr. Oubouzar explained:

> Nowhere does the draft Plan—which after all is a UN document—mention this decision [the UN General Assembly's April 1974 decision concerning natural resources]. It gives too much emphasis to demography and fertility in its analysis and in its proposed solutions.

[10] Material concerning the World Population Conference is taken from daily issues of the *Planet* published during the conference between August 20 and 29, 1974. The core staff of the newspaper consisted of members of the International Planned Parenthood Federation.

On August 28, however, members of the Working Group voted to retain paragraphs urging underdeveloped nations to produce objectives and policies that would reduce birth rates to an average of 30 per thousand by 1985. The People's Republic of China's motions for deletion of "target figures" and for inclusion of a clause indicating that nations should be permitted to increase their populations if they desired to do so were challenged by delegates from the Philippines and Indonesia. After the defeat of these motions, the Working Group voted 57-19 for a text that included the statement:

> In the light of the principles of this Plan of Action, countries which consider their birth rates detrimental to their national purposes are invited to consider setting quantitative goals and implementing policies that may lead to the attainment of such goals by 1985. Nothing herein should interfere with the sovereignty of any government to adopt or not to adopt such quantitative goals.

As its meetings continued, the Working Group accepted many amendments that pointed to economic and social influences upon high birth rates in underdeveloped nations. Delegates' increased awareness of the complex factors that affect population levels was indicated by acceptance of amendments calling for protection of migrant workers, resettlement of refugees, resolution of urban problems, and elevation of women's legal status.

Although the World Population Conference in Bucharest furnished indications that both opponents and advocates of world population planning have become more aware that the topic cannot be treated in isolation from other considerations, intensified activities of American and multilateral agencies directed by the Population Establishment continue to suggest that neo-Malthusian goals retain the prominence that they have acquired in recent years. It is in this sense that World Population Year, 1974, in spite of events at the Bucharest conference, has not ceased to serve the aim of "world population stabilization."

MALTHUS REAPPRAISED

According to the Population Establishment and its hired technicians, overpopulation severely threatens poor nations, presumably leading to depletion of resources, overcrowding, starvation, and social unrest. Doomsday models—from Malthus' geometric versus arithmetic progressions to Paul Ehrlich's eco-catastrophes or the systems dynamics projections prepared by the "Limits to Growth" team at the Massachusetts Institute of Technology—share the gloomy belief that social or technologic advances only postpone disaster instead of contributing potential solutions for humanity's predicaments.

Increasingly, the poor throughout the world have been blamed on two counts: (a) they breed too much; and (b) they demand more than they produce. In the present-day vision of American financiers and industrialists, humanity's rising expectations imply future explosions, and counterarguments are carefully developed according to data supposedly selected independently of political systems or sets of social values. Economic and social inequities are often treated as merely peripheral factors, and ultimately it is claimed that civilization cannot survive unless zero population growth, zero energy growth, and their counterparts are quickly instituted.

Variations upon Malthus' "eternal laws of nature" often embody conclusions that human numbers incessantly press against available resources. Impoverishment, famine, and unrest are then portrayed as "inevitable" menaces unless consumption and numbers are subjected to harsh controls.

Malthus' eternal laws include the so-called law of diminishing returns, whereby the earth's finite capacities limit the ultimate results of human capital and labor inputs. With its imperfections, humanity is exhorted to adjust to these "laws," and poverty can be conveniently reinterpreted as a consequence of "insufficient labor demand."

For Malthus, the wages-prices-profits structures of capitalism were also eternal, but, unlike many of his contemporary heirs, Malthus did not attempt to disguise the enormous gap between social classes:

> The most permanent cause of poverty has little or no direct relation to forms of government or the unequal division of property, and, as the rich do not in reality possess the power of finding employment and maintenance for the poor, the poor cannot in the nature of things possess the right to demand them. . . .

Whereas Malthus used the "principle of population" to falsify the contradictions that he recognized, his contemporary heirs often treat those contradictions as phenomena that can easily be erased by development or plans of action. The large numbers who are presently marginal to the capitalist mode of production are designated targets for strategies intended to restrict consumption of precious resources. In essence, the poor are urged by the owners of wealth to keep their numbers to a minimum when jobs are unavailable, and their past contributions to accumulated surplus value are dismissed as an irrelevant matter.

Because of the social consequences that can arise from the overwhelming contradiction between workers and owners, today's financiers and industrialists are prepared to increase or reduce their "charity" according to immediate needs for maintaining the capitalist mode of production. When the actual numbers of poor are great enough to evoke the possibility of social upheaval, Malthus' "true laws of nature" are quickly invoked.

Present-day analysts who revive Malthus' precepts, though they profess to be mere suppliers of data and forecasts rather than policy makers, carefully avoid investigation of the factors which produce a highly asymmetrical distribution of wealth, within individual nations or on a world scale. "Scientific findings," in turn, are utilized to divert attention from capitalism's exploitative nature and, when possible, to persuade the oppressed that they themselves are responsible for poverty and misery.

For example, mass migration from the countryside to cities is explained in relation to prolific breeding, or "pressure on the land," but not in relation to economic structures whereby the metropolis bleeds outlying rural areas of their natural resources and labor power. On a larger scale, the "world population problem" is treated primarily as one of rapid population increase in the Third World, and it is denied that an international economic order has arisen upon colonial and neocolonial confiscation of resources and surplus value.

Since that system depends upon a continuous flooding of markets with profitable items, underdeveloped nations are confronted by severely limited availability of goods, services, and capital. In particular, health, nutrition, and education are subjected to restrictions, since these can furnish little in the way of profits.

CONCLUSION

Pronouncements of impending doom, even when they allude to present shortages and famines in the Third World, do not trace the true roots of these phenomena, nor do they point toward means for increasing production of goods and services that are so desperately required. Instead, shrinkage of sustenance is treated as if it bore no relation to world price systems and the flow of profits to wealthy minorities. For the Population Establishment, the multiple miseries of the Third World are merely catalogued as additional evidence of the need for worldwide population control.

It has often been observed that the United States contains 6 per cent of the world's population, but consumes more than 50 per cent of its raw materials. Instead of speaking in terms of redistribution of wealth, Malthus' modern disciples prefer to speak in terms of carefully calculated foreign aid to needy nations.

The social relationships that propel the poor toward the margins of production and consumption are kept concealed. In contrast to the planners' "evidence" and projections, contemporary history shows rising mass awareness of the gap between worker and owner. Through this awareness, the oppressed throughout the world become capable of reclaiming and rationally using the wealth that a multinational system of exploitation has extracted from their labors.

REFERENCES

1. Malthus, T. *Essay on the Principle of Population*, Ed. 7. J. M. Dent & Sons, London, 1816. Reprinted in *Population: A Clash of Prophets*, edited by E. Pohlman, p. 160. The New American Library, Inc., New York, 1973.
2. *Marx and Engels on the Population Bomb*, edited by R. L. Meek, Ed. 2. Ramparts Press, Berkeley, California, 1971.
3. Allen, G. A history of eugenics in the class struggle. *Science for the People* 6: 2, March 1974.
4. State of the Union Message, January 1906. Cited in *The United Nations and the Population Question*, R. Symonds and M. Carder, p. 7. McGraw Hill Company, New York, 1973.
5. Sanger, M. *Autobiography*, p. 108. W. W. Norton, New York, 1938.
6. Burch, G. I. Unpublished letter. Cited in *Birth Control in America*, D. Kennedy, p. 119. Yale University, New Haven, 1970.
7. Stoddard, L. *Revolt against Civilization: The Menace of the Under Man*, p. 21. Scribners, New York, 1922.
8. Dublin, L. I. Birth control: What it is doing to America's population. *The Forum* 86: July 1931. Cited in *Population: A Clash of Prophets*, edited by E. Pohlman, p. 10. The New American Library, Inc., New York, 1973.
9. Spengler, J. J. The birth rate—Potential dynamite? *Scribner's Magazine* 92: July-December 1932. Reprinted in *Population: A Clash of Prophets*, edited by E. Pohlman, p. 5. The New American Library, Inc., New York, 1973.
10. Symonds, R., and Carder, M. *The United Nations and the Population Question*, pp. 1-29. McGraw-Hill Book Company, New York, 1973.
11. Keynes, J. M. *Essays in Biography*, p. 120. Macmillan and Company, London, 1933.
12. Osborn, F. *Preface to Eugenics*, p. 42. Harper and Brothers, New York, 1940.
13. Piotrow, P. T. *World Population Crisis: The United States Response*, pp. 31-32. Praeger Publishers, New York, 1973.
14. Stycos, J. M. Cultural checks on birth control use. In *Proceedings of a Round Table at the 1953 Annual Conference of the Milbank Memorial Fund*, p. 63. New York, 1954.
15. Fairchild, H. P. Speech cited in The politics of population: Birth control and the eugenics movement, L. Gordon, *Radical America*, Vol. 8, July-August 1974.
16. *International Approaches to Problems of Underdeveloped Areas*, p. 77. Milbank Memorial Fund, New York, 1948.
17. Acheson, D. Letter of Transmittal to President Truman, July 30, 1949. In *United States Relations with China*, U.S. Department of State, Washington, D.C., 1949.
18. Vogt, W. *Road to Survival*, pp. 238, 281-282. William Sloane Associates, New York, 1949.
19. *Partners in Progress*, p. 46. International Development Advisory Board, Washington, D.C., 1951.
20. Barclay, W., Enright, J., and Reynolds, R. T., Population control in the Third World. *North American Congress on Latin America Newsletter* 4: 8, December 1970. Reprinted in *Population: A Clash of Prophets*, edited by E. Pohlman, pp. 464-483. The New American Library, Inc., New York, 1973.
21. *The Population Council, 1952-1964*, p. 20. Population Council, New York, 1965.
22. Griessemer, T. O. *The Population Bomb*. The Hugh Moore Fund, New York, 1954.

23. Lader, L. *Breeding Ourselves to Death*, pp. 1-37. Ballantine Books, New York, 1970.
24. *The Population Bomb*, p. 3. Population Policy Panel of the Hugh Moore Fund, New York, 1965.
25. *World Population Trends and Problems*, p. 1. U.S. Department of State, Washington, D.C., 1959.
26. Hawkins, E. K. Statement on Behalf of the World Bank Group. International Bank for Reconstruction and Development, Washington, D.C., 1968.
27. *Partners in Development*. Report of the World Bank Commission on International Development, Praeger Publishers, New York, 1969.
28. *U.S. Foreign Assistance in the 1970s: A New Approach*, p. 22. Report to the President from the Task Force on International Development, Washington, D.C., 1970.
29. McNamara, R. S. Address to the University of Notre Dame, May 14, 1969. Reprinted in *Population: A Clash of Prophets*, edited by E. Pohlman, p. 140. The New American Library, Inc., New York, 1973.
30. *Population and the American Future*. The Commission on Population Growth and the American Future. The New American Library, Inc., New York, 1972. Excerpt reprinted in *Population: A Clash of Prophets*, edited by E. Pohlman, p. 233. The New American Library, Inc., New York, 1973.
31. *Population Program Assistance*, pp. 3, 33. U.S. Agency for International Development. U.S. Government Printing Office, Washington, D.C., 1972.
32. Ravenholt, R. T. Facing up to population in 1974. *War on Hunger* 8(1): 6-7, 1974.
33. Johnson, S. Three billion going on seven billion. *Vista* 9(1): 33, 1973.
34. United Nations Fund for Population Activities. *Work Plan: 1972-1975*, paragraph 192, p. 42. New York, undated.
35. United Nations Fund for Population Activities. *Report: 1969-1972*, pp. 22-23. New York, undated.
36. *Le Monde*, August 20, 1974.

Appendix 1

Chronology of the American population control movement[a]

Related Developments in History	Focus of Concern for the Population Establishment	Strategy for Control of World Population	Year	Important Events of American Population Control Movement
Russian Revolution (1917)	Fear of "race suicide"	Birth control "to stop multiplication of the unfit"; more children for the rich and the superior; immigration restriction policies	1921-1945	Establishment of American Birth Control League (1921) Passage of Immigration Restriction Act (1924) Establishment of first research institution on population (1922) India considers national birth control program (1935) Large-scale birth control program approved in U.S. possession Puerto Rico (1937) Merging of eugenics and birth control movements (1940)
Great Depression (1929-1939)	Eugenics			
World War II (1939-1945)				
Independence movement of colonies (1945-)	Scarcity of resources from countries with "exploding" populations	Formulation of strategies to control the "exploding" world population	1946	UN accepts joint Anglo-American proposal for establishment of Population Commission
			1948	Establishment of International Planned Parenthood Federation (IPPF)
Chinese Revolution (1949)			1949	U.S. State Department's Malthusian explanation for the "loss of China"; Vogt's book Road to Survival published
Korean War (1950-1953)				
Cuban Revolution (1959)	Preparation of necessary means to implement strategy of world population control; development of contraceptives, collection of demographic data, social science research to identify determinants of population growth	"Conquest of public opinion" and building of coalition to pressure U.S. government to fund population control programs in developing countries Efforts to win international support for world population control: "population control is necessary condition for development"	1952	Williamsburg Conference for establishment of the Population Council
			1954	World Population Conference (Rome); widespread distribution of Hugh Moore's The Population Bomb
			1958	Ford Foundation grants $9 million to assist India's national family planning program
Alliance for Progress (1961)			1959	Draper Committee urges U.S. government to give foreign aid for control of population in developing countries
			1960	Rockefeller pleas to shift burden of population control from private sector to government

Appendix 1 continued

Related Developments in History	Focus of Concern for the Population Establishment	Strategy for Control of World Population	Year	Important Events of American Population Control Movement
Alliance for Progress (1961) (continued)			1961-1963	Beginning of series of full-page advertisements in major newspaper by Moore Fund to urge public to pressure government to finance world population control programs; advertisements such as "Population Explosion Nullifies Foreign Aid" refer particularly to failure of Alliance for Progress in Latin America
Escalation of Vietnam War	Implementation of population control programs (mainly bilateral programs)	Pressure on developing countries to accept population programs, on developed countries to join in financing them, and on UN to endorse them	1965	President Johnson's historic announcement to "deal with the explosion in world population"; AID begins to fund population control programs; famine in India (1965-1966)
Spread of national liberation movement	Debate of "Will family planning programs succeed?"		1966	UN resolution to assist nations upon request in field of population
			1967-1968	Population control condition ("self-help") tied to U.S. food aid; World Bank Pearson Report coincides with UNA-USA Report and subsequent establishment of UNFPA in 1969
			1969	Moore's Campaign to Check Population Explosion continues from 1967 to 1969, culminating in President Nixon's message to Congress on population
Rise of nationalism and intensified opposition of Third World countries to foreign control of resources. UN Speical Session on Raw Materials and Development; UN Ocean Conference (both in 1974)	Growing recognition of failure of "family planning" approach; need for broad-based "development" approach	Intensification of pressure	1970	Marked increase in AID funding of population control programs in developing countries
		Toward the climax: WPC and adoption of the WPPA; legitimization of global population control	1971	UN designates 1974 as World Population Year and schedules World Population Conference (WPC) in 1974
			1972	Commission on Population Growth and American Future headed by Rockefeller advocates "stabilization" of U.S. population
			1974	World Population Year, World Population Conference, and World Population Plan of Action (WPPA)

[a] This table is based on material from references 10, 13, and 23.

204

PART 4

Corporate Power and Underdevelopment

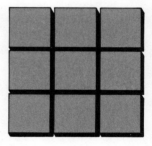

CHAPTER 10

Industrialization and Occupational Health in Underdeveloped Countries
Ray H. Elling

In a field which tends to be eclectic and a-theoretical (epidemiology), this paper attempts to deduct from an examination of developments in the world political economy the groups likely to be at greatest risk. It is a call for serious work on what appears to be a serious problem. The ravages of the past on the health of workers in industrialized nations are recalled. These were times of relatively unorganized, unprotected, unsophisticated laboring forces. The assaults of modern "high" technology are noted. Even with improvements in unionization, protective laws and programs, and increasing sophistication as to occupational hazards, the hazards may be growing in industrialized nations, particularly health hazards such as cancer related to various air pollutants in the workplace. The political economy of industrialization in underdeveloped countries is considered as a prelude to discussing export of expensive and illegal or hazardous work processes and the relationships of working populations in underdeveloped countries to industrialization, particularly that fostered by externally controlled multinational corporations (MNCs). The focus on general community, family, and environmental effects is noted. Examples of healthy and unhealthy industrial work situations in underdeveloped countries are identified and discussed. An hypothesis is offered and qualifications and questions are raised concerning occupational health hazards in internally controlled socialist economies versus internally and externally controlled capitalist economies.

This article appeared, in modified form, in the *Proceedings of the Third National Symposium on Non-Communicable Diseases,* a conference which was held in the German Democratic Republic, April 21-24, 1976.

INDUSTRIALIZED SOCIETIES AND OCCUPATIONAL HEALTH

The wastage of human life during the Industrial Revolution, brought about by child labor, sweat shops, unsafe mines, and other exploitative conditions, has been extensively documented. Engels (1) examined the situation in England. Norman Thomas' comprehensive study of human exploitation in capitalist America (2) includes a chapter on the extremely hazardous lumber industry, and another on mines and miners. In his general chapter on work conditions, Thomas describes the effects on the worker of management's efforts to rationalize and get more out of the capital input. With special reference to the much hated "stretch-out system" in the textile industry, he quotes a report of the Research Department of the United Textile Workers, written in 1932 at the depths of the Great Depression when some 20 percent of those normally gainfully employed were unemployed (2, p. 168):

> In 1920 the maximum load anywhere in the industry was 16 looms. . . . The predominant situation is that where the loom load formerly ranged up to 16, it is now around 72 looms, four and one half times as heavy as it was 12 years ago. . . .
> Even when unskilled workers are brought in to displace experienced weavers there is no decrease, but a tremendous increase in the weaver energy that goes into each yard of cloth. For example: A weaver running 72 looms must ceaselessly patrol a beat 75 yards long. In the course of an eight-hour day, he must walk between 15 and 18 miles. He does more patrolling than any two patrolmen on a city police force. He does this in addition to performing the variety of tasks connected with the weaving process. And he grinds out his 18-mile patrol in a shop with windows and skylights bolted shut, in order that no breath of fresh air may clear the intensely humid fog-like atmosphere, or reduce the 85 percent temperature at which the weave room is kept. These conditions mean more than complete exhaustion at the end of every day of labor. They mean permanent loss of weight, anemia, broken feet, varicose veins and finally, a complete physical breakdown.

In the aftermath of the October Revolution, workers in the Soviet Union were faced with exhortations to outproduce the external capitalist competition. In describing the next stage, Trotsky (3, p. 189) wrote:

> Socialism, after all, does not consist only in the abolition of the exploiters. If people lived more prosperously under the exploiters, more abundantly and freely, and were materially more secure; if they lived better with exploiters than without, then they would say "Bring back the exploiters."
> This means that our task is, without exploiters, to create a system of material prosperity, general security and all-round cultured existence, without which socialism is not socialism. The October Revolution merely laid down the state foundations for socialism; only now are we laying the first bricks. And when we ask ourselves whether we are at this moment producing more goods per unit of labor-power than are produced in other countries, the answer can only be: At present, no, we are producing considerably less—in comparison with America, monstrously less. This question will decide everything. They tried to crush us with their armies, but they failed; they used blockade and famine, but that failed, too. And now we have gone out onto the world market—and this, you know, means that the world market is also creeping up on us. We import foreign goods and export our own. Thereby has begun direct and immediate competition between our fabrics and British ones, our machines and American ones, our grain and North America's.

Improved labor organization (democratic unionization), protective legislation and programs (workmen's compensation, industrial health and safety acts, industrial health programs) and increased sophistication (research and education) have since ameliorated many of the grosser known hazards in industrialized countries. But other measures are slow to be taken. In the U.S., for example, it was not until 1970 that a relatively comprehensive Occupational Safety and Health Act was adopted, and even then, only one definite standard (no more than five fibers of asbestos of five microns length per cubic milliliter of air for an eight-hour exposure, this to be reduced to two fibers in 1976) was stipulated as a part of the law, with others to be adopted administratively as set forth in the law. (See references 4 and 5 for a discussion of the problems and history related to the adoption of this act.)

The problems of establishing standards and adequate enforcement procedures when trained inspection and other personnel and resources are lacking are monumental (6). Furthermore, the increasing complexity and "high" technology of modern industry has led to the recognition of many new hazards, some of which (e.g. vinyl chloride) may be even more dangerous than most previously known health and safety risks. And others, such as asbestos, with a 20-35 year latency period between exposure and the appearance of lung cancer and mesotheliomas, may have only shown the tip of the iceberg of their pathological effects on workers and their families, as well as on community residents exposed to decomposing brake linings and other sources of asbestos fiber (7). In any case, this new awareness is producing a shift from the past concentration on accidents and safety to a concern with air pollution, contact with solvents, noise pollution, and other threats to workers' health (8-10). The 1975 convention of the American Public Health Association was devoted to "Health and Work in America" and a Chart Book (11) was produced for distribution at the meetings to highlight some of the problems. Table 1, based on data from this source (11, p. 71), presents a summary of common occupational carcinogens and indicates the site or organ and type of worker affected. In more specific terms, examples of such effects are:

- Observed deaths from cancer among vinyl chloride workers were more than twice as high as expected deaths (i.e. those observed in the general population of the same age and sex) between 10 and 24 years after first exposure (11, p. 73; 12).
- Meat wrappers working with polyvinyl chloride soft wrap film and price label fumes reported symptoms on work days and improvement on weekends (11, p. 74).
- Construction painters have a significant excess of lung cancer (11, p. 72).
- Among retired asbestos workers, observed deaths from respiratory cancer (58 deaths) greatly exceeded expected deaths (21.7), and for all cancers the rates were 167 vs. 109.4 (11, p. 78; 13).
- Mortality rates from malignant neoplasms of the lung were far higher than expected (15 to 1.5) among those working full-time topside of the oven in one coke plant of a steel mill (11, p. 80; 14).
- Male workers in the rubber industry exhibited an unusually high mortality rate from both stomach cancer and lymphatic leukemia (11, p. 81; 15).

Table 1

Common occupational carcinogens[a]

Agent	Organ Affected	Occupation
Wood dust	Nasal cavity and sinuses	Woodworkers
Leather fibers	Nasal cavity and sinuses; urinary bladder	Leather and shoe workers
Iron oxide	Lung; larynx	Iron ore miners; metal grinders and polishers; silver finishers; iron foundary workers
Nickel	Nasal sinuses; lung	Nickel smelters, mixers, and roasters; electrolysis workers
Arsenic	Skin; lung; liver	Miners; smelters; insecticide makers and sprayers; tanners; chemical workers; oil refiners; vintners
Chromium	Nasal cavity and sinuses; lung; larynx	Chromium producers processors and users; acetylene and aniline workers; bleachers; glass, pottery and linoleum workers; battery makers
Asbestos	Lung (pleural and peritoneal mesothelioma)	Miners; millers; textile, insulation and shipyard workers
Petroleum, petroleum coke, wax, creosote, shale and mineral oils	Nasal cavity; larynx; lung; skin; scrotum	Workers in contact with lubricating, cooling, paraffin or wax fuel oils or coke; rubber fillers; retort workers; textile weavers; diesel jet testers
Mustard gas	Larynx; lung, trachea; bronchi	Mustard gas workers
Vinyl chloride	Liver; brain	Plastic workers
Bis-chloromethyl ether, chloromethyl methyl ether	Lung	Chemical workers
Isopropyl oil	Nasal cavity	Isopropyl oil producers
Coal soot, coal tar, other products of coal combustion	Lung; larynx; skin; scrotum; urinary bladder	Gashouse workers, stokers and producers; asphalt, coal tar and pitch workers; coke oven workers; miners; still cleaners
Benzene	Bone marrow	Explosives, benzene, or rubber cement workers; distillers; dye users; painters; shoemakers
Auramine, benzidine, alpha-Napthylamine, magenta, 4-Aminodiphenyl, 4-Nitrodiphenyl	Urinary bladder	Dyestuffs manufacturers and users; rubber workers (pressmen, filtermen, laborers); textile dyers; paint manufacturers

[a]Source, reference 11, p. 71.

- Carpenters working in New York City showed especially high mortality rates from cancers of the stomach and bladder (11, p. 79; 16).
- In 1965, 12.8 percent of employed bituminous coal miners in Appalachia showed definite x-ray findings of pneumoconiosis, and one-fifth of retired, disabled, and unemployed miners also showed evidence of this disease (11, p. 83; 17).
- Pregnant women working in operating rooms where they were exposed to waste anesthetic gas were far more likely than other pregnant hospital workers to experience spontaneous abortions, and when they delivered, the child was more likely to have some congenital abnormality (11, pp. 84-85; 18).

A recent publication of an occupational health research-action group in Boston (19) lists and classifies the health hazards workers experience from exposure to 61 solvents. Effects of specific agents are listed in relation to skin, brain, peripheral nervous system, liver, kidneys, blood, eyes, nose, and throat, as well as danger of fire and explosion. Three solvents (benzene, chloroform, and trichloroethylene) are identified as causing cancer.

Table 2 (from reference 11, p. 75) gives estimated fatality rates in the U.K. from a variety of causes, by occupation, for selected years.

As Tables 1 and 2 indicate, the occupational health problems created by modern industry are clearly widespread, serious, varied in form, and related to a wide range of agents.

Although social welfare and socialist states may have developed their protective laws earlier and set up far more adequate industrial health services (20), they are by no means immune to the newly discovered hazards of modern high technology. As early as 1949, Soviet researchers reported liver damage among heavily exposed vinyl chloride workers, though this work was not given much attention in other countries. In the U.S.S.R., cancer and other problems have been studied among nickel smelters (21)[1] and threshold limit values have had to be set for a wide variety of substances. (See reference 23 for a comparison of these limits with those in the Federal Republic of Germany.) In fact, competition with outside capitalist economies and "plan fulfillment" (replacing the profit motive of market-oriented capitalism as a motivating force) have combined to make Soviet industry as pollution-prone generally as U.S. industry (24).[2]

---

[1] The Soviet Union is also involved with multinational corporations which themselves may be following apartheid policies and otherwise violating world expectations. Turner (22) cites the case of the British mining company Rio Tinto Zinc developing an open-caste uranium mine in Namibia under the policies and control of South Africa: "Otherwise, the company is in the running for some of the major contracts likely to be available when the Soviet Union hands out contracts to develop some of Siberia's mineral resources. It is unlikely that the Soviets will make an issue of the company's involvement in Namibia" (22, p. 243).

[2] Commoner (24, p. 278) recognizes the potential advantage the U.S.S.R. has over the U.S. in controlling pollution because of its planning structure *if* scientists, policy makers, and others make such control a priority. There is another potential advantage which we will come back to at the end of this paper: the theory of socialism does not require growth whereas capitalism in most views does.

Table 2

Estimated rates of fatality of disease attributed to types of chemical
or physical exposure in the United Kingdom, selected years[a]

Occupation	Cause of Fatality	Rate (Deaths per Million Persons per Year)[b]
Shoe industry (press and finishing rooms)	Nasal cancer	130
Printing trade workers	Cancer of lung and bronchus	About 200
Workers with cutting oils		
Birmingham	Cancer of scrotum	60
Arve district	Cancer of scrotum	400
Wood machinists	Nasal cancer	700
Uranium mining	Cancer of lung	1,500
Coal carbonizers	Bronchitis and cancer of bronchus	2,800
Viscose spinners (ages 45 to 64)	Coronary heart disease (excess)	3,000
Asbestos workers		
Males, smokers	Cancer of lung	2,300
Females, smokers	Cancer of lung	4,100
Rubber mill workers	Cancer of bladder	6,500
Mustard gas manufacturing (figures from Japan, 1929-1945)	Cancer of bronchus	10,400
Cadmium workers	Cancer of prostate (incidence values)	14,000
Amosite asbestos factory	Asbestosis, cancer of lung/pleura	5,300 9,200
Nickel workers (employed before 1925)	Cancer of nasal sinus, cancer of lung	6,600 15,500
β-Naphthylamine manufacturing	Cancer of bladder	24,000

[a]Source, reference 11, p. 75.
[b]Rates are for death, except for the value for cadmium workers which records incidence.

In the German Democratic Republic, the greater availability and use of soft coal as a source of energy, as well as economic pressures similar to those in the U.S.S.R., have led to heavy air pollution. The deleterious effects of industry on man as worker, community resident, and citizen must be identified and more vigorously controlled in all countries if we are to avoid the beginning of large-scale ecological disasters in the next 20 years.[3]

[3] Commoner, after careful and impressive assembly and analysis of the information on world population, resources, and pollution, writes of a 25-year grace period (24, p. 285). He wrote this in 1970-1971.

THE POLITICAL ECONOMY OF INDUSTRIALIZATION
IN THE UNDERDEVELOPED WORLD

Why should we suspect that the occupational health and safety problems associated with industrialization in the so-called underdeveloped countries are and will increasingly become as prevalent and serious, perhaps even more so, than those we have briefly surveyed for developed countries?[4] The answer lies in the general pattern of human and environmental exploitation observed in the relations between the developed and underdeveloped countries, including a vast depopulation (extermination?) of indigenous peoples, much of it in the nineteenth century (28), as well as in special labor, living, and health conditions frequently encountered in underdeveloped countries.

As Figure 1 shows, although the world is producing more and more food and other economic goods, even in relation to its burgeoning population, the concentration of

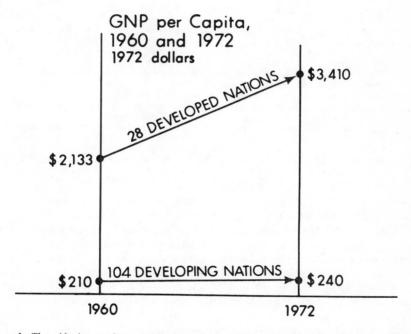

Figure 1. The widening gap between the developed and developing nations. Source, Ruth Sivard, *World Military and Social Expenditures, 1974,* p. 6, Institute for World Order, New York, 1975.

[4] We must caution against necessarily attributing "the good life" to the longer life which goes with "development." On man's need to reassert himself over the technology and dictatorial bureaucracies of so-called "developed" societies see reference 25. We must also caution against the euphemism "developing" being applied to societies in which disparities may be increasing and the overall situation may be becoming increasingly desperate (26, 27).

wealth (as measured by GNP per capita) in 28 countries of the developed world, having 27 percent of the population (1972), has dramatically increased since 1960. The slight increase in average wealth in 104 countries of the underdeveloped world, with 73 percent of the world's population, has occurred at the same time that disparities worldwide and within countries have increased and mass poverty has begun to place limits on growth (26). In short, the U.N.'s First Development Decade has been a failure. In this regard, Barnet and Muller (29, p. 149) quote the now famous remark of President Medici of Brazil: "Brazil is doing well, but the people are not." And summarizing the net results of the World Shopping Center theory offered by the multinational corporations as a solution for world poverty and other problems, they point out that (29, p. 151):

> The evidence of the 1960s is now in. It is an unhappy fact that the development track pursued by the global corporations in those years contributed more to the exacerbation of world poverty, world unemployment and world inequality than to their solution.

Others see a worldwide division of labor developing (30):

> In the recent past we have seen the birth of a world economy and the development of an international division of labor. Although many complex factors have produced this division, and there are variations within it, it is still true that on one side have been those whose economic surplus was being expropriated, on the other those who were expropriating it. This international division of labor allowed the countries which are now rich to develop and multiply their productive resources, while growth was stifled and perverted in many of the countries which are now poor. As perhaps a quarter of the world's population was propelled up to a level of material comfort enjoyed a few generations before only by the aristocracy, fully half the world saw its standard of living stagnate and in some cases (Indonesia, perhaps Bangladesh) even decline. It is impossible to separate the issue of unequal food distribution (which is the question behind the food crisis, not some absolute lack of food) from the acceleration of inequality which the development of the world economy has encouraged. Historically, the food crisis is merely the most recent in a long series of manifestations of inequality between the rich and the poor worlds.

However, this theory of a worldwide division of labor is simply a euphemistic way of identifying human exploitation on a massive scale. Although there is no clear, comprehensive theory of development, it would appear that economic growth to some has meant expropriation from and underdevelopment of others (31).

In the Second Development Decade such use of cheap labor and resources seems bound to continue. The strategy for this decade includes a range of approaches, but heavy emphasis is being placed on industrialization and, increasingly, on the transnational or multinational corporations (22, 29), most of which are controlled by U.S.-based firms and a minority by firms in other developed market economies. As a recent United Nations report (32, p. 188) notes,

> Formerly, the developing countries acquired foreign capital mainly by borrowing in the capital markets of the richer countries and acquired foreign expertise mainly through the services of individuals or managing agencies. This pattern was predominant for investment in infrastructure. Developing countries still acquire foreign capital for their economy through the flotation of loans in foreign markets or through the credits of intergovernmental institutions. They still mobilize foreign technology and entrepreneurship through contracts with individuals and management

firms. However, today, capital, technology, management and access to markets needed for industry flow to a considerable extent to the developing countries through the subsidiaries and affiliates of transnational corporations.

A number of factors are behind this capitalist expansion. In addition to the inherent dynamics forcing competitive capitalist industry to expand, there are a number of conditions surrounding the interaction between developed and under-developed countries that also encourage such expansion. For example, while labor in developed countries has become increasingly better organized and able to command higher wages, labor in underdeveloped countries has been notoriously weak and open to accepting low wages (33). The MNCs are able to offer better wages and fringe benefits than local industry in underdeveloped countries; but these are still far below wages in the "home" country (34, p. 73). Also, the MNCs tend to draw off laborers into the "shallow" (i.e. task specific) special skill development of assembly workers, while more "rounded" artisans are displaced and thrown out of work and industry gets only a narrow temporary base with dislocation and unemployment as later consequences.

While government costs and taxes on industry have risen in developed countries, the client governments of underdeveloped countries have shown a willingness to open their people and other resources to outside exploitation and extraction by providing low tax shelters. To this advantage, the MNCs have added tricks such as purchases from their own home-country subsidiaries at inflated prices as a way of exporting even greater profits without paying taxes. MNC-controlled pharmaceutical subsidiaries in Colombia, for example, were found in 1971 to have profit rates ranging from 38.1 to 962.1 percent; yet for that same year the average profit declared to the Colombian tax authorities was 6.7 percent. In the rubber industry, the effective profit rate was 43 percent, with only 16 percent reported (29, p. 160). Such deceptive practices, including payoffs to government officials willing to blink their eyes as laws and regulations are violated, are widespread, and the recent scandals in Japan, the Netherlands, and other countries concerning payoffs by officials of Lockheed and other firms suggest that they continue.

With what vigor and expertise can occupational health and safety regulations be expected to be upheld, assuming that they exist? While concern over the health and ecological effects of air, water, and land pollution has resulted in increasing controls and costs for control measures in developed countries (in economic terms alone, the cost of environmentally induced disease in the U.S. was placed at $35 billion per year in 1970 (35)), many underdeveloped countries, either ignoring or forgetting that we have a one-world ecology, are actually offering pollution havens. In fact, an official publication of the United Nations (32) actually identifies this as a competitive advantage, and while recognizing the need for better controls, seems also to encourage the transfer of polluting industry from high-pollution congested areas to under-developed countries. Specifically, the publication states (32, pp. 288-289):

> The developed countries, with their large industrial bases, consider pollution of the air, water and soil as environmental problems. In the long term, the shift in the priorities of the developed countries with regard to the environment will affect the international economic structure. The number and complexity of variables that will

come into play render an identification of trends impossible at this stage. However, just as in the field of natural resources, one obvious possibility is the relocation of certain industries from the developed countries with environmental problems to developing countries with few industries, a relatively clean environment and little industrial congestion. . . .

In general, the environmental concerns of the developed countries are in keeping with the desire to achieve a new economic order; that is, the transfer of industries to developing countries may eventually prove to be a positive element contributing to their industrialization. The following three factors are relevant for consideration in an international context:

(a) Capacity of the socio-ecological system to absorb pollutants;
(b) Proximity to renewable natural resources and non-pollutant energy sources;
(c) Reductions in the growth rate of the international transport of raw materials and energy sources (for example, natural gas).

International acknowledgement of the importance of these factors might lead to some redeployment of industries to the developing countries.

The possibility exists that a trend might be set in motion to export pollution from the developed to the developing countries. Adequate preparation on the part of the developing countries in devising and enforcing environmental codes would avoid or minimize this negative aspect. Where developed countries choose to retain highly polluting industries while enforcing stricter pollution controls, the result may also affect the international economic structure. Stricter pollution controls alter production and investment costs in the developed countries; consequently, additional opportunities may arise for competitors in the developing countries where environmental protection does not need to be so stringent and may cost less.

On occasion, attempts to attract outside industry on this basis become quite crude. In Mexico City's English-language newspaper, for example, the state of Mexico placed the following advertisement for polluters:

Relax. We've already prepared the ground for you. If you are thinking of fleeing from the capitol because the new laws for the prevention and control of environmental pollution affect your plant, you can count on us (quoted in reference 29, p. 345).

It seems improbable that the client government of an underdeveloped country which opens its air, land, water, and communities to pollution will be likely to protect its workers from pollution. While the argument has been made that environments in underdeveloped countries have greater "carrying capacity," a world ecological view does not support this, nor could this reasoning be applied to the microenvironment of the workplace. As for the workers in these countries, their carrying capacity is probably *less* for reasons of inadequate nutrition, sanitation, and associated infections and other diseases.

In the rush to attract industry, wealthy individuals and sometimes governments of underdeveloped countries have often provided large shares of the capital. Thus, the resources of the underdeveloped world have served the growth of the multinational corporations in many ways, including cheap labor, ready and cheap raw materials, pollution havens, and even finance capital. The single benefit coming from developed countries through the MNCs has been knowledge, both technical and managerial. It has been what Barnet and Muller call "a system of welfare in reverse" (29, p. 125).

As Turner notes (22, p. 261):

Certainly the drive to control pollution will increase, and the attention currently being paid to auto emissions will be a forerunner of similar assaults, which could even lead to certain industries being put out of business. The richer countries will tend to export their more dirty industries to countries too poor to resist the attractions of the jobs they offer.

Historically, when occupational hazards have become known in developed countries and work conditions "cleaned up," this knowledge and necessary action has not been rapidly transferred to the exploited colonies (36). The example of asbestosis (known long before the recently recognized hazard of lung cancer and mesotheliomas among those exposed to asbestos fibers) is instructive in this regard. As early as 50 A.D., Pliny wrote of dust problems and a disability associated with tiny asbestos fibers. Respirators of a sort were subsequently provided to the slaves who worked the asbestos mines. However, no such protection was provided asbestos workers in the 1800s. It was not until 1900 that the ancient curse was "rediscovered" by the British physician, Montague Murray. By 1918, Canadian and U.S. life insurance companies exhibited their usual foresight and shrewdness by routinely declining to insure asbestos workers. In 1924, the world medical community was more clearly alerted by the work of another British physician, Cooke, who reported a case of respiratory disease leading to the death of a 33-year-old woman—the last of ten asbestos fiber sorters in one factory to die of respiratory disease before the age of 35. He called the disease asbestosis. By 1932, the British government had issued regulations requiring immediate implementation of improved ventilation in every asbestos plant in Great Britain. But the mines for these manufacturing plants were located in the Republic of South Africa! For the next 17 years no health inspector visited these mines. Then Dr. G. W. H. Schepers made the following observations (37):

> During 1949 I made the first official government radiological and clinical survey of the asbestos industry in the North Eastern Transvaal. At that time industrial hygiene in one of these mines and asbestos works was simply deplorable. Exposures were crude and unchecked. I found young children, completely included within large shipping bags, trampling down fluffy amosite asbestos, which all day long came cascading down over their heads. They were kept stepping lively by a burly supervisor with a hefty whip. I believe these children to have had the ultimate of asbestos dust exposure. X-ray revealed several to have radiologic asbestosis with cor pulmonale (right heart failure) before the age of 12. Why Dr. Sluis-Cremer did not see them in his survey ten years later is fairly evident. There was probably not one of them still alive.
>
> In the valley where the mill was located asbestos dust rolled through like the morning mist, and I had a hard time keeping my staff in working trim because of itching skins caused by asbestos adhering to our clothes. Even food at the local hotel was gritty with dust.

In a more recent study of asbestosis in South African asbestos miners, Sluis-Cremer (38) found asbestosis in 35.5 percent of the lungs of miners (44 cases) dying between January 1, 1965 and December 13, 1969; in Northern Transvaal, 83 cases of asbestosis were detected during the same period. He noted that this was an improvement over the 71.5 percent for these areas reported in a study published in 1965. It was also reported in this study that among those miners who died in the two areas, 16.9 and 14.5 percent, respectively, had active tuberculosis.

New awareness of occupational health hazards and enforcement of protective laws have themselves become reasons for industrial runaways from developed countries. In his fine book, *Expendable Americans* (5), recounting the asbestos story, Paul Brodeur cites the case of the Tyler plant, owned by a Pittsburgh-based firm, moving from Texas to Canada. The recent Castleman Report (36)—an especially important source for this paper, which we will cite again when newer hazards are taken up in relation to underdeveloped countries—shows that in 1968, the U.S. manufactured the bulk of its asbestos after receiving most of it in raw form from Quebec mines and in fact exported large amounts to other countries. Of the proportion imported to the U.S., none came from "unregulating" countries. By 1973, overall exports and imports had almost tripled, with the ratio of imports divided by exports rising from 0.285 to 0.321. But what is most significant is that in that same year, 50.1 percent of these imports were coming from unregulating countries, e.g. Mexico and Taiwan (the biggest sources), Venezuela, and Brazil.

Canada supplies most of the asbestos for "Western" industrial countries. Some comes from mines in Rhodesia and South Africa. Mines in the Urals supply U.S.S.R. needs. And China consumes what asbestos is mined there. The strange situation exists that before 1969 the U.S. did most of its own manufacturing of asbestos, obtained largely from mines in Quebec, Canada. With the recognition in the last 10 years of the hazards of cancer from work with asbestos, a significant proportion of the manufacture of asbestos yarn for protective clothing and manufacture of other relatively pure forms of asbestos (the shipping of mixes containing asbestos for concrete and tile from other countries would be too costly) has shifted to those countries without protective occupational health standards and enforcement. Thus, the asbestos is mined in Canada, shipped to Mexico or Taiwan for manufacture, and then shipped to the U.S. for use. Some specifics from the Castleman Report concerning imports of asbestos to the U.S. will be cited in a later section of this paper dealing with new industries in underdeveloped countries.

When "the natives" have on occasion become restless about such exploitation and extraction, military force has always been available in the background. Where abortive uprisings and revolutions have occurred and direct military or other intervention has followed, a repressive police state has been established to maintain control after the intervening forces returned to their home base. The cases of Chile and the Dominican Republic come most obviously to mind. The following quote is illustrative in the case of the Dominican Republic (39, p. 11):

> Troops are ostentatiously present in all the little towns throughout the interior of the country, quartered in the town fort. And as a counterrevolutionary force, the Dominican military has received lavish "assistance" from the Pentagon, ever vigilant to protect the interests of Gulf and Western, Alcoa, Falconbridge Nickel, Chase Manhattan, Bank of America, etc.

For a description of the situation in Chile, see reference 40. The complex picture of intervention, revolt, and counterrevolution in the Arabian states and in Iran is well presented in reference 41. As the National Emergency Civil Liberties Committee records the situation more generally (42, p. 2):

In mid-May ITT's president, Harold Geneen, admitted at a stockholders' meeting to $350,000 sent to rightist forces in Chile for use against the Allende regime, with the encouragement of the CIA. He explained that the purpose was "to preserve a major investment of the company amounting to $135 million for the stockholders, which the company did recover." This, of course, is not the sole explanation, but in Guatemala, Iran, Brazil, as in Chile, the close relations between CIA and specific U.S. business interests determined to maintain domination of local economies have been quite clear. An examination of the record, including the Pentagon Papers, demonstrates that control by American interests of the "rich natural resources" of Southeast Asia was no minor goal in our initial intervention in Indochina. But the people could not be told this. Hence the myths of the cold war were used as cover for the initially secret operations of the CIA, and the later open military expansion when this was not enough to bend the Vietnamese to our will.

For an excellent history of the role of foundation-sponsored public health "assistance" programs in opening foreign lands and peoples up to capitalist exploitation, see reference 43.

While it may be, as an International Labour Office (ILO) report on MNCs (34) suggests, that wages, social welfare, fringe benefits, and working conditions are generally more favorable in MNC-controlled plants than in those of local industry, there are reasons for grave concern as to the effects on workers' health of the high technology of modern industry. The same report calls for additional research before the more favorable work conditions of MNCs can be accepted with assurance, and with regard to the appropriateness of technology, notes that (34, p. 73):

> Much of the technology introduced into developing countries by the multi-national corporation derives directly from the methods used by the corporation in its home country or by its subsidiaries in industrialized countries. It is usually advanced technology, designed for large-scale production and reflecting the fact that in industrialized countries capital is cheap compared with labour. It may therefore be questioned whether the type of technology introduced into a developing country is always well adapted to the new environment.

The poorer nutritional levels of workers associated with higher rates of debilitating disease, the absence of union organization, the lack of official awareness of, concern for, and action in relation to pollution and occupational health hazards, the newness of workers to the industrial environment, the lack of industrial health services and personnel, and still other conditions relating to the underdeveloped countries themselves are all factors leading to the hypothesis that occupational health hazards resulting from industrialization will be at least as great and probably greater in the underdeveloped countries than has been the case in developed countries (44). The situation for Africa was summarized a generation ago in an ILO report as follows (45, pp. 373-374):

> It is clear that the problems of industrial accident prevention and occupational disease control will be felt with increasing urgency in Africa as the economic develop-ment of the various territories progresses, bringing with it new industries and processes involving the use of dangerous machinery or substances, for example, some of the chemicals used in agriculture.
> Even though African workers everywhere have shown a remarkable degree of adaptability to the work done in mechanized industry, it must never be forgotten that many of those who enter modern industrial employment are migrants who have just left their traditional environments and have no prior knowledge of the working

processes to which they are assigned. Such workers cannot be expected to have any clear idea of the hazards involved in their work.

The basic safety rules must therefore be publicized by all available means, e.g. films, radio, posters, pamphlets and talks held in factories.

The authorities should clearly specify in laws and regulations suited to the local conditions of each territory what measures of prevention and protection should be taken to ensure safety and hygiene at workplaces. From the available information, it appears that in some territories there is no legislation on the subject, while in others the law has lagged behind economic and social developments or is still incomplete.

The problem of effective enforcement is undoubtedly one of prime importance and appears to raise considerable difficulties in most territories, for plant inspection personnel is deficient in numbers and not always up to the requisite standards. Inspection services should therefore be developed and should be staffed, apart from the labour inspectors, with sufficient and qualified technical personnel for the inspection of machinery and health conditions in factories.

As regards occupational diseases, the harmful effects of certain dusts of vegetable origin, particularly sisal and cotton, appear to merit further study. Industries processing these materials play such an important part in the economies of some territories that measures to protect the workers employed in them are urgently needed.

Similarly, the use of toxic substances as insecticides or for agricultural purposes constitutes an undeniable danger for workers, as has been discovered in British East Africa, and additional precautions and further research in this field seem to be required.

Of all the occupational diseases, silicosis is at present probably the most serious. The importance of mining in African economies and the size of the mining labour force are such that unceasing vigilance and the study and introduction in mines of the most modern processes aimed at the complete elimination of the dusts which cause silicosis are essential. The experience of countries such as the Belgian Congo, the Union of South Africa and Northern and Southern Rhodesia might afford useful guidance for other territories.

The general improvement of workers' health in Africa is a matter of prime importance. To some extent, then, specific problems affecting workers' health may be appropriately dealt with by general health services. Nevertheless, the setting up of special services to deal with workers' health problems might be usefully considered, at least in some territories. Such services could, among other things, provide leadership in the field of medical assistance to workers, which in certain territories is now largely the responsibility of employers.

EXAMPLES OF GENERAL HEALTH HAZARDS OF INDUSTRIALIZATION IN UNDERDEVELOPED COUNTRIES

There appears to have been more recognition of the broad community health impacts of industrialization (thus indirectly bearing on workers' health) than there has been of the direct impacts of the health of workers at the workplace. The United Nations *Industrial Development Survey* (32), while giving tangential consideration to nonrenewable resources, environmental pollution, and the skill and employment structure of the work force, makes no mention of health conditions directly affecting the worker at the workplace. The ILO volume on *Multinational Enterprises and Social Policy* deals with working conditions in terms of wages, hours, and fringe benefits, but other than suggesting that MNCs may offer higher standards of safety than locally controlled plants, again makes no mention of conditions affecting health on the job (34, p. 73). The major works on MNCs by Barnet and Muller (29) and Turner (22) consider the impacts of rural to urban migration, labor organization, resources, pollution, poverty, unemployment, and governance and political stability, but give only passing recognition to work-related health problems. Turner, for example, notes that there are lower safety standards on the vessels of major multinational shipping corporations operating under "flags of convenience," and he cites the case of the *Torrey Canyon* running aground in the English Channel while operating under the Liberian flag (22, p. 182). Turner also recognizes that one of the attractive features of the rising tourist business for MNCs and underdeveloped countries alike is that (22, p. 211): "It is a clean, safe industry compared to traditional mines and manufacturing. Tourism does not kill or maim its workers, nor does it seriously pollute or devour material resources. All that is needed is to house and feed a few foreign tourists and the money will roll in. Surely that is 'industry without chimneys'."[5] In his important work, *The Closing Circle* (24), Commoner, too, considers the environmental and health impacts of modern industry on the community at large in industrialized countries, but gives little mention to effects on workers' health at the workplace. He writes (24, p. 78):

> Such [single cause-effect, scientific] studies show no specific cause-and-effect relationships apart from a few special cases—a particular form of lung cancer due to asbestos fibers and the effect of certain metals, such as cadmium, on heart disease. However, statistical studies do show that people living in urban polluted air experience more disease than people living in less polluted, usually rural air.

Commoner's focus is on the ecosphere and how soon, given continuance of present population and pollution trends, it can be expected to collapse. This is a very important, but also a very difficult and complex, problem. One wonders whether these overwhelming ecological concerns perhaps distract us from examining and attacking more direct impacts on health at the workplace. A parallel might be found in the United States' avoidance of confronting and solving its social and economic ills by always moving on to some real or imagined "new frontier" (46).

Commoner makes an important general point of the supposed "free" use by industry of biological capital, which is not free at all. He illustrates this not only by reference to the fertility of soil, oxygen, and water, but also notes that (24, p. 272):

> Similarly, chronic, low-level exposure to radiation, mercury, or DDT may shorten a wage earner's life without reducing his income or even incurring extra medical costs

---

[5] The author goes on to count among the hazards of tourism for multinational corporations the close juxtaposition of people from extreme ends of the world scale of wealth and poverty with often different ethnic and racial backgrounds and increasing incidents of violence and building of protective enclaves for tourists: "A significant part of tourism involves shipping rich white pleasure seekers into some of the world's poorest black societies, so it is not at all surprising to find racist reactions to the industry in various parts of the world. . . . The industry is a central point in the argument raging between the 'Afro-Saxon' (i.e. 'Uncle Tom') elites of the area and their militant opponents. After all, what clearer evidence can there be that these rulers have 'sold out' than the erection of luxury hotel and restaurant complexes that exclude local black citizens? The old banana or bauxite industries were bad enough, but at least the beneficiaries were enjoying their dividends back in the United States. But their successors are the people who stay in the expensive Caribbean holiday complexes. They are sitting propaganda targets for anyone wanting to link the area's grinding poverty to the workings of capitalism. Rich, white, and capitalist, they lie in the sun, unconsciously symbolizing the whole structure of oppression as understood by local radicals" (22, p. 220).

during his lifetime. In this case, the cost of pollution is not met by anyone for a long time; the bill is finally paid by exacting the wage earner's premature death, which—apart from the incalculable human anguish—can be reckoned in terms of some number of years of lost income. In this situation, then, during the "free" period, pollutants accumulate in the ecosystem or in a victim's body, but not all the resultant costs are immediately felt. Part of the value represented by the free abuse of the environment is then available to mitigate the economic conflict between capital and labor.

But this is a general point with respect to industry, ecology and human health, and does not particularly direct our attention to health hazards affecting workers at the workplace in underdeveloped countries.

Frequent note has been made of the sometimes disastrous effects of industrialization and commercialization on the health of particular groups outside the work situation proper in underdeveloped countries. The commercialization of infant feeding, for example, has been linked with unsupportable expense to the family, poor sanitation, infectious disease, undesired parity for the mother, and greater economic burdens on the health and well being of the family as a whole.

> The damage that these products [commercial infant feeds] may do in communities that are still successfully breast-feeding their infants is readily apparent, when it is appreciated that in one area of East Africa it would have cost a laborer one-third of his salary to be able to use one of these milks in an adequate quantity to feed his 3-month-old baby (47, p. 56; see also reference 48).

The "dumping" of drugs which are dangerous and outlawed or outdated onto the markets of underdeveloped countries has also been noted (49, p. 26). MNC agribusinesses exploit vast sections of the best land for the export of a single cash crop (e.g. bananas, coffee, etc.), turning farmers into low wage earners who have to import food simply to keep themselves alive. Gradually, a whole country is shifted from a position of relative self-sufficiency to one of extreme dependence and poor nutritional levels. The greatest negative impact is on the women and children, for the lion's share of the family's cash income goes to sustain the man's strength so he can continue to bring in his meager wage (50-53).[6] In addition, industrialization of agriculture has introduced the heavy use of fertilizers and pesticides with disastrous ecological effects and, more pertinent to this paper, with reports of chemically induced disease among agricultural workers (24, pp. 146-153). The spread of bilharzia following the poor planning of the Aswan Dam is well known (55, 56). The world as a whole has seen a 37.4 percent rise between 1950 and 1975 in the proportion of people living in urban areas. In Africa it was 85.6 percent; in Latin America, 47.4 percent, and in Asia, about 80.0 percent (57). Frequent note has been taken of the inadequate sanitation, poor nutrition, and mental health problems stemming from this remarkable and rapid urbanization connected with industrialization where jobs do not materialize for all and only shantytown housing is available (44). There has been rising concern regarding increases in the incidence of cancer and other diseases associated with pollution in the urban areas of underdeveloped countries (58). For an excellent overview of the interrelated problems of smoking, air at work, and community air, see reference 59. There is also conflicting evidence on the exact factors—i.e. whether

---

[6] Bernard Nietschmann deals with the commercialization of turtle hunting and the breakdown of food exchange and human relations among the Miskito Indians in Nicaragua (54).

sociocultural stresses or dietary and other living habits and conditions—involved in the higher blood pressure and higher incidence of coronary heart disease now reported among genetically similar groups living in Western urban areas as opposed to rural settings. Higher rates of coronary heart disease among members of a group living in urban California versus those of the same group living on Guam and another Pacific island, Rota, are reported and the work of others is compared in reference 60.

HAZARDS IN THE INDUSTRIALIZING WORKPLACE IN UNDERDEVELOPED COUNTRIES

This brief review of the general effects of industrialization is not intended to indicate that the problem of direct impacts on the health of workers in the workplaces of underdeveloped countries has been completely ignored or that there are no grounds for concern. A general review of newer as well as older industries is given in reference 61. As Turner describes the situation (22, pp. 192-194):

> Work conditions in the Third World can be atrocious. Wages in South Korea, currently about the lowest in the runaway economies, are about a dollar a day, or around $7 a week. Hours are worse in Hong Kong, where 60 percent of its male workers work a seven-day week, while 52 percent of all employees work ten hours a day or more. Each year some 34,000 children between twelve and fourteen are forced to find work, and a case in which a ten-year-old girl started work at 6:00 a.m. and was still working at 8:50 p.m. is not exceptional. Official estimates are that at least one in four factories in Hong Kong uses child labor and a U.S. consulate official flew home from the colony to run for Congress in order to expose this practice, after a twelve-year-old foster child he had sponsored left school to go to work.
>
> Western unions have spent well over a century trying to eradicate such conditions, and they are not happy to see good work undone by Western multinationals who shift into the Third World to take advantage of conditions outlawed in their parent countries. The Western unions are even more incensed when they see Third World governments competing to make life as difficult as possible for fledgling union movements. In dictatorships like Taiwan, unions have no chance at all, but in other countries where unions have had some rights, there have also been serious government inroads. The incentives for pioneer industries in countries like Singapore and Malaysia specifically guarantee freedom from union trouble for a given number of years, and in 1970 there was the unedifying spectacle of Malaysia tightening its anti-union measures to bring them into line with those of Singapore. In Hong Kong the British administration has a bad record of siding with employers and was responsible for introducing controversial restrictions on picketing.
>
> It is not surprising that Third World union movements are weak. High levels of unemployment do not help matters, and the average government is hostile, seeing the unions as "annoying pressure groups for higher real wages and more advanced services than the economy can afford at a time when investment is a critical need." When a militant union wrote to the International Labor Organization in Geneva complaining about a new piece of anti-union legislation in its country, the complaint reached the ears of the government, which promptly called the leaders to a meeting with the relevant Minister. The unionists were forced to write another letter to the ILO withdrawing their allegations. Having signed, the unionists were told that they were through.

Naturally, the most thoroughly researched occupational health and safety hazards in underdeveloped countries are those of the older industries—e.g. mines (62-66), lumbering (67), textile mills (68-72), and other older type factories (73-78).

Reports of newer types of problems abound, however. Some, such as pesticide poisonings and cancer associated with agricultural chemicals, have emerged with the industrialization of agriculture (79, 80), while other more long-standing problems have intensified or become more evident (81, 82). With regard to the latter process,

- An awareness of new air pollution problems has developed in familiar industries (e.g. steel, auto) (83-85).
- Radiation hazards are now coming to the foreground (86, 87).
- Combined effects of new behaviors (e.g. smoking), urban air pollution, and dusty occupations are demanding attention (88).
- Problems of sociocultural background and the industrialization process, as well as the special problems faced by women workers in Muslim countries, are being noted (89).
- Speculations have developed concerning the relationship between industrialization and mental disorder (90, 91).

These and many other threads of concern run through the picture of occupational health in relation to industry in underdeveloped countries. But given the past history of exploitation of the underdeveloped countries and their people by the developed world, as well as the economic disparities between these parts of the world,[7] special, perhaps primary, attention must be paid to the MNCs and the setting up of hazardous industries in unregulating underdeveloped countries.[8] Evidence in this regard is scarce, but what little there is (such as that presented in the Castleman Reports covering asbestos manufacture (36) and vinyl chloride (93)) is frightening. The carcinogenic

---

[7] The case of Liberia is particularly ironic and tragic. A nation begun in 1822 by blacks who were freed men from the U.S. escaping the slavery of the times, has become, so far as the majority of its population—rubber plantation workers, iron ore miners, and unemployed—are concerned, an economic dependency of large U.S. and West European firms. The earliest on the scene and still the most dominant company is Firestone. One worker with a wife, four children, and relatives who come to stay makes $48 a month after 13 years. "The work is hard and the pay is terrible," he complains. The family lives in a little one-room house. "A power line runs right along the road there, but the company won't let me run a line into the house. So for the last 13 years we've lived in darkness. . . . I'd leave Firestone right away if I could, but there's nowhere else to go." This worker's company-owned hut is one of the better ones. Back from the road the floors are of dust, and there are no modern improvements. Almost all purchases and benefits focus around the hierarchical, patriarchal facilities of "the company." A closely worked out "incentive program" is thought to keep the workers "from getting lazy" as the director of tours explained it. The tappers get one room and no cooking facilities. In an overseer's home there are still no cooking facilities, but there are two rooms. A clerk gets a gas stove. A senior ("native") management person gets an electric stove. The vast majority are at the one room, no stove level. "Each worker is entitled to a free coffin if he's worked here 18 years," Firestone's tour director explains. There is no union. The American managers live in fine modern houses. The "Afro-Saxons" who serve as client government officials have as part of their rewards their own small private rubber plantations and it is to their advantage to keep wages low and discourage unions (92).

[8] The power and prestige and other rewards associated by the client elites of multinational companies in underdeveloped countries with owning "a piece of the action" is perhaps best illustrated by the following story: When the Iman of Oman rose against the Sultan of Muscat and Oman, the Iman said he would agree to terms offered by the Arab League if one of two demands were met: "My first condition is that I get the agency for 'Pepsi-Cola' and my second, if that is impossible, is that I get the Shell agency for distribution of oil products." Unfortunately for peace in the area, the Sultan's uncle had the Pepsi concession and the Sultan's advisor owned the Shell agency but "neither of these worthies would budge" (22, p. 107).

hazards of these materials are relatively newly recognized, but are very serious (94, 95). Nonetheless, a pattern of shifting the production of these materials to unregulating countries seems to have developed.

With the adoption of the Occupational Safety and Health Act in 1970, the U.S. set a definite standard for asbestos in the air breathed by workers—e.g. five fibers of five microns length per cubic milliliter of air (about a thimbleful).[9] In Table 3, we see the response of the MNCs to this new situation. Overall exports and imports of finished asbestos yarns nearly tripled in this period, suggesting the continuing hazard the industrial world faces in this connection. The ratio of imports to exports rose only slightly from 0.2854 in 1968 to a high of 0.4228 in 1970 and 0.3209 in 1973. But the proportion of imports to the U.S. from unregulating countries rose from zero to half of all imports received! These unregulated imports were primarily from Mexico and Taiwan, with increasing amounts also from Brazil and Venezuela.

The vinyl chloride hazard was more recently made widely known.[10] In March 1974, the U.S. Department of Labor set an emergency standard of 50 parts of vinyl chloride gas per million of air. One reaction was for companies to close down or cut back production. A trade newsletter reported that (98, p. 5):

> A 50% cutback in PVC output at its Niagra Falls, N.Y., plant is being undertaken by Goodyear Tire because bringing a 28-year-old unit into compliance with federal standards for worker exposure to vinyl chloride is "economically unfeasible." The move will eliminate 60 of the plant's 440 jobs and halt annual production of 50 million pounds of general-purpose polyvinyl chloride, although specialty resins will continue to be made in an adjacent unit built in 1957. In a separate move, Olin expects to close its 150 million pound-a-year PVC plant at Assonet, Mass., by year's end. Its contract for monomer with PPG Industries expires December 31, and Olin has been unable to line up new supplies. The plant, which employs 200, has been receiving only enough monomer recently to operate at less than 50% of capacity. In a third development, a strike at Uniroyal's PVC plant at Painesville, Ohio, has ended. The company and United Rubber Workers officials have resumed talks over the issue of "working conditions related to vinyl chloride."

The producers of vinyl chloride and polyvinyl chloride are almost all huge MNCs in chemicals, oil, and rubber. The names read like a *Fortune* magazine list of the 500 largest corporations. An inquiry by Castleman to the 30 largest producers yielded replies from only half of them and little information at that. Two companies admitted to having plants in unregulating countries: B. F. Goodrich has plants in Iran, India,

[9] In 1976 it was to go to two fibers. As Castleman points out, this standard may not be safe, since along with every five-micron fiber there are in the immediate vicinity thousands of smaller fibers. "Even at two fibers per milliliter a worker inhales over 10 million asbestos fibers in a day. The two-fiber value is comparable to the standard adopted by the British in 1968. Recent studies showing cancer and asbestosis at less than the two-fiber level have prompted the National Institute of Occupational Safety and Health to recommend further reductions in the standard" (36, p. 6).

[10] However, there is some evidence that a governmental and industry cover-up existed for some months, if not years, before the hazard was publicly recognized. This cover-up is described in the letter to the editor of *Rolling Stone* by Paul Blanc (96) in reference to an earlier article in that journal (97). In any case, Russian researchers first reported a serious problem with vinyl chloride in 1949. Then in 1961, Dow researchers found liver damage in rats with exposures of 500 parts per million. The bad news was out in January 1974, when John Creech, a physician, announced three deaths from angiosarcoma, an extremely rare liver cancer, among workers in a B. F. Goodrich polyvinyl chloride plant in Kentucky.

Table 3

U.S. exports and imports of asbestos textiles, 1968-1973, in pounds[a]

	1968	1969	1970	1971	1972	1973
Total imports ÷ Total exports	0.2854	0.3242	0.4228	0.2494	0.2473	0.3209
Exports—Total	6,899,546	8,804,973	7,465,090	13,346,116	17,286,830	19,195,243
Regulating countries	5,869,239	7,680,063	6,327,276	12,316,360	16,382,014	17,430,226
Unregulating countries	799,052	821,413	873,113	894,898	768,895	1,639,670
Other countries	231,255	303,497	264,701	134,858	135,921	125,347
Imports						
Regulating countries	1,966,196	2,854,059	2,821,705	2,785,214	3,238,538	3,039,579
Unregulating countries	–	180	333,093	543,443	1,035,528	3,121,088
Mexico	–	180	112,491	192,307	489,439	1,214,087
Taiwan	–	–	209,400	311,865	369,990	1,134,310
Venezuela	–	–	–	–	33,841	182,595
Brazil	–	–	11,202	39,271	120,491	545,080
Other	–	–	–	–	21,767	45,016
Other countries	3,444	–	1,120	–	664	–
Total	1,969,640	2,854,239	3,155,918	3,328,657	4,274,730	6,160,667
Percent of imports from unregulating countries[b]	0.00	0.00	10.55	16.33	24.22	50.66

[a] Source, adapted from reference 36.
[b] In a personal communication, Castleman has noted the continuance of this trend in 1974 and 1975.

Mexico, Venezuela, and the Philippines, and Monsanto Chemical has plants in Spain and Mexico. But this information is very incomplete.

What will the next "vinyl chloride" be? Kepone, a deadly material, has already been discovered, but is so lethal, its production will most likely simply be stopped (99). To date, reports have been published on asbestos, fluorides, airborne lead, manganese, particulate polycyclic organic matter, chromium, and vanadium. Reports on nickel, selenium, chlorine and hydrogen chloride, and vapor phase polycyclic organic material are nearly completed. Others under way include copper, arsenic, zinc, and the platinum group metals. Also in process are carbon monoxide, hydrocarbons, nitrogen oxides, and photochemical oxidants. A listing of several others has been submitted by the Environmental Protection Agency for consideration (100). A recent report associates arsenic with lung and other forms of cancer (101). One of the reactions to be most feared by workers in underdeveloped countries is the flight of such hazardous industries to their soil.

The problem of the flight of hazardous industries is of such proportions and so likely to intensify that a bill has been introduced in the U.S. Congress "to establish a Commission on Unemployment Caused by the Dispersion of Hazardous Industry".[11] While such a Commission may study the problem, which will certainly be valuable, little direct help can be expected for U.S. workers, to say nothing of those in unregulating countries.

SUMMARY OF HEALTH PROBLEMS AFFECTING WORKERS IN INDUSTRY IN UNDERDEVELOPED COUNTRIES

It is evident that the health of workers reflects the general health conditions of the population. Thus, workers in underdeveloped countries are often faced with new social-psychological pressures, heavy work loads, and assaults of noise, chemical and air pollution, as well as safety hazards. On top of this, they suffer poor nutritional levels and inadequate housing and sanitation, while their family and neighbors (if not themselves) face heavy burdens of infectious diseases such as diarrhea, malaria, schistosomiasis, tuberculosis, filariasis, leprosy, and the endemic diseases of cholera and smallpox. Given such an epidemiologic context, we can hypothesize that any hazard experienced in industry in developed countries is likely to take a higher toll in disability, disease, and death when transferred to the underdeveloped country.

However, diseases with long latency periods, e.g. cancer stemming from work with asbestos, vinyl chloride and polyvinyl chloride, arsenic, etc., may not show up if workers first succumb to one of the more quick-acting life threats so prevalent in the underdeveloped countries. Thus, we also need to seriously consider hazards known to be operant, but often disguised. To adequately assess the levels of pathology experienced by workers in underdeveloped countries, early signs of long-acting problems as well as indices of short-range threats must be developed. Clearly, the former are essential for better protection of workers in developed countries.

[11] H.R. 9505, 94th Congress, 1st Session introduced by Representative Dominick Daniels. The bill has been referred to the Committee on Education and Labor and hearings were scheduled for June 1976.

Another special characteristic of underdeveloped countries is the lack of adequate occupational health protection. Often this extends into the legal sphere, and in almost all underdeveloped countries, there are not enough active surveillance, protection, and occupational health programs and too few trained personnel at all levels.

The lack of protection for small plants, prevalent in most developed countries, is even more widespread in underdeveloped countries. The ambiguities regarding large industrial plants controlled by MNCs, especially those plants deliberately set up in unregulating underdeveloped countries to avoid protective measures, make it highly questionable whether the newer hazards are any better controlled in large plants.

This lack of protection is, of course, related to the level of consciousness and mobilization of labor, and is thus interwoven with the political-economic system. We will return to this point in our conclusion, identifying it as the most likely direction in which to look for adequate protection of workers in underdeveloped countries, as well as elsewhere.

Recognizing the special conditions in underdeveloped countries—e.g. their epidemiologic context; the lack of protective laws, programs, and personnel; the widespread problem of small plants with no protection; and the need for improved awareness, concern, and understanding among workers and management—the 1970 Symposium on the Health Problems of Industrial Progress in Developing Countries concluded by asserting that (44, p. 376):

> The maintenance of health in industrial communities in the developing countries entails:
> 1. Treatment and prevention of epidemic and endemic communicable diseases, and provision of adequate housing, environmental sanitation, nutrition and social services, including health education of workers and management;
> 2. Prevention of occupational injuries and diseases; including the mechanical, chemical and biological risks in modern agriculture;
> 3. Planning and organization of medical care, including services for small or dispersed working groups;
> 4. Initial and further training for all types of health staff, ensuring an emphasis on preventive as well as curative work;
> 5. Introduction and enforcement of statutory minimum standards of health, safety and medical care in industry.

But these conclusions fail to give recognition to hazards stemming from the unequal political-economic relations between underdeveloped and developed countries, particularly those associated with MNCs and the flight of hazardous industry. Various corrective measures have been considered in this regard, including a proposal by U.S. unions that imports from such companies be banned. But such a solution could be highly impracticable, especially if a material which is hazardous to process is essential and no substitute can be found. One writer has proposed setting up clearly controlled industrial plants for hazardous materials in agreed locations under international ownership and direction, say by a joint ILO/WHO body (102).

I suppose that the workable possibilities of any such arrangement are a long way off. In the meantime, workers in unregulating and poorly protected countries are acquiring a backlog of pathology, and are actually suffering and dying. The most fundamental solution is for the workers themselves to develop an awareness, concern, and consciousness which will lead them to build the kind of economic system and society that will enhance, not simply exploit, human potential. And this leads to our concluding hypothesis.

CONCLUDING HYPOTHESIS AND COMMENT

This paper is not the proper place to develop the conception of self-determining democratic socialism as the most fundamental means of encouraging the protection of workers as an underdeveloped country attempts to industrialize.[12] But experiences in Yugoslavia, Tanzania, Cuba, and China suggest that there is a greater awareness, concern, and mobilization of efforts to protect workers and provide adequate medical and health services in such countries.[13,14] When we look at the rape of countries like Brazil, one cannot help but hypothesize that real protection lies in this direction.

While the fundamental intent of this paper has been to contribute to a greater awareness of and concern for the health conditions of workers, and to stimulate research and action to improve their situation, it is also an exercise in conceptually based epidemiology. Epidemiology has appropriately emphasized field methods and the logic of research design. But its explanatory framework is at best eclectic, if at all existent. There are important exceptions to this characterization, however. One is the seminal piece by Payne (108) identifying poverty as a key complex of conditions associated with the higher incidence and prevalence of ill health in general. In this paper, I have attempted to deduce from an analysis of the world political economy those groups that are likely to be at greatest risk from industrial disease due to the exploitative nature of international capitalism (109, 110), and I have suggested that these groups are to be found among workers in underdeveloped countries.

REFERENCES

1. Engels, F. *The Condition of the Working Class in England in 1844* (English translation). J. W. Lovell Company, New York, 1887 (first edition, 1845, in German).
2. Thomas, N. *Human Exploitation in the United States.* Frederick A. Stokes, New York, 1934.
3. Trotsky, L. *Problems of Everyday Life.* Monad Press, New York, 1973.
4. Wallack, F. *The American Worker, An Endangered Species.* Ballantine Books, New York, 1972.
5. Brodeur, P. *Expendable Americans.* Viking Press, 1974.
6. Corn, M., Assistant Secretary of Labor. Keynote Address, "Work and Health," American Public Health Association Meetings, Chicago, November 1975.
7. Selikoff, I. J., and Hammond, E. C. Environmental cancer in the year 2000. In *Proceedings from 7th National Cancer Conference,* pp. 687-696, Los Angeles, 1973.

[12] On democratic socialism versus market and state forms of capitalism, see Vicente Navarro (103), especially the section "A final note on the convergence theory: The possible replication of class relations in socialist societies."

[13] For a discussion of the extensive health measures for industrial workers in the People's Republic of China, see reference 104 (especially pages 278 and 532), and on the general health services in China, see reference 105.

[14] The industrial situation in Cuba is described in reference 106 and the general health services in reference 107.

8. *Occupational Safety and Health in the Petroleum Industry in the Light of Technical Change. Report III. Petroleum Committee, 8th Session.* International Labour Organization, Geneva, 1973.

9. International Labour Organization, Report V (1) and (2). *Control and Prevention of Occupational Hazards Caused by Carcinogenic Substances and Agents.* International Labour Conference, 59th Session, Geneva, 1974.

10. International Labour Organization, Report VII (1) and (2). *Control and Prevention of Occupational Cancer.* International Labour Conference, 58th Session, Geneva, 1973.

11. *Chart Book. Health and Work in America.* American Public Health Association, Washington, D. C., 1975.

12. Selikoff, I., and Hammond, E. C. Toxicity of vinyl chloride polyvinyl chloride. *Ann. N. Y. Acad. Sci.* 246: 229, 1975.

13. Enterline, P., and Henderson, V. Type of asbestos and respiratory cancer in the asbestos industry. *Arch. Environ. Health* 27: 314, November 1973.

14. Lloyd, J. W. Long term mortality study of steelworkers: V. Respiratory cancer in coke plant workers. *J. Occup. Med.* 13: 53-68, 1971.

15. McMichael, A. J., Andjelkovic, D. A., and Tyroler, H. A. Cancer Mortality Among Rubber Workers: An Epidemiologic Study, Figures 3 and 5. Paper presented to the New York Academy of Sciences Conference on Occupational Carcinogenesis, New York, March 24-28, 1975.

16. Milham, S., Jr. *Mortality Experience of the AFL-CIO United Brotherhood of Carpenters and Joiners of America: 1969-1970,* Table 1. HEW Publication No. (NIOSH) 74-129. U.S. Department of Health, Education, and Welfare, Salt Lake City, July 1974.

17. Lainhart, W. S., Doyle, H. N., Enterline, P. E., Henschel, A., and Kendrick, M. A. *Pneumoconiosis in Appalachian Bituminous Coal Miners,* p. 53. U.S. Department of Health, Education, and Welfare, Cincinnati, 1969.

18. American Society of Anesthesiologists. Occupational disease among operating room personnel: A national study. *Anesthesiology* 41(4): 331-332, 1974.

19. *Survival Kit. A Health and Safety Newsletter,* July-August, 1975. Occupational Health and Safety Project, 639 Massachusetts Avenue, Cambridge, Mass., 02139.

20. Ministerium fuer Gesundheitswesen der Deutschen Demokratischen Republik, *Gesundheitsschutz in der Sowjetunion, Ergebnisse einer Studienreise deutscher Aerzte in die Sowjetunion.* VEB Verlag Volk und Gesundheit, Berlin, 1955.

21. Saknyn, A. V., and Shabynina, N. K. Epidemiology of Malignant Neoplasms in Nickel Smelters. (Institute of Industrial Hygiene and Occupational Disease, Swerdlovsk, U.S.S.R.) GIG TR PROF ZABOL 17(0): 25-29, 1973.

22. Turner, L. *Multinational Companies and the Third World.* Hill and Wang, New York, 1973.

23. Serebryanyi, L. A. Maximum allowable levels of noxious substances at work places adopted in West Germany in June, 1972. (Institute of Industrial Hygiene and Occupational Disease, Academy of Medical Sciences, U.S.S.R., Moscow, U.S.S.R.) GIG TR PROF ZABOL 12: 57-58, 1974.

24. Commoner, B. *The Closing Circle: Nature, Man and Technology.* Alfred Knopf, New York, 1971.

25. Illich, I. *Tools for Conviviality.* Harper and Row, New York, 1973.

26. Myrdal, G. *The Challenge of World Poverty. A World Anti-Poverty Program in Outline.* Random House (Pantheon), New York, 1970.

27. Weintraub, B. The year 2000 in India: Experts paint grim picture. *The New York Times,* p. 3, June 19, 1974.

28. James, W. R. Review of John H. Bodley's *Victims of Progress. WIN* 11: 21, July 24, 1975.

29. Barnet, R. J., and Muller, R. E. *Global Reach.* Simon and Shuster, New York, 1974.

30. Eberstadt, N. Myths of the food crisis. *New York Review of Books* 23: 32-37, February 19, 1976.

31. Brookfield, H. *Interdependent Development.* University of Pittsburgh Press, Pittsburgh, 1975.

32. United Nations Industrial Development Organization. *Industrial Development Survey.* United Nations, New York, 1974.

33. Galenson, W. *Labor in Developing Economies.* University of California Press, Berkeley and Los Angeles, 1962.

34. *Multinational Enterprises and Social Policy.* International Labour Organization, Geneva, 1973.

35. *Medical Tribune* 11: 1, November 16, 1970.
36. Castleman, B. Flight of Hazardous Industries to "Unregulating" Countries. Report for the Maryland Public Interest Research Group. University of Maryland, College Park, Maryland, 1975.
37. Schepers, G. W. H. Discussion in the article by A. Laamanen, L. Noro, and V. Raunio entitled "Observations on atmospheric air pollution caused by asbestos." *Ann. N. Y. Acad. Sci.* 132: 246-249, 1965.
38. Sluis-Cremer, G. K. Asbestosis in South African asbestos miners. *Environ. Res.* 3: 310-319, November 1970.
39. Mulligan, J. E. The Dominican Republic; Police state protection for U.S. corporations. *WIN* 12: 8-12, February 2, 1976.
40. Navarro, V. The underdevelopment of health or the health of underdevelopment. *Int. J. Health Serv.* 4(1): 5-27, 1974.
41. Holliday, F. *Arabia Without Sultans.* Vintage Books, New York, 1974.
42. National Emergency Civil Liberties Committee. *Rights* 22: 2, April-June 1976.
43. Brown, R. E. Public health in imperialism: Early Rockefeller programs at home and abroad. *Am. J. Public Health* 66: 897-902, September 1976.
44. Symposium on the Health Problems of Industrial Progress in Developing Countries. *J. Trop. Med.* part 1, p. 267, November 1970; part 2, concluding p. 379, December 1970.
45. *African Labour Survey.* International Labour Organization, Geneva, 1958.
46. Williams, W. A. *The Great Evasion.* Quadrangle Books, Chicago, 1964.
47. Jelliffe, D. B. Commerciogenic malnutrition. *Food Technology* 25: 55-56, 1971.
48. Arbeits-Gruppe Dritte Welt Bern. Does Nestlé Kill Babies? Postfach 1007, CH-3001, Bern, Switzerland.
49. Makers of drugs assailed in WHO. *New York Times,* June 1, 1975.
50. Conner, C. Hunger: U.S. agribusiness and world famine. *International Socialist Review,* September 1974.
51. Lorza, D., and Jacobson, M., editors. *Food for People Not for Profit.* Ballantine Books, New York, 1975.
52. *Betting on the Strong: The Imperialism of Food Production.* International Peace Research Institute, Oslo, Norway.
53. Horst, T. *At Home Abroad: Domestic and Foreign Operations of the American Food Processing Industry.* Ballinger, Cambridge, Mass., 1974.
54. Nietschmann, B. *Between Land and Water: The Subsistence Ecology of the Miskito Indians, East Nicaragua.* Academic Press, New York, 1973.
55. Hughes, C., and Hunter, J. M. Disease and development in Africa. *Soc. Sci. Med.* 3: 443-493, 1970.
56. Le Haut-Barrage du nil: Une Dure Leçon d'Ecologie. *Science et Vie* 128: 64-67, 1975.
57. Population Chart. The Environmental Defense Fund, Washington, D. C., 1975.
58. Kovi, J., and Heshmat, M. Y. Incidence of cancer in negroes in Washington, D. C. and selected African cities. *Am. J. Epidemiol.* 96: 401-413, 1972.
59. Shy, C. M. Lung cancer and the urban environment; a review. In *Clinical Implications of Air Pollution Research,* edited by A. J. Finkel and W. C. Duel, pp. 3-38. Publishing Sciences Group, for the A.M.A., Acton, Mass., 1976.
60. Reed, D., Labarthe, D., and Stallones, R. Health effects of Westernization and migration among Chamorros. *Am. J. Epidemiol.* 92: 94-112, 1970.
61. Wernsdorfer, G., and Wernsdorfer, W. H. Arbeitsmedizinische Aspekte in den Entwicklungslaendern. *Muenchner Medizinische Wochenschrift* 115: 1321-1328, August 3, 1973.
62. Goldstein, B., and Webster, I. Mixed dust fibrosis in mineworkers. *Inhaled Particles and Vapors* 2: 705-712, 1970.
63. Young, J. K. Pulmonary sarcoidosis in African mineworkers. *Proceedings of the Mine Medical Officers Association* 51: 126-133, May-August 1971.
64. Goldstein, B., and Webster, I. Coal workers' pneumoconiosis in South Africa. *Ann. N. Y. Acad. Sci.* 200: 306-315, December 29, 1972.
65. Hurivitz, L. Medical milestones in the South African mining industry: Valedictory address. *Proceedings of the Mine Medical Officers Association* 51: 47-50, January-April 1972.
66. Thaureauz, B. Occupational carpal lesions in South Moroccan miners. *Maroc Medicine* 535: 284-288, May 1970.
67. Bezjak, V. Histoplasmin tests in Uganda sawmill workers. *Trop. Geogr. Med.* 23: 71-78, March 1971.

68. Kader, A. M. M. Chemico-pathological changes in the liver of industrial workers chronically exposed to cotton dust. *J. Egypt. Med. Assoc.* 54: 489-501, 1971.
69. Khogali, M. A population study in cotton ginnery workers in the Sudan. *Br. J. Ind. Med.* 26: 308-313, October 1969.
70. Mekky, S. Varicose veins in women cotton workers: An epidemiological study in England and Egypt. *Br. Med. J.* 2: 591-595, June 7, 1969.
71. Noweir, M. H. Exposure to noise in the textile industry of the U.A.R. *Am. Ind. Hyg. Assoc. J.* 29: 541-546, November-December 1968.
72. Noweir, M. H. Seasonal exposure to dust in flax processing in Egypt. *Am. Ind. Hyg. Assoc. J.* 36: 318-324, April 1975.
73. el-Sewefy, A. Z., and Awad, S. Chronic bronchitis in an Egyptian ice factory. *J. Egypt. Med. Assoc.* 54: 311-321, 1971.
74. el-Samra, G. H. Hearing loss in boiler makers. *J. Egypt. Med. Assoc.* 53: 812-822, 1970.
75. Dieng, F. Tetraethyl lead and its prevention in an industrial plant in Senegal. *Bull. Soc. Med. Afr. Lang. Fr.* 16: 381, 1971.
76. Sofoluwe, G. O. Urinary delta-amino-levulinic acid determinants among workers charging lead accumulator batteries in Lagos, Nigeria. *Arch. Environ. Health* 23: 18-22, July 1971.
77. Hassan, A. An outbreak of vaccinia in thirteen Egyptian slaughter-house labourers at Cairo. *J. Trop. Med. Hyg.* 73: 51-53, March 1970.
78. Stoke, J. Plumbism in Rhodesia. *Cent. Afr. J. Med.* 21: 119-124, June 1975.
79. Emara, A. M. Occupational health problems in agricultural workers. *J. Egypt. Med. Assoc.* 54: 311-321, 1971.
80. Heyneman, D. Misaid to the Third World: Disease repercussions caused by ecological ignorance. *Can. J. Public Health* 62: 303-313, July-August 1971.
81. Wegesa, P., and Chimatwi, M. B. The impact of increased agricultural activities on the infection rates and densities in an endemic area of onchocerciasis. *East Afr. Med. J.* 48: 433-437, August 1971.
82. Lamont, N. M. A possible form of acute cardiomyopathy as encountered in sugar cane field workers in Tangaat, Natal. *South Afr. Med. J.* 47: 311-315, February 24, 1973.
83. Asbestos: Health risks and their prevention. *Occupational Safety and Health Series, Meeting of Experts on the Safe Use of Asbestos*, pp. 11-18. International Labour Organization, Geneva, December 1973.
84. el-Sadik, Y. M. Exposure to sulphuric acid in manufacture of storage batteries. *J. Occup. Med.* 14: 322-324, March 1972.
85. Osman, H. A. Health problems resulting from prolonged exposure to chemical agents in the rubber industry. *J. Egypt. Public Health Assoc.* 47: 290-311, 1972.
86. Gharbi, H. el-A. Report on the current status of radiation protection in Tunisia: Future prospects. *Tunis Medicine* 49: 295-300, September-October 1971.
87. Basson, J. K., and Selzer, A. Unexpected Radium-226 build-up in pyrite-burning sulphuric acid plants. *Health Physics* 28: 126-127, February 1975.
88. Femi-Pearse, D., Adeniji-Jones, A., and Oke, A. B. Respiratory symptoms and their relationship to cigarette-smoking, dusty occupations, and domestic air pollution: Studies in a random sample of an urban African population. *West Afr. Med. J.* 22: 57-63, 1973.
89. Youssef, N. H. Social structure and the female labor force: The case of women workers in Muslim Middle Eastern countries. *Demography* 8: 427-439, November 1971.
90. Brody, E. B. Psychiatric implications of industrialization and rapid social change. *J. Nerv. Ment. Dis.* 156: 300-305, May 1973.
91. Mustafa, G. Society in relation to mental health in Kenya. *J. Nerv. Ment. Dis.* 156: 295-296, May 1973.
92. Honnold, E. Firestone: American rubber in Liberia. *WIN* 11: 4-7, December 11, 1975.
93. Castleman, B. I. Statement to the U.S. Environmental Protection Agency on the Proposed National Emission Standard for Vinyl Chloride. Environmental Defense Fund, Washington, D. C., February 3, 1976 (reproduced).
94. Handelman, M., and Kotelchuck, D. Corporate cancer. *Health/PAC Bulletin* 50: 2-15, March 1973.
95. Selikoff, I. J. Environmental cancer associated with inorganic micro-particulate air pollution. In *Clinical Implications of Air Pollution Research*, edited by A. J. Finkel and W. C. Duel, pp. 49-66. Publishing Sciences Research Group, for the A.M.A., Acton, Mass., 1976.
96. Blanc, P. Letter to the Editor. *Rolling Stone*, p. 6, February 12, 1976.
97. Klein, J. The plastic coffin of Charlie Arthur. *Rolling Stone*, pp. 43-47, January 15, 1976.

98. *Chemical and Engineering News,* p. 5, November 18, 1974.
99. No date determined for Kepone disposal. *The Nation's Health* 4: 1, February 1976.
100. Griffin, H. E. Keynote Address. In *Clinical Implications of Air Pollution Research,* edited by A. J. Finkel and W. C. Duel. Publishing Sciences Research Group, for the A.M.A., Acton, Mass., 1976.
101. Arsenic exposure linked to lung cancer mortality. *The Nation's Health,* pp. 1-3. American Public Health Association, January 1976.
102. Case, R. A. M. Tumors of the urinary tract as an occupational disease in several industries. *Ann. R. Coll. Surg. Engl.* 39: 213-235, 1966.
103. Navarro, V. The industrialization of fetishism or the fetishism of industrialization: A critique of Ivan Illich. *Soc. Sci. Med.* 9(7): 351-363, 1975.
104. Richman, M. *Industrial Society in Communist China,* pp. 278 and 532. Random House, Vintage Books, New York, 1969.
105. Sidel, V., and Sidel, R. *Serve the People.* Josiah Macy, Jr. Foundation, New York, 1973.
106. Boorstein, E. *The Economic Transformation of Cuba.* Monthly Review Press, New York, 1968.
107. Danielson, R. The Cuban health area and polyclinic: Organizational focus in an emerging system. In *Comparative Health Systems,* edited by R. Elling, pp. 86-102. Supplement to *Inquiry* 12, June 1975.
108. Payne, A. M. M. Innovation out of unity. *Milbank Mem. Fund Q.* 43(4): 397-408, 1965.
109. Chase-Dunn, C. The effects of international economic dependence on development and inequality: A cross-national study. *Am. Sociol. Rev.* 40: 720-738, 1975.
110. Rubinson, R. The world-economy and the distribution of income within states: A cross-national study. *Am. Sociol. Rev.* 41: 638-659, 1976.

CHAPTER 11

Breast-Feeding: The Role of Multinational Corporations in Latin America

Michael B. Bader

Changes in national diet, George Orwell once suggested, are probably more important events in a country's history than changes in dynasty and religion (1). Orwell might have regarded as particularly significant a change in diet which also represents a deep-rooted shift in social mores—the substitution in infant feeding of the bottle for the breast. Moreover, the manipulation of individuals' values by mass media techniques of multinational corporations would have incurred his enmity.

Traditional marketing theory holds that consumer preferences are shaped largely by aggressive advertising methods. Peter F. Drucker (2), noted business management theoretician, observes:

> Markets are not created by God, nature, or economic forces, but by businessmen. . . . Only when the action of businessmen makes [customer wants] effective demand is there a customer, a market. . . . There may have been no [customer] want at all until business created it—by advertising, by salesmanship, or by inventing something new. In every case it is business action that creates the customer.

Threatened by declining birthrates in the developed countries, businessmen look to the creation of infant formula markets in the developing countries to sustain long-term corporate profitability. Literally millions of infants in the developing countries are the unwitting victims of this myopic mentality, what pediatric nutritionist Derrick B. Jelliffe calls "commerciogenic malnutrition" (3).

This paper explores the complex matrix of factors related to the decline in breast-feeding in Latin America. Specifically, we review studies concerning the statistical decline in breast-feeding and the associated immunological, contraceptive, and economic costs. A fascinating and powerful case study of bottle-feeding and infant mortality in rural Chile is presented. Next, the question of cultural imperialism and dependency is addressed. Multinational corporate advertising tactics and current regulation attempts are covered in separate sections. Finally, some suggestions are made concerning public policy to ameliorate this problem, including a consideration of the capacity of nation-states to intervene in marketing channels.

THE DECLINE IN BREAST-FEEDING

Breast-feeding has declined precipitously in the developing countries during the last 30 years (Table 1). For example, 26 years ago, 95 percent of Chilean mothers breast-fed their children beyond the first year; by 1968, only 6 percent did so, and only 20 percent of the babies were being nursed for as long as two months. In Singapore, between 1951 and 1960 there was a decrease from 79 to 42 percent of children in low-income families breast-fed for at least three months; by 1971 only 4 percent of the babies were still nursed at age three months. In the Philippines, 30 percent fewer mothers nursed their babies for twelve months in 1968 than a decade earlier. That manufactured milk formula was substituted for human milk is evidenced in the case of Colombia, where, as breast-feeding of babies declined, milk imports increased rapidly; in 1968, they were seven times greater than the 1964-1967 average (4).

In most low-income countries, the abandonment of breast-feeding is primarily an urban phenomenon, often not so much because urban mothers work as because bottle-feeding is one of the sophistications of city life the urban migrant adopts. In Guatemala, 98 percent of rural Indian babies continue to be nursed after their first birthday, compared with 57 percent of urban children (4). Yet, the efficacy of advertising campaigns for Western-style goods means that urban habits and life-styles have an increased influence on rural societies. In rural Mexico, the decline in breast-feeding is already being felt; between 1960 and 1966 the percentage of babies under six months of age who were fed only breast milk in one rural Mexican community declined from 95 to 73 (4). The concentration of the loss of breast-feeding in urban environments is especially alarming because cities in developing countries are under-going mammoth growth. The urban populations in Venezuela and Mexico, for example, were projected to increase from 47.2 to 65.3 percent and 24.3 to 39.1 percent, respectively, of the total population between 1965 and 1975.[1] This pattern is mirrored throughout Latin America and other parts of the developing world.

What are the causes of the dramatic decline in breast-feeding? Breast-feeding is

[1] Urbanization here is defined as "percentage of population in cities over 20,000." The data are taken from Bruce Russett's *The World Handbook of Political and Social Indicators* (Yale University Press, New Haven, 1965).

Table 1

Extent of breast-feeding in selected countries and years, 1946-1971[a]

Country	Year	Babies Breast-Fed
		%
Chile (at age 13 months)	1960	95
	1968	6
Mexico (at 6 months)	1960	98
	1966	41
Philippines (at 12 months)	1958	64
	1968	45
Singapore (at 3 months)[b]	1951	79
	1971	4
United States (on leaving hospital)	1946	40
	1966	18

[a] This table is adapted from a chart contained in reference 4, p. 91.
[b] Low socioeconomic class only.

often viewed as an old-fashioned or backward custom and, by some, as a vulgar peasant practice. Indeed, anthropologists, struck by the relationship of artificial feeding to societal change, have used the duration of nursing as an inverse measure of acculturation for some countries. In most developing countries, the bottle has become a conspicuous status symbol.

Failure of lactation is one of the responses to the stress of modernization. Among the tensions in a changing environment is the mother's anxiety about her capacity to breast-feed. Her failure to initiate or continue breast-feeding is rarely traced to a physical cause but often to psychophysiological causes that interfere with the key "let-down reflex" which allows the milk to flow. Since estimates are that over 95 percent of all women have the capacity to breast-feed for six months or longer (5), a study on lactation concludes (4), "Social and cultural factors and their psychological and emotional accompaniments were far more important determinants of lactation performance than dietary and nutritional factors."

Changing social attitudes regarding the body reinforce the trend. In the United States, the breast has been gradually transmogrified from its nutritional role into a cosmetic and sexual symbol, and some women fear unjustifiably that breast-feeding will ruin the shape of their breasts. Nursing in public, a common sight a decade ago in most parts of the developing world, is rapidly disappearing, as the modesty accompanying changes in attitude grows. In an effort to reverse this dangerous trend, the Zambian government has issued an advertisement proclaiming that "Breast-Feeding Is Best for Baby," in which a mother in traditional dress nurses her child (1).

Convenience also is a factor in the abandonment of breast-feeding. To free themselves from the constraints of motherhood, women no longer bound by tradition have turned to artificial feeding. Although this is especially true for those who wish to join the organized work force, working mothers comprise only a small portion of those women who have forsaken breast-feeding. In Latin American countries, less than a fourth of women of child-bearing age hold jobs (1), and in one study, conducted in an *urban* area, only 8 percent of the mothers worked outside the home (6).

The health establishment has also encouraged the wholesale defections from breast-feeding. Large quantities of dried skim milk, a copious by-product of the butter industry, have been made available in developing countries under the "Food for Peace" and other international and state institutional feeding programs (1). Medical advice from uninformed or Western-trained doctors and nurses, the provision of supplemental infant foods to new mothers at maternity clinics, and unregulated access to wall space for pro-bottle-feeding posters in clinics, have all exacerbated the problem. Furthermore, health personnel casually distribute free literature printed by infant food companies, literature whose bias is clear (7, p. 3).

The most powerful agents of infant formula promotion are the multinational corporations whose profit statements reflect this trend. Aggressive sales promotion tactics persuade the new mother to change traditional infant feeding practices. In the West Indies, competitive representatives of baby food manufacturers visit the homes of new mothers and give free product samples (6, p. 100). And in Nigeria, women from commercial firms make the rounds of maternity clinics, distributing free samples, while doctors are given supplies for their own children (8). Other methods, such as funding research aimed at establishing scientific acceptance or endorsement of various products, and the sponsoring of pediatric conferences, are usefully employed (7, p. 33). Finally, widespread advertising in professional journals, public newspapers, radio, and billboards has spurred sales growth. The multiplicity of promotional techniques has sparked Derrick Jelliffe to write (9, p. 116):

> The pediatric nutritionist . . . is left increasingly frustrated by the well financed, steam roller, marketing techniques of the food industry to sell totally unaffordable and inappropriate infant foods in impoverished communities, while mouthing sanctimonious platitudes about their world role in improving child nutrition.

Clearly, attempts to reverse this trend will require attention to each of the promotional approaches detailed above.

"IT'S NOT NICE TO FOOL MOTHER NATURE"

In the words of Oliver Wendell Holmes, "the breasts were more skillful at compounding a feeding mixture than the hemispheres of the most learned professor's brain" (4). Holmes' analysis is corroborated by a host of nutritional studies conducted in recent years; these studies uniformly conclude that mother's milk is in many ways the perfect food for the infant. The most exhaustive review of the scientific literature on breast-feeding was conducted by Derrick B. and E. F. Patrice Jelliffe of the University of California at Los Angeles School of Public Health (10). The Jelliffes summarize studies on the biochemical and immunological properties of breast milk, as well as the psychological and economic costs of the trend away from breast-feeding.

Perhaps the most useful contribution of human milk to the infant's long-term health is in the conferring of immunological defenses upon the child. Not only is the bacteria level in breast milk low, especially as compared to the bacteria level in milk delivered from an unsterilized formula bottle, but human milk has inherent anti-infective properties as well. Immunoglobulins transferred to the child through the colostrum, or first few days of mother's milk, provide immunity to certain infectious diseases and help create an intestinal environment inimical to the growth of undesirable pathogenic organisms. The "bifidus factor" in human milk, discovered by György in 1953 and reported in 1967 (11), allows additional protection against diarrheal disease by inhibiting the growth of *Escherichia coli* bacteria. Indeed, a study conducted in a poor rural Guatemalan village substantiated this point (12).

To the extent that reliance on infant formula based on cow's milk reduces the infant's ability to fend off bacterial infection and facilitates the development of diarrheal disease, it contributes to high rates of infant mortality in the developing countries. The results of a 1957-1960 study in rural Punjab, India (13), showed that "at any age when comparisons can be made, case rates for diarrheal disease were lowest among children taking only breast milk and highest for those with the more complex diet of breast milk, other milk, and solid foods." Diarrhea occurred ten times more frequently in a group of non-breast-fed Mexican children than in a group of breast-fed children (6). Moreover, in the years 1950-1953, the Pan American Sanitary Bureau (14) found acute diarrheal disease to be the leading cause of death in eight of seventeen Latin American countries. (This figure includes older children and adults as well as infants.) The compilation of data from this and other studies led the World Health Organization to assert in 1964: "In large parts of the world deaths from diarrheal disease in the general population outnumber those from any other cause" (quoted in reference 15, p. 217).

Since diarrhea results in reduced absorption of nutrients from food, it is commonly associated with infant malnutrition. In 1963, J. E. Gordon noted of his experiences in rural Guatemala: "An episode of acute diarrheal disease commonly precedes kwashiorkor[2] by about four or six weeks" (13). It has been estimated that there are ten to twenty million young children with severe syndromes of kwashiorkor at any one time (16). And it has been amply documented that malnutrition itself is a leading cause of death in developing countries. The inter-American investigation of mortality in childhood showed that in deaths of 35,000 children under five years of age in ten Latin American countries, 57 percent had malnutrition as either the underlying or associated cause of death (14). In addition, malnutrition and infectious disease have been shown to have a synergistic relationship (17).

The protective functions of human milk are, of course, of even greater importance in the developing countries, where in many cases the community is impoverished and where there are low educational levels, highly contaminated environments, and insufficient culinary equipment for the sanitary preparation and storage of food. To prepare bottle formula requires a potable water supply, unpolluted by sewage; in Latin American countries, however, expenditures on water and sewerage are woefully

---

[2] Kwashiorkor is a major severe syndrome of protein-calorie malnutrition, caused by a diet low in protein but containing carbohydrate calories, together with the metabolic ill effects of repeated bacterial, parasitic, and viral infections.

inadequate. In 1970, for example, Colombia allocated only 8.8 percent of its total health expenditures for these facilities, and Venezuela's outlays were only 4.4 percent (18).

In terms of national development, the most meaningful attribute of unimpaired and unsupplemented breast-feeding is its definite contraceptive effect. If, in the first four to six months the infant receives only human milk, the sucking stimulus appears to inhibit ovulation in the mother. In the lactating mother, menstruation and ovulation are delayed from ten weeks to as long as twenty-six months. In Taiwan it was estimated that lactation prevented as many as 20 percent of the births that would have occurred otherwise. In India the same ratio would mean prevention of approximately 810,000 births each year.[3] Jelliffe (16) concludes: "On a worldwide basis, lactation contraception probably has a numerically greater rate of protection from pregnancy than has currently been achieved by technological devices."

Another consideration is the economic significance of declining breast-feeding, which has an impact at both the family and national levels. To purchase an adequate quantity of formula is impossible for the vast majority of families in the developing countries, as it requires one-quarter to one-third of a worker's income (15). As a result the family will often purchase too little of the milk formula, and will overdilute the mixture in the bottle. Since each feeding is too low in its content of calories and nutrients, the result is a slow but inevitable development of nutritional marasmus,[4] which demands prolonged, expensive treatment. Indeed, medical costs are usually ten times greater for bottle-fed babies than for those who are breast-fed (4).

On the national level, the costs for individual families translate into enormous expenditures. For example, the recorded decline in breast-feeding in the Philippines in 1968 alone required the approximate expenditure of the equivalent of $33 million by families or agencies. And in Kenya, it was estimated that the $11.5 million loss in breast milk was equivalent to two-thirds of the health budget, or one-fifth the yearly economic aid (1). In Tanzania, the value of human milk in terms of foreign exchange has been estimated at $22 million per year if substituted with powdered cow's milk or milk formula. This sum is considerably larger than the total budget of the Ministry of Health in that year (7, p. ii). Nutritionist Alan Berg (4) totals the bill for bottle-feeding on the international level with these startling calculations:

> An estimated 87 percent of the world's babies are born in the developing countries, about a quarter of them in urban areas. If 20 percent of the estimated 27 million mothers in urban areas do not breast-feed, the loss in breast milk is $365 million. If half of the other 80 percent do not continue to breast-feed after the first six months, the total loss reaches $780 million. These estimates, however, clearly understate the situation; losses to developing countries are more likely in the billions.

Additionally, in a world of scarce energy and raw materials, the costs in processing,

---

[3] This figure assumes a population growth rate of 2.8 percent per annum. The data are taken from the Overseas Development Council (19, p. 200).

[4] Marasmus, the other main clinical form of protein-calorie malnutrition, usually occurs in the first year of life, and is characterized by wasting of muscle and subcutaneous fat and very low body weight (usually less than 60 percent of standard). It is almost always associated with diarrheal disease.

distributing, preparing, and refrigerating cow's milk formula must be considered. In the United States alone, 70,000 tons of tinplate each year are consumed in the canning of infant formula (16).

Because of its immunological, contraceptive, and economic significance, human milk must be considered as a resource priority in international planning for health, food production, and family planning. We turn now to the concrete example of bottle-feeding and infant mortality in rural Chile.

BOTTLE-FEEDING AND INFANT MORTALITY IN CHILE

One of the most carefully documented studies of infant feeding and infant mortality in Latin America was conducted by Plank and Milanesi (20) of the Harvard School of Public Health in rural Chile in 1960-1970. Ninety-six percent of the women between 15 and 44 years of age in fifteen rural Chilean communities were interviewed in their homes, comprising a sample size of 1712 women.

Even though only 2 percent of the women were not in favor of breast-feeding and more than two-thirds felt it should be continued for at least a year, in practice, only 25 percent of the mothers fed their children exclusively on breast milk by the third month (6) and only 40 percent of the children who had reached the age of one year were receiving any breast milk at all by then (20). Employment of the mother, often cited as an important reason for discontinuing breast-feeding, was an insignificant factor in the communities studied. Of the 17 percent who were gainfully employed, fewer than half worked outside the home, and less than 1 percent claimed that their jobs kept them from breast-feeding.

Infant feeding patterns in the population were largely determined by psychosocial factors, since breast-feeding decreased significantly as maternal education and paternal income rose. The least educated, poorest group (maternal education less than three years, paternal income less than 300 escudos[5]) bottle-fed before age six months in only 35.5 percent of the cases; conversely, the most educated, wealthiest group (maternal education greater than six years, paternal income greater than 500 escudos) bottle-fed in 70.4 percent of the cases, almost twice the frequency as the former group (20).

Of the children being bottle-fed or partially bottle-fed, 66 percent received partially defatted dried milk regularly under the Chilean National Health Service's distribution program (20). It is important to note the complicity of the government health agency here, as other studies have shown that the availability of free milk substitutes is correlated with a decline in nursing.

The results of the study are remarkable. Postneonatal deaths (i.e. deaths occurring after the first month of life) were three times more frequent among those who started bottle-feeding in the first three months than among those exclusively breast-fed during that time (20). Although the investigation did not draw specific correlations between qualitative and quantitative deficiencies associated with bottle-feeding, an investigation carried out by Mönckeberg (6) in rural Chile found bacteriological contamination

---

[5] Ten escudos were worth about U.S. $1.00 in 1970.

in 80 percent of bottles used for feeding babies. Moreover, since bottle-fed children literally lack the intestinal fortitude to fend off bacterial attack, the Chilean study underscores the fact that bottle-feeding often leads to death as a result of diarrheal disease and malnutrition.

Paradoxically, higher income levels were associated with higher mortality rates in the Chilean study. The additional disposable income of these groups was apparently used to purchase milk formula, as higher-income groups tended to begin bottle-feeding at an earlier age. The proportion of infants receiving bottles but no additional foods at six months rose from 34 to 44 percent as income increased; this was paralleled by a rise in infant mortality from 42 to 54 per 1000 infants (20).

Another anomaly is that sanitary conditions—presumably because of their association with income and education—were better in the homes where infant deaths occurred. There were 48.1 postneonatal deaths per 1000 infants in houses with running water (17 percent of the total) as compared with 32.3 in those without it; the rate was 36.0 in houses with some sort of sewage system (83 percent of the total) as compared with 30.0 in those that had none. The families affected lived in less overcrowded conditions than others, with fewer members per room and per bed, and their homes were more likely to be supplied with electricity (20).

Health personnel share directly in the responsibility for alarming infant mortality rates in Chile. The risk of postneonatal death was higher if mothers had visited a private physician or prenatal clinic during pregnancy than if they had professional care only at delivery or not at all: 37.5 as compared with 27.3 per 1000 infants (20). Ironically, the more contact a mother had with health establishments, the greater was the risk to her child's life. We may assume that this fact is in part explained by the distribution and promotion of infant formula by health personnel at the clinics. This catalog of paradoxes is summarized by Plank and Milanesi (20) in their concluding statement:

> The inverse relationships of the infant mortality rates to family income, environmental factors, and medical care reinforce the conclusion that the differential mortality observed was attributable to bottle feeding and neglect of supplementary foods.

The Chilean case demonstrates that higher standards of living (as defined in conventional economic terms) are not necessarily associated with a better quality of life for individuals and families in developing countries. Next, we consider briefly the question of imperialism—political, economic, and cultural—as a background to multinational corporations' advertising practices in the infant formula industry.

THE "COCA-COLONIZATION" OF THE WORLD

In the midst of Lenin's classic work, *Imperialism, the Highest Stage of Capitalism* (21), lies a quotation from Cecil Rhodes, millionaire founder of the British colony of Rhodesia:

> . . . We colonial statesmen must acquire new lands to settle the surplus population, to provide new markets for the goods produced by them in the factories and mines.

In Lenin's view, Rhodes was merely articulating an endemic feature of capitalism: the tendency to seek out new markets abroad in the face of declining profits at home. In this section, we will examine the underconsumption hypothesis which underlies much of the modern analysis of imperialism, and the more subtle concept of cultural imperialism, which argues that consumer tastes in foreign markets are inevitably shaped by the exigencies of production in the metropole.

The underconsumption hypothesis was first developed by Simonde de Sismondi, a Swiss historian, and later elaborated by the German, Rodbertus. The basic argument was really quite uncomplicated: highly developed capitalist economies simply tended to produce more than they could consume. The solution to this problem seemed to lie in expanded foreign investment opportunities overseas, where new markets could take up the slack in consumption in the capitalist nations (22, pp. 36-37).

Although Karl Marx himself never developed a formal economic theory of imperialism, Marx's disciples, John Hobson and Rosa Luxemburg, did. These theories are critically examined in *The Question of Imperialism*, a 1973 analysis of the political economy of dominance and dependence by Benjamin J. Cohen (22) of the Fletcher School of Law and Diplomacy. Cohen offers the following operational definition of imperialism (22, p. 15):

> Imperialism refers to those particular relationships between inherently unequal nations which involve effective subjugation and the actual exercise of influence over behavior.

Cohen examines the formation of patterns of tastes in the subjugated countries, as evidenced by the distribution of the public's total expenditure of income. This distribution of expenditures, according to Marxist and radical writers, does not reflect tastes which have been autonomously determined by their citizens and government, but rather reflects the configuration of ideals and values, styles and fashions, generally associated with the system of global capitalism.

Trade transmits the configuration through what is usually called the "demonstration effect" (22, p. 161): many people in poor countries (and often those that can least afford it) attempt to emulate the consumption patterns of rich nations about which they are informed by the media. Tastes are gradually oriented away from home-grown products toward characteristically foreign types of goods. Multinational corporations producing these goods have an incentive to widen and consolidate the market via investment in merchandising facilities and sales promotion. Their aim is to facilitate the spread of a preference for their output throughout the whole of the local economy.

In the opinion of Marxists and radicals, this practice is cultural imperialism, or the destruction of local autonomy; it is often called the "coca-colonization" of the world. The distortion of consumer desires by multinational corporations has a retarding effect on economic development since it represents a misallocation of scarce monetary resources from the standpoint of the welfare of the community at large. These concerns are echoed by Theotonio Dos Santos (23) of the University of Chile, a representative of the "dependency school" of Latin American economists:

The result of dependency is to limit the development of [the dependent nation's] internal market and their technical and cultural capacity, as well as the moral and physical health of their people.

Furthermore, since high-income groups initiate the consumption of infant formula in the dependent countries, and lower-income groups attempt to emulate their values, an internal pattern of cultural imperialism develops. José Moncada Sánchez (24) of Ecuador maintains that only the establishment of strict state controls over marketing channels and possibly direct intervention in publicity media can interrupt this mechanism. We turn now to a comprehensive examination of the means and motives of multinational advertising campaigns to promote bottle-feeding.

THE PROMOTION OF BOTTLE-FEEDING BY MULTINATIONAL CORPORATIONS: HOW ADVERTISING AND THE HEALTH PROFESSIONS HAVE CONTRIBUTED

United States infant milk companies, like their big brothers, the adult food manufacturers, have gone looking for business in developing countries because of disappointing population trends at home. The annual population growth rate in the wealthiest countries of the world is less than one-half the rate in the remainder of the world (19, p. 211) (Table 2).

The low population growth in the 1960s has limited the sales growth of food processing companies in general. In fact, a business survey published in 1973 stated that U.S. food processing companies had reported the lowest annual rate of domestic sales growth (5 percent) of any industry in the survey. And a 1973 article in *Business Week* explained that food processors, "starving for profits," are looking both at overseas markets and at nonfood products and services at home, seeking "renewed opportunities for profitable business" (quoted in 25, p. 128).

Baby-related industries have been even harder hit by population trends in the United States, for although the population is still growing—albeit at a slower rate—the birthrate itself is in a substantial decline. From a 1957 peak of more than 4.3 million births, the annual number of births had declined in 1974 to about 3.1 million. The 1973 birthrate in the United States was the lowest in American history, a fact reflected in business publication headlines such as "The Baby Bust," and "Bad News in Babyland." The decline in the U.S. birthrate—what *Dun's Review* called "too few mouths to feed"—appears to varying degrees throughout the affluent world (quoted in 25, p. 128).

Searching for opportunities to increase profits, then, some baby food companies have diversified into new lines. Others, including the milk companies, have tried to expand markets for their traditional products in those areas of the world where population is still increasing: the Third World countries.

Abbott Laboratories, the pharmaceutical multinational whose Ross Laboratories division manufactures Similac and Isomil formulas for infant feeding, is expanding rapidly overseas, with the pediatric market a major focus. The overseas portion of Abbott's pediatric sales (including formula products and drugs) rose from 14.3 percent in 1969 (overseas pediatric sales of $12.5 million) to 22.2 percent in 1973 ($31.3

Table 2

Gross national product, per capita gross national product, and
population: 1970 levels and 1960-1970 annual growth rates[a]

Area	Per Capita GNP, 1970	Total GNP, 1970	Per Capita GNP Annual Growth Rate, 1960-1970	GNP Annual Growth Rate, 1960-1970	Population, 1970	Population Annual Growth Rate, 1960-1970
	$	$ bil	%	%	mil	%
Rich countries	2,790	2,570	4.4	5.5	920	1.1
Middle-income countries	870	270	4.5	6.5	310	2.0
Poor countries	300	155	3.2	6.0	520	2.8
Very poor countries	120	230	1.8	4.0	1,930	2.2
World	880	3,225	4.1	6.1	3,680	2.0

[a] Source, Richard Jolly, "International dimensions," in Hollis Chenery et al., *Redistribution with Growth*, p. 160, Oxford University Press for World Bank and Institute of Development Studies, University of Sussex, 1974.

million). From 1972 to 1973, Ross expanded domestic sales for the formula products it markets by 9 percent but foreign sales by 32 percent. In Abbott's 1973 annual report, marketing plans for the company's international division were confirmed (quoted in 25, p. 128):

> In essence, our strategy for 1974 remains unchanged: maintain consistent growth in the pharmaceutical area, but exert major thrust at the newer, more dynamic hospital and pediatric markets.

This strategy appears to have been successful: pediatric sales were up 17 percent in 1974, with sales of two infant formula products up 38 percent. Latin American sales comprised 28 percent of total sales for Abbott in 1974 (7, p. 59).

Bristol-Myers, whose Mead Johnson division manufactures Enfamil, Olac, and Prosobee, includes among its problems over the last five years "the sudden decline in the birthrate which affected Enfamil and other pediatric products." Bristol-Myers' international division, with sales up from just over $100 million in 1968 to $400 million in 1974 (quoted in 25, p. 129), is the fastest-growing part of the company. Infant formula constitutes an important segment of the division, according to the 1973 annual report, particularly in Latin America. Indeed, about 40 percent of the total sales of Enfamil is outside the United States. International sales grew 12-18 percent per year during the last decade, compared with 7 percent for domestic. Advertising and product promotion expenses in 1974 totaled $296 million (7, p. 63).

It is significant to note that Abbott and Bristol-Myers allegedly control 90 percent of the infant formula market, which constitutes a virtual monopoly. In December 1974, *Baker Laboratories* (subsidiary: Baker/Beech-Nut Corporation) went out of the infant formula business. On March 13, 1975, Baker brought suit in federal court in Philadelphia against Abbott and Bristol-Myers, charging that they monopolized the infant formula market, and seeking treble damages and a halt to alleged unfair competition (7, p. 61). *Advertising Age,* March 1975, summarized additional allegations contained in the suit (quoted in 7, p. 61):

> Baker has charged the two companies with paying cash grants to hospitals as well as supplying free infant formula in return for the hospital staff feeding newborns these brands and recommending that mothers continue using them at home. The suit also notes that the hospitals distribute promotional literature.

Another multinational involved in the infant formula business is *Nestle,* the world's second largest food company (the first is the Netherland's Unilever). While only 12 percent of its assets are located in developing countries, they account for 20 percent of its sales. Sales in Latin America, where Nestle began operating in 1920, comprise 35 percent of the total. Brazil, Mexico, and Nicaragua have requested Nestle to increase its activities there, especially with respect to the development of local dairying. Nestle's annual report for 1971 underscored the importance of sales in the developing countries (7, pp. 71-72):

> In the developing countries, demographic growth, the rising standard of living and, generally, the endeavors to promote infant nutrition, offer good prospects for our products.

But Nestle has not gone without virulent criticism. Switzerland's "Third World Group" published a pamphlet delicately titled "Nestle Kills Babies," in June 1974. The following month, Nestle brought suit against the group for libel, and court proceedings were expected to ensue. The group intends to defend itself by establishing a clear cause-and-effect chain from bottle-feeding in poor countries to malnutrition and death, and by showing that Nestle's advertising has played a significant role in the switch to the bottle (7, p. 72).

ADVERTISING THROUGH THE MEDIA AND HEALTH PERSONNEL

The first noteworthy study of the role of the advertising and health professions in the promotion of bottle-feeding was completed in 1975 by Ted Greiner of the Cornell University Division of Nutritional Sciences (7). Greiner studied the distribution of infant formula advertisements in public and professional journals and magazines, and the multinational firms' efforts to employ health professionals directly in their sales campaigns.

Greiner's statistics controvert the claim by infant food companies that they direct advertising toward more affluent audiences. He writes (7, p. 6):

> There appears to be a tendency to advertise selectively in low income publications. This should come as no surprise, since advertising funds are targeted toward maximum efficiency.

In addition, broad-based media, such as radio, outdoor displays, general publications, and recently even television, are relied upon. Efforts at reaching target groups (mothers) are confined to promotion through clinics and hospitals, retail outlets, and home visitations using hospital-provided lists of new mothers.

The advertisements themselves are misleading. Many stress that infant formula are "ideal substitutes for mother's milk," an assertion that is directly contradicted by evidence concerning breast milk's unique immunological properties. Nestle even maintains that Pelargon provides "extra-protection" and a "reduction in bottle-borne infections caused by poor hygiene" (7, p. 10). We should recall, however, that 80 percent of the bottles used for infant feeding in the Chilean example were contaminated with bacteria.

Mothers who are unsure if and when to bottle-feed are encouraged by Similac advertisements to use it "right on the first day," despite careful scientific studies testifying to the initial importance of mother's milk because of its special immunological characteristics (7, p. 7). Finally, many imported infant foods stress their origin from a developed country, showing that the charge of cultural imperialism has some justification.

Advertising specifically directed toward health professionals is particularly useful to multinational firms, since 73 percent of physicians find journal papers and articles "preferred sources of information" (7, p. 8). Surprisingly, this is reported to be true of medical journal advertisements as well. Greiner (7, p. 9) found that journals published in developing countries contain "a higher number of infant food ads per issue than journals of comparable date and area of specialty from developed countries."

Free literature on infant care and feeding, distributed by pediatricians to new mothers as part of their child care services, is notorious for its biases. In a "content analysis" of twenty-two infant food publications, Greiner reports that "most receive uniformly low ratings with respect to both space given to and statements made about breast-feeding" (7, p. 12). Ross Laboratories' free infant care and feeding literature, "Breast-Feeding Your Baby" makes twice as many negative statements as positive statements about breast-feeding, and devotes no fewer than one-third of its pages to promoting its formula (7, p. 13).

Two other aspects of health institutions are exploited to promote infant formula: milk nurses and milk banks. A study of the use of these "milk nurses" in Jamaica in 1974 detailed their questionable practices (25, pp. 137-138). Fully trained nurses who also undergo training by the infant food companies are employed to visit all the new mothers whose names are given by area hospitals. The mothers visited often do not have adequate income to feed their children artificially, but, in general, milk nurses do not tell mothers about the costs involved in artificial feeding. The Jamaica Milk Products Nurse, who sells Nestle products, is allowed to enter maternity wards in public hospitals in order to talk to mothers directly. Other nurses make home visits and home deliveries, sometimes on a commission basis. Although they are supposed to give mothers moral support and child care information, the study revealed that "most mothers felt that the nurses had offered very little information unrelated to the company's products" (25, p. 138).

Milk banks are sales outlets for commercial formula products set up in hospitals and clinics that serve the poor. The banks sell infant milk (sometimes imported tax-free) at discount prices to mothers of limited economic resources (25, p. 138). From information collected in 1974 on milk bank operations in Guatemala City and Santo

Domingo, the banks seemed to be a marketing device—generally introduced by the Swiss firm Nestle—aimed at expanding the practice of artificial feeding among the poor without interfering with the normal commercial market.

Even at discount prices, however, commercial substitutes for breast milk are too expensive for the people the milk banks are designed to reach. At Robert Reid Cabral Hospital in Santo Domingo, Nestle's Pelargon sells in a one-pound tin for 90 cents, a 40 percent discount off the retail price. But very few mothers who go to the bank purchase enough formula each month to feed an infant adequately. Fifty mothers at this bank were asked if they could afford to buy a tin of formula every few days (the maximum feeding duration for a one-pound tin); the most common response was that they simply did not buy it that frequently, that instead they "prepared the bottles with less milk and more water and in this way the milk lasted longer" (25, p. 139). Of course, habitual dilution of the formula causes chronic malnutrition of the infant.

These sad facts make the nutritional firms no less candid about their promotional tactics. Abbott Labs' annual report for 1967 proudly proclaims (7, p. 14):

> Not only quality of product, but skillful promotion to pediatricians, general practitioners, and hospitals have enabled Similac to hold its market leadership.

Bristol-Myers' annual report for 1973 states (7, p. 14):

> Mead Johnson [subsidiary of Bristol-Myers] is frequently introduced to new parents by their doctor or in the hospital with the Enfamil Discharge-Pack.

Business Abroad, June 1970, summarizes Nestle's marketing coups (quoted in 7, p. 15):

> In less developed countries, the best form of promoting baby food formulas may well be in clinics which the company sponsors, at which nurses and doctors in its employ offer child-care guidance service. One fruitful by-product of this operation is that at christenings and birthday parties Nestle products often are given as presents.

Clearly, the multinational corporations have sufficiently wooed the health profession to implicate them in their promotional schemes. We move now to an examination of current efforts to monitor and control multinational advertising practices in the infant formula industry.

CURRENT EFFORTS TO REGULATE MULTINATIONAL ADVERTISING OF BOTTLE-FEEDING

Two groups have been most active in inveighing against the practices of multinational infant food corporations. The Interfaith Center on Corporate Responsibility (ICCR), a "sponsored related movement of the National Council of Churches," has encouraged stockholders' inquiries into the marketing vehicles of Abbott Laboratories and the Bristol-Myers Company. The Protein Advisory Group (PAG) of the United Nations System has been instrumental in drafting industry codes of marketing ethics and publishing studies related to the breast versus bottle controversy.

Bristol-Myers has responded to ICCR's charges in a twenty-page report that, in the opinion of this writer, is misleading, distorted, and self-indicting. The report cleverly employs a PAG classification scheme that places fifty countries in twelve general development levels. Bristol-Myers purposefully regroups these development levels to buttress its claim that "over three-fourths of Enfamil sales come from the more 'developed' countries" (26). Yet, a careful analysis of the Bristol-Myers report reveals that those countries which the corporation considers "developed" include over 71 percent of the population of Latin America, an area of the world that is almost invariably regarded as part of the "developing" world.[6] Such semantic manipulations seriously undermine the credibility of Bristol-Myers' defense of its practices.

The report then takes up the specific points of information raised by stockholders. To the question of what kinds of promotional programs are employed, the report answers (26):

> Pediatricians and other medical professionals are the primary audience for technical promotional literature. The Company believes the physician—not the producer of infant formula products—should advise the mother about her infant's feeding and health care.

Yet, in light of Greiner's study showing the complicity of health personnel in infant formula promotion, Bristol-Myers' response is at best self-indicting. Also, with respect to the labelling and the hygienic preparation of infant formula, Bristol-Myers comments (26):

> Mead Johnson formula products throughout the world are labelled in accord with U.S. Food and Drug Administration labelling regulations for such products.... The label of each infant formula product contains complete and explicit directions for the correct storage, preparation, and use of this product.

In no way, however, does this comment deal with the fact that in large parts of the developing world, the "correct" storage and preparation facilities (e.g. refrigerators and stoves) simply do not exist, and large numbers of mothers cannot even read these labels.

Finally, the company asserts that infant formula products are not marketed to marginal-income or illiterate families. Unfortunately, Bristol-Myers neglects to provide statistical proof of this assertion; they merely conjecture (26):

> In each country, regardless of the overall level of development, one segment of the population has sufficient affluence to seek medical services and to demand and pay for top quality products. It is believed that this segment accounts for essentially all Enfamil sales in the "developing" countries.

In sum, the report smacks of the worst forms of multinational corporate sophistry.

The United Nations Protein Advisory Group has assumed leadership in the incipient dialogue between multinationals and stockholders' groups for which ICCR provides investigative support. In 1972 and 1973, PAG held two international seminars for pediatricians and senior representatives of the infant food industry. These meetings

---

[6] The following Latin American countries are grouped with the "developed" countries by the Bristol-Myers report: Mexico, Brazil, Paraguay, Peru, and Colombia. The total population of these countries (Overseas Development Council statistics, 1969) is 173.4 million, which is 71 percent of the total Latin American population of 244.5 million. The PAG classification scheme explicitly calls the countries "developing countries."

led to the issuance of PAG Statement No. 23, "Promotion of special foods (infant formula and processed protein foods) for vulnerable groups" (27, p. 1). One of the recommendations made in the seminars was that PAG should collaborate with industry, the medical and health professions, and national governments to establish regional industry councils that would assess and act on problems related to inappropriate infant and young child feeding practices. The first of these seminars was held in Singapore in November 1974, and generated a number of useful recommendations.

The recommendations included (a) clear policy guidelines for feeding practices for young infants, older infants, and young children; and (b) general proposals to the medical and health professions, industry, and government "for action to promote desirable policies and practices" (27, pp. 1-5). Moreover, the *PAG Bulletin* has faithfully reproduced a host of studies relating to bottle-feeding, malnutrition, and mortality rates, and has significantly aided in the dissemination of other relevant studies on nutrition.

One of the most interesting proposals produced in response to these PAG efforts is the "International Code of Marketing Ethics with Reference to Infant Feeding," submitted by Ross Laboratories. The code consists of guidelines for ethical behavior that amount to a succinct truth-in-advertising statement (27, pp. 23-25). Although this code could be dismissed as the work of wily public relations men, it does seem to signal a heightened awareness of the social responsibility of these corporations in the face of alarming correlations between bottle-feeding and infant mortality.

Unfortunately, PAG's efforts are weakened by the voluntary nature of industrial participation. Bristol-Myers, for example, is not participating in the industry code (28). And in the absence of any legal jurisdiction to enforce these policy guidelines, PAG is effectively powerless to force compliance. Moreover, can an industry so heavily dependent on the growth of its markets in developing countries honestly be expected to give significant weight to a "code of ethics" in the calculation of profits? It seems that we must look elsewhere—to the power of individual or associated nation-states— for the capacity to regulate the multinational infant food corporations.

PEOPLE BEFORE PROFITS—PUBLIC POLICY RECOMMENDATIONS

The decline in breast-feeding in Latin America, in particular, and the developing countries in general has been shown to be a trend whose serious public health consequences mandate a powerful state response. The urgency of the need for strict regulation of marketing practices of multinational infant formula corporations must penetrate both the mass media and professional journals in developing countries. Health personnel training programs throughout the world should be reoriented to emphasize the immunological and nutritional value of breast-feeding. In addition, the same advertising techniques that are responsible for the increase in artificial feeding can be used to counter the trend. Magazines and daytime radio programs directed specifically to women can serve as channels of information. Maternity clinics can be staffed with specialists in infant nutrition trained not by multinational corporations, but by education centers established under the auspices of the United Nations Protein Advisory Group's regional councils.

Under existing international arrangements, only the state has the legal jurisdiction and political power to control product promotion techniques. Each nation must first autonomously determine which Western consumer goods—whether they be automobiles, clothing, appliances, or technology-intensive health products such as pharmaceuticals and infant formula—are critical to its national development plans, and then decide which of these Western technologies should be produced domestically, and which should be imported and marketed under strict regulation. Alfred C. Stepan (29) of Yale University has argued that direct foreign investment for purposes of creating foreign subsidiaries must be subject to a policy of nonautomatic entry, with access to important markets only selectively and conditionally granted to multinational firms. Since declining birthrates in the industrialized countries make access to markets in developing countries crucial to the long-term profitability of infant formula concerns, developing countries should be able to exact many bargaining concessions from them. Among these concessions is compliance with comprehensive marketing codes drafted by local public health officials and state planners. On the regional level also, common market organizations such as the Andean Pact must close existing loopholes with respect to media access (30). Thus, the state can employ a variety of bargaining maneuvers to mitigate the harmful impact of multinational corporations whose advertising efforts shape local consumption patterns.

Stockholders' groups and "corporate responsibility" centers should continue to press industry for details concerning marketing practices, and corporate responses to these inquiries should be carefully scrutinized for misleading analysis and obfuscatory statements. These groups may work through existing legal structures throughout the world to extend "truth in advertising" precedents and to destroy monopolistic tendencies of the food multinationals.

In the final analysis, however, what is needed is the development of an awareness that human milk is an invaluable natural resource uniquely constituted by nature to protect and nourish the infant. The health needs of the *people* in the developing countries must be placed before the cold requirement of healthy *profits* for the multinational infant formula corporations. The "mother's milk" of politics may be money, but money is immaterial when the health of human beings is concerned.

Note Added in Proof—Since this article was written, the Swiss court ruling on Nestle's charges of libel against the Third World Working Group held thirteen members of the Group liable for $130 each for damages. The Group plans to appeal this verdict.

Acknowledgments—I would like to thank Ann Crittenden, Leah Margulies, Ann L. Engelland, and Eleanor M. LeCain for their invaluable assistance in the preparation of this paper.

REFERENCES

1. Wade, N. Bottle feeding: Adverse effects of a Western technology. *Science* 184: 45-48, 1974.
2. Drucker, P. F. *Management,* p. 61. Harper and Row, Publishers, New York, 1974.
3. Jelliffe, D. B. Commerciogenic malnutrition. *Nutr. Rev.* 30(9): 199-205, 1972.
4. Berg, A. *The Nutrition Factor,* pp. 89-106. Brookings Institution, Washington, D. C., 1973.
5. Muller, M. *The Baby Killer,* p. 6. War on Want Pamphlet, London, 1974.

6. Mönckeberg, F. Factors conditioning malnutrition in Latin America, with special reference to Chile. *Bibl. Nutr. Dieta* No. 14, pp. 23-33, 1970.
7. Greiner, T. *The Promotion of Bottle Feeding by Multinational Corporations: How Advertising and the Health Professions Have Contributed.* Cornell University International Nutrition Monograph Series No. 2, Ithaca, New York, 1975.
8. Wennen-Van Der May, C. A. M. The decline of breast feeding in Nigeria. *Trop. Geogr. Med.* 25: 93-96, 1969.
9. Jelliffe, D. B., and Jelliffe, E. F. P. The urban avalanche and child nutrition. *J. Am. Diet. Assoc.* 57(8): 111-118, 1970.
10. Jelliffe, D. B., and Jelliffe, E. F. P. An overview. *Am. J. Clin. Nutr.* 24: 1013-1024, August 1971.
11. György, P. Human milk and resistance to infection. In *Nutrition and Infection,* edited by G. E. W. Wolstenholme and M. O'Connor. Ciba Foundation Study Group No. 31, London, 1967.
12. Mata, L. J., and Urrutia, J. J. Intestinal colonization of breast-fed children in a rural area of low socioeconomic level. *Ann. N.Y. Acad. Sci.* 176: 93-109, January 7, 1971.
13. Gordon, J. E. Weanling diarrhea. *Am. J. Med. Sci.* 245: 345, 1963.
14. Puffer, R. R., and Serrano, C. V. *Patterns of Mortality in Childhood.* Pan-American Health Organization, Washington, D.C., 1973.
15. Scrimshaw, N. S., Taylor, C. E., and Gordon, J. E. *Interactions of Nutrition and Infection.* World Health Organization, Geneva, 1968.
16. Jelliffe, D. B., and Jelliffe, E. F. P. Human milk, nutrition, and the world resource crisis. *Science* 188: 557-561, May 9, 1975.
17. Latham, M. C. Nutrition and infection in national development. *Science* 188: 561-565, May 9, 1975.
18. Navarro, V. The underdevelopment of health or the health of underdevelopment: An analysis of the distribution of human health resources in Latin America. *Int. J. Health Serv.* 4(1): 5-27, 1974.
19. Howe, J., editor. *The United States and World Development—Agenda for Action 1975,* p. 211. Overseas Development Council, Washington, D.C., 1975.
20. Plank, S. J., and Milanesi, M. L. Infant feeding and infant mortality in rural Chile. *Bull. WHO* 48: 203-210, 1973.
21. Lenin, V. I. *Imperialism, the Highest Stage of Capitalism.* International Publishers, New York, 1939.
22. Cohen, B. J. *The Question of Imperialism.* Basic Books, Inc., New York, 1973.
23. Dos Santos, T. The structure of dependence. *American Economic Review* LX(2): 231-236, 1970.
24. Sánchez, J. M. El desarrollo economico y la distribucion del ingreso en el caso Ecuatoriano. In *Economic Survey of Latin America, 1973,* p. 311, by the Economic Commission for Latin America. United Nations, New York, 1975.
25. Ledogar, R. *Hungry for Profits,* pp. 127-145. IDOC, North America, Publishers, New York, 1975.
26. The Infant Formula Marketing Practices of Bristol-Myers Company in Countries Outside the United States, pp. 12-17. Bristol-Myers Company, August 7, 1975 (mimeographed).
27. Protein Advisory Group of the United Nations System. *PAG Bull.* V(1): 1-33, 1975.
28. Margulies, L. Eco-justice task force, Interfaith Center on Corporate Responsibility. Letter to the author, p. 1, October 15, 1975.
29. Stepan, A. C. The state and foreign capital. In *The State and Society: Peru in Comparative Perspective,* Ch. 7. Princeton University Press, Princeton, N.J., forthcoming.
30. Committee of the Agreement of Cartagena (Andean Pact Countries). Decision No. 24— Standard Regime for Treatment of Foreign Capital and for Treatment of Trademarks, Patents, Licenses, and Royalties. Articles 43-44. December 31, 1970.

CHAPTER 12

The Political Economy of Controlling Transnationals: The Pharmaceutical Industry in Sri Lanka, 1972-1976

Sanjaya Lall and Senaka Bibile

This paper attempts to analyze the experience of Sri Lanka in reforming the structure of production, importation, and distribution of pharmaceuticals during the period 1972-1976. Since the pharmaceutical industry is of vital concern for every developing country, and since it is overwhelmingly dominated by transnational corporations (TNCs) that possess considerable market power as well as a proven ability to resist reform, such an analysis can serve two purposes.

First, it can help policy makers in less-developed countries (LDCs) who wish to reform the industry by illustrating the sorts of difficulties, resistance, and pressures they may expect to face, as well as the benefits they may expect to achieve.

The drug industry has aroused considerable controversy in both the home and host countries of the TNCs which dominate it.[1] The U.S. Senate, during about 18 years of intermittent hearings in various subcommittees, has produced volumes of criticism, evaluation, and recommendation, on the basis of which the Food and Drug Administration (FDA) has set up a complex apparatus for controlling the introduction of new drugs, checking their efficacy, regulating advertising and labeling, and, most recently, reducing their cost to federally financed health schemes (although not to the public).

Other developed countries have also instituted controls of different degrees of intensity and comprehensiveness, though the dominant firms have, with the help of

---

[1] Critiques of the international pharmaceutical industry are provided in references 1-5; for a defense, see reference 6.

various groups, managed to thwart substantial reform. Less-developed countries have not been able to institute successfully controls of the types used by advanced countries, and, with the exception of Sri Lanka, they have certainly not been able to achieve complete rationalization of the industry while retaining a basically capitalist system of production. A number of them have tried (Brazil, Pakistan, India, Turkey, and others have undertaken or are proposing to undertake partial reforms), but have not achieved the desired result of providing effective and inexpensive medicines to meet the basic needs of their populations. We believe that, with careful planning, this goal is achievable. The problem is why the effort is so rarely undertaken. The Sri Lanka case sheds light on this.

The second purpose served by our analysis of the Sri Lanka experience is that it can further our understanding of the TNC phenomenon, in particular of the inter-action between these giant firms and the various groups in host LDCs that are concerned with them. While a great deal has been written about the problems raised by TNCs and the means that may be used to control them (7), much of the discussion by "conventional" economists has been conducted in a sociopolitical vacuum which abstracts from the conflict and compromise (or domination) between the interests involved. Many economists ignore the existence of excess profits arising from TNC operations that might be included in the bargaining process. Even when economists admit the existence of such profits, the game-theory approach (i.e. with an enlightened government embodying a clearly defined "national interest" on one side, confronting a politically powerless TNC on the other) generally used to analyze the process of how TNC earnings are distributed between the firms and host governments ignores crucial sociopolitical factors. It is mainly the political economists who have tried to integrate economic, class, social, and ideological factors in their analysis of the TNC-LDC inter-play. Such attempts have not always been successful; the theoretical constructs still need considerable refinement, and there is an unfortunate tendency to overgeneralize from particular situations. Nevertheless, this approach reflects a much clearer grasp of the forces at work. The detailed analysis of one microcosm of the political economy of the TNC-host country conflict can certainly add to our limited knowledge of how such forces work.

A note of caution is necessary, however. One must be very careful in generalizing the experience of the drug industry in Sri Lanka to other countries or other TNC-dominated industries. The small scale of Sri Lanka's economy and its relative industrial backwardness, coupled with relatively high degrees of literacy and political awareness, may limit its relevance to large countries such as Brazil, India, or Pakistan, or even small ones like Nepal. The peculiar nature of the drug industry, with its high tech-nology and powerful promotional practices, its close relationship with the effective buyers (the medical profession), and public and official sensitivity to its products, may similarly render it different from industries whose products are of lesser social importance, whose merits are more objectively assessable, or whose market power is easier to dilute. Despite this, however, we believe that some interesting and important lessons do emerge from the Sri Lanka case which are of general validity, especially as far as the formulation of health and pharmaceutical policies in less-developed countries is concerned.

BACKGROUND TO THE REFORM

Prior to the reforms undertaken in 1972, Sri Lanka's health delivery structure was similar to that of most countries which do not have a national health service or a comprehensive insurance scheme (8). It consisted of a state sector, administered by the Department of Health, which ran hospitals and provided free medicines, and a private sector, where drugs were provided by relatively unregulated local producers and importers. Although there were 14 drug firms in the country, the bulk of their activity, which consisted of simple formulation and packaging of finished pharmaceuticals imported in bulk, was concentrated in over-the-counter (OTC) or "proprietary" drugs sold without prescription. The greatest share of "ethical" or prescription drugs was directly imported into the country in finished form.

Imports for some 800 institutions in the state sector were handled by the Civil Medical Stores (CMS), while those for the private sector were undertaken by 134 local agents of foreign suppliers. The state sector was, until the late 1950s, subjected to the same exuberant promotion and product-differentiation activity that the industry used in selling its products to the private sector, and still uses in most LDCs where official control of promotion is relatively lax.[2] Several thousand brands were presented to doctors, with the accompaniment of heavy advertising, distribution of samples, and visits by detail men. So great was the influence of promotion on information flow that doctors in Sri Lanka hospitals were often unaware of the generic names of the drugs they were prescribing (and thus of which drugs were equivalent in their effects)[3] and of the proper indications and contraindications for their use. Certainly their practice showed an appalling lack of awareness of drug prices and the possibilities for economizing on drug purchasing.

One of the present authors, then professor of pharmacology at the University in Colombo, was asked to help the CMS rationalize drug prescribing. He advised the government to reduce the drugs used to the 500 (in 1000 presentations) that were actually necessary, and to publish a Hospitals' Formulary listing medicines by their proper generic names only and giving full and objective information on their use. It was recommended that a Formulary Committee be appointed to prepare the report and to review it each month, deleting obsolete or unnecessarily toxic drugs and introducing new drugs that had been proven effective.

In 1959, the state sector was rationalized according to advice given in the face of

---

[2] In early years of excess, such promotional activities were used in the developed countries as well. Furthermore, various U.S. Senate hearings, most recently those under Senator Edward Kennedy, have shown that many of these excesses continue today. The U.K. situation was reviewed by the Sainsbury Committee (9) and Coleman (10), and the Canadian situation by Klass (3). The evidence suggests that the U.S. is subjected to the greatest amount of high-pressure promotion; the U.K. has recently experienced a fall in promotion expenditures, mainly as a result of official control.

[3] This often led to situations where, when particular prescribed brands were not available, patients were deprived of that drug or had to engage in long searches, although the pharmacies and hospital dispensaries had stocks of identical medicines under different names. Bibile (8) also notes instances of doctors substituting one brand of a drug for another in the mistaken belief that they were changing the treatment.

considerable opposition from drug companies and doctors, but nothing was done about the private sector. Drugs were purchased and dispensed by generic names in the state system, and the greatly reduced list proved over time not to have had any adverse effects on the hospitals' standards of medical care.

The 1960s witnessed a steady deterioration in Sri Lanka's balance of payments position. The government was compelled to progressively cut allocations of foreign exchange to both the CMS and the private sector. The CMS found, under this pressure, that it could economize on the purchase of the generic drugs listed in the Formulary by "shopping around" on the world market and buying in bulk, rather than depending on its traditional TNC suppliers. The magnitude of savings was enormous, as we shall see later in our discussion of the rationalization of the private sector. Moreover, the experience gained by the CMS in this period was invaluable to the reforms that were to follow.

By 1963, the foreign exchange crisis had grown to such proportions that the government decided to economize on the purchase of drugs in the private sector. Its first step was to reduce the number of drugs imported, a step taken in the belief that this would reduce the total cost of drugs purchased abroad. The 4,000 drugs being used under a far larger number of brand names were cut, on the recommendation of a Drugs Subcommittee, to 2,100.[4] No action was taken, however, to reduce the number of brands under which these could be sold, and the proliferation of differentiated products continued as before. Thus, 23 brands of tetracycline capsules, 12 of chloramphenicol, 12 of tetracycline syrup, and 12 of prednisolone were being imported, and in every case there was wide variation in the prices of generically identical medicines, *with the more expensive and more heavily promoted branded products dominating the market.*[5] Advertising continued unabated and the prices of imports remained unregulated. Not surprisingly, savings on the total import of drugs turned out to be negligible.

From 1965 to 1970, the foreign exchange allocation for drugs was cut from a total of Rs. 33 million (Rs. 20 million for private and Rs. 13 million for CMS imports) to Rs. 24 million (Rs. 14 million and Rs. 10 million, respectively). As population and medical needs had increased steadily and prices had risen over this period, the per capita supply of pharmaceuticals declined drastically. The Prime Minister asked one of the present authors again to advise on the rationalization of the structure, this time to encompass the entire country. A report entitled *The Management of Pharmaceuticals in Ceylon* (13) was produced in collaboration with a member of Parliament. This report drew heavily on experience gained during the 12 years of operating a rationalized CMS list, and called on the expertise of a group of doctors, pharmacologists, and clinical pharmacologists at the University of Sri Lanka. This expertise,

---

[4] There is no record of the number of brands then on the Sri Lanka market, but it probably ranged between 10,000-15,000. According to the Hathi Committee (11), India had some 15,000 drugs, and Brazil and Spain had between 20,000 and 30,000.

[5] This information is based on data collected by the State Pharmaceuticals Corporation on private sector purchasing for early 1972. In a study of the antibiotic markets in the U.S., Brooke (12) found that for well-established and out-of-patent drugs, the more expensive brands invariably dominate the market, with price variations on identical products of up to 1,000 percent being sustained over many years.

drawn from a milieu independent of the drug TNCs, proved to be of crucial significance in providing the complex of skills required to formulate and mount a comprehensive reform program.

Before discussing the implementation of the report, however, let us first describe its main recommendations:

- The channeling of all imports of processed pharmaceuticals and pharmaceutical chemicals through a state trading corporation. Prices of the 18 main categories of processed drugs (70 percent of the CIF (cost, insurance, and freight) value of private sector imports) were compared with those that were being paid by the CMS in 1969 for the same drugs. It was found that the annual actual import bill of Ceylon rupees 11.7 million would have been only Rs. 3.7 million (13, Table II), *a savings of 68 percent,* if the purchases had been made by a centralized agency taking advantage of the price differences in the international drug market and buying in bulk from economical sources.[6] Prices of pharmaceutical chemicals were not compared since the CMS did not handle such imports, but it was assumed (rightly, as it turned out) that similar savings would be available here to a rational and informed buyer.

- Reduction of the number of drugs imported, and amendment of patent laws (Sri Lanka offers strong patent protection in the form of product patents) in order to obtain newer drugs from the least expensive possible sources. It was noted that the university departments of pharmacology were already preparing a rationalized list of drugs which would retain all the therapeutic properties of the previously imported drugs, as well as leaflets informing prescribers of the proper use of the reduced list and attempting to persuade them of the therapeutic efficacy and bioequivalence of generic named drugs. The rationalization and provision of objective information were to be extended to the category of over-the-counter drugs, where, it was noted, several ineffective, unnecessarily expensive, or "irrationally" combined drugs were in common use.[7]

- The replacement of brand names by generic names in the sale and prescribing of medicines, and an end to the promotion of drugs by the manufacturers. The use of generic names would lead to better prescribing practices, while the provision of information on drugs from official sources would only remove the dangers and costs inherent in the extravagant promotional practices of the industry.[8] As there was already an official quarterly publication of the Formulary Committee, the *Formulary Notes,* in existence for precisely this purpose, it was recommended that it be upgraded, better financed, and brought out more often.

---

[6] Of the four most important categories of drugs examined, the cost of analgesics and antirheumatics would have been cut by 88 percent, antimicrobials by 52 percent, antidiabetics by 87 percent, and antihistamines by 79 percent.

[7] Studies by the FDA, based on exhaustive reviews of the literature and clinical trials, have found that up to 60 percent of prescription drugs and, using a smaller sample, up to 75 percent of OTC drugs, lack evidence of effectiveness (14). Many of these drugs have been withdrawn from the U.S. market but continue to be sold in markets with more lax supervision, in developed as well as less-developed countries.

[8] Such dangers and costs include overprescribing, inappropriate prescribing, lack of awareness of adverse reactions, and uneconomic prescribing. They are further discussed in references 2, 5, 14, and 15.

- Future development of local manufacture of pharmaceuticals based on guidelines set by the government. Local manufacturers would produce according to the rationalized drug list, use materials imported by a state trading corporation, and leave promotion and distribution to the state. If they proved recalcitrant, the government would have the power to nationalize them under the provisions of the Sri Lanka State Trading Corporation (Drugs) Act.

The report also contained a number of specific suggestions on countries from which older, commonly used drugs should be imported (i.e. socialist countries of Eastern Europe), and on the training of pharmacists, improvement of quality-control procedures, and a restructuring of the CMS (which had suffered a drastic deterioration in its buying, storage, and distribution procedures).

The Wickremasinghe and Bibile report (13) set the stage for a complete overhaul of the system of drug provision in Sri Lanka. The government decided to establish the State Pharmaceuticals Corporation (SPC) of Sri Lanka (under the honorary chairmanship of one of the present authors), to enlarge the Formulary Committee and rename it the National Formulary Committee, and to hand over all drug importing and the bulk of distribution activities to the Corporation. Not all the recommendations noted above were implemented, and some proved more difficult to effect than has been envisaged. The industry protested strongly and made formal protests to the government but, by and large, the rationalization of the system was carried out. We shall discuss its achievement and limitations later.

MAJOR PARTICIPANTS IN THE REFORM

We can identify six broad groups which were directly or indirectly concerned with drug provision in Sri Lanka, and played a constructive or obstructive role in the implementation of the reform program.

The Government

Sri Lanka had at the time a coalition government made up of three left-wing parties. While certainly not unified in its objectives, the government had a strongly socialistic ideology. It had implemented sweeping land reforms, started several public sector industries, promoted welfare services and equality of incomes, and was committed to a pattern of development of a primarily egalitarian nature. It was also a government in severe economic difficulty, which resulted in two opposing effects: (a) it made it far more willing to take measures to economize on pharmaceutical purchases along the lines described above; and (b) it made it more vulnerable to economic pressure from those opposed to the reform (i.e. the aid-donor countries whose TNCs were threatened).

The government was, of course, neither monolithic in its structure nor fully consistent in its strategy. The very fact that it was a coalition meant that its ideological positions shifted with the shifting fortunes of its constituent parties, thus affecting the political underpinnings of the entire policy. Since a clear and strong political direction is absolutely vital in any such policy, any change of direction clearly could weaken the implementation of difficult portions of the reform, leaving the lower sections of the government (i.e. the SPC) at variance with the apex (the Prime Minister's office). Until 1975, the Prime Minister fully supported her Minister of Industry and the SPC in their reform programs, but with growing political problems and food shortages, their paths diverged. The Lanka Sama Samaj Party (LSSP), the most radical party in the coalition, left the government. The Prime Minister, along with powerful sections of the government, moved distinctly to the right, accepted U.S. food aid, and back-tracked slightly on her earlier strong stand on pharmaceutical reform. The Minister of Industry found it increasingly difficult to pursue his former strategy, and the SPC was obliged to compromise on some important elements of the program as originally conceived. Thus, the major achievements of the reform came in its early years; in later ones the momentum slowed perceptibly. The pace of reform had little to do with its objective merits or demerits; it was governed more by the power struggles at the apex.

Local Reformists Outside the Government

This category constituted the main intellectual, technical, and organizational force behind the reform, and comprised a group of highly trained, well-placed, radical-minded academics and doctors who could analyze the benefits of change, argue the case cogently, and provide the technical expertise necessary to implement it. The combination of ideology and expertise with a socialist-minded government was, as long as government support was given, crucial. Many less-developed countries have the expertise and ideology, but in disparate groups of people; others attempt reform at the wrong historical junctures. Then, depending upon who is in power (or close to it), reform tends to be hasty and misconceived, or stalled by the machinery which is to implement it, or simply not undertaken (or reversed).[9]

The Drug Industry

It was to be expected that the drug industry would be categorically opposed to reform. Not only would such rationalization reduce the profitability of expensive branded products, it would set a bad example to other poor countries which were trying to get more medicines from very limited resources. It would be misleading, however, to consider the entire industry in this manner. There are several contradictory forces at work, and it is crucial to differentiate between them.

Local Manufacturers. There are five large TNCs with subsidiaries operating formulation and packaging plants in Sri Lanka: Pfizer (U.S.), Glaxo (U.K.), Warner-

---

[9]There are examples for each of these possibilities. In Pakistan, the abolition of brand names in 1973 was initiated by a left-wing minister. It was introduced too suddenly, the requisite quality tests were not undertaken, doctors were not properly informed, the public was not reeducated, and the experiment failed. In the U.K., a Labour Minister of Health sought to implement the Sainsbury proposals, but the opposition of the industry and the civil service itself led to a weak compromise solution (16). In Brazil, a nationalistic military group abolished drug patents in 1969 and set up the Central de Medicamentos to provide cheap basic drugs to the poor; a change of government and an ideological reversal considerably diluted its original aims (4, 17).

Hudnut (U.S.), Unical (for Burroughs-Wellcome, U.K.), and Reckitt and Colman (U.K.). These account for about 75 percent of local drug production. Two local companies, producing under license for TNCs, account for another 22 percent. The remaining seven producers are small local companies, generally producing preparations for skin application. It is clear that the TNC subsidiaries would be hostile to the rationalization of drug production and promotion (since over half their production consisted of elegantly packaged and heavily advertised minor remedies and vitamins of little therapeutic value to the majority of the population, which could not afford them), and that they would oppose the channeling of imports of pharmaceutical chemicals (which they previously imported from their principals at arbitrary prices) through the SPC. Clearly also, their hostility would be more virulent and effective the greater the support they could expect from their home governments.

The response of local firms would be more ambiguous. On the one hand, they (especially the large firms operating under foreign license) would resent the interference of the SPC in their production and marketing decisions. On the other hand, they would welcome the lowered costs of pharmaceutical chemical imports, the provision of technical expertise by the SPC, the protection given against foreign competition, and the aid provided by the state to promote local enterprise. They may also be more susceptible to local ideological currents, and have a weaker base from which to resist any reform.

Foreign Suppliers. Those TNCs which were previously selling high-priced patented and branded drugs would resent the reform, but would be unable to apply anything but indirect pressure unless they found patent infringements and decided to risk a court action in Sri Lanka against a public corporation. Some TNCs are also competitive suppliers in generic markets, and in this context they would not suffer from the change. (Some, like Roche, which sells extremely expensive tranquilizers and very cheap vitamins, are both.) Smaller foreign companies in capitalist countries which sell by generic names, especially those which do not observe patent laws, would welcome the reform, as would the large public sector companies in socialist and developing countries such as India and Egypt.

Local Dealers. Those who were dependent on the previous structure of the industry for a livelihood (e.g. detail men, importers, and firm representatives) would be bitterly opposed to reform, unless they could be absorbed into the new structure or persuaded of its wider social benefits.

Local Opponents of Reform

There are other interested groups, outside the industry itself, which would oppose reform. The most important of these would be members of the medical "establishment" (the Sri Lanka Medical Association) and the private medical profession, who received various direct (free samples and hospitality) and indirect (attractive advertising, easily digested information from detail men) benefits from the drug companies' promotion, and who were convinced of the superior quality, efficacy, and reliability of the branded products of the large manufacturers. There are two, relatively minor, countervailing factors. First, a certain quantity of very common drugs is provided by doctors in Sri Lanka as part of the consultation fee, and doctors would welcome the lowering of cost for these drugs. Second, a few doctors could be expected to have a strong social conscience, or be aware of the criticisms of the industry voiced in the developed countries, to such an extent as to overcome the conditioning imposed by the industry's promotion.

Some opposition may also be expected from the consumers themselves, who are accustomed to brand names, have been persuaded by the advertising of OTC drugs, or are worried by the reduction in the number of medicines. Much of this opposition would tend to be concentrated in the ranks of the educated elite, who are conscious of branded and advertised drugs and are able to afford them, but its effectiveness would, at least in the Sri Lanka case, be limited by the strength of the dominant ideology and the socialist commitment of the ruling sections of that elite. As the political climate changes, however, this factor may well prove to be of great significance; the next year or two will show the strength of the elite's resistance.

Foreign Opponents of Reform

Since the TNCs as a group are likely to feel threatened by the reform, and since they wield far more power than small firms, it is to be expected that their representative organizations and home governments will do what they can to oppose it. The power that they wield will depend on a number of factors, including the extent of foreign investment (not just in the drug industry) already in the country, the expected inflow of direct investment and aid, and the involvement of the home country in the defense or support of the regime. The more the LDC is dependent upon the home country for aid, investment, or military support, the more pressure the drug industry is likely to bring against drastic reform.

Foreign Supporters of Reform

These are, by their very nature, unlikely to be as powerful in most LDCs as the opponents. Reformist doctors or pharmacologists, charity organizations, and even government bodies (like the FDA) in the developed capitalist countries may give moral support and advice, but are unlikely to be able to influence their own governments if a real threat to foreign investment is perceived. Those in developed socialist countries can, of course, be more helpful in terms of selling drugs and providing technology, but they do not possess either the capital or the advanced know-how of the TNCs. Thus, their support will be most valuable for countries in the first stages of pharmaceutical development and least valuable for those with advanced pharmaceutical industries. For Sri Lanka, with very little local production, the socialist countries may be quite useful; for India, they may be less so. Thus, the former would be freer to implement reform than the latter.

These, then, are the various groups which have an interest in the pharmaceutical industry, and the reactions that we may plausibly expect them to have to a major reform. The outcome is clearly far from determinate. On the contrary, it depends upon a complex interplay of social, political, and economic factors, as well as upon how they exercise their influence by means of ideology, persuasion, bargaining, or straightforward domination. The following discussion can only scratch the surface of this complexity, but we do hope to elaborate upon the political economy of controlling transnationals in this area.

MAJOR ISSUES IN THE REFORM

Acting on the recommendations of the Wickremasinghe and Bibile report (13), the government set up the State Pharmaceuticals Corporation in 1971. It was initially empowered to import processed pharmaceuticals for the private sector, and later also for the CMS, but the patent law was not changed. The SPC was also permitted to import some pharmaceutical chemicals for local manufacturers on a negotiated basis. The principle of changing from brand to generic names was accepted. The promotion of drugs by manufacturers ceased, except for the relatively small proportion of the market for OTC drugs, which were manufactured locally and sold through the existing retail network.

The process of reform may be best examined in terms of four major issues: (a) the centralization of purchase from a rationalized list of finished drugs; (b) the purchase of pharmaceutical chemicals for local manufacture; (c) the non-observance of patents; and (d) the change from brand to generic names, with the accompanying problems of quality assurance, bioequivalence testing, and provision of independent information.

Centralized Purchase from a Rationalized List

The State Pharmaceuticals Corporation was faced with two immediate major tasks: to reduce the several thousand brands of the 2100 drugs being imported to a reasonable number without detriment to therapeutics, and to undertake the task of buying drugs of adequate quality economically on world markets, replacing the 134 private importers which had previously done this.

The National Formulary Committee was entrusted with the task of rationalizing the drug list for the private sector along the lines which had been used for the state sector in 1959. Three main criteria were used: (a) the deletion of imitative drugs which added nothing to the therapeutic value of particular drugs that were to be chosen on the basis of economy; (b) the deletion of a large number of "irrational" fixed combination drugs (similar to the FDA's action in the U.S.) where good practice required the flexible use of single drugs; and (c) the deletion of drugs without clear therapeutic value or with high toxicity (8). The number of drugs was reduced from 2100 to 600, and further reductions are being considered. Since brand names were almost entirely (but, as we shall see, not completely) abolished, the profusion of brands practically disappeared, drug prices were greatly reduced, and there is no evidence that health services were at all adversely affected.

The main initiators of the rationalization of the drug list were academic pharmacologists and clinicians. It was clear to them that such a reduced list was conducive to better prescribing and to economizing on purchase. The main opponents of the reduction were the medical establishment, the local drug companies and their dependents, private importers, and, in a few cases, consumers. Complaints were made by some doctors of interference with their professional judgment, by drug companies and importers of the loss of therapeutically desirable drugs, and by consumers of the loss of familiar brands. The tactics of the opposition ranged from publishing adverse reports in the press and direct protests to the government, to organizing "symposia" of opponents and stirring up popular resentment through rumor and insinuation (powerful weapons on a small island). There was little attempt to produce scientific evidence for opposing particular deletions, and many went uncontested; but over the years a great deal of heat was generated by doctors and drug representatives about the restricted drug list and the activities of the SPC.

There were two ways of effecting a compromise on the rationalized list. The most important was to induct leading private practitioners into the National Formulary Committee and the tender board of the SPC, and make them a responsible party to the decision-making process. In the Committee they could be exposed to scientific evidence based on clinical trials and the findings of other countries; the conflict would then become localized and partly shorn of its emotional trappings, and the doctors outside would have a much weaker case to argue. The second way was simply to give in on drugs where feeling ran exceptionally high,[10] in exchange for more acceptable deletions. As time passed and the doctors became accustomed to working with the reduced list, without obvious detriment to health care, the process of rationalization became somewhat easier. However, with the departure of the LSSP from the government in 1975 and the weakening of government support for the SPC's reforms, criticism grew more strident where vested interests were concerned. The local representatives of TNCs voiced more open protest in the newspapers, and doctors were able to force additional concessions from the Formulary Committee on the retention of particular branded drug imports. The progress of rationalization, while not reversed, was certainly slowed down in 1976. The battle is still being waged, and its final outcome will depend on political developments in 1977 and thereafter.

The second immediate task faced by the SPC was to replace the private import system for finished pharmaceuticals. This clearly required a great deal of careful planning, quality checks, inventory control, and so on before implementation. The SPC studied the pattern of private sector imports for 6 months in 1972, and started by taking over about one-third of these imports. This proportion was increased as the SPC gained experience, and by the end of 1973 it had taken over all imports.

Since the purpose of the exercise was to economize without compromising on quality or therapeutic benefits, the SPC had to take several factors into account. First, some drugs were so new that they were effectively monopolized by the innovator; on these, termed "monopoly quotations" (about 26 percent in terms of value in 1973 and 22 percent in 1975), the SPC could only bargain for better terms (but from a weak position) until a competitor (usually a non-patent observing firm) appeared and offered the drug more cheaply at satisfactory quality.

Second, price quotations on older drugs could be obtained from a number of

[10]This was the case with soluble aspirin, which has no therapeutic advantage over ordinary aspirin but costs three times as much. The detail men for the local TNC subsidiaries concerned mounted an intensive campaign, via the doctors, to have the drug retained. So powerful was this campaign that the National Formulary Committee was forced to retain the drug, which continues to dominate the private aspirin market.

264 / Lall and Bibile

producers throughout the world. The maintenance of quality required that any small generic drug producer seriously considered had to provide a certificate of quality plus an independent certificate of quality from a reliable laboratory (e.g. the Haffkine Institute in India), an agent (e.g. the General Superintendence Company of Geneva), or an official body (e.g. the PARCOST program in Ontario, Canada). It was only after such certification that a low-price bid would be accepted. The savings to the country of "shopping around" and obtaining better information about market conditions were usually substantial, as we shall see.

Third, in some cases, traditional TNC suppliers or other TNCs would themselves quote the best price, substantially reducing their earlier price. There was, in other words, a distinct benefit to be gained from bargaining apart from simply "shopping around." This benefit also applied to some traditional East European suppliers, and not just TNCs. Recourse to public sector firms clearly does not obviate the necessity of acting as a "rational" consumer.

By 1975, the market shares of various supplying countries had changed dramatically as compared to pre-SPC days in early 1973: the U.K. supplied 16 percent of imports in 1975 (47 percent in 1973), the U.S. 2 percent (16 percent); India 17 percent (7 percent); Hong Kong 6 percent (0.5 percent); Japan 7 percent (0.2 percent); and Poland, Hungary, and Czechoslovakia together 10 percent (0.4). Switzerland and West Germany proved themselves to be competitive and maintained their former shares of 7-9 percent, although some former TNC suppliers were replaced by small generic manufacturers from these countries.

We shall not detail procedures for tendering, control of ordering and shipping, storage, and so on, which are fascinating but not relevant to the present discussion. Two points should be briefly noted, however. First, almost no drugs were purchased from Italy, the best known source of inexpensive drugs (because it does not observe patents on drugs), simply because the SPC lacked information on the manufacturing practices of the cheaper generic producers who quoted on tender. Second, the tendering system was far from ideal. Small manufacturers in the U.S., for instance, never submitted bids, partly because they were not aware of the tenders, and partly because they prefer to bid anonymously for tenders channeled through their trade association (quite separate from the U.S. Pharmaceutical Manufacturers' Association, which represents the TNCs) rather than openly under their own names, because of fear of commercial retaliation by the big TNCs which are also important customers.[11]

Resistance to the SPC buying procedures came from several sources. First, the TNCs themselves, finding the very basis of their oligopolistic pricing and profitability cut, mounted a campaign to persuade the government and the doctors to reject low-price drugs. In a letter to the Prime Minister, Joseph Stetler, President of the U.S. Pharmaceutical Manufacturers' Association (representing the TNCs), argued forcefully against various aspects of the reform program. The letter was delivered to the Sri Lanka ambassador in Washington, D.C., and transmitted to the Prime Minister and

---

[11] In his study of the U.S. antibiotic market, Brooke (12) notes that many large firms buy finished drugs from small manufacturers and then sell them under their own brands at much higher prices than generic equivalents sold by their suppliers. It is not surprising, therefore, that these suppliers would not want to openly undercut their "big brothers" in the world market.

several Ministries concerned. In it, Stetler took the following position on buying drugs economically in the world market (18):

> The restraints and prohibitions placed on the industry, and particularly affecting the world-wide, research-based major producers, would not only inhibit the growth of an indigenous pharmaceutical manufacturing base in Sri Lanka, but would also have a number of corollary consequences. Some that might be anticipated are:
> 1) World-wide tender purchasing by SPC does not guarantee availability of drugs or raw materials, their availability at the time or pricing desired by SPC, or assurance that they would be, in fact, less expensive than those available to companies.
> 2) Those companies having high investments in research and development and quality control would be discouraged from bidding; sources without such expenses or quality control standards would more likely submit low bids. . . .
> 6) Finally, the action calls in question the Government's position with respect to all foreign investment in Sri Lanka.

Stetler's arguments sound persuasive, and the veiled threat of point 6 is rather formidable. Yet events have proved the first two points completely wrong. Worldwide tendering was shown to be amenable to strict quality standards, inventory, and forecasting control, and far cheaper than the previous "free" system. Research-based TNCs showed no aversion to bidding; many of them continued to submit high-cost bids up to 1976, in spite of never winning a tender for commonly available drugs. When they were asked to quote prices for the new drugs on which they had effective monopoly, they were as willing to supply the SPC as they had been to supply private importers. Thus, one tends to question the veracity of Stetler's claim in his concluding paragraph (18, p. 6) to be concerned with the effects "not only on the pharmaceutical industry and on all private industry in Sri Lanka, but potentially for the health of all its citizens."

There was, of course, very little "muscle" to back up the Pharmaceutical Manufacturers' Association's threats, since the U.S. had relatively few investments in Sri Lanka and the TNCs themselves had no intention of boycotting the SPC. Other developed countries did not raise even an official murmur. However, the industry could wield more pressure *within* the country, through its importers and salesmen. A widespread and insidious campaign denigrating low-cost suppliers was launched. And a second source of opposition, the private practitioners, was drawn into the campaign. Drugs were reported to be ineffective, substandard, or toxic, but little empirical evidence was produced. The SPC always checked the quality of drugs reputed to be faulty, and in cases where such defects as unsatisfactory sugar coating, poor labeling, inappropriate ointment base, etc., were found, the products were immediately recalled and replaced. In some, relatively rare, cases, where the manufacturing firm was thought to be negligent, it was "blacklisted" and barred from tendering.

The important point to note is that there is *always* a risk of particular batches of drugs being defective, even with the strict controls exercised in the U.S., for example. The evidence from the U.S. does not support the claim that large manufacturers have a better record on drug recalls than small generic ones. Concerning its 1974-1975 recalls, the FDA points out (19):

> The list [of 224 recalls] reveals the names of many large and small manufacturers, and the agency is unable to conclude from this list that there is any clear difference between these two groups based on recalls.

In Sri Lanka also, recalls involved large firms (e.g. Roche's tetracycline, Pfizer's penicillin tablets, and Burroughs-Wellcome's malt syrup) as well as small ones. The medical establishment, however, seized upon and publicized the latter, while keeping silent about the former. Physician distrust of lower-priced, unbranded drugs is a universal phenomenon and, indeed, is one of the main fruits of the expensive promotion undertaken by the big firms.[12] This accounts for the latter's products continuing to command far higher prices than those of small firms, even when there is no scientific basis to differentiate between them, or when, as in some cases, they are identical products with different labels. The reaction in Sri Lanka was, therefore, entirely to be expected.

There is no easy way to counteract the opposition, and it still continues among sections of the medical profession. However, some progress has been achieved by two methods. First, doctors were sent literature based on clinical and recall evidence to persuade them that cheaper drugs are not necessarily bad. While such "re-education" was bound to be slow, it did show some success, especially among younger doctors. Second, a few high-priced drugs were permitted to be sold alongside much cheaper equivalents, and patients were found to switch to the latter in the course of a year or so. When the less expensive product was found equally effective, demand for the other gradually disappeared, and it could be removed without protest.

Purchase of Pharmaceutical Chemicals
for Local Manufacture

The reform of finished drug imports proved far easier than that of buying pharmaceutical chemicals for local manufacture. One of the original purposes of setting up the SPC had been to economize on the cost of importing bulk chemicals as well as finished drugs. In April 1973, the SPC prepared a "34-drug program" in which a limited beginning would be made with 34 (of a total of 225) locally formulated drugs, whereby the chemicals would be imported on the basis of worldwide tenders by the Corporation. However, if the manufacturer was already buying materials at prices comparable to the best SPC tenders, it would be allowed to continue as before. For instance, when one local firm was buying vitamin raw materials from Roche, the cheapest supplier, and continued doing so, other producers were made to follow suit. The program aimed:

- to increase the local processing of drugs,
- to reduce the cost of imported chemicals, saving an estimated Rs. 3 million out of Rs. 9 million on the 34 drugs, and
- to work existing factories, which were running at well below capacity, at full capacity and in two shifts.

The SPC found that the installed capacity (at single-shift) of the seven large producers could manufacture 750 million tablets annually, but was only producing

---

[12] The cost of promotion per doctor in the U.S. came to about $5000 per annum in 1970, the bulk of it on detail men. There are about ten doctors per detail man in the U.S., as compared to five in Colombia and only three in Mexico, Guatemala, and Brazil (5, p. 122), a striking illustration of the relative intensity of promotion in developing countries.

300 million; the total tablet requirement of Sri Lanka was 1000 million. Similarly, installed capacity for capsules was 40 million, actual production was 6 million, and total requirement was 120 million. Thus, the entire requirement of tablets and capsules could have been met by increasing the number of shifts to two or three without adding further capacity; Sri Lanka would have saved considerable foreign exchange by formulating and packaging pharmaceuticals domestically.

The seven small local producers responded favorably; the five TNC subsidiaries, however, showed resistance. Initially, they simply refused to respond, until in December 1973 the Director of Regulation of Industries issued a stiff warning. Glaxo then accepted the program in principle, but the others did not. In May 1974, after further pressure and more warnings from the Ministries of Finance, Industries and Scientific Affairs, and Health, two other TNCs (Reckitt and Colman, and Unical) agreed to cooperate. Pfizer held out a little longer, but then followed the others in agreeing to the program in principle. Agreement in principle was, however, quite a different matter from cooperation in practice. Four TNCs started a further series of delaying maneuvers, asking for further discussion, clarification, and changes. An SPC official noted (20):

> As a result, Unical tabletting capacity, which is 90 million a year in one shift, is lying idle; Reckitt and Colman, which has a 165 million tabletting capacity a year, is making only 45 million tablets, and not making the 90 million tablets of aspirin required in the SPC programme. Recently the SPC made an urgent appeal to Pfizer to make tetracycline capsules required in the cholera epidemic and offered quality tested raw materials and capsules. Pfizer delayed, raising one query after another, as is usual with them. The urgency of the situation has not concerned them in the least.

The outcome of Pfizer's refusal to encapsulate SPC-imported material (from Hoechst of West Germany) during the epidemic was that the tetracycline lay unused in SPC stores and Pfizer equipment lay idle, while tetracycline capsules had to be airlifted to the country at enormous expense.

By 1975, only 14 of the 34 drugs were being produced according to the program. The situation had improved slightly by the end of 1976, but Pfizer was still refusing to use material imported by the SPC, Glaxo had just agreed to start producing 7 drugs, and the other TNCs had not yet launched into actual manufacture with SPC materials. The final outcome of the battle, especially with Pfizer, is still unclear, but that company's refusal and stalling have enabled it to hold out for over 3½ years against a host government's clear intent and policy.

Two questions then arise: Why did Pfizer hold out? And how did it manage to get away with it?

The "why" is easily answered. Pfizer was buying tetracycline from its parent firm at a CIF price of $99 per kilo, when raw material of equivalent quality was being offered to the SPC by Hoechst (an even bigger transnational) at $20 per kilo. This is a classic example of transfer-pricing behavior, where the usual defense used by TNCs, in terms of quality (Hoechst could hardly be accused of poor quality products) or of reaping a return on research and development (the drug has long been out of patent and is technologically well diffused) could not possibly be justified. Glaxo was engaged in identical practice: its chlorpheniramine imports cost $411 per kilo from the parent firm and $53 from Halewood (a small British firm).

The "how" is more complicated. The initial stalling and resistance of the transnationals was to be expected. It may also have been expected that the U.K. firms would, in the absence of outside support, ultimately accede to the demands of the host government. The fact that the one large U.S. TNC held out may be traced to two factors. The first, and apparently determining one was pressure brought by the U.S. government to protect Pfizer. By the end of 1974, the SPC, with the strong support of the Minister of Industries, was recommending nationalization of Pfizer to ensure its compliance. The reaction of the U.S. was swift and, as it turned out, decisive in preventing such a measure. The U.S. Ambassador personally intervened with the Prime Minister in the matter, and, while we can only speculate as to the nature of his intervention, the dependence of Sri Lanka on U.S. aid (food aid had just become crucial) may have figured largely. The chairman of the SPC was ordered to "continue negotiating" with Pfizer; no further disciplinary action was taken. Pfizer is still holding out in the hope that the forthcoming elections (mid-1977) will bring a government which is more "reasonable" in its pricing arrangements with its parent company. In the interim, of course, the government's move to the right has strengthened the TNC's resolve to minimize their compliance with the 34-drug program, and there is a real danger that the whole plan may be jeopardized by a leadership unwilling to take the necessary political measures to discipline TNCs.

The second factor, perhaps a minor one, affecting Pfizer's attitude may have been the hard line taken by the Pharmaceutical Manufacturers' Association. In his letter to the Prime Minister, Stetler argued strongly against channeling raw materials through a state agency (18):

> We submit that it is entirely inconsistent with the drug manufacturer's responsibility [for quality] to withhold from it the right to select its source of supply for raw and partially finished materials. . . . Inconsistency in source of raw material for any given drug would produce a wide range of medical and therapeutic problems, as well as production, sampling and testing difficulties.

While the second point is valid if the raw materials were indeed of poor or variable quality, the stress laid on bioavailability (which we will discuss later) is almost certainly misleading. The familiar "bogeyman" of the drug TNCs' promotion, i.e. the small supplier of poor quality, cheap merchandise, keeps reappearing in different guises, and no amount of evidence to the contrary makes him go away. The Pfizer tetracycline episode provides a perfect example; the quality of materials was in fact one of the main delaying devices used by the firm in its refusal to use the Hoechst chemicals.

Stetler goes on to argue, "With companies reduced to a service operation [i.e. not choosing their own raw materials], the flow of information concerning new technology and scientific development through the private sector would be impaired or cut off" (18). This charge deserves to be taken more seriously. While various TNCs have quoted for raw material tenders, and this represents the sale of "embodied" technology produced by pharmaceutical research and development, there may exist a distinct problem concerning the transfer of new technology to set up new plants for drug production. The problem is not very pressing, however, for Sri Lanka. The SPC is considering setting up a plant for formulating several products, and has received various offers for the supply of technology. Of these, one of the most attractive seems to be from Indian Drugs and Pharmaceuticals Limited, an enormous and highly sophisticated public sector manufacturer. No equity participation is demanded; the turn-key job will be done on a cost-and-commission basis. Whatever the merits of this offer, it certainly does not seem that the reform program has set back the country's industrialization process in the slightest.

A note of caution is necessary, however. Sri Lanka is just starting to manufacture drugs, and technology is relatively easily available at this stage. The cooperation of TNCs may be more of a constraint to countries at the level of India or Mexico, for example. These countries should consider Stetler's warning seriously, and explore alternative sources of technology from developed capitalist countries, socialist countries, and other LDCs before launching on a program which antagonizes TNCs. The solution to aim at would be not to accede to the TNCs' desire for a "free" market, but to create conditions in which suitably regulated local enterprises could buy technology from TNCs at appropriate fees.

Patents

In spite of the recommendations of Wickremasinghe and Bibile (13), the government did nothing to amend the strong patent protection that it offers to drug processes and products. The SPC decided, however, to buy patented drugs from non-patent-observing sources. Propranolol, patented by Imperial Chemical Industries, was available from Polfa (Poland) at U.S. $7.6 thousand instead of the $27.3 thousand charged by the patent holder for the quantity needed by Sri Lanka, a savings of 72 percent. Diazepam, patented by Roche, was available from Ranbaxy (India) for less than $200, while the TNC quoted $7760, a savings of 97 percent (this was an extreme case, but savings were always substantial).

The patent holders (e.g. ICI and Roche) realized, of course, that patent laws were not being observed and sent warning letters to the SPC which were forwarded to the Minister of Industries, but none of them has yet taken the SPC to court. TNCs generally are aggressive litigants when patents are threatened; however, the prospect of fighting a state corporation in a socialist-minded regime clearly did not appeal to them. If the regime changes, there may well be a spate of infringement cases. However, Argentina provides an interesting parallel. In 1970, the Supreme Court of Argentina ruled that a local firm which imported an American Cyanamid-patented chemical from Italy was acting in the public interest (4, pp. 63-64). The law in Argentina was not changed, but the precedent set allowed several other local firms to break the legal monopoly and import drugs at a fraction of the previous cost. The TNCs involved are dragging their feet about suing; a similar outcome is possible in Sri Lanka.

The patent issue is a highly sensitive one for the pharmaceutical industry. It is one of the few major industries which depends on patents for effectively guarding its technological innovations and which is in the forefront of all battles to strengthen and extend patent monopolies. However, while it is clear that the TNCs need patents to reap an overall reward from their expensive and risky research and development, the benefit a small developing country receives from offering patent protection is far from clear. It certainly pays much higher prices than it needs to; every new drug has effective competitors from non-patent-observing bases within 3-4 years, and a worldwide buying service can save enormous sums by shopping around. What, then, does it gain? Stetler (18, p. 4) answers forcefully:

> Such protections [on patents and trademarks] provide a major incentive for producers to make new medicines available to smaller markets, such as Sri Lanka, where product exclusivity is a compensation for low per capita income and a variety of business risks which otherwise would make the market unattractive. Patent protection is a strong inducement, not only for direct investment, but for the transfer of technology and know-how licenses. . . . The major international trend is to strengthen rather than weaken patents and industrial property protection.

As with Stetler's other arguments, this is a mixture of half-truths and exaggerations. First, there is no evidence that Sri Lanka would be unable to obtain the latest medicines if it did not offer patent protection. Second, there is no evidence that non-observance of pharmaceutical patents inhibits the inflow of capital or technology: neither Brazil nor Italy has patents on drugs, yet in both cases the TNCs have been investing heavily, buying up local firms, and selling their latest products. Third, there are several exceptions to the "major international trend" Stetler describes: India has considerably weakened drug patents, as has Argentina; Brazil has abolished them; the United Nations Conference on Trade and Development is negotiating major revisions to the Paris Convention.

Stetler does not mention the main reason for retaining drug patents: to promote innovation. But he clearly realizes the futility of making this point to a country which constitutes a minuscule portion of the world drug market. It is doubtful, in fact, whether this argument would even apply to *all* LDCs taken together for a large part of drug innovation which is aimed at "rich man's diseases" (e.g. cancer, heart and psychotropic illnesses), and for which LDCs constitute less than 10-15 percent of world sales. For innovation specifically directed at tropical diseases, some form of guaranteed returns would of course be needed, but a system of universal patents for drugs does not seem to be the most advantageous from the LDCs' point of view (21).

The increasing tendency in LDCs to weaken the application of patent laws on drugs has worried TNCs (even the Canadian government has relaxed the laws somewhat). But, in contrast to a threat to direct investments, it is not an issue on which their home governments can act directly. Moreover, even TNCs are prepared to accept a few aberrations as long as they are allowed to operate freely in other ways, and thus retain their market dominance and profitability. In the longer run, therefore, the counterattack will probably concentrate on marketing elements of the reform rather than on the patent issue.

Brand versus Generic Names, Quality,
Bioequivalence, and Promotion

The mechanism of promotion and marketing in the drug industry is at the heart of the market power exercised by the large firms, and thus must be the core of a program to lower their prices. The profitability of the TNCs depends on their ability to introduce "new" drugs (i.e. genuine innovations, duplicates, or combinations), impress brand names upon the consciousness of doctors, and persuade them of the superior performance and quality of their products. So rapid has been the introduction of "new" drugs, so powerful the promotion system of the large companies, and so close the relationship built up with the medical profession that doctors in most countries are virtually dependent on the firms themselves for information about new therapies, are unaware of the economics of prescribing, and are convinced of the superiority of branded products. The situation is rather worse in LDCs than in developed countries. In the latter, "consumerism," the growth of official concern, and a better awareness on the part of doctors have provided a weak but growing countervailing force. In LDCs, belief in international brand names is stronger, official attempts to provide objective information weaker, and consumerism still nascent.

Reform of the marketing system requires tackling two distinct problems: first, ensuring that the cheaper generic products are of adequate quality and are biologically equivalent with the branded products of the TNCs; and, second, ensuring that the change from brand to generic names is accepted by prescribers, who are provided information on the proper use of drugs by means other than private brand promotion.

Let us now briefly return to the issue of bioequivalence and illustrate how it was used to hamper the SPC's program. While the SPC took every feasible means to ensure that the drug imports were of adequate quality, the industry tried to prevent the acceptance of these drugs by claiming that inexpensive generic drugs were not bioequivalent with expensive branded products. It insisted that the generic producers' alleged lack of stringent quality control rendered their products therapeutically less effective or ineffective, even if they met the chemical requirements laid down for the relevant drugs (12, 22). Doctors are, as we have noted, predisposed to accept this on the basis of the scantiest evidence, and the TNCs did their best to strengthen that belief. Two examples will further illustrate the problem.

The first example concerns tetracycline. In late 1976, Bibile (23) noted:

> The prevailing impression among many doctors in Sri Lanka is that tetracycline supplied by the SPC is either ineffective or not as effective as it used to be when this drug was imported by the private sector. As a result some doctors even administer double the usual dose of this drug in an attempt to control bacterial infections. . . . [Locally capsulated tetracycline imported from Hoechst] was tested before it was capsulated and tested again after capsulating (by the Drugs Quality Control Laboratory of the Ministry of Health) before it was released on the market. Even so the SPC received complaints of clinical inefficacy of tetracycline although none of the complaints was accompanied by any evidence.

Detailed examination by a bacteriologist at the General Hospital in Colombo found that the problem lay not with the quality of the drug, but with its serious overuse for minor ailments which had led to resistance to the drug. The bacteriologist commented (24), "The problem of drug resistant strains of staphylococci is a worldwide problem and develops because of the widespread use of antibiotics and the abuse of antibiotics. Our figures may be higher than in other countries since tetracycline is freely prescribed by all Government Medical Officers, by General Practitioners and Ayurvedic Practitioners." Doctors were placing the blame for their predilection to prescribe antibiotics freely, even for the common cold, on the buying policies of the

SPC, despite the fact that in most developed countries such overuse had become widely recognized as a cause of the reduced effectiveness of drugs.

The second example involves the industry's move to more overt attacks on the SPC. In September 1973, Mr. C. Ponnalagan, a local representative of one of the drug TNCs, published a letter in the *Ceylon Daily News* (25) arguing that since the FDA in the United States had recalled a certain batch of generic oxytetracycline for not producing the desired blood levels, branded products of "reputed manufacturers" were more reliable and should be purchased even if they were more expensive. He also asserted that "most of the drugs imported [by the SPC] are not even tested for their chemical equivalency."

The argument was misleading, and the assertion was simply wrong. As the chairman of the SPC pointed out in the same paper the next day, U.S. drug recall data did *not* support the claim that small generic producers were more prone to recalls than large brand-name producers. The SPC did not import any drugs that did not carry quality certificates from abroad, and also tested imports locally in the Ministry of Health's Quality Control Laboratory. Bioequivalence *was* a problem, *but only for 25 drugs on the rationalized import list.* These were imported from traditional sources until bioequivalence testing could establish the equivalence of cheaper suppliers. Despite these assurances and scientific evidence, however, *criticism and distrust of generic drugs continue to this day.*

Bioequivalence is a problem that plagues reform programs everywhere, and TNCs constantly seize upon it to prevent major changes from taking place. Stetler (18, p. 3) argued that "It is now widely accepted, on the basis of chemical and other analytical tests, that the assumption of therapeutic equivalency in medicines is unsupportable. . . . The conclusion, we submit, is that 'generic equivalency' in medicines is a misconception which has now been refuted." If this were indeed so, a buyer would have no option but to continue to depend on large TNCs with products of proven efficacy. But is it? As with his other arguments, Stetler stretches the evidence to defend the status quo.

Where very careful and detailed tests are not utilized, it is true that for certain drugs chemically identical products may produce different bioavailability. Different bioavailability may or may not indicate therapeutic inequivalence; only trials can establish this. Moreover, the number of drugs where nonequivalence constitutes a therapeutic problem is small. The most recent tests of the FDA, which can hardly be faulted for a lack of exhaustive study (in fact, Stetler quotes a former FDA authority), have narrowed the list to 24, and a report of the U.S. Office of Technology Assessment (22) notes that the methodology and experimental procedures required for bioequivalence studies are available from that Office. This report (22) also notes that "drug products meeting the standards and falling into categories for which evidence of equivalent bioavailability is not essential can be considered as interchangeable and listed as such. . . ."

Stetler and the industry are attempting to confuse the government (and the medical profession) with half-truths, conveyed in scientific jargon, which no one but a trained pharmacologist could evaluate. Drug TNCs try very hard to establish generic inequivalence, and are on occasion not above manufacturing the evidence. To quote one example (12, p. 42),

In 1968, *JAMA* [*Journal of the American Medical Association*] published an editorial critical of generic products. That same issue contained an article on the generic formulation of the anti-diabetic drug tolbutamide. The generic product was compounded with less than the standard amount of agent and the article claimed that the generic formulation was far less effective than the tolbutamide marketed by Upjohn under the name Orinase. The paper, entitled "The Generic Inequivalence of Drugs," was written by a member of the Upjohn staff. The inferior product had never been marketed, had never been proposed for clinical use, and had been developed for this article by the Upjohn laboratory.

Bioavailability is a problem requiring expert understanding and exhaustive scientific testing, but it does *not* raise fundamental barriers to a rationalization program: what better evidence of this than the fact that the FDA is launching (naturally, in the face of fierce opposition from big drug firms) its Maximum Allowable Cost program to promote generic purchasing by government-financed health programs in the U.S.? In the Sri Lanka context, however, it is clear that the reform program would have encountered insuperable difficulties had it not been directed by experts having the knowledge necessary to counter the propaganda of the TNCs and the entrenched prejudice of the doctors. If bioavailability had not been checked and the results not made known, even on a few drugs, the whole program could have been jeopardized. Doctors, being generally suspicious of the reform, would have raised much stronger protest than they did. Consumers would have joined them, and the TNCs would have been back in business.

The efforts of the FDA to establish drug interchangeability and reduce the cost of its own health programs proved crucial in providing the example, techniques, and findings necessary to the rationalization in Sri Lanka. The "openness" of the American system, with its detailed published accounts of the operations of the drug industry and of the results of the FDA's exhaustive clinical and scientific tests, thus bore (unlikely) fruit in Sri Lanka. The FDA is instinctively sympathetic to the needs of consumers, and potential reformers would do well to draw upon its experience. It would be interesting, however, to see whether the FDA would be willing, and able, to provide positive and explicit support for reform in the face of opposition from U.S.-based TNCs.

The change from brand to generic names faces other problems.[13] Patients from the affluent minority have a strong belief in well-known brand names, not just for OTC drugs but also for prescription drugs with which they have become familiar. In a few cases, the demand for particular brands was so entrenched in Sri Lanka that the SPC had to give in, even when much cheaper generic substitutes were available. The strategy of the SPC was then, as noted previously, to sell both products at their respective prices and let economic rationality win out over a period of time. This strategy seems to have been fairly successful.

A greater problem was posed by the doctors, who had become so accustomed to

---

[13] The SPC managed, by means of the gradual pace of change and some compromise, to avoid an all-out battle with local firms. In Pakistan, however, local subsidiaries of TNCs opposed the generic scheme bitterly; Ciba-Geigy even sold out its local operations in 1973 in protest, and "pressure from other firms led to extended permission for the use of brand-named products for 18 months after the implementation of the Act [Drug (Generic Names) Act, 1973]" (26, p. 59). Thus, hasty and inadequate planning was compounded by poor political strategy.

prescribing by brand name that they were unaware of the generic names of several drugs. The change in their habits thus had to be gradual and had to be accompanied by a minor process of reeducation. The SPC provided cross-reference lists of brand and generic names to doctors. For old drugs, the changeover was relatively easy since generic names had become more familiar as a number of competing brands had emerged; for new drugs, it took longer. In the interim the SPC permitted brand names on packages, but they had to be displayed less prominently (in half the size) than the generic names. As the traditional sources of supply were replaced and prescribing habits changed, the majority of brand names were dropped. Some brand-name products are still sold, mainly those which are new and still under the effective monopoly of a TNC.

While promotion was still allowed for OTC drugs made by local manufacturers, it virtually disappeared for drugs imported by the SPC. With the disappearance of promotion, the distribution of free samples, hospitality, and visits by representatives also practically stopped. According to Stetler (18, p. 5) this led to the problem that "the information function on drug research and applicability now performed by companies through their medical and marketing representatives [was] eliminated. Doctors and pharmacists in remote locations, and even in urban areas, may be hard put to fill this information gap."

Stetler was certainly right that an "information gap" was created. The SPC has attempted to fill the gap by publishing and distributing two quarterlies: one edited by the National Formulary Committee, called *The Prescriber*, and the other edited by the Independent Medical Practitioners' Association (private practitioners), called *Sri Lanka Practitioner*. These publications carry the latest information on the rational use of drugs, drawing upon the state of the art and science internationally, and contain scientific findings on the indications, contraindications, and adverse reactions to drugs. While these publications are not as glossy or seductive as the TNCs' promotional literature, the following points favor their continued use as a means of disseminating information:

- First, with the reduced list of drugs and the use of generic names, the need for information was also greatly reduced. The flow of "new" drugs is far less than under the free market system. The removal of the profusion of brand names makes the informational task much easier.
- Second, the information provided by TNCs is not renowned for its objectivity. It is intended to persuade as well as inform, and often contains exaggerated claims, suppression of adverse reactions, incorrect indications, and the implicit denigration of competitors' products. The potential for misinformation is much greater in LDCs, where authorities are relatively lax. Silverman (5) has collected a horrifying compendium of data on the misinformation practiced by U.S. drug companies in Latin America, greatly extending and strengthening earlier findings by Ledogar (4). Focusing on seven major categories of pharmaceuticals, Silverman describes the variety of labeling and promotional practices used in different Latin American countries as compared to the U.S., and he concludes (5, p. 106):

> It is abundantly clear that there are glaring differences in the ways in which the same multinational pharmaceutical companies describe essentially the same drug products to physicians in the United States and to their medical colleagues in Latin America. This holds not only for global corporations headquartered in the United States. It is true also for such companies based in Switzerland, France, West Germany and other nations. . . . With few exceptions, the indications included [in Latin America] in the reference books are far more extensive, but the listing of hazards are curtailed, glossed over, or totally omitted. In some cases, only trivial side effects are described, while serious or possibly fatal reactions are not mentioned.

A strong case can therefore be made for official control of this "information function," even in the absence of broader reform. In the context of a broad reform, of course, the case is overwhelming.

- Third, provision of official information is far less expensive than TNC promotion. As it is the consumer who pays in either case, there are certainly grounds for economizing on this score. The SPC has decided to provide, in partnership with the Ministry of Health, the two "official" publications free of charge to all medical practitioners.

The people in Sri Lanka who are most unhappy about the abolition of private drug promotion have been the local detail men and importers, for whom it had provided a comfortable livelihood. Many private practitioners regret the loss of free samples and glossy, easily digestible literature on new drugs. However, because this is not an issue that can be publicly aired, their annoyance is diverted into channels such as complaints about drug quality. A number of physicians do, however, accept the social desirability of channeling information through neutral publications. In fact, the SPC publishes such a journal on behalf of private practitioners, undercutting those who would argue for a return to the old system.

ACHIEVEMENTS OF THE REFORM

We have already described the achievements of the reform in terms of reducing the number of drugs and abolishing brand names. This section will deal with some of the more tangible benefits.

Table 1 shows the savings achieved on selected drugs by the centralized purchase of finished pharmaceuticals. It gives the number of private sector suppliers before the SPC takeover and the number of tenders received for the drug afterwards, the average weighted price paid before and the ensuing tender price, and the value of SPC purchases for the second half of 1972 and the percentage of savings achieved over what the same purchases would have cost under the old system. In 1972, the SPC took over the import of 52 drugs, and achieved an overall saving of more than 40 percent; some of the drugs shown in the table have been selected to illustrate the more dramatic savings.

It should be noted that the number of tenders received has always been higher than the number of actual suppliers before the takeover. The SPC was able to introduce a much stronger competitive element into the market than had existed previously.

Table 1

Savings in Ceylon rupees achieved by the SPC takeover of finished drug imports in Sri Lanka, 1972[a]

Drug	Private Sector, January-June 1972		State Pharmaceuticals Corporation, July-December 1972			
	No. of Suppliers	Average Weighted Price per 1000	No. of Tenders	Actual Price	Value of Purchase (Rs. 000)	Percent Savings
Tetracycline caps. (250 mg)	23	74.26	44	40.77	531.5	45.1
Chloramphenicol caps. (250 mg)	12	64.88	41	46.26	208.2	28.7
Sulfadimidine tabs.	7	22.62	31	11.60	112.7	48.7
Neomycin tabs.	2	791.80	9	149.00	1.8	81.2
Phenylbutazone tabs. (100 mg)	5	43.09	36	7.48	7.7	82.6
Phenylbutazone tabs. (200 mg)	8	79.88	37	11.76	33.2	85.3
Chloroquine tabs.	6	41.68	34	28.23	14.1	32.3
Metronidazole tabs.	5	170.02	21	22.26	17.7	86.9
Aspirin tabs.	7	8.50	32	3.14	40.8	63.1
Chlorpromazine tabs. (25 mg)	2	48.86	29	6.30	3.1	87.1
Hydrochlorothiazide tabs.	1	139.40	3	10.98	3.3	92.2
Tolbutamide tabs.	1	55.80	19	16.00	4.0	71.3

[a]The 1972 rate of exchange was U.S. $1 = Ceylon Rs. 6.18.

The bulk of its savings resulted, however, simply from "shopping around" and disregarding brand names and, where relevant, patent protection. In most cases, moreover, the lowest tender was *not* accepted. Suppliers of the very cheapest drugs tended to be of dubious quality and manufacturing practice, and the SPC always obtained independent certification of quality before awarding a tender. Even so, the savings were considerable.

The benefit to the consumer showed up directly in price reductions. As distribution and retail margins have been determined for some time by the government, a reduction in CIF prices led to a proportionate reduction in the final price to the patient.

A glance at Table 2 shows that similar savings were achieved in the import of pharmaceutical chemicals for local formulation. We noted earlier that some of these imports were previously from the parent companies of the subsidiaries (Pfizer and Glaxo), and high prices simply represented the clandestine transfer of profits abroad. However, it should be apparent that high prices reflect not so much the existence of transnational investments and intrafirm operations as that of a strong element of monopoly power in the final product market, based on the technological and marketing practices of the large firms. Thus, Beecham was able to charge an independent local firm extremely high prices for cloxacillin and ampicillin. Yet, when faced with the prospect of competition in a market where its brand name did not matter and where the buyer had information on alternatives, Beecham was prepared to cut its prices by about 80 percent in each case.

If bids submitted by traditional TNC suppliers are any indication of what the suppliers would have continued to charge Sri Lanka, it appears that the SPC has continued to save considerable sums of foreign exchange year after year. In fact,

Table 2

Imports of intermediate chemicals by the private sector in 1972 and the SPC in 1973 in Sri Lanka: Comparison of costs per kilo and savings in U.S.$ by the SPC

Intermediate Chemical	Private Sector, 1972		SPC, 1973		Savings as Percent of Original Cost
	Supplier	CIF Cost per Kilo	Supplier	CIF Cost per Kilo	
Tolbutamide	Hoechst	40.62	Hoechst	19.24	52.6
			Polfa	2.52	93.8
Paracetamol	Sterling	3.24	Phone Poulenc	2.76	14.8
Chlorpropamide	Pfizer	126.21	Pliva	9.46	92.5
Aspirin	Glaxo	1.16	Polfa	0.99	14.7
Magnesium hydroxide	Sterling	5.18	Nichiman	0.61	88.2
Prednisolone	Organon	632.68	Roussell	321.77	49.1
Chloramphenicol	Boehringer	25.24	Lepetit	15.46	38.7
Cloxacillin	Beecham	606.47	Beecham	135.96	77.6
Ampicillin	Beecham	569.90	Beecham	95.11	83.3
Tetracycline	Pfizer	98.87	Hoechst	19.72	80.1
Chlorpheniramine	Glaxo	411.00	Halewood	52.53	87.3

as its tendering procedures have become more efficient and broad-based, the market it faces has become more competitive. Furthermore, as the SPC organization has grown (e.g. employment rose from 103 in 1973 to 330 in 1976), it has become financially self-reliant. It pays market rates of interest, a "contribution" to the government as well as taxes, and has made a healthy profit every period since the second year of its operation.

Another benefit of the reform was achieved by banning or restricting the use of particular drugs. In his study of drug TNCs in Latin America, Ledogar (4) names some drugs which were exceptionally toxic but which were being promoted and sold without proper warning. In contrast, let us look at a few examples to see how the reform helped Sri Lanka:

- *Dithiazanine Iodide.* By the mid-1960s, this drug had been banned in the U.S. and France. Yet, according to Ledogar, "In the areas outside the jurisdiction of the FDA, Pfizer's marketing tactics have not been interfered with in the same way. Under brand names like Netocyd and Dilbrin, the drug was being promoted in many countries of Latin America as late as 1974 as a broad-spectrum anti-parasitic agent" (4, pp. 30-31). Pfizer was also promoting its extensive use in Sri Lanka until 1972, when the National Formulary Committee banned it on the basis of the U.S. evidence.
- *Dipyrone.* A pain-killer with toxic side effects, dipyrone is severely restricted in its use in the U.S. and banned in Australia (4, pp. 31-32). Yet it is sold by several TNCs in Latin America as a completely safe analgesic. In 1972, Winthrop's Conmel was the 20th most popular ethical drug in Colombia. It has been banned in Sri Lanka, except in the rarely used injectable form necessary for bringing down high fever in patients who cannot take oral medication.
- *Long-Acting Sulfonamides.* These drugs have also been banned or severely restricted in the U.S. and many European countries because of the associated fatal Stevens-Johnson syndrome and other severe allergic reactions, but they have been heavily promoted and sold without adequate warning in Latin America. They were removed from the market in Sri Lanka, but only after a long battle with the drug companies in which the doctors, armed with literature provided by the detail men, sided with the firms.

Other examples could be given, but our point has been made. Let us now conclude our discussion on the political economy of TNC reform.

CONCLUSIONS

What has been learned from the Sri Lanka experience? And are the lessons valuable for other less-developed countries? We shall attempt to answer these questions in the concluding remarks which follow:

1. Sri Lanka has benefited in several significant ways from its reform of the international drug industry. Drugs are now much less expensive, undesirable and ineffective drugs have been excluded, and prescribing practices should show more rationality once the effects of the cumulative promotion of the firms have been counteracted.

2. The process of reform is extremely complex and difficult. Nonetheless, it *can* be successfully implemented given the appropriate combination of technical skills, a strong and socialist-minded government, gradual, carefully planned and well-propagated change, and insistence on quality assurance.

3. It can be concluded that reform is much easier in terms of controlling imports of finished drugs than those of pharmaceutical chemicals, not because of the nature of the product but because of the attitudes of the TNCs concerned. They are willing to bid in worldwide tenders and occasionally sell inexpensive drugs, but they resent any attempt to channel their intrafirm trade through the state. It follows that the larger the direct investment of TNCs in a particular country, the more difficult it will be to implement reform of local production. Sri Lanka found it relatively easy to change the status quo simply because the structure was small and undeveloped.

4. TNCs can bring several forms of pressure to bear upon the most committed government. They can use threats and persuasion from abroad; they can get their home governments to support them in cases where nationalization is threatened; they can restrict their future investments; and, most important, they can use their powerful alliance with doctors.

5. Even without pressure from TNCs, doctors are reluctant to accept a reformed drug delivery system. There are real problems posed by the quality of inexpensive drugs and bioequivalence which governments must face and overcome. Doctors must be persuaded that the new system is trustworthy, and their conversion requires time, education, and determination. Furthermore, since they are used to a powerful promotion system, which has to be replaced by a less attractive (but cheaper and more objective) information-provision system, the change has to be gradual.

6. Locally owned industry has been proven amenable to reform in Sri Lanka, but this is no indication of how it would react in countries where it is larger, better established, and able to promote its own drugs effectively. It is likely that in a country where such industry is profitable and successful (e.g. Argentina), it would fight reform, especially of the marketing system, just as hard as TNCs do. This does not rule out the likelihood of local firms asking partial reforms which strengthen their position vis-à-vis foreign competitors. (The proposed Indian reforms clearly have this sort of flavor.)

7. The local elite and the doctors accepted radical reforms on drugs and in other matters in Sri Lanka largely due to the mass pressure which had installed a socialist government in a landslide electoral victory in 1970. The importance of political direction cannot be overemphasized: the SPC made its major achievements before 1975, when the government had a unified socialist ideology. From 1975 onward, the government shifted its course, succumbed to local and foreign-vested interests, and enabled the critics to slow down or halt the pace of reform, especially as far as local production was concerned. With the reemergence of right-wing forces, it is to be expected that the elite, and especially the medical establishment, will try to revert to the old system of TNC-dominated drug provision. The lessons of this are of vital significance: it is difficult to imagine a government in a developing country undertaking or implementing a genuine reform of drug TNCs in the absence of a long-term and powerful socialist base and ideology. The internal and external constellation of opposing forces would otherwise be too strong.

8. It has been noted that the development of domestic industry is not adversely affected by reform in the early stages of development since a great deal of technology is available and there are few economies of scale (meaning capital requirements are low). At later stages, however, a reduction of TNC investment and technology may be more of a real threat, and has to be carefully considered. Economies of scale do become important in the production of intermediate chemicals, and the technology is often held monopolistically.

Lessons for Other LDCs

The list of conditions under which a comprehensive reform of the pharmaceutical industry is likely to succeed is, therefore, long and restrictive. There are not many developing countries which at present have the ability, the willingness, or the patience to launch and carry through such a program. Attempts at reform are, of course, widespread, but their achievements are often piecemeal and lopsided because one or the other ingredient for success is lacking. India, for instance, may take a tough line with TNCs and force them to accept local ownership and sell technology to domestic firms; given the strength of private firms as a whole and the lack of political direction, however, it is unlikely to achieve much by way of reducing the number of drugs on the market or abolishing brand names. Pakistan is even less likely to undertake reform because of the disastrous results of its ill-planned generic drug program. Brazil and Mexico both have a very powerful TNC presence and a strong influence on policy from the home countries of the TNCs; thus, no major reform policy is likely to get sufficient political support. Countries like Argentina have a strong indigenous sector which relies heavily on brand name promotion, and which will resist any encroachment on this source of profitability.

In sum, we do not expect any major changes to take place in the developing world in the system of drug delivery. The main changes are, in fact, occurring in the rich countries like the U.S., France, Sweden, Germany, and the U.K. It is they who may first achieve some real reform, and it is they who will probably set the pace for change in the Third World. Certainly the emerging political-economic climate of the Third World does not bode well for comprehensive independent reform there.

POSTSCRIPT: DEVELOPMENTS IN 1977

Unfortunately, the trends which became evident in late 1976 seem to have been strengthened in the first four months of this year. After the Sri Lanka Communist Party left the coalition government in protest over its handling of a general strike at the end of 1976, the swing to the right became even more pronounced. By the end of February, some Parliamentarians of the Sri Lanka Freedom Party had resigned from the government. More significantly, the Minister of Industries, a stalwart supporter of the SPC, also resigned in protest of the right-wing policies of the Prime Minister; he specifically stated that, among other things, he had recommended the takeover of drug TNCs but the proposal had been shelved. One of the present authors has resigned from the chairmanship of the SPC, protesting the lack of government support for SPC policies and the growing bitterness of the opposition from vested interests. He also noted the increasing disenchantment among the staff of the Corporation, and the danger that this may lead to a deterioration in its former levels of efficiency, honesty, and dedication. The coming months will determine whether or not Sri Lanka retains the valuable gains of the reform, and whether or not the TNCs and their supporters can reestablish their former hegemony.

Acknowledgments—We are grateful to the State Pharmaceuticals Corporation, Sri Lanka, for permission to publish the findings of our research concerning its operations and to T. Attapattu for collecting the statistical material. We also wish to thank Ajit Singh for his comments on an earlier draft. The authors retain full responsibility for the content of this paper, a version of which first appeared in *World Development*, Vol. 5, No. 7, July 1977.

REFERENCES

1. Lall, S. The international pharmaceutical industry and less developed countries, with special reference to India. *Oxford Bulletin of Economics and Statistics* 36(3): 143-172, 1974.
2. Lall, S. *Major Issues in Transfer of Technology to Developing Countries: A Case Study of the Pharmaceutical Industry* (TD/B/C.6/4). U.N. Conference on Trade and Development, Geneva, 1975.
3. Klass, A. *There's Gold in Them Thar Pills.* Penguin, Harmondsworth, 1975.
4. Ledogar, R. J. *Hungry for Profits: The U.S. Food and Drug Multinationals in Latin America.* IDOC/North America, New York, 1975.
5. Silverman, M. *The Drugging of the Americas.* University of California Press, Berkeley, 1976.
6. Reekie, W. D. *The Economics of the Pharmaceutical Industry.* Macmillan, London, 1975.
7. Lall, S., and Streeten, P. P. *Foreign Investment, Transnationals and Developing Countries.* Macmillan, London, 1977.
8. Bibile, S. *A Case Study of Pharmaceutical Policies in Sri Lanka* (TD/B/C.6/21). U.N. Conference on Trade and Development, Geneva, 1977.
9. Sainsbury Committee. *Report of the Committee of Enquiry into the Relationship of the Pharmaceutical Industry with the NHS, 1965-67.* Her Majesty's Stationery Office, London, 1967.
10. Coleman, V. *The Medicine Men.* Temple Smith, London, 1975.
11. Hathi Committee. *Report of the Committee on Drug and Pharmaceutical Industry.* Ministry of Petroleum and Chemicals, New Delhi, 1975.
12. Brooke, P. A. *Resistant Prices: A Study of Competitive Strains in the Antibiotics Markets.* Council on Economic Priorities, New York, 1975.
13. Wickremasinghe, S. A., and Bibile, S. *The Management of Pharmaceuticals in Ceylon.* Industrial Development Board of Ceylon, Colombo, 1971.
14. Rucker, T. D. Economic aspects of drug overuse. *Med. Ann. D.C.* 42(12): 609-614, 1973.
15. Speight, N. Cost effectiveness and drug therapy. *Trop. Doct.* 13: 89-92, April 1975.
16. Lang, R. W. *The Politics of Drugs: A Comparative Study of the British and Canadian Pharmaceutical Industries, 1930-70.* Saxon House, London, 1974.
17. Evans, P. B. Foreign investment and industrial transformation: A Brazilian case study. *Journal of Development Economics* 3(2): 119-139, 1976.
18. Stetler, C. J. Letter to the Prime Minister of Sri Lanka, May 10, 1973.
19. United States Food and Drug Administration. *Federal Register* 40(120): 26147, 1975.
20. Edirimanasinghe, S. M. 34 Drug Programme: A Summary of Negotiations with Local Manufacturers. Minutes of Managing Director, SPC, Colombo, November 1974.
21. Lall, S. *The Development of the Pharmaceutical Industry in Developing Countries: Problems and Prospects.* U.N. Industrial Development Organization, Vienna, forthcoming.
22. Office of Technology Assessment. *Drug Bioequivalence—A Report of the OTA Bioequivalence Study Panel.* Government Printing Office, Washington, D.C., 1974.

282 / Lall and Bibile

23. Bibile, S. Tetracyclines in Sri Lanka. *The Prescriber* 5(1): 1, 1976.
24. Mahendra, M. Resistance to tetracycline. *Sri Lanka Practitioner* 1: 37, 1976.
25. Ponnalagan, C. Letter in the *Ceylon Daily News,* September 11, 1973.
26. Heller, T. *Poor Health, Rich Profits: Multinational Drug Companies and the Third World.* Spokesman Books, London, 1977.

CONTRIBUTORS

MICHAEL B. BADER is a 1977 graduate of Yale University, where he was enrolled in an honors program entitled "Scholars of the House," under whose auspices he conducted research on the international politics of the Ethiopian famine of 1972-1974. His first article, "Breast Feeding: The Role of Multinational Corporations in Latin America," was published in this *Journal* in November 1976. Mr. Bader plans to attend graduate schools in medicine and international law.

NICOLE BALL is currently writing a book on the socioeconomic and political causes of disaster. From 1971 to 1976 she was a research fellow at the Institute for the study of International Organization at the University of Sussex, where she received an M.A. in international relations in 1971. Her publications include "The Myth of the Natural Disaster" (*The Ecologist* (U.K.), 1975) and "Understanding the Causes of African Famine" (*Journal of Modern African Studies*, 1976).

SENAKA BIBILE was, until his recent death, professor of pharmacology at the University of Sri Lanka, where he had worked since 1947. He received a first class honors degree in medicine in 1945 and a doctorate of philosophy in pharmacology from the University of Edinburgh in 1952. Dr. Bibile's research work has been chiefly in clinical pharmacology. During the past 18 years he advised the Ministry of Health, Government of Sri Lanka, on rationalizing the use of drugs. His advice led to the writing of a Ceylon Hospitals' Formulary and the creation of a Formulary Committee in 1960, and subsequently to the creation of the State Pharmaceuticals Corporation in 1971. He acted as chairman of this Corporation from its inception until early 1977.

JAIME BREILH is a professor in the Department of Social and Preventive Medicine at the Medical School of the Central University of Quito and coordinator of the Health Branch of the recently formed National Ecuadorian Research Team on Child Welfare Problems. Dr. Breilh obtained a Diploma in Epidemiology and Health Statistics from the London School of Tropical Medicine and a Master's degree in Science and Social Medicine from the Autonomous Metropolitan University of Mexico. After completing his duties as director of a rural health subcenter during his first postgraduate year of social medical service, he became a member of the teaching staff of the School of Medicine of Quito, working in various service-teaching and educational reform programs in the fields of social medicine and epidemiology. As such, he participated as coordinator in the formation of a new program of medical education which links work and learning and puts that process in direct contact with the health-disease problems of the people. The Central University of Quito, the Autonomous Metropolitan University of Mexico, and the Autonomous National University of Mexico have published several of his works and papers which have criticized the conventional organization of medical education and the official health system and have proposed a reconceptualization of the theoretical foundation of the epidemiological studies.

Presently, as part of a Latin American group of epidemiologists, he is completing a critical study of the conventional epidemiological method and implementing research projects which emphasize the historical nature of the health-disease process and, correspondently, a new methodological model to develop such a conceptual basis.

MICHEL CHOSSUDOVSKY is currently an associate professor of political economy at the University of Ottawa. He has previously taught at academic institutions in Chile, Argentina, Peru, Senegal, and Venezuela. Dr. Chossudovsky received a Ph.D. in economics from the University of North Carolina in 1971. He has been consultant to several governmental and international organizations, including the World Health Organization, the International Labor Office, and the Canadian International Development Agency. Dr. Chossudovsky is the author of a volume entitled *La Miseria en Venezuela* (Vadell Editores, Valencia 1977), a study on poverty in Venezuela which includes analyses of nutrition and of the health sector. He has also written several articles on the political economy of repression in Latin America. Dr. Chossudovsky is currently undertaking a study on poverty and the health sector in Latin America in the context of a United Nations Economic Commission for Latin America research project on critical poverty in Latin America.

PETER J. DONALDSON received his Ph.D. in sociology from Brown University. At present, he is a staff associate at the Population Council assigned to Seoul, Korea, where he serves as the Council's representative and a consultant to the Korean Institute for Family Planning and the Korean Development Institute. Prior to coming to Korea he worked for four years in Thailand, first at Mahidol University's Institute for Population and Social Research and later at the Thai Ministry of Public Health. His research interests include family planning research and evaluation, population policy, and the study of health care delivery systems.

RAY H. ELLING is professor of sociology and director of the Program in Cross-National Studies of Health Systems in the Department of Community Medicine and Health Care, University of Connecticut, Farmington. He received his Ph.D. in medical sociology from Yale in 1958. He has taught at Harvard, Cornell, and the University of Pittsburgh, and served as chief of the World Health Organization's Behavioural Sciences Unit. His work has been primarily on the sociology of medical care organization. Dr. Elling edited the volume *National Health Care: Issues and Problems in Socialized Medicine,* and prepared with R. F. Martin the research monograph *Health and Health Care for the Urban Poor.* He also edited the volume *Comparative Health Systems,* which appeared as a supplement to *Inquiry* in 1975. An additional monograph, *Cross-National Study of Health Systems, Political Economies and Health,* and a two-volume annotated bibliography on this same subject, were published in 1980.

ERLAND HOFSTEN is a chief demographer at the Swedish Central Bureau of Statistics. He attended the University of Stockholm, and in 1952 received his Ph.D. from Uppsala University. Dr. Hofsten has served as assistant professor at the University of Stockholm. In 1972-1973 he was director of the United Nations-sponsored Regional Institute for Population Studies in Ghana. Other international assigments included work in India in 1958-1959 and in Singapore and Malaysia in 1955-1956. Dr. Hofsten's primary research interests are in the fields of labor statistics and demography.

SANJAYA LALL has been a research officer at the Oxford University Institute of Economics and Statistics since 1968. From 1965 to 1968, he worked as an economist for the World Bank in Washington, D.C. Mr. Lall received a first class honors degree in politics, philosophy, and economics from Oxford University in 1963, and a bachelor of philosophy degree in economics from Oxford in 1965. Author of an annotated bibliography on foreign investment, Mr. Lall is about to publish a book on transnationals and developing countries. He serves as a consultant to several international agencies on problems of foreign investment and the pharmaceutical industry.

BONNIE MASS received a Bachelor of Arts degree and teaching certificate from the University of Georgia in 1964, and since that time she has taught in the states of Georgia and North Carolina. In 1973, she taught at the Women's Center School in Cambridge, Massachusetts. During her discussions concerning women's issues, she became involved in researching the varied social ramifications of birth control movements as they have evolved historically and as they are developing today. On this subject, she has published a monograph, *Political Economy of Population Control in Latin America,* and she has contributed articles to *Science for the People* and other periodicals. Jointly with others, she has prepared a report on population control in Latin America for the January 1975 session of the international Bertrand Russell Tribunal in Brussels.

VICENTE NAVARRO is presently professor of health and social policy at the Johns Hopkins University. He is advisor to several governments and international agencies, as well as to labor organizations in many countries. A founder of the International Study Group on Political Economy of Medical Care and the founder and editor-in-chief of the *International Journal of Health Services,* he has written extensively on sociology, political sociology, and the political economy of medical and social services. Dr. Navarro is the author of *Medicine under Capitalism; Social Security and Medicine in the USSR: A Marxist Critique,* and *Class Struggle, the State and Medicine: An Historical and Contemporary Analysis of the Medical Sector in Great Britain;* and the editor of the collection *Health and Medical Care in the U.S.: A Critical Analysis.*

MICHAEL TAUSSIG is an assistant professor in the Department of Anthropology at the University of Michigan and has also worked as a medical doctor in Australia and England. He is at present working on the social benefits of indigenous and folk medicine in South West Colombia, in relation to the health hazards of the spreading market economy in the same area. With the collaboration of Anna Rubbo, he has written a book on the social history of the Cauca Valley, Colombia, *Esclavitud y Libertad en el Valle de Río Cauca* (La Rosca, Bogotá, 1975).

MITTBANQUG